OXFORD CLASSICAL MONOGRAPHS

*Published under the supervision of a Committee of the
Faculty of Literae Humaniores in the University of Oxford*

The aim of the Oxford Classical Monographs series is to publish books based on the best theses on Greek and Latin literature, ancient history, and ancient philosophy examined by the Faculty Board of Literae Humaniores.

Theseus, Tragedy and the Athenian Empire

◆

SOPHIE MILLS

CLARENDON PRESS · OXFORD

1997

Oxford University Press, Great Clarendon Street, Oxford OX2 6DP

Oxford New York
Athens Auckland Bangkok Bogota Bombay
Buenos Aires Calcutta Cape Town Dar es Salaam
Delhi Florence Hong Kong Istanbul Karachi
Kuala Lumpur Madras Madrid Melbourne
Mexico City Nairobi Paris Singapore
Taipei Tokyo Toronto Warsaw
and associated companies in
Berlin Ibadan

Oxford is a trade mark of Oxford University Press

Published in the United States
by Oxford University Press Inc., New York

British Library Cataloguing in Publication Data
Data available

Library of Congress Cataloging in Publication Data
Theseus, tragedy, and the Athenian Empire / Sophie Mills.
(Oxford classical monographs)
Originally presented as the author's thesis (D. Phil.—Oxford).
Includes bibliographical references.
1. Greek drama (Tragedy)—History and criticism.   2. Theseus
(Greek mythology) in literature.   3. Athens (Greece)—Civilization.
4. Imperialism in literature.   5. Sophocles. Oedipus at Colonus.
6. Aeschylus. Suppliants. 7. Euripides. Hippolytus. I. Title.
II. Series.
PA3136.M55   1997   882'.0109351—dc21   97–14789
ISBN 0–19–815063–6

1 3 5 7 9 10 8 6 4 2

Typeset by Hope Services (Abingdon) Ltd.
Printed in Great Britain on acid-free paper by
Biddles Ltd., Guildford & King's Lynn

ACKNOWLEDGEMENTS

My greatest thanks must go to Professor Sir Hugh Lloyd-Jones and to Dr Robert Parker for their invaluable instruction, help and encouragement in supervising the Oxford D.Phil. thesis which forms the basis of this book; to my examiners, Dr Nicholas Richardson and Dr Richard Buxton, and to Dr Oliver Taplin, whose shrewd and kindly advice helped me so much in the metamorphosis of a thesis into a book. I must also express gratitude to the Fellows of Somerville College, who elected me to the Joanna Randall-Maciver Junior Research Fellowship, enabling me to finish the thesis and embark on its transformation in thoroughly pleasant surroundings. Last, but not least, I must thank everyone who has had to live with this publication over the long years of its gestation; especially Mrs Kate Mills, Dr Michael Dewar, Dr Julia Griffin and Dr Naomi Stephan; also Gillian Carrington, Gillian Cloke, Victoria Elliott, Claire Martin and Theresa Wise. Finally, thanks must go to Nayyir Bayyan, secretary of the Classics department, and Mike Honeycutt of the computer centre at UNC-Asheville, who assisted in producing the typescript.

I would like to thank the following publishers for permission to reprint extracts from texts for which they hold the copyright. Oxford University Press for selected quotations from Oxford Classical Texts of Aeschylus, ed. D. L. Page (1972); Homer, vols. 1–3, ed. D. B. Monro and T. W. Allen (first published 1902, 1908); Euripides, vols. 1 and 2, ed. J. Diggle (1981, 1984) and vol. 3, ed. G. Murray (first published 1909); *Fragmenta Hesiodea*, ed. R. Merkelbach, M. L. West (1967); Sophocles, ed. H. Lloyd-Jones, N. G. Wilson (1990); Thucydides, ed. H. S. Jones (first published 1900); Virgil, ed. R. Mynors (1969); also *Poetarum Melicorum Graecorum Fragmenta*, ed. M. Davies (1991) and *Iambi et Elegi Graeci ante Alexandrum Cantati*, ed. M. L. West (1989); Clarendon Press editions of Euripides' *Hippolytus*, ed. W. S. Barrett (1964) and Euripides' *Heracles*, ed. G. W. Bond (1981); *Euripides*, by C. Collard (1989); and *Inventing the Barbarian*, by E. M. Hall (1989); all by permission of Oxford University Press.

Oxford University Press (New York) for selected quotations from *Theseus and Athens*, by H. J. Walker (Oxford, 1995). Georg Olms Verlag for use of H. Diels and W. Kranz, *Fragmente der Vorsokratiker*, 11th edn. (Zurich and Berlin, 1964), ii, 285–6. The Egypt Exploration Society for the texts of *Oxyrhynchus Papyri* 1241, 2078 and 3531. B. G. Teubner for Pindar, *Carmina cum Fragmentis*, ed. B. Snell (Leipzig, 1970) and Bacchylides, *Carmina cum Fragmentis*, ed. B. Snell (Leipzig, 1971), and for selected quotation of the fragments of Euripides from *Tragicorum Graecorum Fragmenta*, ed. A. Nauck and B. Snell, 2nd edn. (1964). Vandenhoeck and Ruprecht for quotation of texts from volumes 1, 3 and 4 of *Tragicorum Graecorum Fragmenta*, ed. B. Snell, R. Kannicht and S. Radt (Göttingen, 1971–85). Harvard University Press for permission to quote from the following Loeb editions: Lysias: *Orations*, trans. W. M. R. Lamb (1940); Isocrates: *Orations*, vols. 1, 2 and 3, trans. G. Norlin (1928–45); Pausanias, *Description of Greece*, vol. 2, trans. W. H. S. Jones and H. A. Ormerod (1960); Plutarch, *Lives*, vol. 1, trans. B. Perrin (1967); Plato, *Works*, vol. 12, trans. W. M. R. Lamb (1955): also quotations from *The Invention of Athens*, by Nicole Loraux, copyright 1986 by the President and Fellows of Harvard College, reprinted by permission of Harvard University Press.

I should like to dedicate this book to Somerville College, and especially to Nan Dunbar and Miriam Griffin, in gratitude for everything.

S.M.

University of North Carolina at Asheville
1996

CONTENTS

ABBREVIATIONS

I have been unable to take anything more than selective notice of publications that reached me after 1993, and take this opportunity to apologize for any glaring omissions. All translations of Greek are my own; they are designed for the Greekless reader and have no pretensions beyond this function. All abbreviations follow the conventions laid down in the Année Philologique, and the following may also be noted:

ABV	*Attic Black-Figure Vase Painters*, J. D. Beazley (Oxford, 1952).
ARV²	*Attic Red-Figure Vase Painters*, J. D. Beazley, 2nd edn. (Oxford, 1963).
Diels and Kranz	*Die Fragmente der Vorsokratiker*, 6th edn., H. Diels and W. Kranz (Berlin, 1951).
FGrH	*Die Fragmente der griechischen Historiker*, ed. F. Jacoby (Berlin, 1923–58).
LIMC	*Lexicon Iconographicum Mythologiae Classicae* (Zurich, 1981–).
PMGF	*Poetarum Melicorum Graecorum Fragmenta*, ed. M. Davies (Oxford, 1991).
RE	*Paulys Real-Encyclopaedie der classischen Altertumswissenschaft*, ed. G. Wissowa (Stuttgart, 1894–1978).
TGF	*Tragicorum Graecorum Fragmenta*, ed. A. Nauck with a supplement by B. Snell (Hildesheim, 1964).
TGrF	*Tragicorum Graecorum Fragmenta*, ed. B. Snell, R. Kannicht and S. Radt (Göttingen, 1971–85).
Thompson	S. Thompson, *Motif Index of Folk Literature: A Classification of Narrative Elements in Folktale, Ballads, Myths, Fables, Mediaeval Romances, Exempla, Fabliaux, Jest Books and Local Legends*, 6 vols. (Copenhagen, 1955–8).

I

Images of Theseus before Tragedy

I.I INTRODUCTION

Every human being experiences a continuous interplay between past and present, because only by constantly referring to what is known already can the present be understood and preparations for the future be made. Something similar is true of human societies, for which the past can be defined as comprising certain events, personalities or institutions which are considered by most people to have a continuing relevance for their present and future prosperity.[1] The function of this past is essentially aetiological because it purports to explain what has made the society what it is: it defines the nature of the society for its members, and the past is used as a guide to the future to encourage certain values and types of conduct. In the Greek world especially, what past generations were has a direct bearing on current ones, and particularly outstanding individuals or groups, whether from recent history or the heroic past, can be made to stand as allegedly typical examples of the prowess of the city as a whole, exemplifying behaviour which should be 'natural' for all its members. It need hardly be said that this so-called 'national character' prescribes behaviour at least as much as it describes it, and that it is not necessarily fixed or free from contradictions, in spite of the way that it is usually presented, as something natural, time-honoured and self-evidently right.

The figures of myth are particularly important in the self-definition of the city and its understanding of the world, because myths concern the distant past and can be retold in different ways, according to the examples that the society needs to draw from them.[2] Athenian literature abounds in references to the qualities

[1] Because this past must be readily comprehensible to a large number of people, only a few major events will tend to be repeatedly emphasized, and those in a rather broad outline, avoiding detail.

[2] Cf. Bremmer 1987: 5, and now Walker 1995: 6.

supposedly typical of the Athenian national character, and to exemplary characters from myth and history who exhibited them. Long before the fifth century, the most famous mythological Athenian was Theseus, whose triumphs, above all over the Minotaur in Crete, symbolized and represented a time-honoured Athenian heroic prowess. The most detailed depictions of Theseus as a national hero and representative of Athens' past are found, however, in fifth-century Athenian tragedy, a genre in which myths were presented to the whole city in a contemporary form,[3] and whose function, like that of myth itself, was partly educational. This book seeks to trace the process by which the figure of Theseus in the public genre of tragedy is moulded according to certain public, 'official' Athenian perceptions of the Athenian national character, so that he comes to represent the idealized imperial Athens, the city of justice and mercy that is familiar from a substantial body of Athenian writing about Athens. First, however, it is necessary to trace the earlier development of his role in Athens, and the process by which an individual hero, who originally represented nothing but himself, comes to represent collective Athenian virtue. Theseus' role in the story of the Minotaur and certain other tales is not as complex as his role in tragedy, but the mighty killer of monsters is a direct ancestor of Theseus the humane, democratic king of tragedy who stands against all forms of tyranny.

I.2 THESEUS BEFORE TRAGEDY: HEROES AND MORALITY

Theseus is associated with Attica and Trozen from earliest times,[4] yet he is also known in early narrative from outside Attica, and, like any mythological important hero, he also has striking adventures outside the regions in which he is located.[5] Such a combination

[3] Cf. Vernant 1988: 9.

[4] He abducts Helen and hides her at Aphidna in Attica, while the story of the Minotaur is told exclusively from an Athenian point of view: Bethe 1910: 222. The unanimity of all sources that Trozen, not Athens, was Theseus' birthplace indicates the antiquity of the association: Herter 1936: 203–7; Sourvinou-Inwood 1979: 20–1. Walker 1995: 9, 12–13 rightly refutes Herter's theory that Theseus is originally an Ionian hero, although his claim, 12 f., 55, that the story of Theseus' birth at Trozen is only a 5th-cent. invention is very dubious: see Sourvinou-Inwood 1971 and 1979: 20–1.

[5] In Crete, Thessaly, and perhaps Phocis: Hes. 298 M–W makes him the lover of Aegle, daughter of Panopeus, whose name may suggest a Phocian connection: Wolgensinger 1935: 31.

automatically makes him an attractive candidate for development
as a representative of Athens' past; more so, in fact, than Athenian
heroes such as Cecrops or Erechtheus, whose activities are confined
to Attica.[6] However, once his reputation becomes part of Athens'
reputation after a consistent link has been forged between them, it
is important that his deeds are suitable reflections of attributes
deemed to be Athenian and models for Athens. In some of his earliest appearances in eighth- and seventh-century literature and art,
he is distinctly ambiguous as a symbol of Athenian prowess:
although he was one of the fighters against the uncivilized Centaurs
with his Thessalian friend Peirithous, he also assisted him in a disastrous attempt to abduct the queen of the underworld, and he
himself carried out a scarcely less disastrous abduction of Helen.
Even his most magnificent exploit of killing the Minotaur in Crete,
so that Athens was liberated from king Minos' oppression, was followed by an act of ingratitude and treachery to the king's daughter
Ariadne, whose help to him in killing the monster was rewarded by
abandonment by Theseus as he made his way back to Athens.

Because the past as it is encapsulated in what is passed down in
mythology can be given an explanatory, educational function as it
is brought to bear on the present and future, offering advice to
those whose knowledge is inevitably limited,[7] anxiety about the
ethical content of what is remembered and told must naturally
creep in: already in the sixth century Xenophanes complains about
the unedifying portrayal of the gods in Homer and Hesiod, while
Theagenes of Rhegium is credited with allegorizing Homer, probably in an attempt to explain away the apparent immorality of the
gods.[8] The discrepancy between what is passed on in myths and the
conditions of ordinary human life frequently creates an interplay
between the restrictions which are placed on human conduct and
the relative immunity of the gods from such restrictions.[9] Heroes
such as Theseus are the middle term between gods, whose power is

[6] Kearns 1989: 89. For Menestheus, the Athenian leader in Homer, see §1.3.2.

[7] The process occurs right from the first in Greek literature: at *Il.* 9. 529–600,
Phoenix advises Achilles by means of the story of Meleager; at *Il.* 24. 602 ff. Achilles
admonishes Priam. The other side of the coin is the heroes' desire to gain immortality via the stories that are remembered: see *Il.* 6. 357 ff., *Od.* 8. 579 ff.

[8] Xenophanes, 21 B 11–16 DK with Untersteiner 1956: pp. cxxi–cxxxiii,
Theagenes: Diels and Kranz i, 51–2, and see also Bažant 1982: 30.

[9] The interplay can be implicit, as in much of the *Iliad* in which the 'easily-living
gods' contrast with 'wretched mortals', or rather more explicit: esp. Eur. *Hipp.* 120,
HF 1341–6, *Ba.* 1348.

vast, and men, whose power is nothing in comparison. The nature of a hero is to be better and stronger than ordinary men: he is by definition, 'one of the men of old', whose prowess can only be imagined by the men of the present who lack anything near it.[10] Distance from the present can be linked with a distance from the everyday behaviour, including morality, which is necessary for the successful operation of human society. Only Theseus is special enough to conquer the Minotaur or to fight the Centaurs; but by the same token, only he is special enough to help Peirithous in the fantastically impious abduction of Kore. The case of Ariadne is perhaps slightly different, because it is a more human, romantic story of love and betrayal, but even here he goes against the ordinary obligations of human life.

However, heroes remain subject to higher powers and so they are punished for their transgressions. Ordinary people can only look on, and consider them as examples in a dual sense. First, their civilizing powers allay anxiety about the dangers in the world and give us hope that we will not be destroyed by what is Other, affirming the human and familiar over the dangers of the world around us.[11] Second, the heroes' transgressions reaffirm the importance of the behaviour fit for ordinary human beings in everyday society by the sufferings they incur. Myth in Greek and other cultures offers its audience material which is removed from them in time and often space, but which is also close by its bearing on their experience of the world, enabling them to be instructed, but at some distance.[12]

The earliest stories in which Theseus appears exemplify his heroic ambivalence as both a civilizer and a breaker of ordinary boundaries who suffers punishment for it. In this ambivalence, he is not dissimilar to Heracles, and the pair have some common attributes. Both are of semi-divine parentage and are 'men of old'

---

[10] Nestor makes this point explicitly at *Il.* 1. 262 ff., and it is a commonplace that the men of the past are better than those now: cf. *Il.* 4. 405 ff. They are naturally bigger: Hdt. 1. 68, Plut. *Thes.* 36. 2. On the essential ambivalence of the hero, see Brelich 1958: 229–83.

[11] Kirk 1974: 85, 203–6; Henderson 1964: 110–28; cf. also Segal 1974. The predominating form in the Theseus stories is that of the civilizing myth: for parallels, see S. Thompson 1955–8, vol. i, s.v. 'culture hero', A500–A599 and 'monsters', vol. vi, 283.

[12] See also the illuminating remarks made by Kearns 1989: 133–7 on the fundamental connection between heroes and the city.

who lived before the Trojan War:[13] the adventures with which they are associated tend to lack the historical veneer of those of the heroes of the Trojan War, being instead of a more fabulous nature, as they fight mythical monsters and encounter death. However, although Theseus is prone to abduct women, he never has the appetite for food and sex in huge amounts at a time which is a stock characteristic of Heracles;[14] nothing he does corresponds to the violence of Heracles' murder of his guest-friend Iphitus, nor does he follow Heracles' example in getting drunk, like the half-wild Cyclops or Centaurs.[15] Equally, Heracles is the only hero magnificent enough to achieve Olympian status.[16] Neither side of Heracles is very amenable to the process of sanitization and domestication which is necessary for a national representative and which shapes the figure of Theseus during the sixth and fifth centuries. Heracles never loses his early fabulousness and 'otherness': Theseus can, so that the timeless, untouchable and exceptional hero turns into a national hero, a reflection of something close at hand and attainable in some measure for every Athenian.[17] It is significant that though Theseus is of semi-divine parentage in early myth, tragedy, with the exception of the *Hippolytus*, will always prefer him to be Aegeus' son.

Where Theseus is simply one of the 'men of old', he is much like other gods and heroes, who are not bound to follow the ordinary

[13] *Il.* 1. 265; *Od.* 11. 321, 631; implied also by *Il.* 3. 144. His name is one of those short names ending in -ευς which are generally assumed to belong to an older strand of mythology than those of many of the heroes who play a dominant part in the Homeric poems: Kretschmer 1912: 305–6; Nilsson 1932: 26; cf. also Kirk 1962: 118. The name itself may be pre-Greek (Von Kamptz 1982: 123–4; Masson 1972: 287–9; *contra* Herter 1936: 233–5) but it appears as an ordinary name of 'Mycenean' Greek on late 13th-cent. records of land tenure from Pylos (En 74, l. 5 and Eo 276, l. 4; nos. 115 and 120 in Ventris and Chadwick 1973: 243 f.; see also A. M. Davies 1963: 327). Its appearance as an ordinary name in the 13th cent. may provide a *terminus post quem* for the stories of Theseus the hero: Herter 1939: 258; Kirk 1962: 137–8: Vermeule 1958: 105.

[14] Heracles could get through Thespius' fifty daughters in one night (Paus. 9. 27. 7): such an excess of appetite and strength is characteristic of him, but not of Theseus.

[15] Centaurs drinking: *Od.* 21. 295 ff.; Heracles: Panyassis, frs. 12–14D, with Matthews 1974: 74–8.

[16] Webster 1972: 260–2. Even though he is powerful enough to fight the gods (*Il.* 5. 393–404, cf. Hes. *Thg.* 314, *Il.* 15. 25, Panyassis 21D), he is still protected by Athena and made immortal.

[17] Such a process works best with heroes, because their power is limited: any attempt to make Zeus follow ordinary human ideas of justice and morality is doomed to failure in the light of human experience.

rules of society, but his adoption as the national hero and representative of Athens means that he can no longer be sufficiently distanced as an educational example; hence any deeds which conflict
with what Athenians need to believe about their representative
(and therefore themselves) must be pushed into the background or
sanitized in Athenian literature, although for non-Athenians they
are less disturbing and can be retained. When the Theseus myth is
developed in the second half of the sixth century, the vast majority
of the newer tales conform to the pattern of the Minotaur story, of
lone hero conquering danger for the benefit of others: the interest
of the inventors and audiences of these stories is clearly in Theseus
as a moralized, civilizing hero; a safe and morally unchallengeable
reflection of typical Athenian behaviour.

I.3 THE EARLIEST EXPLOITS OF THESEUS

Although Heracles is a far more important hero than Theseus, even
at Athens, until the sixth century, there is sufficient fragmentary
literary and artistic evidence to show that Theseus' abduction of
Helen, his ill-fated journey to the underworld, the Cretan adventure and the Centauromachy are all familiar stories before the sixth
century and that they are not confined to Athenian narratives. They
were known to the authors of early Greek lyric and of the cyclic
epics, the *Cypria*, *Little Iliad* and *Iliupersis*,[18] and to the artists who
drew on their work long before Athenian interest brought about the
elaboration of the myth.[19]

---

[18] The *Little Iliad* is usually ascribed to Lesches of Mytilene, and the *Iliupersis*,
to Arctinus of Miletus: for full testimonia, see Bernabé 1987: 71–6. The origins of
the *Cypria* are disputed: the Atticisms contained in the extant fragments do not
prove an Attic origin (cf. M. Davies 1989: 93–4), nor can its subject matter (*pace*
Bethe 1922: 339–41). Athenaeus 682d–e associates it with Cyprus or Halicarnassus,
although the fragments contain little Cypriot dialect. It is listed as an Ionian epic in
Schmid and Stählin 1929: 195–221; also Jouan 1966: 22–5.

[19] Although the language and some of the content of the fragments of the cyclic
poems date them after Homer and Hesiod (cf. M. Davies 1989), artistic evidence
suggests that earlier versions were current as early as the 7th cent.: Johansen 1967:
26–8, 35–7, 39; Jouan 1966: 15; Huxley 1969: 136; Walker 1995: 15–20; cf. also
J. Griffin 1977.

1.3.1 *Theseus and Helen*

The incompatibility of Theseus' rape of Helen with canonical Homeric chronology is an indication of the story's antiquity.[20] It is linked with Peirithous' attempted abduction of Kore at least as early as Pindar and almost certainly earlier, by Alcman.[21] The earliest possible artistic representation of the story dates from the first quarter of the seventh century, and it was sufficiently well known to be included in the mythological compendia on the chest of Cypselus (Paus. 5. 19. 3), and the throne of Bathycles (Paus. 3. 18. 15).[22] The full version of the story runs thus:[23] Theseus and Peirithous thought that since they were both the sons of gods, both should have divine wives, so decided to help each other abduct Helen for Theseus and the queen of the underworld for Peirithous. Theseus took Helen and hid her with his mother Aethra or his associate Aphidnus at Aphidna or Athens,[24] causing an invasion by the

[20] It may antedate Paris' more famous exploit: Becker 1939: 148; Kakridis 1971: 30 n. 31. Later writers improve the chronology—if not the moral content—by making her into a little girl at the time: Hellanicus *FGrH* 4 168; Apollod. *Ep.* 1. 23; ΣLycophr. 513. However, the tradition that Iphigeneia was the daughter of Theseus and Helen was known already to Stesichorus: Paus. 2. 22. 6 and see Shapiro 1992: 232–3. Helen is prone to being abducted, and it is usually assumed that the facts of cult lie behind the form of her myth: Herter 1939: 193–203; Nilsson 1950: 528–32, 1932: 73–6; Becker 1939: 138–43. It has also been suggested that Theseus' own tendency to abduct ex-goddesses like Helen and Ariadne, may reflect an original ἱερὸς γάμος in Cretan religion, but although abduction by Theseus may be common to Helen and Ariadne, the stories have become individualized and entirely differentiated from one another by the time we see them, even if they were once versions of the same story: for theories of the relationship of these myths to early religion, see Nilsson 1932: 170–1; Clota 1957; Butterworth 1966: 4, 174–86.

[21] Alcman 21 *PMGF*: ΣAD *Il.* 3. 242 says that he only told the story 'in part', but Paus. 1. 41. 4 ascribes to Alcman the details that Theseus promised to help Peirithous in the underworld, and that he was absent from Attica when the Dioscuri came, so that I assume that he did connect the two abductions with one another; cf. also fr. 22 *PMGF*; Pind. fr. 243, 258 Sn.; Hellanicus *FGrH* 4 F134 (cf. 143, 168), who probably drew on early sources: Jacoby 1949: 223. Later sources: D.S. 4. 63; Plut. *Thes.* 32. 4; Apollod. *Ep.* 1. 23; Hyg. 79. On the episode, see Herter 1939: 263–6; Brommer 1982: 93–7. The abduction of Helen is assigned to the Cypria as fr. 12 by M. Davies 1988: 39; Becker 1939: 36; *contra* Van der Valk 1964: 351.

[22] See *LIMC* 4. 1, s.v. 'Helene', 507–13 and Ghali-Kahil 1955: 309–12; more sceptically, Fittschen 1969: 161 ff.

[23] For the reconstruction, cf. Severyns 1928: 273–5.

[24] Aphidna: Hdt. 9. 73; Isoc. *Hel.* 19; D.S. 4. 63. 3; Paus. 2. 22. 6. Athens: Apollod. *Ep.* 1. 23; Hyg. 79; ΣLycophr. 501. ΣAD on *Il.* 3. 242 combine the two, and the caption on the Chest of Cypselus ran, Τυνδαρίδα Ἑλέναν φερέτον, Αἴθραν δ' ἔλκειτον | Ἀθάναθεν ('they take Helen, Tyndareus' daughter and drag Aethra from Athens'), emended by Bergk to Ἀφιδνάθεν: Hitzig and Blümner 1901: ii, 411–

Dioscuri (joined, in later sources, by Attic enemies of Theseus)[25] when he was away, presumably because he had already gone to Hades with Peirithous: Castor was wounded, but they succeeded in finding Helen and captured Aethra in revenge.

The tale does not reflect well on Theseus, not so much because he abducted Helen,[26] but because the abduction caused an enemy invasion of his country. There is a consistent tradition that he was not present to save his defenceless mother from suffering and humiliation, and the triumph of the Dioscuri is central to the story in Alcman and also in early Peloponnesian art.[27] It is not hard to see why the original tale should have become unfitting for Theseus' later incarnation as an Athenian statesman, and was given less and less prominence: it does feature on fifth-century vases, but only rarely, tragedy and monumental art ignore it, and later sources indicate that it could be seen as a blemish on Theseus' reputation.[28] One significant exception to the comparative neglect of the story in later Athens is on a late fifth-century vase on which his liaison with Helen is at last sanctioned by law and the gods: young and handsome, he marries a splendidly dressed Helen, with her mother, the brothers who had once invaded Attica to retrieve her, and his divine father (amongst others) in attendance.[29]

412. Aphidna is probably primary: it was an important Mycenean citadel and all the connections of Helen and Iphigeneia are with NE Attica: Kearns 1989: 34 n. 121, 158; Herter 1936: 195–6 and Ghali-Kahil 1955: 308; Walker 1995: 28 n. 56: on Aphidna, see Hope Simpson 1981: 51; cf. also Wilamowitz 1925: 236 n. 2.

[25] Decelus and Titacus in Hdt. 9. 73; Academus in Plut. *Thes.* 32. 5. Like Aphidnus and Theseus' hostile cousins the Pallantidae, they are eponyms of regions in Attica. Later sources link their role with Theseus' unification of Attica, and although the actual form of these stories is entirely anachronistic, such conflicts may reflect a time before Attica was unified: Herter 1936: 197–200, 1939: 263.

[26] Images of Theseus as an irresistible male can coexist with more earnest portrayals of Theseus the national representative, certainly in the sixth century, and on the 20 or so 5th-cent. vases portraying the abduction, he is a handsome ephebe, not Hellanicus' dirty old man: Shapiro 1992: 233–4. The two types of Theseus may even complement one another: Shapiro 1991: 136 and Garland 1992: 98; see also Neils 1981 and 1987: 40–1. For a robust attitude to abduction, compare Hdt. 1. 4. 2.

[27] Neils 1987: 20–1. Cantarelli 1974: 486 is surely wrong to think that the absence of Theseus diminishes the Dioscuri, since Alcman appears to have included this detail in his hymn of praise to them. In one version of the myth, which may reflect Athens' hostility to Megara, Theseus is present to meet the invaders: Paus. 1. 41. 4; Plut. *Thes.* 32. 6 (Hereas *FGrH* 486 F2) with Ampolo and Manfredini 1988: 255.

[28] Isoc. *Hel.* 18; D.S. 4. 63. 5. A not dissimilar shift of emphasis happens in stories of Theseus and the Amazons.

[29] Greco 1985–6. See also *LIMC* 4. 1, no. 35 by Polygnotus, *c.*430–420 (cf. nos. 48–52); Shapiro 1992*b*, esp. 234 f.

Some time before the composition of the *Little Iliad* and *Iliupersis*, the story acquires a sequel in which Theseus' sons, Acamas and Demophon, come to Troy and rescue their grandmother from captivity there as Helen's servant.[30] This may simply have been a later rationalizing addition to the core of the old abduction story, but at Athens it comes to overshadow the older tale. Not only does the rescue of Aethra attest the filial piety of Athenians (cf. [Dem.] 60. 29), but it also enlarges Athens' disappointingly minor role in Homer[31] by bringing the Theseidae into the magic circle of the Iliadic heroes. Although they were entirely unknown to Homer, and even the cyclic poets only seem to know of their mission to rescue their grandmother, and retain the Homeric Menestheus as the Athenian leader in battle (cf. *Il.* 2. 522, 4. 327, 12. 331–7, 373), Menestheus lacked the heroic dash which made Theseus a worthy Athenian national representative,[32] and Theseus' sons represent the city at Troy in the fifth century, because their father's appeal was so great.[33] In tragedy likewise, Theseus (or Demophon in Euripides' *Heraclidae*), not

[30] *Little Iliad* 23D; *Iliup.* 4 and 11D. Αἴθρη Πιτθῆος θυγάτηρ ('Aethra, daughter of Pittheus') is one of Helen's servants at *Il.* 3. 144, but the chronological difficulties of the line caused Aristarchus to athetize it: *ΣIl.* 3. 144, 7. 10, cf. Eustathius 951. 10, *ΣIl.* 13. 626 with Erbse 1979. Most commentators follow him: see, however Ameis, Hentze and Cauer 1913: 119; Wilamowitz 1925: 236; Ghali-Kahil 1955: 306. The story was sufficiently well known for Stesichorus (193; cf. 205) to put his own stamp on it by having Demophon carried to Egypt with the Th[estia]dae on his return from Troy. According to *PMGF* 223, the daughters of Tyndareus were made διγάμους τε καὶ τριγάμους . . . | καὶ λιπεσάνδρας ('twice- and thrice-married, and deserters of their husbands'). Helen's third husband is either Deiphobus or (less probably) Theseus: Podlecki 1971*b*: 324; also Bowra 1963: 251–2.

[31] Keenly felt, although the Persian Wars were an acceptable substitute for Homeric glories: cf. Hdt. 9. 27, Thuc. 2. 41. 4, Plut. *Cim.* 7; *FGrH* 392 F16; [Dem.] 60. 10; Isoc. 4. 83; Hyperid. *Epitaph.* 35 f.

[32] He is certainly no Achilles, although his very obscurity may indicate that he is a genuinely ancient Athenian figure, perhaps a Mycenean king remembered in oral tradition: Page 1959: 145–7, 173 n. 79, 272 n. 52; Kirk 1985: 206. His place in Homer means that he is never entirely forgotten: he represents Athens as one of Helen's suitors in Hes. 200. 3 (generally dated to *c.*600–570), and he appears on a sixth century black figure kantharos, along with Achilles and other more famous Homeric characters: Zschietzschmann 1931; see also n. 62 below. He appears rarely in 5th-cent. art (see *LIMC* 6. 1, 473–5), but it is he, not Theseus, to whom the Athenians are compared on the Herm dedicated by Cimon after the battle of Eion and he acquires a role as Theseus' enemy in the 5th cent.: see below.

[33] Eur. *Tro.* 31 with *Σ*; *I.A.* 248; S. *Phil.* 562. There was a statue of the wooden horse on the Acropolis which contained Menestheus and the Theseidae: Paus. 1. 23. 8. For a full list of representations of Acamas in the 5th cent., see Kron 1976: 141–70.

Menestheus, is the king of Athens; Acamas is, of course, one of the tribal eponyms chosen by Cleisthenes. Sixth-century vases show the Theseidae setting out for Troy, and it is perhaps not meant to be clear that their purpose is the rescue of their grandmother rather than proper Homeric combat.[34] The act of filial piety even adorned the Parthenon: presumably one was not meant to wonder why Aethra needed to be rescued in the first place. It is a consistent feature of the treatment of the Theseus myth at Athens that prominence is given to the parts of it which are suitable examples of 'typically' Athenian behaviour, and other stories are pushed into the background. This is particularly true when he appears on the tragic stage: it would be difficult to associate the Theseus of most tragedy with the treacherous and impious abductor of early myth. By being brought to life by tragedy, the Theseus who appears as a representative of Athens before an audience of Athenians and foreigners blots out any other, less praiseworthy images of Theseus (or, perhaps, of Athens) that any of the audience might have.[35]

1.3.2 *Theseus in Hades*

The easiest explanation for Theseus' own failure to go after his mother is that he had already met with disaster while fulfilling his side of the bargain with Peirithous in accompanying him down to the underworld. In the most common version of the story, the two abductors were tricked into sitting down, whereupon they were bound fast for eternity.[36] A meeting with death is a classic motif of

[34] Kron 1976: 153. Note especially London BM 173, on which the ethnic $A\Theta E$ appears on Acamas' shield; also Berlin F1720 by Exekias, *c*.530, which pays them the compliment of pairing them with Heracles and the lion. See Kron 1976: 148 and pl. 19. 2 and Shapiro 1989: 148. The Theseidae appear in Trojan scenes in art throughout the fifth century: see *LIMC* 1. 1, 435–46.

[35] For the relation between the Theseus of most tragedy and the Theseus of the Hippolytus plays, see §§6.3 and 6.5, and for the relationship between the Athenian image of Athens and other cities' perceptions, see the end of §2.5.

[36] Already in the 'Hesiodic' poem on their descent which may be the same as the *Minyas*: Paus. 9. 31. 5, 10. 28. 2, 29. 9; Paus. 1. 17. 1–2; Apollod. 2. 5. 12; Hor. *Odes* 4. 7. 28: on the significance of sitting down, see Battegazzore 1970. Homer may allude to the story: *Od.* 11. 631 places Theseus and Peirithous in the underworld, and they are not dissimilar to the notorious evil-doers of *Od.* 11. 576ff., but the problems surrounding the transmission of *Od.* 11 prevent certainty. Hereas of Megara alleged that the line had been added by Peisistratus to *Odyssey* 11 for the greater glory of Theseus, and, like *Il.* 3. 144, its Homeric authenticity has been doubted: see, however, Wilamowitz 1884: 141; Herter 1936: 201; Hoekstra and Heubeck 1989: 88. In Panyassis 9 they sit on rocks which eat into their flesh (cf. Apollod. *Ep.* 1. 23) and Attic vase painters also portray this version: see *LIMC* 5. 1 s.v. 'Herakles and Theseus' no. 3515.

traditional tales of heroes and it is popular in early epic; usually, the civilizing hero withstands an encounter that ordinary mortals—by definition—cannot,[37] but Theseus and Peirithous fail to do so. It is clear that they have been punished for what they should not have done, just as Peirithous' father Ixion was punished for a similar act of wickedness towards Hera (Pind. *P*. 2. 21–41; [Eur.] *Peirithous* fr. 1). They must be punished for the heroic hubris that leads them even to think that they deserve divine wives, quite apart from taking their own steps to acquire them. Yet again, however, some story-tellers were unable to leave the pair sitting in Hades for ever, just as Aethra could not be with Helen for ever: from the early sixth century, a version is known, even outside Attica, in which Heracles comes to rescue them both.[38] It is possible that this story was originally intended to enhance the heroism of Heracles (who also saved Prometheus) rather than to whitewash the reputations of the two abductors, but it does have the result of making their crime look less serious, and from this version developed the most commonly attested form of the story in which Theseus is rescued by Heracles, but Peirithous is imprisoned forever so that blame for the whole unfortunate incident is fixed firmly on him.[39] This is the version that was most palatable to the Athenians, but it could never be unambiguously flattering to their national hero: Heracles' rescue of Theseus associates him with the supreme panhellenic hero so that they are comrades in a dangerous place, but it leaves him in his debt

[37] Heracles is the most famous classical example: Hom. *Il.* 5. 397; 8. 369; *Od.* 11. 623. A poem may have been devoted to his catabasis: Lloyd-Jones 1967: 227–9. On catabasis in general, see Ganschienietz 1919, esp. 2395–418; Clark 1979, esp. 79–94, 125–45.

[38] On an inscribed shield band from Olympia, *c*.580 on which Theseus' name is unusually in a Doric form: Kunze 1950: 112ff.; see also *LIMC* 5. 2, 182 and Brommer 1982: 101–2. According to Tzetz. *Chil.* in Cramer 1886: iii, 359,22 Euripides, presumably in the *Peirithous*, had both men rescued by Heracles; as also D.S. 4. 26; Hyg. 79.

[39] Theseus saved, Peirithous not: D.S. 4. 26. 1; Apollod. *Ep.* 1. 23–4; Plut. *Thes.* 35; Paus. 1. 17. 4; Aristid. 40. 7; cf. *Σ*Ar. *Ran.* 142. In Apollod. 2. 5. 12, who also distinguishes between the two, Heracles and Theseus ascend via Theseus' home town of Trozen: it has been suggested that an Attic Catabasis of Heracles may lie behind this account: Norden 1926: 5 and n. 2; Lloyd-Jones 1967: 206–29, esp. 211, who dates it *c*.550. In Hes. 280 M–W, Meleager is appalled at Peirithous' desire for a divine wife but seems to approve of Theseus, calling him Ἀθηναίων βουληφόρε ('Athenian counsellor', l. 26). Linguistic evidence suggests that the poem originates from Attica, and it is datable to the early 6th cent. It may be making a moral distinction between Theseus and Peirithous, but it is so fragmentary that conclusions must remain uncertain: see Merkelbach 1950, 1952.

and in the wrong. The problem is subtly explored more than once in tragedy, but there were also less complex attempts to save Theseus' credit, so that he tries to dissuade Peirithous from the enterprise, and when that fails, he accompanies him purely out of loyalty.[40]

Later, a rationalized and less disturbing account of his end was offered, in which he was banished from Attica by enemies and died on Skyros by slipping or being pushed off a cliff by king Lycomedes: this tradition lies behind Cimon's retrieval of the bones of Theseus from Skyros in 475. Although the full story is only found in late sources,[41] in view of the consistent preference for versions of the story in which Theseus does not end his days in Hades, it is very probable that the story of his death on Skyros antedates the discovery of his bones. Not only does the story remove Theseus from any transgression, but it also explains why Menestheus is the leader of the Athenians in Homer.[42] The story has been highly politicized in all surviving accounts, so that its earliest form is irrecoverable. Theseus can be presented as the unlucky victim of his own political correctness in synoikizing Attica and founding democracy, which brought the enmity of the aristocrats whose power he had diminished upon him,[43] but there are also anti-Thesean or anti-democratic versions of the story in which the act of synoikizing Attica and bringing democracy is linked with,

[40] Dissuasion: Isoc. 10. 20, D.S. 4. 63. 4 and Aelian *V.H.* 4. 5. Loyalty: S. *OC* 1593, and see Chapter 5. Outside Attica the older stories could be told: Polygnotus painted their eternal imprisonment amongst other scenes, probably inspired by the *Minyas*, on the Lesche of the Cnidians: Robert 1892: 64. There is a potentially comic aspect in having Heracles rescue Theseus by pulling him bodily from the rock: *Σ*Ar. *Eq.* 1368 and the Suda, s.v. λίσποι say that Athenians have small bottoms because Theseus left a piece of his in the rock when Heracles rescued him. However, this scholiast also offers more seemly explanations of the neatness of the Athenian bottom. *ARV²* 1086, 1 (*LIMC* 4. 1 3516) flatters Theseus' dignity by having him lift himself from the rock without Heracles' assistance.

[41] Paus. 1. 17. 3; Plut. *Thes.* 32–3; *Σ*Aristid., 561D; *Σ*Ar. *Plut.* 627a.

[42] Kron 1976: 142. See Hellan. *FGrH* 323a F21; D.S. 4. 63; Paus. 1. 17. 6; Apollod. *Ep.* 1. 23 f. They are enemies at least from the early fifth century: see the interpretation by Neils 1987: 85 of *ARV²* 259,1, *c.*480.

[43] *Σ*Ar. *Plut.* 627a; Plut. *Thes.* 32. Association of synoikism and democracy: Theophr. 26. 2; Dem. 57. 75; Isoc. *Hel.* 35. Hellanicus narrated the abduction of Helen and the overthrow of Theseus by Menestheus, but how democratic a framework he cast it in is unknowable: Jacoby 1954 on *FGrH* 323a F21; J. K. Davies 1971: 81. The pattern of the punishment of a statesman by the people in spite of his services to them is influenced by democratic ideologies, because it reassures the *demos* of their authority over their leaders: Thomas 1989: 199.

and discredited by, the abduction of Helen or the murder of his cousins the Pallantidae, for which he is punished by the enemy invasion as in the earlier story.[44] Herodotus preserves an account which may date from the Peloponnesian war, to judge from its (pro-Spartan?) aetiological slant, which is decidedly unflattering to Athens' national hero: Decelus led the Dioscuri to Helen's hiding-place in Attica because he was angry at Theseus' hubris (whether over the synoikism or simply the abduction is unknown) as a result of which Decelea was favoured by Sparta.[45] It may be significant that a non-Athenian can talk so openly of the 'hubris' of Theseus, and it is interesting that he never entirely manages to shake off the less flattering stories, in spite of the Theseus who is usually presented in tragedy to an audience of Athenian citizens and foreigners as the mouthpiece of conventional Athenian ideals and as a representative of an idealized Athens.

1.3.3 *Theseus in Crete*

Theseus' earliest exploits exhibit a pattern of failure modified by sequels which transform them into moral successes. The abduction of Helen becomes a story of family piety, the hubristic journey to the underworld, a story of loyalty between friends. Subsequent chapters will show how important the exhibition of such loyalties is for the moral credit of the national representative and the city-state itself that he represents. Of at least equal importance with loyalty to family and friends is prowess in combat, and no other Athenian hero faced and surmounted as great a challenge as the Minotaur. Most of the elements of the developed story in its best-known form are demonstrably in place at least from the seventh century and seem to be as famous outside Attica as within it. Androgeos, the son of Minos of Crete had met his death in Attica,[46] and Minos

---

[44] *Σ*Ar. *Plut.* 627a; Plut. *Thes.* 32 in which Menestheus the first demagogue works to remove Theseus from power, aided by the Dioscuri and the disgruntled aristocrats of Attica. His account may reflect a speech of the oligarch Antiphon: Cantarelli 1974: 480–3; Gianfrancesco 1975.

[45] Hdt. 9. 73: hence the Deceleans have προεδρία and ἀτέλεια at Sparta and the Academy was not invaded in the Peloponnesian War: see Ampolo and Manfredini 1988: 254; Masaracchia 1978: 190. The structure of the story is similar in Plut. *Thes.* 32 where Academus plays the part of Decelus.

[46] Probably already in [Hes.], fr. 144–7: 145 sets Ἀν]δρόγεων (l. 9) with Μίνωϊ (l. 10) in the context of the birth of the Minotaur (ll. 15–17): see also Philoch. *FGrH* 328 F17; Plut. *Thes.* 16. 1; D.S. 4. 60. 4; Paus. 1. 27. 10; Apollod. 3. 15. 7–8; Hyg. 41; *Σ*[Pl.] *Minos* 321a. Note also *POxy* 2452, fr. 73 (Sophocles' *Theseus*). Huxley 1969: 120, notes Hesiod's strikingly unfavourable attitude to Theseus.

punished the Athenians by forcing them to send seven youths and seven maidens[47] to be devoured by his half-bull, half-man off-spring who lived in the labyrinth, a terrifying maze of passages from which no one could ever escape.[48] To survive the dangers posed by the Minotaur and the labyrinth, Theseus must prove himself twice over in slightly different ways. Ariadne, Minos' daughter, fell in love with Theseus and gave him a ball of thread[49] so that he could find his way back out of the labyrinth when he had killed the monster; in return, Theseus was to take her with him when he left Crete. Theseus killed the Minotaur, thereby freeing Athens from the tribute for ever, and escaped from Crete with his benefactress: however, on the way back, at Dia or Naxos,[50] he abandoned her. His return was greeted by the suicide of his father Aegeus, because Theseus had broken his promise to him that he would change the sails of his ship from black to white if he was suc-cessful in Crete. Meanwhile, in the most usual form of the story, Dionysus (never any other god) rescues Ariadne and marries her.[51]

This version of the story in which Theseus is ungrateful and treacherous dominates later tradition (its potential as a narrative is

[47] Already in Sappho, ap. Serv. *Aen.* 6. 21. For a possible connection with initia-tory rituals, see Brelich 1958: 240–2; Jeanmaire 1939: 227–383.

[48] Although Linear B tablet Kn Gg702 refers to the 'mistress of the labyrinth' (po-ti-ni-ja da-pu$_2$-ri-to-jo), the relationship between this and the function of the labyrinth in the myth of Theseus is unknown. Labyrinths are, from earliest times, symbols of difficulty and perplexity: Reed 1990.

[49] The youths, the thread and the Minotaur are associated already on a mid-7th-cent. amphora in Basel: Neils 1987: 22 n. 88, and some interpreters suggest that there are even earlier representations of the Theseus and Ariadne story: see Neils 1987: 19. Oddly, there is nothing in Athenian art before the later sixth century: see *LIMC* 3. 1, 1053–4, nos. 16–21, whose scheme occurs already on five mid-7th-cent. Corinthian gold plaques (*LIMC* 3. 1, 1055, no. 37). Cf. Neils, 22–3 and n. 90.

[50] Dia, Hom. *Od.* 11. 321–5, Naxos thereafter. See next note.

[51] The bibliography on Ariadne is extensive: helpful treatments include Pallat 1891; Nilsson 1950: 523–8; M. L. West 1966: 418; Webster 1966; Hoog 1973; Eisner 1977; Blech 1982: 259 ff. For the association with Dionysus, see also Herter 1939: 256–7 and Kerényi 1976: 108. In Hes. *Thg.* 947 f. she is his bride and *Od.* 11. 321 ff. may also presuppose this. Although the passages themselves may be no older than the sixth century (M. L. West 1966), it is often thought that her connection with the god is primary, and that, like Helen, her cult as a goddess lies behind her myth: reli-gious factors external to the myth would then explain why she cannot go to Athens with Theseus. The fertility of Naxos and its association with Dionysus may also have contributed to the development of the myth: Webster 1966: 23. The pair may be associated on a 7th-cent. Melian amphora: *LIMC* 3. 1, s.v. Dionysus, no. 708, 482. Other 6th-cent. portrayals are not lacking: see 482–8, and nos. 709–17, 756–60, 763–9, 771–5.

obvious),[52] and is already to be found in Hesiod or the Catalogue and the *Cypria*. Hesiod says that he deserted Ariadne: δεινὸς γάρ μιν ἔτειρεν ἔρως Πανοπηΐδος Αἴγλης ('for a terrible love of Aegle, Panopeus' daughter, pained him').[53] The portrayal was so potentially offensive to Athens that Hereas of Megara could claim that Peisistratus had had the line removed from the text of Hesiod.[54] In the *Cypria*, Nestor told the story of Theseus and Ariadne as part of a digression to console Menelaus for the loss of Helen, and Homeric scholiasts say that according to the *neoteroi* (hence, presumably, the *Cypria*), Ariadne was abandoned on Naxos by Theseus, but was rescued by Dionysus, who married her.[55] What happened to Theseus is not mentioned, but one may suspect that Menelaus would have been most effectively consoled by a story which had an unhappy ending for the abductor. Later sources link the abandonment of Ariadne with Aegeus' suicide.[56] Plutarch reports a tradition that Aegeus fathered Theseus in defiance of the Delphic oracle, which could explain why he has to die (indirectly) at his son's hands, and may also shed light on Theseus' rather chequered career in early myth. Such a framework should antedate the development of the Theseus story as a national myth:[57] hence it is

[52] Cf. Wolgensinger 1935: 18: compare the story of Jason and Medea or Scylla and Minos.

[53] Hes. 147 and 298 M–W and cf. Athenaeus 557b: 'Theseus married Hippe and Aegle, because of whom he broke his oaths to Ariadne, as says Cercops.' Whether Cercops, or Hesiod, or both, told this story is unclear, but Athen. 503d exhibits a similar confusion concerning Cercops' authorship of the *Aegimius*. The *Aegimius* may have included a digression on the worthlessness of lovers' oaths; Hes. 299 refers to Jason's oath, 294 and 296 to Io: cf. also fr. 124 M–W (187 Rz.) which Rzach assigns to the *Aegimius*. If Theseus appeared as a typically faithless lover in the *Aegimius*' list, this might explain later confusion between Cercops and Hesiod: see Huxley 1969: 107–9; Schwartz 1960: 261–3. Possibly relevant is Theognis l. 1231, who mentions Theseus, with Ajax, as a victim of ἀτασθαλίη brought about by love.

[54] Plut. *Thes.* 20. 1–2 (= FGrH 486 F1). We need not take the accusation seriously: no ancient textual critic seems to have done so, and Megarian Homeric scholarship had a highly political bias: cf. FGrH 485 F6, Strabo 9. 1. 10 and Plut. *Sol.* 10. 1, with Scott 1911 and Davison 1955: 16–18. It is interesting, however, that both this allegation and Hereas' other claim, that Peisistratus inserted l. 631 into *Odyssey* 11 for Theseus' glory, concern parts of the Theseus myth which did need careful handling in Athenian literature.

[55] Proclus *Chrestomathia* 103. 23; ΣOd. 11. 325: on this episode see Severyns 1928: 281–3 and Jouan 1966: 384–6.

[56] Cat. 64. 227ff.; D.S. 4. 61. 4; Apollod. *Ep.* 1. 9–10; Hyg. 41, 43. Little can be made of Simonides 550–1 (*PMGF*), which referred to the colour of Theseus' sails and to Aegeus' death. On this episode of the *Cypria* see Jouan 1966: 384–6.

[57] Plut. *Thes.* 3. 1; Comp. *Thes.* 5. 2, with Ampolo and Manfredini 1988:

possible that the *Cypria* linked the desertion of Ariadne with the death of Aegeus, to Theseus' discredit, but even if the two cannot be connected, it is certain that the *Cypria* did not portray Theseus in a flattering light.

Killing the Minotaur makes Theseus a civilizer and also the liberator of his people, an ideal national hero: from the middle of the sixth century, some vase paintings include Athena in the combat with the Minotaur[58] and her attendance is an economical means of indicating both the justice of Theseus' combat and his Athenian origins. That he fights and wins in a foreign land is particularly to his credit, especially in a land such as Crete which appears as a mysterious, slightly threatening place in early Greek poetry.[59] He is not the only hero to undergo trials on the edges of the known world, but more than Odysseus or Heracles, Theseus is fighting as much on behalf of his country and to save its young people as in an individual capacity. This Theseus predominates in fifth-century public representations in which he exercises his individual prowess on behalf of the community he represents. This kind of heroism is not unique: even the most individualistic among the Homeric heroes does not operate in isolation from a community, but it is hard not to feel that there is a difference in emphasis between the exploits of the Homeric heroes and Theseus' encounter with the Minotaur.

Moreover, his heroic altruism can extend beyond his immediate community. On the famous vase of Clitias and Ergotimos (*c*.570)[60] which seems to show the aftermath of the Minotauromachy, a ship

199–200. Like the Oedipus story, the story would also explain how fathers must be succeeded by sons: Bremmer 1987: 48; Calame 1990: 123, 257.

[58] *ABV* 104,126, *c*.560–550: *ABV* 163,2 (*LIMC* 3. 1, 1054, no. 28), *c*.540.

[59] Hoekstra and Heubeck 1989: 179. Our oldest sources are ambivalent towards Crete: Minos is a remarkable figure (*Od.* 11. 568, 19. 179, Hes. fr. 141, 144 M–W), but Crete is also the home of liars (*Od.* 13. 256, 14. 199). Compare also *Hom.h.Dem.* 123 with Richardson 1979: 188. It is conceivable that this image reflects memories of Cretan domination in the Aegean, but this is, of course, not to concur with euhemeristic attempts to turn the Theseus myth into history so that its structure reflects the historical ending of Cretan power over the islands. It is most unlikely that an account of any historical conquest of Crete would have taken an entirely symbolic form, and in spite of the Athenian focus of the Theseus myth, it does not seem to have been Athenians who made the decisive conquest of Crete, if indeed there was such a conquest: Herter 1936: 216; Blegen 1940. On the so-called 'Minoan thalassocracy', see the papers collected in Hägg and Marinatos 1984 and the scepticism of Starr 1955.

[60] The so-called François vase: *ABV* 76,1. See Minto 1960: 42–58; Beazley 1986: 24–33 with pl. 27, 1–3.

is drawn up, from which emerge the twice-seven youths and maidens in a joyous dance led by a Theseus who combines martial prowess with grace and culture: he wears a costume like that of Apollo and he carries a lyre.[61] From the names which the artist has given the twice-seven, it would appear that Theseus did not only save the youth of Attica: Eleusis and Salamis are both represented,[62] which may be significant in an era in which Athens was both using the Eleusinian mysteries for her benefit and seeking to bolster her growing dominance over the Saronic Gulf and her possession of Salamis. Later chapters will explore the political implications of the altruism which places those whom Athens has helped very firmly in the city's debt, but it is striking that these tendencies are to be found even in the early sixth century, particularly if the dance is intended to be the crane dance on Delos, whose *aetion* in later sources was the victory over the Minotaur.[63] The vase may just antedate Peisistratus' reign, and Athenian interest in Delos can be traced back at least to Solon; thus the scene may be an early manifestation of the increase in connections between Delos and Athenian heroes in the Peisistratean age and of Athens' political

[61] As he does on the chest of Cypselus (Paus. 5. 19. 1) and in other early portrayals from the late 7th cent. on: *LIMC* 3. 1, 1056, nos. 47a–49. Note also the fragment listed as Anacreon 99 by Bergk: ἀγχοῦ δ᾽ Αἰγείδεω Θησέος ἐστὶ λύρη ('near Theseus, son of Aegeus, is the lyre'). For the importance of the combination of strength and grace, cf. Shapiro 1991: 126.

[62] Eleusis: Daidouchos; Salamis: Epiboia, daughter of Alcathous of Megara and the mother of Ajax (Pind. *Isthm.* 45), assuming that Epiboia, Eriboia and Periboia are one and the same. Phereboia is a wife of Theseus in Plut. *Thes.* 29. 3. Similar tendencies can be found in the list of the twice seven given by Servius commenting on V. *Aen.* 6. 21, although the preponderance of Athenian deme-names suggests that his source was a post-Cleisthenic *Theseid*, and he includes various eponyms of Athenian families: Wilamowitz 1893: 278–9. Antiochos on the vase is presumably the eponym of the later Cleisthenic tribe. There is also a girl called Menestho, presumably in an attempt to integrate Menestheus into the Theseus legend: Menestheus appears in Servius' list, and in Philochorus, Theseus saves a Menesthes who is the grandson of Sciros: see Jacoby 1954: 441–2 on *FGrH* 328 F111. But there were other traditions: the names of the twice seven on *ABV* 163,2 by Glaucytes and Archicles have nothing in common with these two lists.

[63] Call. hymn 4. 307f.; Plut. *Thes.* 21; Hesych. s.v. Δηλιακὸς Βωμός; Pollux, *Onom.* 4. 101; *ΣIl.* 18. 591. The dance itself is probably of very ancient origins: Herter 1939: 259f.; Lawler 1964: 46–8; see also Gallet de Santerre 1958: 181ff. To my mind, Neils's observation, 1987: 26 n. 113, that a joyous dance as soon as the ship has landed is only appropriate for the dance on Delos is decisive against interpreting the scene as a victory dance on Crete. For Crete: Friis Johansen 1945, followed by Walker 1995: 43; Beazley 1986: 31. For Delos: de la Coste-Messelière 1947; Herter 1973: 1143; Neils 1987: 26. On the scene in general: Brommer 1982: 83–6. *ABV* 77,3, 5 and 9 are fragments of another victory dance by Clitias.

interest in the island.[64] The combination of the Delian setting and Theseus' appearance as the saviour of the defenceless Athenians on a vase on which feats of the supreme hero Achilles predominate,[65] may be a product both of increasing Athenian self-confidence and of Theseus' growing importance as representative of Athens' glorious deeds abroad and nearer home.

The desertion of Ariadne and the indirect murder of Aegeus contrast strongly with the liberation of Athens, and the ungrateful, untrustworthy parricide that emerges from them cannot be a national representative because he violates principles of loyalty which no Greek could ignore. Athens could scarcely censor such well-established stories, and the *Cypria* as a whole remained popular as a poem there,[66] but the nature of myth facilitates the invention of new versions to 'set the record straight', shifting the emphasis of the narrative as required, just as the abduction of Helen turns into the dutiful rescue of Aethra. Quite a few of the stories that begin to be told from the late sixth century concern Theseus' exemplary relationship with his father and Athens.[67] Pherecydes (*FGrH* 3 F148, *c*.470) carefully explains that Theseus left Ariadne because Athena appeared to him and told him that he had to do so![68] Meanwhile Ariadne, Minos and Crete can be treated unflatteringly so that Minos is a tyrant whose rule is justly overthrown by Theseus. Ariadne is perhaps not entirely blameless in her relations with Theseus: Pherecydes 148 points out that *she* fell in love with *him*, and certainly Isoc. 12. 193 condemns the Amazon Antiope for betraying her country because of her love for Theseus.[69]

---

[64] Gallet de Santerre 1958: 285–7, 303–5.

[65] The link is made again in the 470s: Isler-Kerényi 1972, cf. Neils 1987: 87.

[66] Schmid-Stählin 1929: 210 n. 4; Jouan 1966: 30.

[67] Although *ARV*[2] 1269,5, *c*.430, shows Aegeus consulting the oracle about having children, and E. *Med.* 717 mentions it, 5th-cent. Athens ignores the disobedience to that oracle which leads ultimately to his death.

[68] For Pherecydes' date, cf. Jacoby 1947*a*. This version appears on vase paintings roughly contemporary with his histories: see Neils 1987: 83 on *ARV*[2] 252,52; p. 100 on *ARV*[2] 405,1; also the later *ARV*[2] 1184,4, *c*.430. *ARV*[2] 927,2 also of the 470s seems also to have been influenced by the apologetic Athenian version of the story and may reflect Ion of Chios' account of the foundation of Chios: Jacoby 1947*b*. The myth of Dionysus and Ariadne remains popular throughout the 5th cent., perhaps partly because it draws attention away from her ill-fated liaison with Theseus.

[69] [Pl.] *Minos* 320e, Strabo 10. 4. 1 and Plut. *Thes.* 16. 3 note the venom with which Athenian literature treats Minos: see also the remarks of Calame 1990: 213–21. It is conceivable that *Od.* 11. 321 ff. reflects attempts to sanitize Theseus'

1.4 THE THESEID

Scenes of the Minotauromachy comprise the vast majority of the 5 per cent of Athenian vase painting which portrays Theseus at this time, and reach a height of popularity around 540–530.[70] Towards the end of the century, however, appears a new series of exploits which have the same essential significance as the Minotauromachy in making Theseus a civilizer and benefactor of humanity: they are also Athens' 'answer' to the labours of Heracles,[71] although their introverted, Athenian emphasis, which ties Theseus closely to the Saronic Gulf and Athens, contrasts with the panhellenic range of Heracles, whose adventures are fully developed before those of Theseus. This cycle appears quite suddenly on vases in fully developed form after *c*.510, but the earliest example dates from nearer 520.[72] Poetry tends to inspire artistic representation, rather than the other way round,[73] and although the testimonia for an epic poem about Theseus are meagre, it is often thought that the Theseus cycle in art illustrates an epic poem which should be datable certainly before 510 and probably before 520.[74] Although the

dealings with Ariadne. It is in a part of the book which is generally reckoned to be late, and the Attic form of Dionysus' name at l. 324 is often regarded as suspicious: V. Bérard 1946: 96; Bolling 1925: 240–1; Wilamowitz 1884: 149; *contra* Herter 1939: 258 n. 55. Here, uniquely, Ariadne is killed by the orders of a vengeful Dionysus before she reaches Athens and Theseus does not abandon her. The most obvious reason for the god's hostility would be that she had been unfaithful to him with Theseus (cf. also E. *Hipp.* 339), but there is no hint that Theseus, associated with Athens at l. 323, suffered as well: the claims of *ΣOd.* 11. 325 and Eustath. *Od.* 11. 324, which inculpate both of them for making love in Dionysus' shrine may be wrong. Alternatively, Calame 1990: 244–5 suggests that, like Callisto, Ariadne was punished for losing her virginity. Moreover, in this passage, Minos is not the lawgiver of *Od.* 11. 568f. but 'baneful' (322, cf. *Il.* 2. 723; 15. 630; 17. 21), no doubt because of the tribute. See also §§6.4, 7.1.2 and 7.5.2 on Cretan women in *Hippolytus* and the lost tragedies, and for the ideological slant of Athenian accounts of Minos' thalassocracy, see Starr 1955: 290.

[70] Boardman 1975: 1. There are over 300 in black figure: Brommer 1982: 37; Young 1972: 133–9.

[71] Cf. Nilsson 1951: 56, 1953: 748.

[72] Villa Giulia 20760, *ARV*[2] 83,14 by Skythes: Neils 1987: 34–5 and fig. 7–8.

[73] Friis Johansen 1967: 35–9.

[74] Herter 1939: 282–5 with bibliography, n. 183. Wilamowitz 1925: 234 n. 2 doubts its existence, as, most recently, does Walker 1995: 38–9, but see Jacoby 1949: 394–5, who dates it to the third quarter of the 6th cent.; cf. 1947*a*: 31–3 n. 46. The testimonia are admittedly scanty: Plut. *Thes.* 28. 1 and *Σ*Pind. *Ol.* 3. 50b refer to the 'author of the *Theseid*', and the scholiast lists this author before Peisander and Pherecydes, which may suggest an early date, as may its author's anonymity: cf. Bernabé 1987: 136; also Herter 1973: 1046. Arist. *Poet.* 1451[a]16f. mentions 'those of

Theseus myth is only expanded at the end of the sixth century, he
and his family do seem to have featured in mythical narrative at
Athens before this time. An inscribed fragment by Exekias, *c*.540,
portrays a bearded, mature Theseus, quite unlike the Theseus of
later artistic representations, who may be greeting his sons or giving them his blessing as they set out for Troy.[75] If he and his sons
were already representing Athens on sixth-century vases, the
appearance of the Theseus cycle may be less surprising than has
sometimes been thought,[76] especially if there was already a sixth-
century shrine of Theseus.[77] The sheer numbers of Minotauromachy vases might also indicate that he was a figure of some
interest at Athens before the invention of the Theseus cycle.[78] The
earliest literary source for the cycle is Bacchylides 18 (19–30), probably written, like poem 17 which is discussed at the end of this

the poets who have written a *Herakleid* and a *Theseid*', but some of these are evidently much later than the sixth century: M. L. West 1972: ii, 61. Denying the existence of a 6th-cent. *Theseid* means that Pherecydes' account of Theseus will be the
first known literary account of him, which seems too late, given that the cycle vases
form such a unity and that Bacchylides 18's laconic treatment of the cycle presupposes that his audience is entirely familiar with the myth: it is possible, as Jacoby
suggests, that Pherecydes based his own account on the poem (denied by Neils 1987:
12, but on doubtful grounds).

[75] *ABV* 143,1; another Exekian fragment preserves part of a picture of Acamas:
Malibu Getty Museum 78. AE. 305: see Shapiro 1989: 147–8 and pls. 66c, 66d. Cf.
n. 34 above.

[76] Barrett 1964: 3 n. 1; Shapiro 1989: 145, who argues for active interest in
Theseus even in the Solonian period: cf. Kearns 1989: 110; Gauer 1968: 64. Certain
parts of the Theseus myth are compatible with currency in the earlier 6th cent.,
although they would be equally compatible with a later origin. It is possible, for
example, that the Salaminioi were connected with Theseus and the Oschophoria at
their incorporation at Athens in the early 6th cent.: Jacoby 1954: 296; Kearns 1989:
39, 97 f. Again, the myth that Ennea Hodoi was Acamas' wife's dowry (Aeschin. 2.
31; *Σ*Lycophron 495; Plut. *Thes.* 34. 1) could originate in Peisistratus' Thracian
connections: Nilsson 1953: 746–7 and cf. Kearns 1989: 89. *Ath.Pol.* 3 and Plut.
Thes. 24–6 ascribe the foundation of the aristocratic order to Theseus, contrary to
normal democratic tradition: Sarkady 1969 would date the tradition to a time when
the aristocratic state still existed.

[77] *Ath.Pol.* 15. 4, although Rhodes 1981: 210–11 is sceptical. See, however,
Herter 1939: 285–6; Shapiro 1989: 145; Walker 1995: 21–2, with bibliography; for
possible archaeological evidence, Koumanoudes 1976.

[78] Boardman 1975 contrasts Theseus' frequency with that of Heracles who
appears on 44 per cent of all vases at this time, but these percentages cover up a wide
variation in frequency of individual deeds. The victories over the Nemean lion and
over the Amazons account for 20 per cent of all his appearances in black figure:
Webster 1972: 66. The Heracles myth was elaborated before that of Theseus, and it
is not surprising that they inspired more vase paintings, but this need not mean that
Theseus was unimportant.

chapter, in the early years of the Delian League. The poem treats Theseus' adventures in such a laconic way that we must assume that the cycle is entirely familiar to its audience by this time.

The cycle is embedded in a very familiar framework, of the quest for a father and the tests that a young man must undergo to prove his heroic worth, and it also conveniently brings Theseus from his birthplace in Trozen to Athens. Aegeus had left his sword and sandals under a rock there for Theseus to take when he was old enough to come to Athens to find him,[79] and on his journey to him around the Saronic Gulf, Theseus cleared the way of the hazards to travellers that had previously made the road impossibly dangerous. The deeds of his youth prefigure his greater triumph at Crete and, like the victory over the Minotaur, his victory over the brigands of the Saronic Gulf actively benefits other human beings, particularly travellers and strangers who are by their nature vulnerable, imposing safety and order on danger and chaos. In making a journey by land, rather than simply sailing across the Gulf, and performing heroic and beneficial deeds along the way, Theseus marks out the territory, from the Isthmus to Athens itself, to which his city could justly lay claim. It is slightly paradoxical that Theseus' birth outside Athens is, in fact, more useful to his city than an Athenian birth would have been.[80]

The core of the cycle comprises five similar opponents,[81] Sinis-Pityokamptes on the Isthmus, the Crommyonian Sow, Sciron at Megara, Cercyon at Eleusis and Procrustes at Erineus or Korydallos.[82] Each of them was made memorable by his inventive techniques of killing travellers: Sinis-Pityokamptes used pine trees to catapult them to their deaths;[83] Sciron asked them to wash his

[79] Already portrayed on *ARV*[2] 141,1 of the late 6th cent.: Sourvinou-Inwood 1971 (but see Neils 1987: 123 n. 530).

[80] Such claims may explain why his Trozenian origin remains fixed in the myth: *contra* Nilsson 1953: 747, followed by Walker 1995: 12, who rightly points out (p. 42) that the Theseus cycle is shaped, in part, by Athenian fantasies of having the whole Isthmus under Athenian control (cf. Calame 1990: 224).

[81] For full iconographic details, see Taylor 1981, Brommer 1982 and Neils 1987; on the significance of the cycle as a whole, Brelich 1956, and for more modern examples of such beings, Lawson 1910.

[82] Plut. *Thes.* 6. 3 begins with Periphetes-Korynetes of Epidaurus, but our earliest literary source, Bacchylides 18, which is usually dated to the early years of the Delian League, starts with Sinis: Periphetes is probably a later addition to the cycle, not before *c*.460, to make it up to half a dodecathlon like that of Heracles: Herter 1939: 280. On Periphetes, see Neils 1987: 97 ff.; Brommer 1982: 3–5.

[83] Brommer 1982: 6–8; J. Schmidt 1929: 238–44. First on *ARV*[2] 108,27, *c*.510 in

feet and then kicked them off the cliff into the jaws of a man-eating tortoise;[84] Procrustes mutilated all those who slept on his bed with a hammer;[85] Cercyon specialized in lethal wrestling matches.[86] Theseus turns all their evil techniques against them by forcing them to suffer exactly as they made others suffer, combining physical strength with intelligence and moral righteousness as he will do in a more complex way in tragedy, and as the city of Athens itself did in Athenian ideology.[87] Once Theseus reaches Athens, he undergoes further tests in which he triumphs; an ambush set up for him by his cousins, the Pallantidae, who wish Aegeus to remain childless so that they can succeed him on the Athenian throne,[88] and an encounter with the bull which was harassing the inhabitants of Marathon.[89] Pictures of Theseus and the bull are especially pop-

company with the Minotaur, Procrustes, Sciron and Cercyon: Neils 1987: 37 and fig. 10–11. The motif can be found in other traditional tales: H. 1522. 1 and S135 (Thompson). See also Tillyard 1913; Farnell 1900: 39; Herter 1973: 1070.

[84] Brommer 1982: 14–18; van der Kolf 1929: 537–45. First probably on a cup by Scythes, c.510: Neils 1987: no. 2, p. 36 and fig. 9.

[85] He is variously named Damastes-Procrustes: Plut. *Thes.* 11; Procrustes-Polypemon: Paus. 1. 38. 5. Bacchylides calls him Procoptas 'of Polypemon': Brommer 1982: 22–6; van der Kolf 1957: 599, 609–13; 1952: 1790–1; Herter 1973: 1078. Cf. Thompson, G313 and F531. 4. 10; cf. D631. 3. 7. The scene probably first appears on Scythes' cup of c.510 (see previous note) on which, however, Theseus attacks him with a sword, not the canonical hammer: Neils 1987: 46 intriguingly compares the iconography of an archaic votive group (Athens, Acropolis Museum 145 and 370), tentatively identified as a portrayal of Theseus with Procrustes, with the chastisement of *Adikia* by *Dike* on *ARV²* 11,3 (*CVA* 2 Austria 2, pl. 51).

[86] The scene first appears on *ARV²* 108,27, c.510. Wrestling with a giant is itself not uncommon in traditional stories: culture heroes must perform great feats of strength and skill and Greek heroes are often athletes: Thompson H1562; Brelich 1958: 94–106. Heracles' wrestling match with Antaeus first appears c.530: Brommer 1984: 38–41.

[87] See Chapter 2. The moralizing and civilizing elements are especially strong in Bacchylides 18: Theseus conquers the violent (ὑπέρβιος) Sinis, l. 19, the 'man-killing' sow, l. 23, and the reckless (ἀτάσθαλος) Sciron, l. 24.

[88] ΣEur. *Hipp.* 35, Plut. *Thes.* 3 and 13 with Brommer 1982: 137–9. They are pale compared with the opponents of the Saronic Gulf, but quite well-established in the tradition: they appear on vases (*ARV²* 259,1, c.480, with Neils 1987: 85), perhaps on the Treasury of the Athenians at Delphi, and they may probably be identified with the giants that Theseus is fighting in Heraclean style on the Hephaesteion: Neils 1987: 50 and 126 with older literature. In literature, they are mentioned in Sophocles *Aegeus* 24R; Theseus has to spend a year in Trozen for killing them in E. *Hipp.* 35, and their murder is turned even more to his discredit in ΣAr. *Plut.* 627a.

[89] The bull appears in the cycle certainly from c.510 on *ARV²* 108,27 and is perhaps shown already on Cab.Méd. 174, *ABV* 315,2, c.550: Schefold 1978: 164; Kron 1976: 128; Taylor 1981: 82. However, a bull scene of c.515 (*ARV²* 172,4: Neils 1987: 32, 144–5) portrays a nude youth inscribed Heracles, so that this must remain a possible identification for the earlier picture.

ular at Athens, no doubt because subduing a bull is a dangerous and heroic act which Heracles himself had performed, and many later sources identify the Cretan bull and the bull of Marathon as the same beast.[90]

Similarly, the inclusion of the Crommyonian sow in the cycle probably owes something to Heracles' Erymanthian boar,[91] but though she appears on the earliest cycle vase, she is less popular than the others, and is transformed in later literature into a disreputable old woman.[92] Apart from the sow, Theseus' enemies are all in human form. Humanized opponents are more common among some of the later stories about Heracles as well,[93] and as time goes on, the Saronic cycle and adventures such as the Centauromachy and Amazonomachy, in which Theseus fights as one of a group, come to be more popular as examples of his heroism than the original, but archaic combat with the monstrous Minotaur.[94] The Theseus of tragedy is also less of a fighter against mythical monsters than against monstrous human cruelty and impiety, and is a less fantastic and distanced figure than his original incarnation.

Sinis and Procrustes seem to be no more than bogymen, whose names indicate their evil activities,[95] but both Sciron and Cercyon had an independent existence outside the Saronic cycle. Plutarch (*Thes.* 10) records a Megarian tradition according to which Sciron was a great and good polemarch, and Choerilus, an older contemporary of Aeschylus, wrote a tragedy about Cercyon's daughter Alope who was the mother of Hippothoon, the eponym of the Athenian tribe which retained strong Eleusinian connections. Such

[90] Brommer 1982: 27–34. In the account of Apollod. *Ep.* 1. 5. 6, Medea is Theseus' wicked stepmother who sends him against the bull before Aegeus recognizes him in an attempt to kill him. This variant is found on vases from *c.*460: it may be of older origin, but the evidence is extremely hard to evaluate and will be discussed in full in Chapter 7. For now it is enough to note that the Pallantidae and Medea have a similar function in the story: both make a wicked and vain attempt to break the association between Theseus and his father and thus Theseus and his city.

[91] Madrid 10915 (*ABV* 606,25) may link the two: Taylor 1981: 104.

[92] Plut. *Thes.* 9. 2. Apollod. *Ep.* 1. 1: Brommer 1982: 9–13. From *c.*480 (first on *ARV²* 431,47) an old woman is included in the scene: see Neils 1987: 94.

[93] Webster 1972: 261.

[94] The Minotauromachy is subsumed into the cycle, along with the Marathonian bull (first Ashmolean V303 (*ARV²* 120,7)) and becomes old-fashioned: Neils 1987: 43, cf. 66.

[95] Sinis is 'the harmer' (cf. Hesychius, s.v. σίνεϲ) or 'Pityokamptes', the Pine-bender; Procrustes and Procoptas are both 'the one who beats out', Damastes, 'he who lays people low', derived from προκρούω and προκόπτω and δαμάζω respectively.

a subject has obvious contemporary interest if the play is near in time to the Cleisthenic tribal reforms.[96] If his grandson was sufficiently important to be a tribal eponym, Cercyon and his family must have been developed as characters before *c*.510 when he first appears in the cycle of Theseus' adversaries.[97] The popularity of the Sciron myth at Athens may have been boosted by the enmity between Athens and Megara[98] but the resemblance between mythological structure and history is general and ideological, rather than specific. By killing Sciron, Theseus does not come to rule Megara or Salamis, but rather, by giving him a taste of his own medicine, he restores the rules of civilized behaviour. To end the reign of terror of Sciron and all the others is to be a truly civilizing Athenian like those described by Aeschylus at *Eumenides* 13 as κελευθοποιοί (road-makers).

Although there are exceptions to the rule, pictures of the cycle tend to make Theseus and his opponents the literal antitypes of one another: larger, bearded, unkempt men are routed every time by the clean-cut, all-Athenian youth Theseus. His youth in these paintings contrasts with his appearance as a wise adult king in tragedy, but in both manifestations he is idealized as befits a national representative.[99] The accomplishment against all odds of a dangerous mission against evil by a young, lone hero is a potent motif which shapes countless stories, ancient and modern.[100] Its

[96] If it is true that Phrynichus was the first to bring women onto the stage (Snell 1971: 67), the play will not be earlier than *c*.510. For the story, see Hyg. 187; Paus. 1. 14. 3; Kron 1976: 177–80; also Ch. 7 below. Pherecydes 147 mentions her in an unknown context. Cercyon was probably treated unflatteringly: Athens only knows him for his lethal wrestling matches and his cruelty to Alope.

[97] Kron 1976: 30. In Hyg. 187, Theseus gives Eleusis to Hippothoon at his request; Istrus *FGrH* 334 F10 makes Hippothoon Theseus' son.

[98] Mythological propaganda was certainly one of Athens' weapons in the fight for Salamis: see Plut. *Sol.* 10. 1, and compare the Megarian anti-Athenian textual criticism cited above; also Hes. 204. 44 M–W with Legon 1981: 101; Nilsson 1951: 56–8; Kearns 1989: 116; Jacoby 1955: 429–31; see also Walker 1995: 12.

[99] Similarly Achilles and, after *c*.500, Triptolemus undergo a transformation from bearded man to youth: Friis Johansen 1967: 230, and on the importance of youth as an ideal at Athens see C. Bérard 1989: 71. Theseus' habitual nakedness may also be intended to recall the customs of the palaestra: Neils 1987: 37, cf. 72. Although Heracles contrasts with the youthful Theseus by retaining his appearance as an older man, from *c*.530, he is shown as a lyre-player, so that, like Theseus, he becomes a hero pre-eminent in more than sheer strength: *LIMC* 4. 1, nos. 1438–54 with Shapiro 1989: 60.

[100] Rank 1964; Bettelheim 1976: 26–7, 112; Kirk 1974: 156, 204, 162. Brelich 1958: 124–9 stresses the link between Greek folk tales of this form and tribal initiations and rites of passage.

power depends on the ability of the audience to sympathize with the trials and triumphs of the hero, even to the point of identifying themselves with him. The tendency to identify with an Athenian hero, benefiting humanity as he journeys to his father along the road to Athens must be particularly strong for Athenians, as it will be in tragedy when Theseus the Athenian is often presented as the sole defender of Greek civilization. A national hero such as Theseus is useful as an embodiment of the best qualities of the nation in its own eyes: his image is itself dependent on the idealized image of Athens and can be recreated as that image changes, so as to present consistently an ideal standard of conduct.[101]

I.5 ATHENS' RISE TO PROMINENCE IN GREECE

The sixth century sees an increase in the importance of Athens in the Greek world, and a corresponding increase in Athenian self-consciousness and confidence at home.[102] At the end of the previous century, Athens was important enough to take part in the Sacred War and to be awarded Sigeum by Periander; early in the next century the city was eventually successful in the lengthy dispute with Megara over the possession of Salamis,[103] while in the mid-sixth century, Croesus' appeal for help to Athens as well as Sparta, whose reputation was far longer established, indicates that Athens' reputation had spread even beyond Greece. The purification of Delos undertaken by the tyrants is a particular assertion of Athens' Ionian consciousness which is manifested especially at the end of the century when—briefly—Athens took on the mantle of the champion of the Ionians against Persian might.[104] Symbolic parallels can be made between the deeds of Theseus the civilizer, who boldly volunteers for danger, and the active foreign policy of Athens. A similar manifestation of the symbolic portrayal of

[101] Gastaldi 1977: 284; Osborne 1983: 67.

[102] Many of the poems of Solon betray a strong Athenian consciousness: see e.g. Solon 2W. The introduction of Athenian owl coinage is similarly revealing: Kraay 1956: 58–63. See also Shapiro 1989: 18–24, for a general appreciation of the national significance of the Panathenaea, traditionally inaugurated in 566/5; also Andrewes 1982*a*: 410–11. On the later 6th-cent. temple on the Acropolis (530–20), Athena is portrayed unmistakably as a national goddess: Boersma 1970: 20–1.

[103] I follow the account of Andrewes 1982*b*: 360–91 and 1982*a*: 392–416.

[104] Croesus: Hdt. 1. 59, cf. 1. 53. 3 where Croesus is advised to seek help from 'the most powerful of the Greeks'. Ionian revolt: Hdt. 5. 99; Ionian consciousness is shown already in Solon 4.

Athens as a civilizing city is found in the popularity of Triptolemos of Eleusis as another Athenian hero at this time:[105] he is shown as the distributor of ears of corn to others, and therefore as the patron of the civilized art of agriculture for the good of humanity. Patterns that are dominant in the ideology of fifth-century Athens are already being laid down,[106] and these parallels foreshadow the symbolic relationship between Theseus and Athens which predominates in tragedy.

The development of a sense of Athenian national pride and of the uniqueness of the Athenian 'national character' is closely bound up both with the need to acquire a unique and glorious past as a forerunner of the glorious present, and also with the notion of the unification of Attica under Theseus.[107] The Athenians' belief that they were autochthonous precluded foundation myths of the usual kind, and so the synoikist of Attica will be a founding hero. Theseus is often credited with the synoikism, and his mythical role as the unifier of Attica with Athens at its centre has been seen as a symbolic reflection both of Peisistratus' historical achievements and those of Cleisthenes,[108] but the dominant conception behind both of these is the necessity that Attica should be a unity, both as an ideological ideal, conveniently traceable to one founder,[109] and as a historical process which can be traced in the political and religious develop-

[105] Shapiro 1989: 67–83. The initiation of Heracles at the Eleusinian mysteries links the great panhellenic hero with something specifically Athenian, and Attic vases connected with it are found from c.590 on.

[106] These patterns may be connected with the emphasis on 'usefulness' that is manifested in early Greek poetry: cf. Donlan 1973: 149.

[107] Of course a council of Athenians did not suddenly decide to adopt Theseus as a representative; but myth is such a potent source of examples that by a gradual, hardly conscious, process, Theseus may have emerged as the most suitable example. Cf. Taylor 1981: 81; Kjellberg 1922: 247; Shapiro 1989: 144. This first wave of 'national consciousness' may be compared with the increased interest in the older heroes of Attica in the last quarter of the 5th cent.: Boersma 1970: 87–8; cf. Webster 1972: 258.

[108] Theseus and Peisistratus are good monarchs who defeat aristocrats to unify Attica; Peisistratus promoted the Panathenaea and Theseus is associated with the Synoikia: Hignett 1952: 123; Andrewes 1956: 8, 114; Bicknell 1972: 60. Cleisthenes and Theseus are both responsible for the real unification of Attica: Jacoby 1949: 394 n. 23; Sourvinou-Inwood 1971: 99; Kearns 1989: 117; although he is never credited with having altered the tribes, which one might expect.

[109] Jacoby 1954: 392–9, commenting on *FGrH* 328 F94, which attributes the first synoikism to Cecrops. Sources for the founders of early Athenian institutions are not unanimous: the fact of their having had an individual founder is more important than who that individual was.

ments of the sixth century.[110] The festival of the Synoikia antedates Cleisthenes,[111] and his reorganization of Attica essentially continues the process which Peisistratus also encouraged in his support for the Panathenaea and Dionysia and his promotion of state cults.[112] Theseus' alleged role is symbolic more of the general process than of individuals' contributions to it.

Symbolic of Athenian national consciousness too is the gradual adjustment in relations between Heracles and Theseus throughout the sixth century. Although they have common attributes and are associated in art, even outside Attica, from the early sixth century,[113] Heracles is by far the greater hero everywhere down to the sixth century (and remains so outside Athens). It is he, not Theseus, who features on the old buildings of the Acropolis and at Athena's side in the gigantomachy on her temple, *c*.530–520:[114] and as we have seen, early narratives associating Heracles and Theseus assign an inferior role to Theseus in the story of his unsuccessful mission to the underworld. However, in spite of Athena's favour,[115] Heracles' panhellenic importance, and also his tendency to excess, debar him from suitability as an Athenian national hero. By the first quarter of the fifth century 13 per cent of all extant vase painting has Theseus as its subject while Heracles' appearances have declined from 44 down to 19 per cent, but he remains great and important as a hero, and always more important in cult than Theseus.[116] The exploits of Theseus are developed so as to catch some of his reflected glory, and he is even given the chance to surpass his role model.[117] The *Theseid* mentioned the Cerynian hind

[110] The process stems partly from a gradual centralization of the citizens' political lives in the middle of the town: Vernant 1975: 44–64. The agora begins to be the centre of Athenian political life from the end of the 7th cent.: Thompson and Wycherley 1972: 17.

[111] Hornblower 1982: 79 n. 9, citing Sokolowski 1969: *Supp.* 10A 31 f.

[112] Andrewes 1982*a*: 410–15.

[113] See especially Boardman 1982: 2–3.

[114] Boersma 1970: 20–1; Friis Johansen 1945: 56; Shapiro 1989: 21–4.

[115] *Il.* 8. 362: see especially Shapiro 1989: 157–63; also Woodford 1971: 214. He is also associated with her in early Corinthian art: Beckel 1961: 65.

[116] Statistics: Boardman 1975: 1; cult: Woodford 1971: 211–12. Walker 1995: 51–2 makes too absolute a distinction between Athenian attitudes to Heracles and Theseus before, and after, 510.

[117] Brommer 1982: 132; Gastaldi 1977: 285. He is explicitly Theseus' role model in Plut. *Thes.* 6. 5 f. (cf. 25. 4, 29. 3) where Sinis and the rest are adversaries who had escaped Heracles' notice. Thus I take a fundamentally different line from John Boardman in his series of articles 1972, 1975, 1978*a*, 1978*b*, 1982, 1984, in which he

(*Σ*Pind. *Ol*. 3. 50b): presumably Theseus helped Heracles to capture it—a story otherwise unknown—partly to share his glory, but
also to redress the balance of services rendered to him by Heracles
in the underworld. Many of Theseus' feats resemble those of
Heracles, and are modelled on them, but some attempt is made at
differentiation between the two: Heracles fights the Cretan bull,
Theseus, the Marathonian bull, and although the iconography of
the two is not entirely distinct in early portrayals, by the early classical period vase painters tend to show Heracles preparing to master the bull by brute force, while Theseus is often shown after the
event, with a masterful, but relaxed demeanour.[118] Theseus often
accomplishes his victories over Sinis and the rest with grace and
ease: this is not always so with Heracles because he is not the ideal
representative of Athens.

From the late sixth century Theseus takes on poses very similar
to those of the statue of the tyrannicides Harmodios and
Aristogeiton,[119] and these poses are common for him in the next
century,[120] but already on Scythes' Villa Giulia cup which probably antedates the statue, he is in the Aristogeiton stance, which is

uses evidence from vase paintings to suggest that Heracles was a Peisistratid political symbol whose popularity diminishes after the fall of the tyrants. Independently,
but to the same end, Schefold 1946, cf. 1978, suggested that Theseus is an
Alcmaeonid hero; also Jacoby 1949: 394–5; Sourvinou-Inwood 1979: 48–51; Kearns
1989: 115–17. The link between Peisistratus and Heracles is now widely accepted—
as e.g. Andrewes 1982*a*: 400—but I shall argue elsewhere that 'party-political' art
transmitted by such symbols is an unknown concept in 6th-cent. Greece. For recent
expressions of scepticism concerning political vase paintings, see Osborne 1983;
R. M. Cook 1987; Shapiro 1989: 15–16; Blok 1990. In any case, vase painting may
be a less reliable guide to public sentiment than monumental buildings (as
Boardman 1982: 2–3 notes): Athena lends her support to Theseus comparatively
rarely on vases (Brommer 1982: 30–1, cf. 17), but the public profession of her support on the Delphic metope indicates that he is indeed a national hero: Neils 1987:
126; cf. Beckel 1961: 67–71. For the most recent discussion of the problem, see
Walker 1995: 35–47, with whose refutation of the 'Peisistratus–Theseus' equation I
entirely agree, although I think he underestimates Athenian interest in Theseus
under the Peisistratids: Theseus does not represent Peisistratus, but his popularity
clearly increases under the tyrants and before 510.

[118] Shefton 1962: 348, 367–8.
[119] Kardara 1951; Taylor 1981: esp. 78–146, assuming that the statue by Critios
and Nesiotes which dates from the 470s was essentially the same as the lost statue
erected in 510 by Antenor: Becatti 1937.
[120] For example on the Theseion (see below) and on the Hephaesteion (*c*.450),
where he was shown in the 'Aristogeiton' pose, defeating giants (perhaps the
Pallantidae) while in the western centauromachy, he was probably in the centre, in
the 'Harmodios' position: C. H. Morgan 1962: 222 and pls. 82a–d.

that of Heracles on several cups of 530–520.[121] If Heracles' stance is the original inspiration behind the pose, then both Theseus and the tyrannicides would be assimilated into his tradition as a saviour of humanity: Heracles kills lions and hydras; Theseus the Minotaur and the brigands of the Saronic Gulf; and Harmodius and Aristogeiton, the tyrants. Since Theseus and the tyrannicides become more important than Heracles in the political context of the Athenian democracy, these poses lose their Heraclean origins so as to be typical of Theseus and the supposed founders of the democracy as one national symbol is equated with another.[122]

The culmination of the process of adjustment between Theseus and Heracles is to be found in Euripides' *Heracles*, but it is already clear on the metopes of the Treasury erected by the Athenians at Delphi,[123] on whose southern, more prominent side Theseus is portrayed with Athena in a meeting which is otherwise unique to Heracles.[124] Heracles and Theseus are associates, as in earlier representations, but the deeds of the non-Athenian hero are now relegated to the north side of the temple, and Athena's special attention is turned to Theseus in the midst of a magnificent and expanded version of the cycle.[125] The erection of such a building at the international centre of politics, religion and tourism indicates national pride and Theseus' prominence must indicate that he is a national symbol of Athens.[126]

[121] Taylor 1981: 43–6.

[122] Harmodios and Aristogeiton were a useful symbol of the new regime because the Athenians needed a purely Athenian account of the end of the tyranny, quite separate from the realities of the Spartan intervention and Delphic corruption. Hence they were commemorated by a statue in 510/9 (Pliny *HN* 34. 4. 17) even though no one then could have thought that they literally ended the tyranny: Thomas 1989: 260.

[123] Estimates of its date range from *c.*520 to after 490, but I follow Dinsmoor 1946 (also Fuchs and Floren 1987: 248 n. 2; *contra* Boardman 1982) in dating it after *c.*510 and perhaps before *c.*500, to judge from certain vases of the turn of the century which seem to have been influenced by its iconography: Neils 1987: 42, 49, 53, 56. Audiat 1933: 85–91 attempts to refute the stylistic dating, not wholly convincingly.

[124] Boardman 1982: 4.

[125] It comprised the defeats of Sinis, probably Procrustes, Cercyon and Sciron: Theseus' encounter with Athena was probably in the middle, followed by an indeterminate victory, the capture of the bull, the killing of the Minotaur, and lastly, Theseus and an Amazon: see de la Coste-Messelière 1957. The Hephaesteion renews their association: Theseus takes the north and south sides, Heracles, the east, with a centauromachy on the west: for the Hephaesteion see Sauer 1899; Dinsmoor 1941; C. H. Morgan 1962*a* and *b*; Thompson 1966*a*.

[126] Thus he could not be chosen as one of Cleisthenes' tribal eponyms: a Theseis tribe, like a Herakleis tribe, would have unbalanced their equality, although his

1.6 CENTAURS AND AMAZONS

No less important than Theseus' combats with individuals are the
exploits in which he is one of a collective of heroes. Centaurs are
fabulous creatures of the past, only semi-civilized and a threat to
men, and the great heroes of old have done humanity a service by
removing this threat.[127] If *Il.* 1. 265 is genuinely Homeric, even
Nestor is proud of having fought alongside great men as Theseus
and Peirithous who performed such a service; even if it is not,
Theseus is a Centauromachist at l. 182 of the description of the battle of the Lapiths and the Centaurs of 178–190 of the *Shield of
Heracles*, and on Clitias' and Ergotimos' roughly contemporary
vase.[128] Like the Centaurs, the Amazons are the sort of opponents
that Greek heroes must defeat to prove their heroism: they are not
Greek, they live on the margins of the civilized, Greek world—in
this they may resemble Minos—and their customs are not those of
Greeks.[129] They are no negligible threat and to conquer them is to
reassert one's own superior civilization. Amazonomachy is a popular theme in Attic black figure ware long before the Persian Wars
and Heracles' earliest Amazonomachy dates from the late seventh
century.[130] True to form, however, Theseus' first encounter with
an Amazon is not in battle, but follows the Ariadne–Helen–Kore

family feature prominently among the eponyms: Kron 1976: 244, Garland 1992: 89,
and on the criteria for the selection of the eponyms, especially Kearns 1989: 80–92.

[127] In Homer they are φῆρες ('beasts'), and must be driven away, at *Il.* 1. 268, 2.
742. At *Od.* 21. 295–304, like the Cyclops, they cannot hold their wine. Scenes of
men fighting creatures who are half horse and half man can be traced at least to the
last quarter of the 8th cent.: Fittschen 1969: 111 f.; Brommer 1982: 104–5; Kirk
1985: 80.

[128] The line Θησέα τ' Αἰγείδην ἐπιείκελον ἀθανάτοισι ('Theseus, son of Aegeus,
like the immortals') is absent from many manuscripts and Bm4 calls it νόθος,
although Paus. 10. 29. 10, Eust. 75. 42 and Dio Chrys. 57. 1 all know it as Homeric.
Most scholars assume that it has been transferred to the *Iliad* from the *Shield of
Heracles*, dated *c*.570, where it is certainly genuine: Russo 1950: 34–5, 120, followed
by Walker 1995: 19–20; cf. Herter 1936: 222 for various critical opinions. The line
is, however, unexceptionable in its context in the *Iliad* and Van der Valk 1964 makes
a case for accepting it on the assumption that Aristarchus first omitted it and that his
omissions are sometimes made on purely subjective grounds: this view has been
challenged by Apthorp 1982, but see West 1982: 1. For the scene on Clitias' and
Ergotimos' vase, see Minto 1960: 59–79; Weizsäcker 1877; Beazley 1986: 32.

[129] Brommer 1982: 115. For general treatments of the meaning of the Amazon
myth, see Tyrell 1984; Hardwick 1990; also Hall 1989: 34, 52–4. As the historical
world is further explored, so the Amazons move further east: Huxley 1960.

[130] *LIMC* 1. 1, 587, no. 1. For early Amazonomachies, see von Bothmer 1957:
6–29; Shapiro 1983.

pattern, as he carries off Antiope:[131] it would appear that his encounter with the Amazons was not originally merely a doublet of that of Heracles.[132]

The scene was portrayed on the temple of Apollo at Eretria at the end of the sixth century,[133] where it is apparently sanctioned by Athena who occupies a prominent place in the middle of the pediment.[134] The abduction of a non-Greek woman is evidently more acceptable than the others. Like the abduction of Helen which brought Theseus' enemies into Attica, it naturally leads to an Amazon invasion, but this time the abductor successfully repels his enemies and Theseus marries the Amazon and has children by her.[135] In most accounts, he marries Phaedra after the death of the Amazon, but Plutarch reports that in the *Theseid*, he puts Antiope aside for Phaedra: she is angry and summons her fellow Amazons to the wedding where Heracles saves Theseus and his guests from the marauding women.[136] Both versions emphasize Theseus' success in taming an untameable warrior woman: either her love for

[131] Peirithous often helps him, as in other abductions, cf. Pindar fr. 175 Sn.; see also Pherecydes 152. On Antiope, see Brommer 1982: 110–14; on Theseus and the rest of the Amazons, 115–23; also von Bothmer 1957: 127–8. Hofkes-Brukker 1966 argues that the love of Theseus and Antiope is portrayed already on a relief from Olympia of *c*.570.

[132] According to Plut. *Thes.* 26, most writers say that Theseus' expedition to the east took place after that of Heracles, although Philochorus (*FGrH* 328 F110) says that they went together and Antiope was Theseus' prize for valour, thus exonerating him from the charge of abduction. Gastaldi 1977: 290 and Wolgensinger 1935: 43 both see a difference between Heracles' martial Amazonomachies and the more sexually tinged contests of Theseus.

[133] Von Bothmer 1957: 124–31 dates it *c*.515, Shapiro 1991: 134, in the last decade of the century. Boardman 1982: 12 dates it later still, because he interprets the abduction symbolically in the context of the help given to the Ionian revolt by Athens and Eretria. However, the story appears on vases which probably antedate the temple: see Neils 1981 and 1987: 32–3; von Bothmer 1957: 89, 126. A very early 5th-cent. base of an acroterion from Ceos also portrays the scene: *LIMC* i. 1, 857, no. 3.

[134] In the same way Poseidon sometimes appears on vases to help his son: Heimberg 1968: 53–8; von Bothmer 1957: 127. For the friendship between Athens and Eretria, Auberson and Schefold 1972: 29.

[135] Stesichorus names Demophon's mother Iope, and Pindar, Antiope. The Amazon invasion was probably one explanation for the presence of so-called Amazons' graves around the city: Preller and Robert 1921: 733; Herter 1936: 200, 219; Wolgensinger 1935: 43; Barrett 1964: 8 n. 2.

[136] Plut. *Thes.* 28; cf. Apollod. *Ep.* 1. 17. In later tradition Theseus himself kills Antiope: Ov. *Her.* 4. 117; Sen. *Ph.* 227, 927; Hyg. 241. Naturally, there is no hint of this in the *Hippolytus*. With Gastaldi 1977: 293 I take the uprising of the Amazons to be part of the *Theseid*, not a separate poem.

him causes the invasion or, when the Amazons come to bring her back, she fights on the Greeks' side before settling down to mother-hood.[137] In this story, both aspects of Theseus play a part: he is a vigorous young man who is irresistible even to an Amazon, but also the successful incorporation of Antiope into a city to which she was originally hostile parallels the welcome offered by Athens to out-siders—even dangerous ones—in tragedy; it is often Theseus, in his role as ideal representative of the city, who welcomes such people. The idea that Athens is uniquely a city open to all is a matter of pride in public pronouncements.[138] The Hellenicized Amazon, for whom Theseus was more precious than her sisters, may have been portrayed in the Amazonomachy on the Theseion.[139]

After the Persian wars, however, the abduction seems to be deemed inappropriate, and it is turned into a Minotaur-Cycle type of deed so that the invasion becomes an aggressive attack success-fully repelled by Athens.[140] By the time of Euripides' *Hippolytus*, the Amazon is not even Theseus' legitimate wife, and although there are representations in which Antiope fights for the Greeks, there are also slightly later vases, which may reflect her demotion in status, on which Theseus attacks an Antiope.[141] It seems certain that the change is influenced by Athens' experience of an enemy invasion in the Persian wars, so that it becomes unpatriotic for Theseus to have an Amazon bride. If the *Theseid* mentioned by Plutarch was a sixth-century production, however, then the Amazon invasion of Attica must already have been known before the Persian wars, and will resemble other ancient stories about invasions of Attica by Eleusinians and Thracians, who provide a

[137] Paus. 1. 2. 1; Plut. *Thes.* 27. 4. Hegias of Trozen (ap. Paus. 1. 2. 1) reports that Heracles could not take Themiscyra by force, but when Theseus came to help him, Antiope fell in love with him and opened the gates!

[138] Cf. Thuc. 2. 39. 1 with chapter two below: also Kearns 1989: 54 on the sig-nificance of welcoming foreign heroes into the city.

[139] If NY 07. 286. 86, *ARV*² 616. 3 reflects its murals: Barron 1972: 34–6, cf. 39. The friendly Amazon appears on vases: von Bothmer 1957: 166–70 and *LIMC* 1. 1, s.v. 'Amazons', nos. 295–303. Hofkes-Brukker 1966: 17 sees Antiope's support for the Greeks on *ABV* 362,32 of *c.*520–510.

[140] Hdt. 9. 27; Aesch. *Eum.* 685–90 with Sommerstein 1989: 214; Barrett 1964: 4; Tyrell 1984: 13–16; Gastaldi 1977: 293. Only two abduction scenes date after 490, when the Eretrian pediment was destroyed: Brommer 1982: 112.

[141] Barron 1972: 39 suggests that these vases reflect the Amazonomachy of the Stoa Poikile. Even on the Athenian Treasury Theseus kills an Amazon, rather than abducting one, presumably so that his prowess equals that of Heracles: de la Coste-Messelière 1957: 70–81; pls. 27–30.

foreign threat which a united Athens can be shown to have surmounted.[142] The story has its own form and the reality of the
Persian invasion shapes it only in part: both wars are defensive, but
no more detailed analogy is ever worked out. The symbolism transcends historical and political events in the narrower sense,[143]
because it is of such a basic kind, fulfilling the need for self-definition, self-assertion and self-praise by the conquest of what is foreign, dangerous and uncivilized: in this context, the Saronic cycle,
the Amazonomachy and the defeat of Persia in 479 can be made to
have much the same 'meaning'. It is not surprising that in the fifth
century the defeat of the Amazons is popular, not only as one of
Theseus' deeds, but, like the defeat of Persia, as one of the great
heroic deeds of the Athenian people as a whole.[145] Both the
Amazons and the Centaurs stand at a general symbolic level for
what is undesirable and un-Athenian, while Theseus and his fellows are interchangeable with the people of Attica as a whole,
because of the possibilities of connecting past and present through
myth, especially in public art and literature.[146]

---

[142] Kearns 1989: 113–15, and for the Eleusinian wars, Simms 1983. Whatever the
historical reality behind these wars, there is also a distinct 'mythical' reality residing
in the details that are subsequently remembered and repeated by subsequent generations, just as there is a 'mythical' version of the Persian Wars which is far from
identical with what happened historically: see also §1.7.

[143] Hölscher 1973: 45 and 71–3. Even Antiope can be dressed either as a barbarian or as a hoplite (as on *ABV* 367,93) and the identification between Amazons and
Persians is never absolute and consistent: Shapiro 1983: 106; cf. Boardman 1982: 6.

[144] Cf. Hall 1989: 100; see also Thomas 1989: 196–213.

[145] On the treatment of the Amazonomachy in the funeral orations, see §2.4
below. Amazonomachy is portrayed on the Theseion, the Stoa Poikile (along with
the taking of Troy) and on the Acropolis on the shield of Athena, the pedestal of
Olympian Zeus (Paus. 1. 17. 2) and the metopes of the Parthenon (the Attic version):
the eastern battle was on the rods of the throne of Olympian Zeus, on which Theseus
appears as Heracles' ally (Paus. 5. 11. 4). See von Bothmer 1957: ch. 10; *LIMC* 1. 1,
s.v. 'Amazons'; cf. Barron 1972: 35. Centauromachy is also a stock theme of public
art, on the Parthenon and on the Hephaesteion, on which Theseus is dominant, but
the Centaurs themselves are too fantastic to be made into invaders of Attica.

[146] The feats of individual heroes are matched with the collective
Amazonomachy on the east side of the Delphic Treasury, whether it is the Attic
Amazonomachy (as Hofkes-Brukker 1966: 17f.) or the eastern battle. If the Amazon
invasion of Attica featured in the Theseus myth before the Persian wars, the Attic
battle must remain a possibility, and the association of Heracles and Theseus does
not automatically imply that the eastern combat must be have been intended:
Brommer 1982: 117 n. 8; *contra* Boardman 1982: 12f.

1.7 ATHENS AND THESEUS AFTER THE PERSIAN WARS

The image of Athens as an active, civilizing city—a fundamentally
appealing self-image—is established long before the Persian wars,
shaping, and being shaped by, the Theseus myth and others.[147]
The Athenians risked all at Marathon, and even more at Salamis,
because they were already ideologically disposed to doing so. The
ideal image of Athens as civilizer and protector which influenced
the decision to oppose the Persians is fostered by the victory resulting from that decision and, after the wars, especially by the appeal
of the Ionians to Athens to become their champion both against
Persia and the hubris of Pausanias.[148] In the decade following the
Persian wars, the pre-existing image of Athens the civilizer is confirmed once and for all by the interconnection between current,
recent and past military triumphs and the symbolic image which
shapes Theseus the national hero and which shaped the original
responses to Persia and other enemies in the first place. The notion
that Athens is a civilizing city is of fundamental importance for an
understanding of the ideology of the Athenian empire which
strongly influences the characterization of Theseus in tragedy.

This era sees an outpouring in public literature and art of subjects of various degrees of direct relation to the Athenian achievement:[149] also probably datable to this time is the establishment of
the funeral oration, in which an ideal of the nature of Athens is presented explicitly to Athenians, offering the audience a lesson for the
future out of the recent and distant pasts, and interpreting historical realities through a filter of ideology as proof of the rightness of

---

[147] Calame 1990, esp. pp. 1–68, discusses at length the working of symbolic
processes in the life of the community.

[148] Hdt. 8. 132, 9. 90; Thuc. 1. 95. 1–2, cf. 75. 2; Plut. *Cim.* 6, 8. 2, 12, *Arist.*
23–25. 1; D.S. 11. 44. 6. One might make an analogy between the actions of the
Athenians in the Persian wars and those of the kings in suppliant drama—the preferred image of Theseus in tragedy—in daring to sacrifice the well-being of their city
for the higher good.

[149] There was debate at Athens about whether Marathon or Salamis was the
greater battle: Plato *Laws* 707b–c; cf. Hdt. 7. 139; Plut. *Arist.* 2 and 16, *Them.* 20; cf.
Cim. 5. Cimon and Themistocles seemed to have used these battles to wage a propaganda war against one another in the 470s through art or literature relating to
them: Jacoby 1945: 161–85; Amandry 1960; Forrest 1960: 235–7; Podlecki 1966:
8–26, 1968, 1975a: 35–7 and 1975b; Rhodes 1981: 288–9. It should, however, be
borne in mind that the art and literature which concerns the great battles has equal
relevance to the whole Athenian people who fought them: this has relevance for the
reception of the bones of Theseus at Athens; see below.

that ideology. Public art and literature tend to look for paradigms of contemporary reality in the mythical, rather than the more recent, past. The distance achieved by comparing the contemporary with events far in the past, rather than events of recent history, dignifies the present and idealizes it, smoothing away any awkwardnesses in the contemporary situation, and providing a version of events which is acceptable to every Athenian. Similarly, nearly all tragedy dramatizes events of the distant past while making them contemporary,[150] and Theseus in tragedy can voice the ideals of Athens or represent a unique prowess which has an immediate relation to every Athenian. He is a mouthpiece for the conventional ideals of the contemporary city, but it is important that he is located in the past, because this establishes the authority of what he says and offers the audience the sense that the city now is the same as it has always been: such continuity is persuasive and reassuring.[151]

It is particularly appropriate, and perhaps hardly accidental, that it is in this era that the bones of the Athenian national hero are brought back from Skyros to Athens to be buried in the middle of the city, like those of a founding hero, thus making literal the link between Theseus and Athens that was expressed symbolically in the Saronic cycle. It is likely that the Theseia festival was also given particular prominence at this time.[152] The glorious task was accomplished by Cimon and was sanctioned by the Delphic oracle.[153] It is

[150] The various relations of myth and contemporary reality will be discussed in more detail in subsequent chapters. For the relation between myth, history and tragedy, see also Hall 1989: 62–9. I agree with her that there is a distinction in Greek thought between what we call myth and history, although I would rather think of the distinction in terms of the recent and distant pasts.

[151] In the same way the Athenians are explicitly equated with their Homeric ancestor Menestheus on the Herms dedicated by Cimon after his campaign at Eion in 476–5, the first time that the Greeks attacked Persia under Athenian leadership: on Eion see Plut. *Cim*. 8. 1; Thuc. 1. 98. 1; How and Wells on Hdt. 7. 107 and *Σ*Aeschin. 2. 31; cf. also Plut. *Thes*. 36. 1. Smart 1967 follows Diodorus 11. 60. 2 in dating it to 469, but see Barron 1972: 20 n. 4. For the Eion epigrams, see Aeschin. 3. 183–5 and Plut. *Cim*. 7. 4–6, with Blamire 1989: 112–14: Jacoby 1945; Wade-Gery 1933.

[152] Herter 1939: 293–5; Deubner 1932: 224–6; Walker 1995: 57. On the important, but late-attested role of the ephebes at the Theseia, see Herter 1973: 1226–9.

[153] Plut. *Cim*. 8. 3–7; Plut. *Thes*. 36. In the *Theseus*, the expedition is a direct response to the oracle by the Athenian people; in the *Cimon*, the oracle is brought into an account of the conquest of Skyros and the pirates of the Aegean, which casts Cimon as a civilizing hero in the Thesean mode, while also acting for his own glory. Plutarch's purpose differs from passage to passage, and it is unwise to base firm conclusions about the relation of state and individual on either account, as Blamire 1989 and Podlecki 1971 do. Cf. next note.

an important indication of the status of Theseus at this time that Delphi demanded the return of his bones. Evidently he was regarded as the coming hero; and this is understandable for the national hero of a city whose prestige in the Greek world was so high. Although the expedition was of political benefit to Cimon (cf. Plut. *Cim.* 8. 7), it is not possible to draw too clear a line between his private interests and the enthusiasms of the Athenian people,[154] since Theseus was not Cimon's creation but a national hero of importance to the Athenians long before the 470s.[155]

The murals of the Theseion, built (or rebuilt if there was a sixth-century building) for the preservation of the bones are notable for their balance of Theseus as a hero in collective combats which are standard ways of speaking metaphorically about the prowess and goodness of the city, and Theseus as an individual hero.[156] In the portrayal of Theseus in public art and literature, a balance is often struck between individualism and collectivity—of obvious rele-

[154] As, rightly, Walker 1995: 56–61. Although the retrieval of the bones is often seen as Cimon's private enterprise, the conquest of Skyros may have been a state enterprise: Podlecki 1971: 142 points out that Skyros would be strategically useful to the Athenians, and the Dolopians there had given earth and water to the Persians, and Forrest 1956 mentions a dedication which refers to the Athenians and their allies carrying something back to their homeland after receiving an oracle from Delphi. Its date would suit the expedition to retrieve Theseus' bones; if this is its context, it may be an ordinary public dedication after the event. Barron 1972: 21 suggests that work may have already started on the Theseion, in accordance with the oracle, before the final conquest of Skyros. If so, the interest of Athens as a whole in the campaign is clear. For a slightly different account, see Blamire 1989: 120.

[155] Even if Cimon did believe that he was a descendant of Theseus: Ajax, whose mother is commonly Eriboia, is Cimon's ancestor in the Philaid genealogy given by Pherecydes 2. Pherec. 153 says that Theseus married a Phereboia: if this is another form of Eriboia, Pherecydes may have made Theseus the father of Ajax by Eriboia, and thus the ancestor of the Philaids: Barron 1980; Thomas 1989: 162–9. Both the Cimonids and the Phytalidai who were associated with the cult of Theseus (Plut. *Thes.* 12, 23. 5) lived at Lakiadai. The identification of the mother of Ajax with the Eriboia who went with Theseus to Crete would be obvious, although no fifth-century source says that this Eriboia was one of Theseus' loves, and in Bacchylides 17, the violent lust of Minos for Eriboia contrasts with Theseus' respect for the young girl, whose honour he is determined to save, out of high ideals, rather than any erotic interest. Even if Cimon did claim Theseus as an ancestor, it is not clear that such a claim was as important to Athens at large as it was to Cimon: all Athenians are in some sense Theseidae, and by this date he could not be tied to one or two individuals. Cf. also §3.3 n. 58.

[156] For the testimonia, Wycherley 1957: 113–19; Thompson and Wycherley 1972: 124–6. It was a large shrine: cf. Thuc. 6. 61. 2; Andoc. *Myst.* 45. Appropriately for Theseus' reputation as a fighter against oppression, it was a place of asylum for slaves: Ar. *Eq.* 1312, frs. 567, 458–9; see also *FGrH* 328 F177.

vance to the democracy—which gives his public a chance both to identify with him and also with the groups in which he participates.[157] Here he is represented in groups of heroes as a Centauromachist[158] and Amazonomachist,[159] but in the centauromachy, his individual prowess is highlighted by his having killed a centaur in the midst of an undecided battle.[160]

Contrasting with these two collective representations was a painting of Theseus' meeting with his divine parents under the sea: although Theseus' fights against oppressors continue to be popular in the first quarter of the fifth century, his meetings with his parents, both divine and mortal, become strikingly popular with vasepainters at this time.[161] Theseus goes to Athens to meet Aegeus, surmounting dangers along the road to prove his worth, and in the same way, he must brave the dangers of the sea to prove himself as Poseidon's son. His arrival in Athens is the culmination of his labours around the Isthmus, and reinforces his Athenian identity, as well as Athens' claims to political dominance in the region. His triumphs over the oppressors of humanity make him a worthy role model and prefiguration for his Athenian audience,[162] while the

---

[157] Neils 1987: 129, comments on the preference in public art from the 450s to the 430s for collective actions rather than those of individual heroes, such as Theseus, but this tendency can be seen already in the 470s and is implicit in much tragedy which focuses on Athens.

[158] Originally, the battle takes place outside (cf. Shefton 1962: 338–44, 355–65), but in this representation they may have been brawling indoors at Peirithous' wedding feast. This variant adds to the ethical significance of the scene, so that Theseus and his fellows are the protectors of civilized customs: Barron 1972: 25–31, working from New York 07. 286. 84 (ARV^2 613. 1); Woodford 1974: 160–1.

[159] Probably the Attic battle, rather than the eastern campaign: Barron 1972: 33.

[160] Paus. 1. 17. 2. Various reconstructions place him in tyrannicidal iconography: Shefton 1962: 338–44f.; Barron 1972: 27–9; Taylor 1981: 148ff.; Harrison 1972: 353–78; for a possible prototype of Theseus, see Woodford 1974: 160, and pls. 14–15.

[161] Neils 1987: 82, 95–7, 106–7; Brommer 1982: 78 and cf. A. H. Smith 1898. In the earliest representation of Theseus and his divine parents (Louvre G104), Amphitrite takes centre stage, while on slightly later vases, Poseidon is dominant, e.g. the Tricase vase and Paris Cab.Méd. 418 (ARV^2 260,2; Neils 1987: fig. 40). A cup of c.480, NY Met. 53. 11. 4, 1970: 46 (Neils 1987: 97, fig. 48) portrays Theseus with Poseidon and Amphitrite and also his reception by Athena on the Acropolis. For the combination of Poseidon and Theseus' mortal parents, compare Paris Cab.Méd. 571, c.480–470, ARV^2 386(a), and London BM E264 (ARV^2 579,1), c.460–450, with Kron 1976: 135; Neils 1989: 106–7.

[162] Cf. Neils 1989: 107. The image of Theseus the saviour is especially notable on the contemporary ARV^2 257,11 (Neils 1989: 84–5), which features Theseus and the Minotaur and three of the Athenian mothers.

meeting between Theseus and his divine parents reinforces the idea
which may well antedate the Persian wars, and which was certainly
confirmed by Athens' victory in them, that Theseus and Athens
itself are especially favoured by the gods. Theseus' meeting with
his mortal parent is an expression of Athenian claims to power by
land; that with his sea-god father expresses Athenian claims to
power by sea,[163] and in the early years of the Delian League, the
emphasis on Theseus' divine paternity is revealing.[164] By identifying with the national hero, every Athenian could have a share in the
protection of Poseidon, whose relationship with Theseus must
have seemed especially credible after the miraculous success of 480,
and the choice of this scene as a decoration of the wall of the
Theseion is highly significant.[165]

His meeting with his divine parents is also the subject of a
roughly contemporary poem of Bacchylides (17),[166] whose
Theseus represents a kind of intermediate stage between the hero
of early narratives and the ideal Athenian of later tragedy, in that he
exemplifies the best of human ethical virtue, and yet retains the
religious element of divine parentage that is notably missing in the

[163] Cf. Walker 1995: 95.

[164] On a contemporary amphora now in Zurich (Neils 1987: 87 with Isler-
Kerényi 1972), Achilles and Thetis with six Nereids bearing his armour are portrayed: on the other side, another six women meet a youth, who is probably
Theseus, and present him with garlands. The equation of Theseus with Achilles ele-
vates Theseus to the status of one of the greatest heroes of the Greeks, as one might
expect in the triumphant days after the defeat of Persia, although in a less explicit
form the equation was already made on the François vase, some eighty years previously.

[165] Paus. 1. 17. 2–4 follows the description of the paintings of the Theseion with
an account of Theseus' death. It seems most unlikely that his rescue from Hades was
an appropriate subject for the shrine of the heroized Theseus and in any case, this
passage does not sound like a description of a picture: Robert 1895: 47. The scene
did appear on the Lesche of the Cnidians, but this was not a shrine to Theseus, nor,
for a Cnidian audience, is Theseus a national representative or reflection, but merely
one of the men of old who had done a memorable, if dreadful, deed. Hence I doubt
the suggestion of Six 1919, expanded upon by E. Simon 1963, that a crater by the
Niobid painter of *c*.460 reflects a picture in the Theseion, even if—as is doubtful—
it does portray Theseus and Peirithous in the underworld: *LIMC* 5. 1, 182 regards
the interpretation as uncertain.

[166] And Bacchylides 18 dramatizes Theseus' journey to Athens to meet his
human father, Aegeus. Poems 17 and 18 are conventionally dated to the early years
of the Delian League, but their Theseus has so much in common with those of earlier art and later literature, and a date as early as 490 or as late as the 460s (cf. D. A.
Schmidt 1990: 30–1) cannot be excluded. On Bacchylides' career, see Jebb 1905:
2f.; Körte 1918, esp. 140ff.; Severyns 1933.

Theseus of most tragedy. The poem opens on board the ship of King Minos, which is carrying the twice-seven Athenians to Crete to be sacrificed to the Minotaur. One of the Athenian girls, Eriboia, attracts the unwelcome attentions of King Minos (13), whose ship it is, but at her cry of distress, Theseus springs to the rescue, and reprimands the Cretan king for his unlovely conduct, speaking sternly, but not rudely to a man who is his senior,[167] reminding him that he should behave with justice and restraint (20–46).[168] Theseus' treatment of Eriboia, unlike that of Ariadne, is suitable for celebration, and roughly contemporary with Bacchylides' story is Pherecydes' version of the Ariadne story which is careful to exonerate Theseus from the charge of treachery.[169] In reply, Minos attempts to reassert his supremacy on the ship by challenging the younger, apparently inferior man to a contest of genealogy. He proves that he is the son of Zeus by requesting thunder from his divine father (53–5, cf. 71), and then offers Theseus what he thinks is an impossible challenge which will rid him of the Athenian do-gooder for ever: he takes a ring from his finger, throws it into the sea, and orders Theseus to fetch it (60–6, 76f.).[170] Theseus does not

[167] Compare the moderation of the Theseus of *OC* 907f. and E. *Supp.* 724–5.

[168] The importance of what is essentially a minor incident—no more than a prelude to the great story of the triumph over the Minotaur—is greatly increased by Bacchylides' strongly Homericizing language, and Theseus acquires the stature of an authentic Homeric hero, the type who can give as good as he gets in contests, physical or genealogical, with opposing heroes. On Bacchylides and Homer, see Buss 1913; Jebb 1905: 81–2; Segal 1976; cf. Lefkowitz 1969.

[169] *FGrH*3 148 (cf. §1.3.3). Compare also the apologetic versions of the Theseus and Ariadne story on the roughly contemporary *ARV*[2] 252,52 (Neils 1989: 83) and *ARV*[2] 405,1 (Neils 1989: 100); also the later crater (*ARV*[2] 1184,4, *c.*430): see §7.5.2. Jacoby 1947*b*: 6–7 connects Ion's account of the foundation of Chios (ap. Plut. *Thes.* 20), which may have used material from Pherecydes, with a vase of the 470s (*ARV*[2] 927,2; Bernard 1986: 1057, no. 53). On one side, Ariadne hands two children (Oenopion and Staphylus?) to a nymph, while on the other, Theseus appears to be remonstrating with Athena. The implication may be that Ariadne must marry Dionysus, leaving Theseus' children: if so, this vase also will have been influenced by the Athenian version of the story.

[170] In his lawless handling of Eriboia, his apparent disregard for the justice which Theseus urges upon him, and his cruelty, Bacchylides' Minos conforms to the portrayal of him which is standard in Athenian tragedy: see Ch. 7 n. 4; cf. Maniet 1941; *contra* Giesekam 1977*a*: 242–6. This may seem strange, given that Bacchylides himself calls Minos the ancestor of the Ceans (1. 112ff.), for whose chorus poem 17 was written (17. 130f.). However, Ceos was only 13 miles (20 km.) away from Athens, and had long-lived connections with the more powerful city (see Sokolowski *LSCG* 1969: 188–91; *LIMC* 1. 1, 857, no. 3; Pridik 1892: 24–33; cf. Jebb 1905: 5–6; Severyns 1933: 56–9). Above all, Ceos fought alongside the Athenians at Artemisium and Salamis (Hdt. 8. 1, 46. 2; cf. Thuc. 7. 57. 4): especially if the poem

hesitate for a second and, showing the active courage that encomia
of Athens hold to be typical of the city, plunges into the water, to
everyone's astonishment (81–5). The second half of the poem
describes Theseus' reception in his father Poseidon's underwater
kingdom, where he is welcomed and given gifts by his stepmother
Amphitrite.[171] The poem ends as Theseus rises up from the ocean,
entirely unharmed, to the wonder of all (119ff.). Bacchylides'
Theseus, like that of tragedy, is a courageous defender of the
oppressed, who will always stand up for what is right, however formidable his enemies; the ideal Athens follows exactly the same
principles.[172]

Theseus' appearance on the Stoa Poikile (completed *c*.460),[173]
marks the very last stage in his metaphorical journey to Athens, and
the choice of pictures on the building as a whole conforms to preferences already discussed. Like the Theseion, it may have a connection with Cimon, but again, the subjects of its murals have a
general, public significance for all those who had experienced the
attack of the Persians and the Athenian triumph.[174] All its murals

was written in the early years of the Delian league, when the Athenian hegemony
was still popular, the theme of an Athenian standing up to a tyrant is an inspiring
subject with some contemporary relevance. Moreover, in this poem Bacchylides
makes no effort to link Minos with Ceos, so that he is, in effect, a different character from the Minos who is the ancestor of the Ceans: see also §§6.4 and 6.5.

[171] On a crater from Bologna of *c*.440, an extremely young Theseus is being carried by a Triton down to Amphitrite, who offers him a crown. It is often suggested
that this vase reflects the iconography of the painting in the Theseion: Robert 1898:
143; cf. Brommer 1982: 81–2, 85; *contra* Jacobsthal 1911. On a 6th-cent. black figure plate influenced by Athenian art, although of Thasian origin, a young ephebe
holds a javelin and peacefully rides a sea monster. If the scene does not represent
Heracles and Triton, it may possibly be intended to represent the story told by
Bacchylides: Weill 1959; but see Brommer 1982: 78. If this is the case, it is striking
that this part of Bacchylides' story, at least, long antedates its first extant representation in literature.

[172] Bacchylides even associates Theseus' quintessentially Athenian behaviour
with Athens by having the patron goddess of Athens attend the ship (l. 7). She has
no independent role in the adventure, but her presence hints that powers benevolent
to Athens and Theseus are not far away. Athena is sometimes included on vases portraying Theseus' heroic feats, but there is also an unusually close comparison to be
made between Bacchylides 17 and Euphronius' cup of *c*.500–490 (Louvre G104) on
which Theseus is greeted by Amphitrite with Athena in attendance behind them.

[173] See Wycherley 1957: 31–47; H. A. Thompson 1950: 327–9 for archaeological
details; also Wycherley 1953.

[174] Its alternative name was the Peisianacteion, after Cimon's brother-in-law:
J. K. Davies 1971: 378; Jeffery 1965: 41–2. However, the precise nature of any
Cimonian influence on its construction is unclear: Boersma 1970: 55–7; cf.
Thompson and Wycherley 1972: 90; also Robert 1895: 8; Kron 1976: 218. Aeschin.

show Greeks fighting non-Greeks, or Athenians against non-Athenians, and Pausanias implies that they were arranged so that pictures of the two historical battles, of Oenoe and Marathon,[175] flanked the two mythical ones, yet another Amazonomachy, and the taking of Troy.[176]

The Marathon picture is remarkable for placing contemporary persons in the same picture as the gods and heroes, so as to make the Athenians' achievement as impressive as those of the great heroes of the past. The story of their victory at Marathon is constructed as a tale of virtue rewarded and wrongdoing punished and the triumph of David over Goliath, very much like many of the Theseus stories. Harpocration says that Micon was arraigned for painting the Athenian fighters as smaller than the Persians, and if it is true at least that they were smaller, we should recall as a parallel the many Theseus cycle vases on which Theseus conquers huge adult males. Thanks to Athens' courage and the help of the gods and heroes, justice is done against all the odds: Pausanias names Athena, Heracles, Theseus, Marathon and Echetlus as the divine champions of the city. Heracles and Theseus are both associated with Marathon, where Athena too was worshipped as the local goddess Athena Hellotis (*ΣP. Ol.* 13. 56a), and the three form a group of long-standing association for the welfare of Athens. Theseus was

3. 186 says that the Athenian people would not allow Miltiades' name to be inscribed on the picture of Marathon, and it is reported that the people gave Polygnotus citizenship for his work on the Stoa: Harpocration s.v. Polygnotus; cf. Plut. *Cim.* 4. 6; Plin. *HN* 35. 38. Hölscher 1973: 74–8 suggests that the portrayal of historical characters and events indicates that the Stoa was Cimon's private dedication, since the state did not fund statues of individuals at this time: cf. Dem. 20. 70, 23. 196; Plin. *HN* 34. 17. However, the battle of Marathon was uniquely relevant to every Athenian who had lived through it. The Marathon picture contrasts with an offering at Delphi, which consisted of statues of Athena and Apollo, most of the Athenian *phyle* heroes, and also Theseus, Codrus, Phyleus/Philaus/Neileus and Miltiades: Paus. 10. 1. 1 with Hitzig and Blümner 1901: vol. iii, 677–8. This is more likely to have been a private dedication by Cimon: D. Kluwe 1965: 21; E. Kluwe 1968: 679. The glory of Athens still underlies the dedication, but the Philaid element is strikingly dominant, especially if we read 'Philaus' for the 'Phyleus' of the manuscripts: Vidal-Naquet 1986; Kearns 1989: 81–2, 205.

[175] Oenoe: Paus. 1. 15, but there are great difficulties in accepting his evidence: Jeffery 1965; Meiggs 1972: 96–7f., 469–71; Boersma 1970: 56; Vickers and Francis 1985. Marathon: Aelian *Nat.An.* 7. 38; Paus. 5. 2. 6; Plin. *HN* 35. 57. See Robert 1895: 4; Delvoye 1960: 803.

[176] Harrison 1972: 364; Vickers and Francis 1985: 106. Amazonomachy: Ar. *Lys.* 679 with *Σ*; Arrian *Anab.* 7. 135; Plin. *HN* 35. 9. Troy: Paus. 1. 15; Harpocration, s.v. Polygnotus; Plut. *Cim.* 4. 6.

portrayed in a striking manner, 'coming up from the ground'. Now that his bones were in the Theseion, he could be imagined to have been in Attic soil in 490, even if this was strictly speaking anachronistic. At last he had achieved autochthony and could defend his people:[177] the battle of Marathon was especially appropriate for his appearance, since it could easily be transformed into a purely Athenian victory.[178] Theseus, as a truly democratic hero, is, however, only one of the heroes who, along with their Athenian successors, made victory possible in a morally and divinely sanctioned rejection of the forces of tyranny.[179] The eternal gods, the heroes and the ephemeral men of the present all fight for the same ideal, and Theseus is as closely linked with the ordinary Athenian soldiers as with the commanders, in a magnificent blend of past and present which unites all forms and eras of Athenian prowess. This is an appropriate moment at which to leave Theseus and to turn to what is said of the nature of the Athens for which he was fighting.

[177] Gauer 1968: 117; Hölscher 1973: 62. Herodotus' account of Marathon is unique in not depending only on the picture itself (cf. Massaro 1978: 469), and probably in having had some of the Marathonomachoi as its source. Uncharacteristically he ignores the apparition: was it, in fact, an invention of the painter for whom Theseus was an essential symbol of Athenian identity, prowess and good fortune?

[178] The glory of Salamis had to be shared with other states, and the panhellenic battle of Plataea gets the least attention of all at Athens: Loraux 1973: 20–2, 27–8.

[179] Cf. Aelian *Nat.An.* 12. 38; Luc. *Jup.* 32; Himerius 10. 2, 2. 21. To my mind, the collectivity of the picture loosens the ties that are often assumed to link Theseus and the picture of Miltiades (hence Cimon). It is very far from certain that they were near one another in the painting: Robert 1895: 17, cf. 34 and 45, puts him in the centre; see also Hölscher 1973: 62. However, Massaro 1978: 467, makes a very different, but equally plausible reconstruction and Harrison 1972: 363–4 places Theseus and Miltiades at opposite ends of the picture.

2

The Athenian Image of Athens

2.1 INTRODUCTION

Much of the first book of Thucydides' *History of the Peloponnesian War* is devoted to examining the relationship between the outbreak of the war and the growth of the Athenian empire. The first extended exploration of the links between them is presented in the account of the debate at Sparta (Thuc. 1. 66–88) which was convened to discuss the incidents at Epidamnus and Potidaea, where Athenians and Corinthians had recently come into conflict with one another. The Corinthians open the discussion, and try to frighten the Spartans into making war on Athens by painting a formidable portrait of their common enemy. For them, the Athenian empire is intimately connected with the national character of the Athenians (Thuc. 1. 70), who are a uniquely active, aggressive people, never still, but always taking risks and striving to do better: their limitless ambition and energy are manifested in an unceasing expansion which is a direct threat to Sparta and the whole of Greece. The speech of the Athenians which follows agrees in essence with that made by the Corinthians, although at least in its first half (Thuc. 1. 73–75. 2), Athenian activity is presented in a more flattering light. In Athenian mouths, the indiscriminate military aggression of which the Corinthians complain (Thuc. 1. 70. 3 f. and 5 f.) becomes exceptional courage and enthusiasm for Greece (Thuc. 1. 73. 4–74). Similarly, the Corinthians complain that the Athenians are παρὰ δύναμιν τολμηταί[1] καὶ παρὰ γνώμην κινδυνευταί: the Athenians who stayed to fight the Persians in 480 BC in spite of the desperate situation in the city (Thuc. 1. 74. 2) might indeed be described as 'daring beyond their power and ready to take risks against their better judgement'. It is this very courage that makes them worthy recipients of an empire which, they say, was a gift from the other

---

[1] For the implications of τόλμα, agreed both by Athenians and their enemies to be especially characteristic of Athens, see below, 67.

Greeks who invited them to be their leaders after the Persian Wars, and it is only natural for them to wish to retain it (Thuc. 1. 75. 1–2, 76. 2). Underneath the accusations and counter-justifications which overlay the portrayals of Athens in these two speeches, there lies a large measure of agreement between the Athenians and their enemies concerning what is characteristic of Athens.

Thucydides' Athenians no less than his Corinthians talk of the Athenians as a homogeneous mass, and imply that there is complete consensus among them; but it is, of course, impossible to believe that every individual in a citizen body should fit one stereotype, or without exception accept particular modes of conduct as 'normal' or 'right'. Not every Athenian was an ardent democrat, and there were 'quiet Athenians' who were hostile or indifferent to the activity that Thucydides' Corinthians and Athenians regard as specifically Athenian. The emphasis laid by various writers on the importance of free speech and discussion in the assembly at Athens must indicate that there was plenty of room for debate on public policy, and that it was not necessarily determined by universally recognized and accepted criteria of 'typically Athenian' action, whatever Thucydides' characters may imply.[2] Any attempt to consider the relationship between ideas of 'Athens' or 'the Athenians' and their actual connection with the beliefs and behaviour of individual Athenians is therefore problematic. The assumption that the behaviour of individuals was guided by certain beliefs about their city which were actively meaningful to them can, at best, only be based on inferences and probability, and the very attempt to analyse 'the ideal image of Athens' may make it appear a more clearly defined concept than was in fact the case. If this is so, then any attempt to consider Theseus as a tragic hero embodying typical characteristics of Athens will also be of uncertain value, especially if it is claimed that his portrayal has a specifically educational function for audiences.

In spite of all these caveats, however, a number of probabilities, based variously on social and historical factors and literary evidence, do all seem to point in the same direction. First, in a society in which membership of a comparatively small city state was so

---

[2] On 'quiet Athenians', see Carter 1986, Boegehold 1982; free speech at Athens: Thuc. 2. 37. 1, 2. 40. 2; E. *Supp.* 438 ff.; Dem. 60. 26 etc. For a lucid statement of the difficulties surrounding the consideration of the influence of speeches about Athens on Athenian citizens, see Loraux 1986: 11–13, 75–9.

central to the existence of individuals, determining their social status and demanding certain observances in return, a conception of national identity, of what distinguished Athenians from others, based on both specific institutions and vaguer beliefs concerning the superiority of their polis to others, is likely to be prominent by virtue of the prominence of the institution of the polis. Athenian citizens were distinguished from the numerous non-Athenians who lived in the city by having sole access to decision-making in the assemblies, a task that assumed increasing importance as the volume of public business increased throughout the fifth century, especially after the 470s. Making decisions about the city was thus an essential part of being a citizen, and those who made the decisions had also to be ready to die for them on the battlefield.[3] There is, therefore, a tight link between citizenship, personal social status, decision-making concerning the community and the obligations demanded by membership of the polis, which is likely to have promoted, rather than to have suppressed, the creation of certain beliefs about it and of precepts concerning the kind of conduct typical or ideal for Athenians.

Contemporary Athenian democratic ideology itself, like Thucydides, tends to present 'the Athenians' or 'the δῆμος' as a unified body:[4] even if what is said of these bodies is not literal evidence for the way that all Athenians acted and thought, there is an extensive body of material concerning the characteristics or behaviour regarded as typical or ideal Athenian conduct which reveals a high degree of agreement among writers—in various genres, with various purposes, over a wide span of time—as to its nature and components. If such material was never meaningful to a representatively large section of the population, then its continuous repetition and reproduction, which is indicated by the striking continuity between images of Athens in the fifth century and the fourth century, and even (although evidence is much scantier) in the sixth century, is harder to explain.

The only extant fifth-century writer who is explicitly and consistently concerned with the nature of Athenian self-perception is Thucydides, and admittedly, parts of his picture of Athens are at

---

[3] See Boegehold 1994: 7; cf. Wallace 1994: 127; Loraux 1986: 13; Patterson 1981: 83.

[4] Ober 1994: 109–10 in Boegehold and Scafuro 1994.

odds with the portrait given by other sources.[5] However, what is said of Athens in Herodotus, Gorgias' funeral speech (82 F6 DK) and tragedies with Athenian themes tallies very closely with the more abundant fourth-century sources such as the funeral speeches attributed to Lysias (Lys. 2) and Demosthenes (Dem. 60), and that of Hyperides; Isocrates' encomia of Athens in the *Panegyricus* (Isoc. 4) and *Panathenaicus* (Isoc. 12), and of Theseus himself in the *Helen* (Isoc. 10); and the funeral oration contained in the Platonic *Menexenus*.[6] It is, of course, potentially risky to assume that what is said about Athens in the fourth century will be identical to what was said in the fifth, since the fourth-century orators are looking back to the great days of Athens: because they had lived through Sparta's heavier-handed regime, and now perhaps hankered after a second chance at empire, their view of Athens, and especially Athenian domination of the Aegean, might be thought to be excessively idealized (cf. Isoc. 4. 99). This is certainly the impression gained from an initial comparison of the later sources with Thucydides' hard-headed account of some aspects of the fifth-century empire. It is, however, undeniable that the Athenian military exploits which are the standard paradigms of the ideal Athens and Athenian military work in the fourth century are apparently familiar as such in the fifth century. The canon of exemplary Athenian military action in fourth-century encomia of Athens includes the reception of the children of Heracles at Athens, the burial of the seven against Thebes by Athenians and the Athenian resistance to the Amazons. Herodotus' account of the speech of the Athenians before the battle of Plataea (9. 27) uses precisely those three examples in order to establish Athens' right to lead the right wing of the army there. Although it is unlikely that he is reporting verbatim what was said before the battle of 479, the speech shows

[5] For a brief discussion of Thucydides' complex attitude to the Athenian empire, see below.

[6] The speech is prefaced by a distinctly sarcastic introduction, but this does not exclude it from consideration as evidence. It was taken quite seriously by the Athenians of Cicero's day—among whom it was recited annually (Cic. *Orat.* 151)—and the difference between what it says about Athens and what other encomia say is essentially one of degree rather than quality. The key to its tone is perhaps to be found in Socrates' comments on the embellishment of the truth by orators to cater for the Athenian public's taste for flattery (*Mx.* 234c–235d); but even if its author intended to ridicule the claims of the *epitaphioi* concerning Athens by exaggerating them, the caricature can assist the reconstruction of the original and its intended effect: see Clavaud 1980, esp. 117–18; Loraux 1974.

that these examples were familiar at least in the second half of the fifth century,[7] and it is probable that most, if not all, of them were familiar as stories of Athens' past before the Persian wars, even if they were not yet perceived as the quintessential examples of Athenian action.[8] By the fourth century, they were very obviously clichés, but both Herodotus and Thucydides hint that they, along with Athens' part in the Persian war itself, may have been hackneyed even by their day.[9] The reception of the Heraclidae, the burial of the seven and Erechtheus' stand against the Thracians (another paradigmatic exploit) are also dramatized by fifth-century tragedians. Although it is ostensibly very different from them, close analysis of Pericles' funeral oration reveals that out of thirty-nine topoi common to the later speeches of this genre, thirty-one can already be found in some form in Thucydides.[10] Furthermore, topoi such as the uniqueness of Athenian civilization, Athenian intelligence and the obedience to the laws and the constant resistance to oppression and injustice are common not only to Pericles' funeral speech and later encomiasts,[11] but also to fifth-century tragedy—notably the Theseus plays—and to some passages of Thucydides and Herodotus which discuss Athens. There is therefore quite a large body of fifth-century material of various types whose view of Athens is very similar to those expounded by later encomia.[12]

[7] This passage so closely resembles later funeral orations that it may have been composed under the influence of the genre: How and Wells 1912: ii. 297. Moreover, 'alone', they say, did we crush the insolence of Eurystheus: encomiasts of Athens commonly view all Athenian action as the deeds of unaided warriors against all oppression, although in itself, the theme and its appeal long antedates the Persian wars: see below.

[8] For the dating of the Amazon story, see Preller and Robert 1920: ii. 2, 730–3; for the story of the seven against Thebes, Jacoby 1954: 444; see also Preller and Robert 1920: ii. 1. 140–1. Pherecydes (*FGrH* 3 F84) recounts the reception of the Heraclidae.

[9] Hdt. 9. 73. 4–5; Thuc. 1. 73. 2, 2. 36. 4, 5. 89, 6. 83. 2. Later sources: Lys. 2. 11, Pl. *Mx.* 239b; Dem. 60. 9.

[10] Ziolkowski 1981, esp. 133; Loraux 1986: 246 doubts the value of this kind of methodology, but see below.

[11] Thucydidean reminiscences are especially strong in the *Menexenus* and Isocrates' *Panegyricus*: compare Thuc. 2. 65. 9 with *Mx.* 238d–e; Thuc. 2. 37. 1 with *Mx.* 238d; Thuc. 1. 74. 3 with Isoc. 4. 97; Thuc. 1. 76. 1 and 4 with Isoc. 4. 102; Thuc. 1. 77. 6 with Isoc. 4. 106. Some of these topoi survive even to Aristides' *Panathenaicus*: see Aristid. *Panath.* 8–9, 25–30, 32–9, 43–8, 50–1, 78–82, 110 (cf. 335), 179, 227–8, 330–41, 356–64, 384–6 with Day 1980: 172–80.

[12] Loraux 1986: 252ff. argues that there is a detectable difference between the 5th- and 4th-cent. images of Athens (cf. Hornblower 1991: 295), in that Athenian

Conversely, although Isocrates' *Panegyricus* is naturally concerned to minimize the injustices inflicted by the Athenian empire, what he does admit (above all, in the treatment of Melos and Scione) tallies with Thucydides' more damning account, and though Isocrates concentrates on Spartan atrocities while Thucydides chooses to highlight abuses of power by Athens, the historian does not suppress brutality on the other side (Thuc. 3. 52–68, 4. 80), even if he makes no direct comment on it. Although Thucydides and Isocrates are writing from different points of view, they are essentially telling the same story. Thucydides' attitude to the Athenian portrait of Athens is ambivalent and Isocrates' is not, but the apparent contradiction between them originates not so much from the difference between their dates of birth as from two opposing attitudes to a common and conventional Athenian self-perception. Hence, although one must allow for some exaggeration in individual instances in the fourth-century orators, I assume that the same basic tendencies underlie fifth- and fourth-century accounts of the nature of Athens, that the majority of fifth-century Athenians would have understood and endorsed the ideology behind them—and that Thucydides' apparently schizophrenic presentation is in fact deliberate.[13]

The *epitaphioi logoi* spoken over those who had died fighting for Athens must form the basis of any consideration of the Athenian image of Athens because they present a picture of the idealized Athens in its most concentrated (even exaggerated) form, making concrete what is merely implied elsewhere.[14] Such speeches cannot

military power is dominant in Pericles and Lysias, whereas the Athens of later writers becomes a cultural, not a military leader. However, she does admit (258, nn. 186 and 187) that the cultural superiority of Athens is already a theme of 5th-cent. tragedy: see below, *passim*, and note esp. A. *Eum.* 869, 917 ff.; E. *Med.* 830 f.; Schroeder 1914: 19–23. Even if later *epitaphioi* are forced to take the diminution of Athenian military might into account, Athenian cultural superiority is still familiar to 5th-cent. thought about Athens outside funeral speeches, whose evidence should not be viewed in a vacuum, but as one manifestation of an image of Athens as the ideal city whose power is allied to every virtue: cf. n. 14 below. In any case, the military triumphs of Athens still bulk large in later encomia. I will argue below that the ideal Athens is portrayed consistently both before and after the Persian wars as a civilizing city, and that the military and the cultural are not separable from one another.

[13] In this assumption I follow de Romilly 1963: 240; Loraux 1986 who mingles Thucydides with later speeches, in spite of 252 ff.; by implication, Thomas 1989: 200, 234; see also Brunt 1978, esp. 161–2.

[14] The best treatment of the funeral speech is that of Loraux 1986, although her approach is not beyond criticism. It is not always easy to determine whether she

be detached from entirely practical aims.[15] To judge from the highly impersonal tone common to nearly all of them and the manner in which they concentrate on the efforts of the Athenians as a body, rather than of individuals, their speakers were aiming to encourage community feeling and identity with the city as a whole.[16] The man who spoke the oration was chosen by the citizens as their best representative (Thuc. 2. 34. 6), so that what he said is likely to have reflected and promoted an image of the city considered acceptable to the widest number of citizens possible.[17] Most importantly, since such speeches are designed to console mourners, they must justify the deaths of their loved ones on behalf of Athens by an appeal to the higher good of the city and they must also

considers that the *epitaphioi* stand apart from the rest of the life of the city or that they influence and reflect Athenian ideas of Athens which are not confined to any particular literary genre. Especially if the latter is the case, her methodology rather exacerbates the difficulties inherent in trying to draw fixed conclusions from five specimens of a genre spread over a century, because she places equal weight on what is not said in the funeral speeches, as on what is said (cf. 221 n. 3). Where so little remains of what is said, the conversion of the unsaid into the unsayable seems questionable, especially since (in spite of pp. 11, 46–8) she concentrates on the funeral speech to the exclusion of other relevant evidence from other literary genres whose inclusion would modify her conclusions: cf. n. 12 above. Although the extant specimens of funeral speeches share many topoi with one another, they also differ from one another in style and tone, and I suspect that even in this very formalized genre, there may have been more room for variation (avoiding anything actually controversial) than critics often assume. In this chapter, therefore, I concentrate equally on all literary forms which praise the ideal Athens and deliberately combine them to form one synthesized version of the Athenian ideal (cf. previous note).

[15] Cf. Loraux 1986: 98; *contra* Nilsson 1951: 87 ff., but see below, n. 23. Most evidence makes the battle of Plataea the *terminus post* and Drabescus the *terminus ante* for the date of the first funeral oration, and by the 470s, all the elements of the rite of public burial described by Thuc. 2. 34. 1 are attested. Although they contain stories whose origins antedate the Persian wars (cf. §1.2), the combination of these stories of Athenian action against oppressors is most intelligible in the aftermath of these wars: Ziolkowski 1983: 11–24; Thomas 1989: 207, 213; see also the long discussion by Loraux 1986: 28–30, 56–67. Clairmont 1983: 7–15 links the establishment of the ceremony with the recovery of Theseus' bones, but the resemblance is not especially strong: Loraux 1986: 29 and n. 89, 357. On rather later inscriptions of the second century (*IG* II[2] 1006. 23, 1008. 17, 1009. 4, 1028. 19 f., 1029. 13, 1030. 9. 18 f. and 1034. 22) the Theseia are closely linked with the *epitaphios agon*. Clairmont 1983: 23 ff. suggests that the Epitaphia were inspired by the Theseia: see also Schroeder 1914: 75; Day 1980: 175. How far 2nd-cent. practice reflects that of the 5th cent. is, however, unclear: Jacoby 1944: 61 f.; Loraux 1986: 357 with bibliography.

[16] Loraux 1986: 65–9, 110 f.; Thomas 1989: 203–37; see also Rusten 1989: 161–2, 172–6.

[17] The context of mourning would, in any case, demand concentration on fundamentally uncontroversial themes: Thomas 1989: 196, 200–38, esp. 203–5.

convince their hearers that they should be willing, in their turn, to emulate those who have died for it (cf. Thuc. 2. 43. 1): thus the city must be portrayed as an ideal worth dying for. Especially significant is the way that such speeches interweave past and present, so that an allegedly typical essence of Athens and truly Athenian action is created. The recently dead are made into the most recent representatives of a timeless tradition of courageous and right action on behalf of the city. By insisting on the continuity between the past and the present, the speeches imply both that Athens has always been (and will always be) the same, and thus that ideal Athenian conduct is fixed and obvious and could not be otherwise. The exaltation of the particular details of the present to the level of the natural and eternal is an essential technique of encomia of Athens: in fact it is necessary for the successful function of any system of ideas, especially those which can have no concrete proof.[18] When presented to the Athenian citizens in a speech after which there is no discussion, and which essentially tells them 'this is what you are by virtue of being where you are', the encomium more readily becomes the natural order, removing everyday doubts and giving its audience a sense of pride in belonging to a worthy community.[19]

It is unlikely either that the *epitaphioi* could have voiced ideas which were entirely unfamiliar at other times in the year and in other circumstances, or that there is strictly a one-way traffic from the funeral speeches to other literary genres.[20] Long before the establishment of the funeral speech as a literary form, rudiments of the conception of the ideal Athens can be seen in the stories about Theseus discussed in the previous chapter, especially revised versions which remove him from any suspicion of bad behaviour, and the picture of the ideal Athens which is most fully expressed in the *epitaphioi* is already familiar to fifth-century tragedy, whether brief and self-contained reference is made to it, as in the short eulogy of Athens at E. *Med.* 824–65, or it shapes the structure and action of whole plays, such as those in which Theseus plays a part. The polis is as important as a context for understanding tragedy as it is for the

---

[18] For the technique, see de Romilly 1979: 69–71; Loraux 1986: 120–1, 129; Thomas 1989: 232–7; cf. also Cic. *Orat.* 36. 126 f.

[19] Cf. Loraux 1986: 90, 198, 277; Landmann 1974: 68.

[20] As Loraux 1986: 11, 263 seems to assume, but compare my reservations above, n. 12.

funeral speeches, and, like them, tragedy must be counted as a form of public education.[21] The plays themselves often handle themes related to the polis, but even before the performances, the generals poured libations, the tribute of the allies was displayed,[22] the names of the city's benefactors were announced and there was a parade of the war orphans whom the state had educated. As in the case of the *epitaphioi*, there exists a close connection, entirely unfamiliar in modern society, between the individual citizen and the public life of the city.

Although the funeral orations and some tragedy contain our fullest evidence for the nature of the ideal Athens, no less important is the matter-of-fact and laconic way in which Herodotus refers to certain images of Athens which are standard in encomia, as though they were well-known facts. Such images must have had a wide currency beyond their more formal expression in the funeral speeches.[23] Again, in the fourth century, Isocrates uses the enco-miasts' image of Athens as a serious basis for political argument. Even comedy can contain a kind of 'anti-encomium' of Athens, which necessitates that its audience is familiar with an ideal Athens and what is typical, institutionally and otherwise, of it. The context of comic performance, where what was normally unsayable was allowed, may paradoxically affirm that images of the ideal Athens were important to, and prevalent among, its Athenian audience.[24]

---

[21] Cf. Landmann 1974: 68. Heath 1987 argues strenuously that tragedy is pri-marily concerned with emotion rather than intellect. His approach is a welcome cor-rective to the over-intellectualizing approach of some critics, but it is possible to believe both that tragedy was not concerned with intricate intellectual, philosophi-cal and religious questions (cf. Heath 1987: 47), and that the genre did function edu-cationally in a wider sense. Indeed, public education of this kind could only be of a rather general kind. See also pp. 45–6, 71 where he admits arguments which tell in favour of the educational aspects of tragedy.

[22] Isoc. 8. 82 cites this as a source of exceptional annoyance to the allies. For the background to the Dionysia, see Goldhill 1987; also now Connor 1990.

[23] e.g. Hdt. 1. 60, 5. 82. 2, 7. 161; cf. also 7. 139, which presupposes that the idea that the Athenians saved Greece was familiar, even if unwelcome, to other Greeks. Nilsson 1951: 87 ff. claims that the political importance of funeral speeches was neg-ligible, but if they were merely empty words, devoid of real meaning, why do their ideas occur in so many different sources of different types?

[24] For example, compare the praise of Athens in Pind. fr. 76 with the mockery of the Athenians' fondness for this kind of thing in Ar. *Ach.* 626 f.; Ar. *Eq.* 1111–19 mocks the power of the people under the democracy; the economic benefits gained from the empire which Pericles sanitizes (Thuc. 2. 38. 2) are cynically reinterpreted by Ar. *Vesp.* 520. Ar. *Ach.* 505 f. contrasts the Dionysia with the Lenaea, which no foreigners attended and in whose plays a more critical eye could be cast on the city:

Finally, and by no means least importantly as a proof of the relation between ideas of Athens and their historical influence, when one compares accounts of Athenian foreign policy in the fifth century with the stereotypes of 'typical' Athenian behaviour, it is clear how a direct connection could be made between Athenian action in Greece and the idealized image of Athens as the city whose energy and desire for action never fail. Thucydides' account of the Pentecontaetia (1. 87–117) especially highlights the continuity between the image of Athens presented at the debate at Sparta and historical events: his concentration on the gradual growth of Athenian power abroad and presentation of an almost unbroken catalogue of Athenian expansion makes the fear felt by Athens' enemies in 432 BC seem entirely reasonable; in particular, the indefatigable courage of the Athenians against the Corinthians and Aeginetans (Thuc. 1. 105–6) resembles the remarkable conduct regarded as 'typical' of the city in the debate at Sparta. It would be at least economical to suppose that the ideal forms of Athenian action which encomia present had some active influence on the discussion of questions such as whether to fight or not, or whether to expand or stay quiet.

When evidence from various the sources is combined, a surprisingly unified picture of the ideal Athens emerges, and though the image of Athens that they portray has no room for individuals and could not be a fully comprehensive picture of a city, it is certainly a consistent picture of one particular image. It is hard to believe that it could have been so prevalent and consistent in literature without having had some influence in real life, especially given that its fullest expression is in the obviously educational, exhortatory genre of the funeral oration. I assume therefore that the funeral speeches contain an extreme and highly formalized version of an ideology which, in a less extreme form, pervades mainstream Athenian thought about Athens and Athenian identity. They both reflect and influence certain images of the city: there is no division between these two functions. The images of Athens which will be explored

it is no accident that Theseus' dramatic appearances are confined almost exclusively to tragedy (cf. §7.1.1). For the problematic relationship between comedy and reality, see Halliwell 1991. Loraux 1986: 304–7 suggests that comedy mocks the funeral oration even if mockery of such a sacred thing could not be explicit: I would say, rather, that the mockery is directed much more generally against all perceptions of the idealized Athens, as it is against many other serious things, notably the Peloponnesian War itself (e.g. Ar. *Ach.* 513 ff., 595 ff.).

below are vital as a background for understanding the portrayal of
Theseus in tragedy where he represents the city.

2.2 ATHENIAN IDEALS OF ATHENS: MODELS AND PRELIMINARIES

Ideals externally imposed by society tend to be internalized by
individuals (unless, of course, they are really repellent) to con-
tribute to their own personal sense of self-definition and belonging
in the world. Pride in belonging to a worthy group can bolster an
individual's self-esteem, and some groups inculcate a sense of
power in their members, a sense that as part of an influential group
they have some influence and control on the world around them.
However, power itself is usually not enough: it must normally be
used in the service of morally acceptable conduct so that the individual feels that what he is doing is in accord with higher ideals
such as what is 'just' or 'natural'. As will be shown, the Athenian
construction of the ideal Athens has particular attractions for individual Athenians (and is therefore likely to have had a real influence
on their attitude to the world) because its outlines are so close to the
way that individuals even now prefer to see themselves, and their
attractions enable them to be easily incorporated in Athenian official ideals and passed down through the generations.

A very widespread type of story, which takes as many different
forms in the modern world as in the ancient world, is the story of
the lone hero with a moral mission, whose rightness is thrown into
relief by the wickedness of those who try (and ultimately fail) to
oppose him.[25] The story of Theseus' civilizing adventures is
formed around this structure, as we saw in Chapter 1, and the
appeal of all such stories to an audience depends on their being able
to identify themselves to some degree with the hero, the righteous
lone individual who is vulnerable (at least for a time) to the forces
of the dangerous Other—an image attractive for every individual in
his relations with others. The Greek victory over Persia is constructed as this kind of story whose structure is exactly the same as
other paradigmatic myths of Athenian action to be discussed

---

[25] See Thompson H1200–550, L300–99 and 400–99 on the importance of heroes
and villains in folk-tales; the articles of Peneff and Passerini in Samuel and
Thompson 1990 on the influence of such 'folk-tale' structures on the way that
people tend to construct their own life histories; also V. Turner 1974.

below: the good underdogs conquer evil oppressors in spite of their superior strength, because the gods are on their side and Greek justice (δίκη) will always win against foreign injustice or oppression (ὕβρις).[26] Victory against all the odds is especially attractive because it can so easily be interpreted as a reward for moral virtue: although it is possible to imagine boasting of an unjustly gained victory or one guaranteed by sheer physical force, victory where the results are very far from certain is a highly desirable sign of (and reward for) excellence (ἀρετή), moral and otherwise.

Athens' contribution to the war of δίκη against ὕβρις was particularly important and, at least in the immediate aftermath of the Persian Wars, it was acknowledged as such outside the city, even in the face of the claims of other states to have saved the Greeks.[27] The ensuing growth of the Athenian empire was recognized to be a result of the Persian Wars, and thus it is that much later Athenian military action is viewed through the filter of the virtuous campaigns of 490–478, in which Athenians were clearly fighting for justice against wicked oppressors. Athens' behaviour in the Persian Wars confirmed rather than created the image of Athens as the city which always fights against oppression. The previous chapter traced the connection between the growth in interest in Theseus and ideas of Athens as a civilizing city long before 490 BC, but the victory over the Persians gives particular credibility to the idea that Athenians are active fighters for justice and civilization. The paradigm of the civilizing hero lies behind many different aspects of what is said of Athens in encomiastic literature.

The ideal Athens is functioning as model and example for its audience through tragedy as early as 458 BC, in the conclusion of Aeschylus' *Oresteia* trilogy. In the *Eumenides*, Orestes leaves an unending cycle of blood feud at Argos and, after wanderings through Greece (*Eum.* 239), comes at last to Athens.[28] Orestes himself has contributed to the bloodshed by killing his mother to avenge her murder of his father. His matricide is just because it was commanded by Apollo's oracle (A. *Cho.* 900; 985–9; 1044–8), but it

[26] Cf. Loraux 1986: 146, 165: for emphasis on the wickedness of Xerxes' expedition, cf. A. *Pers.* 740ff.; Hdt. 7. 22–4, 189, 8. 65; Lys. 2. 29; Isoc. 4. 90.

[27] Cf. Hdt. 7. 139; W. C. West 1970, esp. 278–9; Starr 1962.

[28] All roads 'naturally' lead to Athens: compare the words of the suppliants in E. *Hcld.* 185ff., *Supp.* 187–9 and S. *OC* 84ff., 258–65. For all of them Athens is the last resort of the desperate. Other Greek cities either cause conflict or fail to resolve it: Athens is the only city capable of resolving such a conflict.

is simultaneously a terrible deed demanding punishment from the Erinyes, who guard the order of society against violations such as kin-murder (A. *Eum.* 333–96, 490–565) with a strict unbending justice that cannot accommodate the ambiguous nature of a crime which was simultaneously right and wrong. The Argive chorus at the end of the *Choephoroi* can see no means of resolving the conflict between the two views of the matricide; but the impossible will be accomplished by Orestes' move to Athens. Thanks to its patron goddess Athena and the unique wisdom of the Athenians, to whom she delegates the task of judgement, the conflicting claims are considered and a compromise is found. The Erinyes are persuaded to reside at Athens as guardians of society connected with the newly-founded court of the Areopagus, while the Athenian jury is able to add mercy to their justice in order to save Orestes. Both persuasion and mercy are important in a murder court, in which the fundamental principle of returning like for like is refined and made flexible by the addition of human reason to judge conflicting claims. Indeed, the existence of such a court could be seen as essential to a civilized society.[29] The conception of Athens as the city of persuasion, mercy and flexibility was fundamental to the idealized self-perception of democratic Athens as the most truly civilized city in Greece. The Athens of the *Eumenides* is also a place of courage and intelligence.[30] It takes courage as well as wisdom even to help a man who has incurred the wrath of the Erinyes, let alone to invite such terrifying goddesses into the city, and the clever daring of Athens will be rewarded both on a human and on a divine level: thus Orestes gratefully rewards the Athenians with an eternal alliance with Argos (*Eum.* 762–77), and the appeased Erinyes promise to protect Athenian society (*Eum.* 938–1010, esp. 961). It is clear that in its treatment of Athens the *Eumenides* is structured around the pattern of ἀρετή and reward which shapes the feats of many heroes, including Theseus, and on a broader ideological plane, the relationship of fifth-century Athens to the rest of the Greek world. The next three chapters will explore the working of the pattern of ἀρετή and reward in the figure of Theseus in Euripides' *Suppliants* and *Heracles* and Sophocles' *Oedipus at Colonus*. The *Suppliants*

[29] Dover 1957: 234–5, cf. A. *Eum.* 704 f. Persuasion of Erinyes: esp. A. *Eum.* 794 f. 885, 970. On the establishment of laws at Athens, cf. Isoc. 4. 39; Lys. 2. 19.

[30] Pericles comments on the exclusively Athenian combination of courage and intelligence: Thuc. 2. 40. 3, and see also below.

focuses on an established Athenian myth and presents Athenian ideological claims explicitly. The other plays are also shaped by the myth of the ideal Athens, but they focus primarily on themes which have nothing to do with Athens, whose role in them is apparently due to innovation by Athenian playwrights.[31] They are therefore especially interesting as examples of myths reinvented in the ideal image of Athens and also as examples of a metaphorical Athenian expansionism in myth that was paralleled by Athenian political reality.

2.3 COLLECTIVE AND INDIVIDUAL IN ATHENIAN SELF-PRESENTATION

Although the Athens of the *Eumenides* is the city of Theseus (*Eum.* 1026, cf. 402, 685 ff.), neither he nor any individual Athenian king appears;[32] and the role assigned to Theseus in later plays is here divided between Athena and the Athenian jurors. A named individual figure such as Theseus, or even his less glamorous sons, on the Athenian jury in the *Eumenides* would have detracted from the anonymous collectivity of the citizen jurors which is so important in the trial scene. Moreover it is clear that a human king, even the king of Athens, cannot be placed on an equal footing with divinities such as the Erinyes. Therefore the reason, moderation and the 'fairness' of a collective democratic Athenian vote will acquit Orestes, and Athena will provide divine authority for the acquittal. There is no place for Theseus here.[33] In this emphasis on the collective, the *Eumenides* is unusual among tragedies (though characteristic, perhaps, of the political climate after Ephialtes' reforms) in being closer to the conventions of much public art than later tragedy was. The collective anonymity of the jurors in the

[31] For pro-Athenian innovations in the *Eumenides*, see Sommerstein 1989: 1–6, esp. 5.

[32] Even if the 'children of Theseus' of 399–402 are Demophon and Acamas, they have no share in the action of the play, and the phrase may simply mean 'the Athenians', as 'children of Hephaestus' obviously does at *Eum.* 13.

[33] See also Frey 1947: 20–3. I disagree with Loraux 1986: 65–6, who denies that Theseus was ever associated with democracy in the fifth century (cf. §3.3) and associates his absence from the funeral speeches with a reaction against his alleged association with Cimon: if so, it is surely odd that Aeschylus should have mentioned him at all in the *Eumenides*. He was also a major character in Aeschylus' *Eleusinioi*, whose dating is uncertain, but, like the *Eumenides*, it included an Athenian–Argive alliance, and could therefore be dated after Cimon's period of eclipse.

Eumenides more closely resembles that of the Amazonomachists and Centauromachists on the murals of the Theseion and Stoa Poikile, or pictures of Greeks fighting Orientals and Centaurs on the Parthenon, in which it is impossible to identify any individuals, because concentration on the feats of any individuals would detract from the collective representation which exemplified the unity and splendour of the whole city.[34] Such scenes of individual subordination to a larger body have their real-life counterpart in the imperatives of fighting for the city, and the collectivity of the dead citizen-soldiers is celebrated in the city's tribute to them in the funeral oration as an example of collective action. Material addressed to a community and intended to encourage sacrifices for that community naturally tends to dwell on examples in which a collective, rather than individuals, is shown to act. It is more usually in the nature of tragedy to set individuals against one another;[35] and thus the mythical exploits which belong to the Athenians in *epitaphioi* and some public art tend to be ascribed to individuals such as Theseus in most tragedies.

Essentially the nature of Athens remains constant, but whether the individual or the collective is preferred will tend to depend on genre: thus in the tragic version of the funeral speech over the Argive dead of E. *Supp.* 857 ff., the strongly collective focus of the historical funeral orations is transformed into an account of the prowess of individual leaders, because of the requirements imposed by tragedy. Precisely because the focus of tragedy which includes Athenian heroes tends to be Athens, rather than individual heroes who represent the city, Theseus is not its exclusive representative: thus in the *Eumenides* he does not appear at all, his son appears in Euripides' *Heraclidae* and in the *Hippolytus* Theseus himself no longer represents Athens. Where he is the representative of Athens in tragedy, Theseus embodies Athenian civilization in all its manifestations, so that he is usually less an individual character with his own fate than a symbol of Athenian virtue. He is consistently given characteristics which are considered as especially commendable in Athenian (and often Greek) thought, and such characteristics are usually marked as uniquely Athenian, by means of a contrast, sometimes implicit, sometimes absolutely explicit, between Theseus and the tragic representatives of other Greek cities. His

[34] Neils 1987: 129, 140; Boardman 1985: 247–52.
[35] Cf. Zuntz 1955: 13–14; Loraux 1986: 107.

Athenian origin is then emphasized so as to suggest that he is a typical Athenian thanks to his origins. All Athenians, all of whom are Theseidae, can and should try to live up to the virtues of their representatives—Theseus and those anonymous Athenians whose deeds are recounted in the *epitaphioi*. As with the *epitaphioi*, representation of the city of Athens as an example to the audience is primary: Theseus, like the recently dead in the *epitaphioi*, is merely an example of certain timeless and typical Athenian virtues.[36]

2.4 THE IDEAL ATHENS

There are five classic examples of Athenian prowess, and all of them celebrate the assertion of justice and order over the forces of disorder and injustice by the civilizing Athenians.[37] In the first two, hostile foreigners are repelled by the united forces of Athens: neither the Amazons nor the Thracians led by Eumolpus are strong enough to impose their violence on the city. Past and present are assimilated to make one common ideal exemplifying unchanging Athenian morality and power, so that these mythical foreigners, especially the Amazons, are partly assimilated to the historical Persian invaders. For example, Lysias' Amazons had enslaved many nations (4–6), and on hearing of Athens' greatness, they marched against her. However, they proved no match for brave men (ἀγαθοὶ ἄνδρες) at Athens and were punished for their greed and foolishness (ἄνοια). Very similar claims are made about Xerxes: he too was foolish, inexperienced and lacking experience of brave men (ἄπειρος ἀνδρῶν ἀγαθῶν (27)). By their unjust greed for Athens' land, the Amazons lost their own, just as the Persians were ignominiously routed. Naturally the *epitaphioi* say nothing of Theseus' abduction of Antiope, which was known to the author of the *Theseid* as the cause of the invasion (cf. Plut. *Thes.* 28. 1); for Aeschylus (*Eum.* 686), the Amazon invasion was not an honourable attempt to recover a lost sister, but simply a display of ill-nature

---

[36] Loraux 1986: 270–9, 283, cf. 104 ff. explores the highly collective focus of the *epitaphioi*, and suggests that there is rather a tension between the needs of the polis and those of individuals. If such a tension is recognized and resented, it might work against acceptance of the ideals promulgated by such speeches. However, such possible tensions are only one side of the coin: the polis also gives its citizens a welcome sense of belonging to something that is clearly worth some personal sacrifice.

[37] Still of value as a collection of evidence is Schroeder 1914. See also Landmann 1974: 76–7; Ziolkowski 1981: 74–137; Loraux 1986; Thomas 1989: 207–13.

(φθόνος) towards Theseus. Occasionally, the Amazon is characterized as a 'bad girl', who falls in love with Theseus because she is a
non-Greek and therefore has no self-control:[38] thus she is severely
but justly punished by the defeat of her people. All these are morality tales, not history, and they are structurally akin to the stories of
Theseus' triumphs over the brigands of the Saronic Gulf, in which
the strong and wicked are discomfited by means of the *lex talionis*
used in the service of Athenian civilization.[39]

The other great exemplary deeds of Athens are the return of the
bodies of the Argive dead to Adrastus when the Thebans refused to
let him bury them, and the help given to the Heraclidae against
their enemy Eurystheus: tragedy assigns them to Theseus and
Demophon respectively, while they belong to 'the Athenians' in
more collective literary forms. As with the stories of invasion and
resistance, Athens' military prowess is an important element in
these stories, but the battles fought on behalf of the Heraclidae and
the Argives are often characterized as a regrettable consequence of
enemy intransigence and as undesirable in themselves. What they
illustrate above all is Athens' unique moral sense in pursuing the
justified claims of such suppliants according to the law of Greece
which is also classified as divinely sanctioned law. Thus Lysias
(7–11) describes the bodies of the Argive dead refused burial by the
Thebans as Ἑλληνικοῦ νόμου στερηθέντες ('deprived of Hellenic
custom') and Theban action as θεοὺς ἀσεβεῖσθαι ('impiety towards
the gods').[40] Athens' military might is used in the service of civilization, and it would be wrong to make too sharp a division
between the two. Encomia of Athens consistently portray the city
as unique among all other Greek cities in upholding laws which all
Greeks should have the moral sense to support automatically and
unquestioningly, and thus as the only truly Greek city. Athens is a
super-Greek city, the education of Greece (παίδευσις Ἑλλάδος),[41]

---

[38] Isoc. 12. 193. In *FGrH* 391 F4 in which Demophon deserts Phyllis as his
father deserted Ariadne, Phyllis is said to display a similar *akrasia* towards him
which exonerates him from the charge of desertion. Ariadne herself may be portrayed in a similarly unflattering light: see also §§7.1.2, 7.5.2.

[39] The story of Euripides' *Heraclidae* is similar: Athens saves the suppliants and
Eurystheus himself ends up as a suppliant. Cf. Isoc. 4. 59–60; 12. 194. See also
below.

[40] Lys. 2. 7–11, esp. 9; cf. Isoc. 12. 55, 170, 174. See esp. Ch. 3 below.

[41] Thuc. 2. 41. 1, echoed in Isoc. 4. 50 (although Hornblower 1991: 307–8 denies
that there are any cultural implications in Thucydides' claim). Lys. 2. 22 and Isoc.
4. 68 both say that the Amazons thought that the conquest of Athens would mean

and hence Theseus, the representative of the city in tragedy, is a kind of super-Greek. Only he is amply endowed with all four cardinal Greek virtues, and other characters can simply look on and admire, rather than emulate or equal his achievements. The Athenians are never tempted into violence or over-confidence ($\H{v}\beta\rho\iota\varsigma$) in spite of their obvious superiority, unlike inferior or barbarian nations: moderation ($\sigma\omega\phi\rho\sigma\acute{v}\nu\eta$), after all, is one of these cardinal virtues,[42] and the hallmark of all their actions is the impartial pursuit of justice.[43] This is an ideal which is attractive to many individuals in their relations with others, but it is also useful for the public ideology of an expanding, imperial power of Athens' type. Unlike many imperial powers, Athens could not claim real cultural or racial differences as alleged reasons for her superiority over subject cities: the assertion that Athenians are more Greek, upholding Greek principles more assiduously than others, and that Athenian domination is entirely deserved by virtue of the goodness of those dominating is clearly useful. Since the difference between Greek and barbarian was so obvious, Athenian self-definition was more effectively served by the claim that Athenians were different from their Greek peers.[44]

The exaggerated claims of the encomia, which I interpret as extreme manifestations of a broader national pride which exists both before and after the fifth century, are worth some discussion because of their relation to the portrayal of Theseus in tragedy. They focus above all on the civilizing power of Athens in all its forms, because of the universal appeal of the 'civilizing hero' and because of its particular convenience in justifying Athenian expansion: once these claims are conceived they are too attractive to be abandoned, even after the fall of the empire. Anchises' expression of the Roman ideal *parcere subiectis et debellare superbos* (V. *Aen.* 6. 853) could be applied without any qualification to Athenian action in encomiastic literature and to Theseus' actions in tragedy. Sparing the humble and conquering the proud demand strength

the conquest of all of Greece: compare the Athenocentric conception of the Persian expedition against Greece as punishment for Athens at Hdt. 5. 105; cf. 7. 139.

[42] Cf. Pl. *Rep.* 427e10–11. Needless to say, many of her enemies thought exactly the opposite: see e.g. Thuc. 1. 84. 1.

[43] Impartiality: esp. Lys. 2. 8–10. The restraint of Theseus in victory is commented on with awe at E. *Supp.* 724–5; cf. Lys. 2. 10. See also below.

[44] Cf. Loraux 1986: 88–90, 165. She also links the birth of the funeral speech with the time when Greeks start to fight other Greeks (62, cf. 95).

and intelligence, and those who adopt this ideal lay claim to possession of both simultaneously (cf. Thuc. 2. 40. 3). Strength is necessary to conquer those who deserve it, but when pardon is desirable, then strength may be laid aside and the image of the merciful conqueror who stays his hand comes into play. Intelligence is necessary to make the choice between punishment or mercy. οὗτοι γὰρ ἐκέκτηντο ἔνθεον μὲν τὴν ἀρετήν . . . τοῦτον νομίζοντες θειότατον καὶ κοινότατον νόμον, τὸ δέον ἐν τῷ δέοντι καὶ λέγειν καὶ ποιεῖν <καὶ ἐᾶν> καὶ δισσὰ ἀσκήσαντες μάλιστα ὧν δεῖ, γνώμην <καὶ ῥώμην> . . . [45] Even Gorgias, the least 'serious' of the *epitaphios*-writers, but an expert in the techniques of persuasion, singles out the importance of γνώμη and ῥώμη (if the supplement is correct) and of doing τὸ δέον ἐν τῷ δέοντι, which is a sort of perfection.

Just as the Athenians exploited to their own advantage their special connection with the cult of Eleusis which was important for all of Greece, so Athenian encomia of Athens in the *epitaphioi* attribute to Athens the origin or fullest flowering of certain qualities or possessions which all Greeks considered particularly Greek or particularly worth possessing.[46] Agriculture is often a symbol of civilized life in Greek thought,[47] and thus encomia of the ideal Athens attribute to the city the origin of corn and the olive.[48] Isoc. 4. 28 makes the civilizing element particularly striking: Demeter gives Athens the products which are responsible for our not living like animals (οἳ τοῦ μὴ θηριωδῶς ζῆν ἡμᾶς αἴτιοι γεγόνασι).[49] The

[45] Gorgias, 82F6 DK: 'These men possessed divine excellence . . . thinking that this was the most divine and common law, to say what ought to be said at the right time, and to be silent, and to act, and to leave things alone, practising two things of especial importance, intelligence <and strength> . . . '

[46] Isoc. 4. 33. Conversely, all bad things belong to other peoples: cf. Hall 1989: 103.

[47] As already in Hom. *Od.* 9. 118–35: its demands are fundamental to social stability, and the practices of farming, in which human will is imposed on the landscape, are analogous to the feats of a civilizing hero.

[48] The discovery of corn is obviously related to the interest in Triptolemus and Eleusis long before the development of the empire: Shapiro 1989: 76–7; Day 1980: 15–38. On the symbolic value of olives, see Detienne 1970 and cf. Hdt. 5. 82. 2; S. *OC* 694; Dem. 60. 5; Pl. *Mx.* 238a. Fire, another pre-eminent symbol of technological progress, is also associated with Athens: Plut. *Cim.* 10. 7. Hephaestus and Athena are associated already at Hymn *Hom.* 20. 2–4, and the cult of Prometheus is unique to Athens: Guthrie 1957: 97–8; cf. Grossmann 1950: 114–19.

[49] Pl. *Mx.* 237d puts the contrast between Athenian civilization and non-Athenian barbarity in a more striking form: Attica was producing corn and olives, and the human race itself, but other lands could only manage dangerous wild animals: there is a parallel in V. *Geo.* 2. 140–4.

earth is personified as a mother who provides food, so it can even be suggested that the origin of the human race itself is in mother Attica, and thence because human beings are the creation of the gods, that Athenians must be especially close to the gods.[50] All Athenians are the children of this mother: they are purely Athenian, and, by definition, what is purely Athenian is given authority by being based on divine championship rather than subjective human principles. Athenian civilization is uniquely long-lived because of Athenian autochthony. Uniquely in Greece, Attica has always been inhabited by the same race, who have never had to drive anyone out of their land.[51] Thus Athens is a uniquely just city and a city with a uniquely ancient pedigree, which can trace its birth back to the creation of humanity itself.[52] It is not surprising, then, that Athens is said to have discovered not only the symbols of civilized and law-abiding life such as agriculture, but the very laws of Greece which themselves 'naturally' conform to a higher, transcendent principle of justice.[53] As a thoroughly law-abiding place, Athens has always been different from other cities in Greece, which (in spite of Theseus' own mitigated parricide) can be called the home of incest, parricide and other staples of Greek mythology (Isoc. 12. 121–4; Nepos, *Epaminondas* 15. 6.) Because of this eternal justice it is uniquely fit to deal with all invasions of the lawless and uncivilized, whether they are Amazons, Thracians or Persians, on behalf of the rest of Greece. Past, present and future, Athens essentially remains the same. As will become clear in the next three

[50] Earth as mother: Dem. 60. 5, Isoc. 4. 25, 12. 125, Lys. 2. 17, Pl. *Mx.* 237b–c: Attica as origin of human race: Dem. 60. 5; Isoc. 12. 124, 206, 4. 33; typically, Pl. *Mx.* 237d–e, 238d takes things further: Clavaud 1980: 118. It is true that there is nothing of this in Thucydides, and Athenian civilization is instead subordinated to Athenian power (cf. Hornblower 1991: 307–8), but since Hdt. 5. 82. 2 calmly ascribes the origin of the olive to Attica, I am not convinced that more extravagant claims could not have been made in the 5th cent. by those more sympathetic to them than Thucydides.

[51] The idea is already familiar to Hdt. 7. 161; also Thuc. 2. 36. 1; Lys. 2. 17–18, in which autochthony, democracy and justice are closely linked; Dem. 60. 4f.; Pl. *Mx.* 237c, 245c–d; Isoc. 4. 24, 12. 124, 206; Hyperid. 7; Lycurg. *Leoc.* 83. In the autochthony topos, Theseus' Trozenian origins are conveniently ignored.

[52] Homeric origins must be insignificant in comparison: cf. Dem. 60. 10. Isoc. 4. 83, 186; Hyperid. 35, and Isoc. 12. 202ff. (cf. 153) contrasts the Athenians with the Spartans who had inhabited the Peloponnese for a mere 700 years: cf. Loraux 1986: 69f.

[53] The first murder court is established at Athens in the *Eumenides*: cf. Isoc. 4. 40; D.L. 5. 17. Again Pl. *Mx.* 238b takes the topos to bizarre extremes, so that the Athenians are the givers of the gods to others.

chapters, the figure of Theseus in tragedy, embodying the perfection of an eternal unchanging Athenian civilization, is both a reassuring model and a justification of Athens' current status in the Greek world. It has often been noted that the fifth century sees an increasing preference in Athens for the portrayal of Athenians as the aristocrats of the Greek world, and the appeal to nature or what is fixed by tradition is essentially aristocratic. The attraction for Athenians in being able to claim that certain virtues are innate in the national character is obvious.[54]

The generosity of the Athenians, whether in taking it upon themselves to repel the uncivilized from Greece, or in offering the benefits of Athenian civilization to all, is a fundamental part of the Athenian self-image: θεοφιλῶς and φιλανθρώπως ('with love for the gods and men') did Athens share the benefits of civilization with others,[55] making of them her friends. To have plenty of friends is good, and indicates one's own moral worth; and correspondingly, it is shameful to have none.[56] Reciprocity is essential in friendship, and although it is shameful to think explicitly of the return while offering someone else a service,[57] it was acknowledged that a benefactor puts the person he has helped into his debt, and is owed a return. In the highly competitive society of Greece, the altruism of benefactors is matched only by the keenness of those they have helped to repay their obligations.[58] Thucydides' Pericles says, of what was often an aggressive imperialistic policy, 'it is not by receiving benefits that we make our friends, but by giving them' (Thuc. 2. 40. 4), and this is revealing, both of Greek attitudes to friendship, and of the modes of thought which strongly influence

[54] Isoc. 4. 63 and 99 suggests that Athenian autochthony entitles Athens to hegemony over Greece: cf. Loraux 1981, esp. 35–6; 1986: 148–9, 277 ff.; also Thomas 1989: 217–18. In itself, however, autochthony is not purely aristocratic: Connor 1994: 38. See also below, 70–2.

[55] Isoc. 4. 29. Note again the connection of divine and human is important and runs right through Athenian ideology: see also below, 75–8.

[56] Many friends: Arist. *EN* 1155ᵃ30; no friends: Isoc. 1. 16, Hes. *WD* 715. Respect for friends is ranked with respect for the gods, the laws and one's parents: Gorgias, F6, l. 11; Isoc. 1. 16; cf. Hes. *WD* 327–34. The emphasis on the morality of friendship is especially strong in the *Heracles*: see §4.4 below, *passim*.

[57] Reciprocity: Arist. *EN* 1155ᵇ27–34; 1156ᵇ–1157ᵃ9; Pl. *Lys.* 212c–d; shameful to think of the return: Arist. *EN* 1162ᵇ36.

[58] Ar. *EN* 1167ᵇ17–1168ᵃ27: those who receive benefits are in their benefactors' debt; 1162ᵇ5–14 admits that there is an element of competition in friendship. For friendship in Greece, see esp. Blundell 1989: 21–59.

the portrayal of Theseus in tragedy.[59] In this context the treatment
of the rescue of the Heraclidae is especially interesting. As we have
seen, Heracles was the greatest of the Greek heroes and had saved
Theseus from the underworld. Neither of these facts was especially
welcome to a city seeking to be the greatest in Greece, and so, while
it can sometimes be acknowledged that Demophon is simply repay-
ing a debt (E. *Hcld.* 215 ff., 240–2), more often it is presented as
another example of active Athenian prowess. In effect it becomes
an assertion of Athenian superiority over Greece's greatest hero: in
spite of all Heracles had done for humanity, it was to Athens that
his children had to look for rescue.[60]

The appeal of generously granting help when implored is apparent at Athens even before the Persian wars, as Athens accepted the
obligations attendant on being the Ionians' mother-city and helped
their friends and kinsmen in answer to their appeal.[61] After the
Persian wars and in the campaigns of the 470s, Athens, not Sparta,
led Greek forces against the barbarians in the 'new Trojan War',
and this position of pre-eminence in fighting on others' behalf for
the freedom of all Greece was highly attractive to them: it was not
one that they could relinquish later on. Civilizing heroes such as
Heracles and their own Theseus endured toils (πόνος) for the benefit of humanity and were honoured for it: thus within Athens it can
be argued that the empire is a deserved honour because of Athenian
πόνος.[62] Nicole Loraux makes a further comparison between the

[59] Compare especially Theseus' treatment of Adrastus and Heracles in the
Suppliants (esp. 513 ff.) and *Heracles* of Euripides with Loraux 1986: 81–2 on the
way in which Athens' insistence on looking after her 'friends' (rarely, even 'allies' in
the *epitaphioi*) reduces them to the status of clients, forced to leave all initiative to
Athens: 'All greatness is solitary [cf. below, n. 103], and Athens would much rather
have suppliants, on whom it may lavish compassion, than effective allies.'

[60] As Dem. 60. 8, which notes that they are the saviours of the saviour, an idea
implicit in much of Euripides' *Heracles*; Lys. 2. 13–16, where Heracles' services are
actually denied; cf. Isoc. 4. 61, although 56 admits that Heracles did help humanity.
Thus even Sparta owes her existence to Athens: Landmann 1974: 77. See the end of
§§4.4 and 7.6.2 on the various means employed of shifting emphasis away from
Heracles' prowess and onto that of Theseus.

[61] Hdt. 5. 97: contrast the failure of their appeal to Sparta's leadership of Greece
and kinship with the Ionians at 5. 49. Herodotus does not dwell on the Athenians'
subsequent abandonment of their noble role after the burning of Ephesus (5. 103).

[62] Thuc. 2. 36. 2, 62. 3, 64. 3; also 63. 1, but already honour and κλέος (glory) are
mingled with fear (cf. below, p. 80); E. *Supp.* 576; Lys. 2. 43, 55, 57; Isoc. 12. 128,
and on the connection between κλέος and πόνος, cf. Carter 1986: 1–25. The portrait
of the soft Ionians who refuse to undertake πόνος in the Ionian revolt (Hdt. 6. 12) is
partly a defence of the Athenians from the charge of abandoning their allies.

position of *prostatai* of Greece which the Athenians desired and
that of Achilles in relation to the Greek army at Troy. The Homeric
hero defines himself through his services to the community by
being both the protector of those less strong and brave than he is,
and also the role model for others. Because the heroes take more
risks than anyone else to protect the community, they are entitled
to ask for more honour from it, just so long as they prove themselves by continuing to take risks on its behalf.[63] In a similar way,
the empire of which Athens was leader and protector is a concrete
proof of Athens' worth; but it obliges Athenians both to explain the
claims of Athens to pre-eminence in Greece, in encomia, and—
more dangerously for some of the more vulnerable cities in
Greece—to maintain their reputation for activity and risk-taking
by continuous expansion.

Heroes are above all admired. There is an element of admiration,
if not approval, even in the hostile portraits of Athens offered by
Thucydides' Corinthians and pseudo-Xenophon's *Athenaion
Politeia*, and it is clear that even the ambivalent Thucydides was far
from immune to it. It is also a source of pride to the Athenians that
other Greeks should accept their rule.[64] [Xen.] *Ath.Pol.* 1. 17–18
claims that Athenians are flattered by the constant stream of allies
to Athens, and although the metics faced political disadvantages at
Athens, and were never treated as equals,[65] life in Athens was still
attractive to them. That a disadvantaged life in Athens was preferable to life with full political rights in their own cities will be
another contributing element to the image of the city presented by
encomia, that Athens was a kind of élite city, a magic circle fully
open only to those of pure ancestry. In spite of the real restrictions
on citizenship, the lives of the metics could be held up as 'proof' of
the openness of the city, its greatness, and Athens' generosity in
sharing it with others,[66] even though the contrast in status between

[63] Hom. *Il.* 12. 310–28; cf. Loraux 1978: 811–13. The image of Achilles as the
mother bird who gives everything to her children, keeping nothing for herself (*Il.* 9.
323 ff.), is perhaps especially attractive for such a city which so tirelessly helps its
friends. It is also, of course, a profoundly aristocratic image. Pericles commends an
Achillean short life with glory for the Athenian empire: Thuc. 2. 64. 3–4 with
Gomme 1956: 125–7.

[64] Cf. Thuc. 2. 41. 2, 63. 1, 64. 3, 6. 31, 7. 63. 3; Ar. *Vesp.* 656–63, 711, with
Forrest 1975: 17–29; Loraux 1986: 84–7, cf. 290; de Romilly 1963: 101.

[65] Whitehead 1977, esp. 35–57, 69–80.

[66] Unlike Sparta: Thuc. 2. 39. 1; cf. 6. 31. 6, 7. 63. 3; Isoc. 4. 41–2; with a different emphasis, [Xen.] *Ath.Pol.* 1. 12. See also Loraux 1986: 19.

the metics and the full Athenian citizens can also be used to 'prove' Athenian superiority. In the same way, the Theseus of tragedy will always accept suppliants at Athens, and fight for them, although they are his inferiors in various ways. The actions of Theseus and those of the Athenians can be described in very similar language: he is held to have made all dangers his own, and offered all benefits to others, just as the Athenians are commonly said to have made war which was common (κοινός), their own business (ἴδιος).[67]

The loyalty of Athens to friends was a vital part of Athenian imperial ideology. It created obligations between Athens the creditor and the indebted allies, from whom absolute obedience could be demanded, and such expectations were partly founded on historical reality, which made a potent 'proof' of their rightness.[68] In the early years of the Delian league, Athenian conduct in 480 was accepted as a reason for the allies' loyalty, and time and time again, defensive Athenian imperialists use this to justify the continuing existence of Athenian imperial domination, unaware of, or ignoring, the idea that their credit could have been used up.[69] The altruism shown by the Athenians on behalf of their weaker Greek friends in the Persian Wars comes to colour all Athenian military action, and all military action is a necessary manifestation of Athenian ἀρετή, because of the unchanging ideal Athens, where everything is always the same. In the idealizing mode, every deed, past and present, undertaken by Athens can be regarded as selfless intervention for the common good on behalf of the weaker simply because it is Athenian action.[70]

[67] Theseus: Isoc. 10. 36. Athenians: Lys. 2. 44; Dem. 60. 10; Isoc. 4. 86, cf. 57. On suppliants, see also 76–7 below.

[68] Obedience: Thuc. 1. 18. 2, 73. 2, 2. 40. 4; Lys. 2. 20–6, 42; Isoc. 4. 71–3 and 12. 49–51. The historical 'proof' is, of course, partial and entirely Athenocentric: cf. Loraux 1986: 155–8.

[69] Thuc. 1. 73. 8, confirmed by the historical excursus of 94. 4–7; 3. 10. 2; 6. 34. 5, cf. 76. 3; Hdt. 7. 139; Isoc. 4. 72, 12. 49–52, 67; even the less bellicose Isoc. 8. 30. But it is possible to be too cynical about this. The Spartans refused to enslave the Athenians at the end of the Peloponnesian War because of what they once did for Greece: Xen. *Hell*. 2. 2. 20.

[70] Pl. *Mx*. 244e; Isoc. 4. 52–3; cf. Walters 1980: 6–9 and below, §3.4 *passim*. The military ideology of the Roman empire operated similarly: Brunt 1978: 175–8. Compare also the following: 'The benefits that English rule has conferred upon mankind in the past . . . her arm has always been raised in the cause of liberty, of justice and of truth. In the great continent of Africa . . . England is the only country which has never failed to turn an attentive ear to the cries of the down-trodden and oppressed . . . It is our rule [in India] . . . which stands between countless millions and every kind of oppression, tyranny and wrong' (Drage 1890: 10).

In sharp contrast to Athens, the Spartans were unwilling to take part in foreign campaigns. In Spartan terms, this translates as moderation and self-control as against Athenian interference (πολυπραγμοσύνη),[71] but Athenians call it slowness and stupidity. Athens' bravery is active and glamorous, based on intelligence, speed and initiative. The speed of the Athenians in the Persian Wars, as opposed to Spartan slowness, is used as another justification of the possession of the empire.[72] It was 'more useful' for Greece than anything done by Sparta, just as Theseus' deeds are 'more useful' than those of Heracles (Isoc. 10. 24). Athenian military action is commonly described by both the Athenians and their enemies as τόλμα—in fact a morally ambiguous term, comprising both exceptional courage to do what others dare not, and rashness, courage to do what one should not do.[73] In the ideal Athens, it is filtered through Athenian wisdom, so that no mistakes are ever made, but the common consensus of Athens and Athens' enemies on the daring of Athens tellingly illustrates the moral ambiguity surrounding the empire. The ideal τόλμα is the sort of courage that Theseus is made to show, a courage which is used voluntarily for the good of others.[74] It is supremely individual, and linked to individual intelligence, but it is also determined by a set of unbreakable rules of behaviour, in Greek ideology common only to Greeks, in Athenian ideology common only to Athenians.[75] Sparta's form of courage can also be classified as selfish, unlike the noble struggles of Athens on behalf of Greece. Athens takes on her full share of deeds, and they are deeds of the right sort, because they are not

---

[71] For the term, see Adkins 1976: 301–27; also Ehrenberg 1947 and, more sceptically, Allison 1979.

[72] Athens' speed: Lys. 2. 23, 26; Isoc. 4. 87, 12. 170; Hyperid. 24: Loraux 1986: 158–9; Thomas 1989: 222.

[73] Carter 1986: 12. Thucydides explicitly contrasts the Athenian character with that of the Spartans who lack it: οἱ μὲν ὀξεῖς, οἱ δὲ βραδεῖς καὶ οἱ μὲν ἐπιχειρηταί, οἱ δὲ ἄτολμοι ('these swift, those slow, and these enterprising, those cautious': 8. 96. 4–5; cf. 1. 69. 5, 70. 3). Like Athens' speed, Athenian daring in the Persian wars also justifies the possession of the empire: Thuc. 1. 74. 2. See also Dover 1970: 355.

[74] Compare Isoc. 10. 25: none of the Greeks except Theseus dared (ἐτόλμων) to withstand the Marathonian bull.

[75] Other people's daring is mere ignorance (ἀμαθία) because it lacks intelligence: Thuc. 2. 40. 3. Athenian obedience to certain laws without coercion: Hdt. 7. 104; Thuc. 2. 37. 3, with Landmann 1974: 83: on the nature of Pericles' unwritten laws (ἄγραφοι νόμοι), see below, n. 118. In traditional stereotypes, democracy suffers from lack of self-control (ἀκολασία, as [Xen.] *Ath.Pol.* 1. 5, 10), but the ideal Athens avoids all the usual pitfalls.

self-regarding, but concerned with helping others.[76] Similarly, Theseus is always ready to expend effort on helping others when they have been wronged and deserve his help.

As Thucydides sees (2. 63. 2), military intervention, whether it is called helping friends or πολυπραγμοσύνη[77] is by definition essential to an empire like that of the Athenians which is constantly expanding, because the ideal image of the city is fixed as the place whose greatness depends on continuous and successful action in the outside world. There was no moment at which Heracles or Achilles could retire, and in the same way, Athenian action defines the Athenians, so that they must maintain and expand their power, while simultaneously justifying such expansions. Alcibiades, encouraging intervention in Sicily, says that Athens should help even those who have done nothing for her: τήν τε ἀρχὴν οὕτως ἐκτησάμεθα ('this is how we got our empire'). This justification nicely illustrates the ambiguity between the idealized and the hard-headed view of Athenian activity.[78] Tragedy deals with Athenian intervention in the purely idealizing mode, providing an unbroken line between past and present via the myths of the idealized Athens. Athenian intervention is presented in a context in which it can only be an unambiguous moral good, as Greeks acting for the good of Greeks, just as Athenians once fought for the good of Greece against Persia, and in turn this helps to validate current Athenian policy. At E. *HF* 266, as Heracles' blameless family await extinction at the hands of the wicked tyrant Lycus, the chorus asks him indignantly, 'Am I interfering (πράσσω πόλλ᾽ ἐγώ) in helping my friends?' Here, of course, it is hardly 'interference' for them to try to help Heracles' condemned family, even though their efforts will be in vain; but this kind of intervention, like those recounted by the funeral orations, can be used to imply that any intervention is legitimate. At E. *Supp.* 575–6, the Theban herald criticizes Theseus, πράσσειν σὺ πόλλ᾽ εἴωθας ἥ τε σὴ πόλις ('You're always interfering, you and that city of yours'): since the context is

---

[76] The selfishness of Sparta can define Athenian selflessness: Thuc. 1. 74. 3, 1. 88; 3. 13. 7 and 4. 40. 3–4; cf. Isoc. 12. 46–8, 228. The complaints of Spartan slowness and selfishness have a basis in historical reality, but they are also strongly influenced by Athenian self-definition, and where it is appropriate for the speaker's purpose Sparta is not condemned: see e.g. Isoc. 4. 86–8.

[77] The two are linked by Ar. *Plut.* 913.

[78] Thuc. 6. 18. 1; cf. Isoc. 12. 164, 4. 52: contrast Hermocrates' cynical view of such help: Thuc. 4. 61. 4, 6. 77. 1. By 18. 3, Alcibiades himself has moved away from all ideas of altruism: if Athens does not rule, it will be ruled.

the burial of the Argives, in which Athenian intervention can only be admirable, Theseus can answer sincerely, τοιγὰρ πονοῦσα πολλὰ πόλλ᾽ εὐδαιμονεῖ ('Yes, and by a lot of hard work we get a lot of happiness').[79] Conversely in the *Heraclidae*, the unsympathetic Theban herald tells Demophon not to intervene in what is not his business as his city is too prone to do (*Hcld.* 253–5), but he is clearly wrong, since Demophon must intervene against a man whose idea of justice involves oppressing suppliants. Thus every sting is taken out of πολυπραγμοσύνη and doubts are cast on the validity of criticisms by Athens' current enemies.

Theseus is himself purged of anything alien to the ideal Athens. In Athenian narratives he cannot desert Ariadne, and he only accompanies Peirithous on the impious mission to the underworld out of loyalty to his friend;[80] even Aethra's servitude to Helen is turned into an image of loyalty and devotion, as the Parthenon portrays her rescue by her grandsons. However, like the fundamental conception of the civilizing city that lies behind so many of the idealized images of Athens, some, at least, of these Athenian stories antedate the Persian wars,[81] and they certainly antedate the full flowering of the empire. The ideal Athens is not simply a creation of the imperial era, and history and ideology are mutually intertwined so as to influence and endorse one another.

Even the thalassocracy, on which Athens' empire depended, can be turned into an example and a proof of the ἀρετή of the city.[82] The Greeks are a sea-faring nation, so since Athens is the best at naval warfare, she is once more the most 'truly Greek' city both in myth and history.[83] The first thalassocrat was traditionally Minos, who also drove out the pirates; and in this respect, he is a mighty civilizer.[84] However, he was also an oppressor of Attica whom

[79] At Thuc. 6. 87. 2, Euphemus almost echoes this in a very different context, where Thucydides seems to be trying to expose the ideals of imperial πολυπραγμοσύνη: πολλὰ δ᾽ ἀναγκάζεσθαι πράσσειν, διότι καὶ πολλὰ φυλασσόμεθα ('forced into plenty of interference, because we have plenty to guard').

[80] Cf. §§1.3.2, 7.6.2.　　　　　　　　　　　　　　[81] See §§1.3–1.3.3.

[82] Connection of thalassocracy and empire: Thuc. 1. 15. 1; of both with the democracy, [Xen.] *Ath.Pol.* 2. 5; cf. Isoc. 12. 115–16.

[83] Note especially Thuc. 2. 41. 4: πᾶσαν μὲν θάλασσαν καὶ γῆν ἐσβατὸν τῇ ἡμετέρᾳ τόλμῃ καταναγκάσαντες γενέσθαι ('by our daring, making every land and sea accessible').

[84] Thuc. 1. 4; cf. Hdt. 3. 120–5; cf. Isoc. 12. 42–4. On the importance of the 'Minoan thalassocracy' for 5th-cent. Athens, see especially Starr 1955: 282–91. The list of thalassocracies preserved in Eusebius may conceivably reflect a Periclean source justifying Athenian claims: Myres 1906 esp. 86, 130.

Theseus conquered, for the good of Athens and the rest of Greece as well. Conquering the conqueror and civilizer puts Theseus on a higher plane of civilization and strength than Minos. Again, an idealized image can be underpinned by historical reality, since the thalassocracy is a result of the Persian Wars and is therefore a just reward for Athens' noble service to Greece at Salamis and proof of the city's worthiness to have it (cf. Hdt. 7. 144. 2). It is no coincidence that it is in the 470s that there is a particular interest in Theseus as Poseidon's son.[85]

Command of the sea gave Athens the economic advantages by which (uniquely) the city could confound the dictum laid down by Solon that no man or state could be self-sufficient. Pericles boasts of the abundance and variety of goods at Athens and of the people's self-sufficiency,[86] and Athens' invincibility is explained by the self-sufficiency of the Athenian people at 2. 41. 1 f. Versatility and self-sufficiency (αὐτάρκεια) were long admired as part of the ancient aristocratic ideal of ἀρετή, because they are qualities not available to all: what is in origin aristocratic is taken over by Athens as quintessentially democratic.[87] At *Il.* 9. 443, the ideal held up to Achilles is μύθων τε ῥητῆρ' ἔμεναι πρηκτῆρά τε ἔργων ('to be a speaker of words and a doer of deeds'): Achilles himself has some trouble combining these two traditionally opposed terms, but in the ideal Athens, λόγος and ἔργον need not contradict one another.[88]

The opposition between word and deed takes many forms in Greek thought, amongst which are peace versus war, intelligence versus physical strength, persuasion versus violence, and civiliza-

---

[85] See § 1.7 on Bacchylides 17. How far the portrayal of Athens as the wise benefactor reflected general sentiment immediately after the Persian wars, and how far it is already a defensive reaction to hostility from the other Greeks is an interesting question: Walters 1980: 10; Kierdorf 1966: 107.

[86] Hdt. 1. 32. 8; Athenian self-sufficiency: Thuc. 2. 36. 3, 38. 2, 41. 1. [Xen.] *Ath.Pol.* 2. 7–12 views the phenomenon from the opposite perspective, contrasting the abundance of goods at Athens with their paucity in other places. Isoc. 4. 42 presents it with a philanthropic twist: the Athenians in their generous self-sufficiency have set up the market for everyone at Peiraeus. Hermippus 63K lists all the goods that pour into Athens: the tone of the passage is unknown, although Aristophanes' presentation of the topos (*Vesp.* 520) is not flattering. His *Holkades*, frr. 428, 430, 431 K.-A. may also have referred to this. See also Loraux 1986: 86–7.

[87] Kakridis 1961: 23–8; see also Loraux 1986: 153–5. Plato *Rep.* 561e comments on the versatility of the democratic man.

[88] Thuc. 2. 40. 3; the Athenians are ἐμπειρότατοι δὲ λόγων καὶ πραγμάτων ('most experienced in words and actions'): Isoc. 8. 52.

tion versus bestiality.[89] Strength on its own can easily be portrayed as mere aggression, and thus, especially in military contexts where it may be necessary to mask aggression with nobler motives, λόγος often has more moral authority than ἔργον. A recurring motif of the Theseus tragedies in which he is confronted with enemies is his reluctance to use mere force against his opponents, and his preference for words. Where his opponents are less civilized than he is and refuse to respond to the more civilized idea of persuasion, Theseus is forced to beat them on their own terms by using force. Because Theseus is Athenian, and versatile both in word and deed,[90] he is able to do this, being neither aggressive nor feeble but perfectly balanced between the two, wisdom tempering power and power underpinning wisdom.[91] There is a tradition that he established the worship of Aphrodite Pandemos and Peitho after he had accomplished the synoikism of Attica.[92] Peitho was originally worshipped in various parts of Greece as the patron of erotic persuasion, but in fifth-century Athens its erotic aspect is lessened and Peitho becomes the goddess of persuasive speech in general.[93] In this way, persuasion is annexed so as to make of it a particularly Athenian, and democratic, quality, and the representatives of Athens in tragedy exemplify its uses for the benefit of others.[94]

The reconciliation of traditional opposites to create a city of total virtue can throw up some interesting paradoxes. We are sometimes told that Athens has a 'mixed constitution', and though it is a democracy, it is also an aristocracy in the sense that the best people rule; that is, it combines the best of so-called Athenian and Spartan constitutional virtues.[95] The fifth century, perhaps from the

[89] For a useful summary of the 'word' and 'deed' opposition, see Parry 1981: 15–21; on persuasion, see Buxton 1982: 58–66.

[90] Implicitly in tragedy, and explicitly at Isoc. 10. 21: οὐδ' ἑνὸς ἐνδεᾶ γενόμενον ἀλλὰ παντελῆ τὴν ἀρετὴν κτησάμενον ('possessing perfect virtue and not lacking any'); cf. Isoc. 12. 165.

[91] The ideal of the mean is important in the 5th cent. (Grossmann 1950: 19–29) but has much older origins: e.g. Solon 5 and 16, Thgn. 331 ff., 945, P. *Pyth*. 11. 51 ff., A. *Eum*. 525 ff. etc. Like many terms of moral approbation it can cover a variety of positions: Dover 1957: 233.

[92] Paus. 1. 22. 3; cf. Isoc. 15. 249.   [93] Cf. Shapiro 1977: 160–2, 257.

[94] Thus Athens is the city where linguistic skills are most developed: Isoc. 4. 48; cf. Lys. 2. 19; significantly, Cleon condemns the importance of speech: Thuc. 3. 38. 4.

[95] Thuc. 2. 37. 1; Pl. *Mx*. 238c–d, with Thomas 1989: 219; on the 'mixed constitution', see Oliver 1955: 37–40. Isoc. 12. 131 denies that Athenian democracy suffers from the ἀκολασία characteristic of democracy in its enemies' eyes.

Persian Wars on, and certainly after Pericles' citizenship laws of 451/0, sees an increasing emphasis on the aristocratic disposition of the Athenians: indeed, the funeral speeches tend to ignore specifically democratic features of the constitution, preferring to speak in vaguer terms, concentrating more on ideas such as government by an élite or the ἀρετή of the people.[96] The idea of aristocracy retained its glamour even in the radical democracy,[97] and the portrayal of Athens as an aristocratic democracy is explained partly by the sense of specialness that it gives to even the most ordinary Athenian, putting him, if just for a little time, on the level of the kings of old, the civilizing heroes, or even the famous Spartan *homoioi*.[98] Tragedies set in Athens are often vague on the constitution of the heroic city, but maintain a sturdy defence of democracy, whose superiority is made clear by the moral contrast between the representative and product of a democracy (often Theseus) and an opposing tyrant/oligarch, with the effect that Athens is under the rule of a good king, while being simultaneously somehow a democracy.[99] This is obviously impossible in strictly logical terms, just as the portrayal of Theseus both as wise, mature king and handsome youth is logically contradictory,[100] but both types of Theseus and this odd constitution are necessary to support Athenian claims to complete virtue and complete civilization.

The combination of opposites to make perfect virtue is only possible for Athens: all other cities fail in some way to achieve it.[101] They can fail outright; and this is frequent in encomia in which Athens is regarded as the only city to be truly civilized. The uniqueness of Athenian civilization is especially striking in

[96] Patterson 1981: 40–83, esp. 82–5, 102–4, 132–3; Loraux 1986: 23–4, 150ff., and esp. 172ff.

[97] Loraux 1986: 217.

[98] Cf. Gomme 1956: 125–6, who comments on the gap between the aristocratic Athenians of the *epitaphioi* and the kinds of characters we see in Aristophanes. See especially Loraux 1986: 172ff., who suggests (212) that the aristocratic representation of the democracy tends to obscure the distinctive qualities of the democratic way of life (whether this is confined to the funeral speeches or in the public life of the city more broadly is not entirely clear). I would guess, however, that the citizens, hearing the vague defences of democracy in the *epitaphioi*, which tend to abstraction and elevation, would mentally supply them with the necessary specific details.

[99] Nationality, character and government are explicitly linked in Pl. *Mx.* 238c and Isoc. 12. 138, and Lys. 33. 7 shows that the Athenians associated possession of an unchanging constitution with the absence of stasis (as Walker 1995: 144).

[100] Cf. Kakridis 1961: 50f. On Theseus and democracy, see also §3.3.

[101] Cf. Isoc. 4. 73; Loraux 1986: 213.

Pericles' *epitaphios* speech: μόνοι γὰρ τόν τε μηδὲν τῶνδε μετέχοντα οὐκ ἀπράγμονα, ἀλλ' ἀχρεῖον νομίζομεν ('we alone think that the man who takes no part in this [sc. politics] is useless, rather than someone who minds his own business': Thuc. 2. 40. 2, cf. Isoc. 4. 109). This is an example both of the λόγος | ἔργον combination unique to the ideal city, and of the annexation by Athens of qualities valued by Greece at large, since in essence it is not so very different from behaviour commended already by Hesiod.[102] Similarly, at 2. 40. 3–4 (cf. 39. 1), Pericles says that Athens acts differently (διαφερόντως) from others: ἐνηντιώμεθα τοῖς πολλοῖς· οὐ γὰρ πάσχοντες εὖ, ἀλλὰ δρῶντες κτώμεθα τοὺς φίλους ('we do the opposite of what most people do; not by receiving benefits, but by giving them do we make friends'). In fact, to excel in benefiting others is, of course, utterly traditional as a definition of male ἀρετή, not at all confined to Athenian ethics, but the uniqueness of Athens' virtues must be stressed for an effective self-definition.[103] The Persian wars 'prove' the uniqueness of the Athenians, since it was their unique moral character which made them take their unique stand against the barbarian hordes, 'few against many'. Once more we may compare the image of the civilizing hero, who defeats not just one, but many, enemies, particularly Theseus the young, lone warrior who opposes violence and danger with his unique sense of right.[104]

Alternatively, non-Athenians may be allowed some virtue, but never complete virtue, or all the various characteristics generally valued in Greek culture. This schematization is perhaps more satisfactory because of the absence of deep cultural differences between the Athenians and their enemies or their subjects.[105] Thus

[102] Hes. *WD* 293–7: Rusten 1989: 154–5.

[103] μόνος used of Athens: Thuc. 2. 41. 2, 1. 70. 7; reversed at 1. 69. 4 ἡσυχάζετε . . . μόνοι ('you [Spartans] alone of the Greeks are inactive'); Lys. 2. 4–7, 20–1, cf. 15, 40; Pl. *Mx.* 240c–d. Of the establishment of the democracy, Lys. 2. 18; Isoc. 4. 56; Pl. *Mx.* 245c. The desire to be unique is not confined to Athens: Xen. *Lac.Pol.* 1. 2, 2. 14, 9. 1, 10. 4; and see Loraux 1986: 166–7 on Sparta's annexation of virtues commonplace among the Greeks.

[104] Athens' lone stand against the barbarian: Hdt. 7. 10, 9. 27; Thuc. 1. 73 ff.; Lys. 2. 20 f.; Dem. 60. 10 f.; Andoc. 1. 10. 7; Lycurg. *Leoc.* 70. 'Few against many': A. *Pers.* 324–5; Hdt. 6. 61–100 and 7. 228 emphasize the vastness of the Persian army; Lys. 2. 40, cf. 22; Dem. 60. 10; Isoc. 4. 96; cf. Pl. *Mx.* 240c–d. On the historical distortions involved in all this, see Walters 1981.

[105] Language, religion and the same customs define what it means to be Greek: Hdt. 8. 144. 2.

Sparta is granted ἔργα, because it would be absurd to deny Spartan military power, and courage (ἀνδρεία) is a cardinal Greek virtue in which all Greeks must outstrip the barbarians. The sting in the tail is that Spartan military might is purely a result of an excessively narrow and strict training, while Athens has time for even better ἔργα, and λόγοι as well: φιλοκαλοῦμέν τε γὰρ μετ' εὐτελείας καὶ φιλοσοφοῦμεν ἄνευ μαλακίας.[106] Athens combines the best of Dorian and Ionian, being neither obsessed with war, nor over-refined as the Ionians traditionally were,[107] and although the word ἁβρός ('delicate') is pejorative when applied to the Persians, it is no longer so when used of Athenians.[108] Athens was the first city to give up carrying weapons καὶ ἀνειμένῃ τῇ διαίτῃ ἐς τὸ τρυφερώτερον μετέστησαν:[109] thanks to their unique intelligence, which can determine τὸ δέον ἐν τῷ δέοντι, Athenians can take the very best of ἁβρότης without succumbing to excess. The word ἁβρός itself is etymologically connected with ἥβη (youth);[110] one may recall the standard portrayal of Theseus as a delicate, sometimes girlish youth who is, however, a great fighter. When Theseus arrived in Athens, he was mocked by the builders of the Delphinion for his girlish appearance: his response was to loose the oxen of a cart standing nearby and to throw them over the temple (Paus. 1. 19. 1–2). This combination of tough and soft, quite different from the stereotype of the dour 'uncivilized' Spartan, is claimed by Athens as uniquely Athenian. The remarkably frequent festivals in Athens exemplify Athens' soft living and flexibility, and they also seem to have democratic associations.[111]

[106] 'We love beauty without extravagance and wisdom without being soft': Thuc. 2. 40. 2. Thuc. 2. 39. 1 notes that the innate courage of the Athenians obviates the need for training, and Gorgias attributes 'innate Ares' to them: see Loraux 1986: 150–1 on the working of this highly aristocratic ideology of non-professionalism, which also influences the figure of Theseus. On the various failings of Sparta (often contrasted with Athens by implication), see Lys. 2. 31–2, Isoc. 4. 92, 12. 46, 198, and esp. 208, 217, complaining about Spartan deficiency in culture, justice and reverence.

[107] Ionians: Xenophanes, DK21 B3. Mixture: [Xen.] *Ath.Pol.* 2. 8–9, 12; Landmann 1974: 87 compares the mixture of Doric and Ionian styles on the Parthenon; also Kakridis 1961: 50–1.

[108] Here I disagree with Hall 1989: 81.

[109] 'And changed to an easier and more luxurious way of life': Thuc. 1. 6. 3: cf. Bacchyl. 18. 1; E. *Med.* 826–7.

[110] Verdenius 1962.

[111] Thuc. 2. 38. 1; Ar. *Nub.* 309; Isoc. 4. 45–6; association with democracy: [Xen.] *Ath.Pol.* 2. 9, 3. 2, 3. 8; Plut. *Per.* 9. 1, 9. 3, 11. 4; Grossmann 1950: 94–8. At S. *OC* 1006 Theseus comes to Oedipus from the middle of a sacrifice to Poseidon.

They are also, of course, proof of Athenian piety. Athenian piety was a fundamental element in the idealized picture of Athens. This is not surprising: everything in mainstream Greek thought returns to the gods, and Thucydides is atypical in this, as in many other ways.[112] The claim that the Athenians, uniquely among ancient imperialists, ignored justifications of empire which relied on divine sanction, relies too much upon Thucydides' cynical and distorted view of the prevailing ideology of imperial Athens.[113] As will be demonstrated in subsequent chapters, the figure of Theseus at Athens is very similar to Virgil's Aeneas, 'outstanding in virtue (*pietas*) and battle (*arma*)' (cf. Isoc. 10. 31). If the gods are just, as mainstream thought undoubtedly liked to believe that they were, it is important that the Athenian empire itself is just.[114]

The close relation of the Athenian empire to the divine has been somewhat obscured by another element which dominates in Pericles' funeral speech, although it is not confined to it: it is another essential constituent of the ideal Athens. Strictly speaking, it does not fit well with traditional piety, but its classification as Athenian is another element in Athenian versatility. This is the belief that humanity does not depend exclusively on the gods, and that human reason is an important agent in human progress.[115] It is necessary that the gods should have sanctioned all Athenian action, especially the establishment of the Athenian empire, but no less necessary that it should also be the rightful reward for the Athenians' own unique efforts.[116] Hence, in Theseus' character, especially in the *Suppliants* and the *Heracles*, we will sometimes find a slightly uneasy mixture of traditional piety and a more progressive 'humanistic' outlook. This humanism is partly influenced by fifth-century scientific thought and is also connected with other

---

[112] Lloyd-Jones 1983: 129–36, esp. 133.

[113] As Grene 1965: 5–6, 30–1; also Brunt 1978: 161–2. Hornblower 1987: 182–3 redresses the balance a little.

[114] Thuc. 5. 105. 2 twists this shockingly so that the Athenians claim they are doing what the gods do, because they are following the law of the stronger: cf. Andrewes 1970: 173–4.

[115] As Xenoph. 21 B18 DK; Anaxag. 59 B21 DK; Democr. 68 B119 DK.

[116] Compare the πόνος topos above. Isoc. 4. 33 describes the Athenians as πρός τε τὰς τέχνας εὐφυεστάτους ὄντας καὶ πρὸς τὰ τῶν θεῶν εὐσέβεστατα διακειμένους ('most naturally disposed to arts and sciences, and most reverently disposed towards the gods'), and 38 f. makes only the vaguest distinction between gifts given by the gods and those given by Athens.

manifestations of democracy.[117] As the majority of the people is given more freedom in government, they acquire a greater sense of personal power, so that what has seemed immutable can, in fact, be altered by human reason.[118] However, the immutability of what is 'natural' or divine remains useful as a proof of Athenian virtues. All Greeks are clever, especially as defined by barbarian stupidity, and wisdom is regarded in Greece as one of the four cardinal Greek virtues. Athenians are naturally the cleverest of the Greeks, and are clever in the right way, producing the right sort of courage: others' courage is merely ignorance (ἀμαθία).[119] Thucydides' Sparta makes a virtue of her ἀμαθία: this has some historical basis in the cultural poverty of the city, but is also a product of the ideological component of Athenian self-definition in relation to other cities.

Athenian claims to wisdom, courage, piety and generosity are especially asserted in tales of the reception of suppliants by Athens and the Athenian kings—especially Theseus in tragedy—who embody the city. The successful reception of a suppliant demands these universally commendable characteristics which Athens liked to consider Athenian, and which Greeks consider Greek. The claims of suppliants are taken seriously in Greece long before the fifth century, and supplication essentially resembles the theoxeny, in which a divinity in unprepossessing disguise tests an unknowing mortal.[120] If the mortal has the wisdom and compassion to pass the test, great benefits are his. Once more, modes of behaviour

[117] See especially Guthrie 1969: iii. 55–84; Farrar 1988: 16–28, 38–9; Meier 1993: 1–39; but see the qualifications of Hornblower 1987: 73–5.

[118] Hdt. 1. 32. 4. Reliance on human reason: Thuc. 1. 142. 9; [Xen] *Ath.Pol.* 1. 2; Democritus 68 B119. See especially Edmunds 1975: 89–142. Grene 1965: 87 comments on the tone of total personal responsibility in Pericles' speech, in which divinity is ignored, although he does at least mention the festivals (2. 38. 1). Hornblower 1991: 302–3 denies that the 'unwritten laws' of 2. 37. 3 have any religious significance, but the context suggests that they have both a social and a religious dimension: the previous clause refers to laws 'for the help of those who have been wronged', such as helping suppliants, which are enjoined both by the laws of Greece and by divine law, and whose observance is considered uniquely Athenian in mainstream ideology.

[119] Cleverness of Athens: cf. Hall 1989: 121; Hdt. 1. 60. 3; cf. Thuc. 1. 68, 70. 2, 142. 8, 2. 40. 1, 41. 1, 62. 5, 8; cf. E. *Med.* 824. Others' ἀμαθία: Thuc. 2. 40. 3, and see also chapter four on ἀμαθία in the *Heracles*.

[120] Kierdorf 1966: 92 f. relates the popularity of the reception of suppliants to the reception by the Athenian commanders of those oppressed by Pausanias' hubris (Plut. *Cim.* 6. 2; Aristid. 23). The reception of the allies may have been seen by Athens as 'typically Athenian', but the importance of receiving suppliants long predates the 470s. The *Odyssey* already contains elements of a theoxeny: Kearns 1982.

regarded as morally commendable in general Greek morality are annexed for the sole credit of the ideal Athens. Such claims are also structured by the relationship of ἀρετή and reward. To receive a suppliant is a pious action, but there is extra credit attached to it, because the potentially dangerous nature of suppliants also demands intelligence and courage from those who receive them. John Gould suggests that when a suppliant, a weak inferior, applies to a stronger superior for protection, the inferior is, in fact, a threat to the integrity of the person supplicated.[121] If so, then it is clear that successfully welcoming suppliants must be a source of pride to Athenians, because it proves that their city's integrity can cope with any number of demands, even from persons who are dangerous both in human terms and potentially in divine terms as well. Like those who pass the test of theoxeny, the Athens which receives suppliants will always gain some benefit from so doing. A benefit gained is especially attractive if—as in the reception of suppliants— it has been preceded by a risk: risk makes a benefit into a deserved reward for personal courage.

Reception of a suppliant also often demands a flexibility, benevolence and ability to see beyond the superficial circumstances of a case, which necessitates the operation of terms such as οἶκτος (pity), ἐπιείκεια (reasonableness) and πειθώ (persuasion).[122] The ideal Athens was the home of such qualities, and they may be

---

[121] J. P. Gould 1973, esp. 100.

[122] On Athenian ἐπιείκεια, see especially de Romilly 1979: 53–63. Cleon condemns them as entirely inappropriate for an imperial power: Thuc. 3. 37. 1–2, 40. 2–4. He is almost the antithesis of the ideal Athenian and his preference for ἀμαθία with σωφροσύνη (3. 37. 3) resembles that of the Spartan Archidamus (1. 84. 1–3); cf. also Ar. *Eq.* 985–6. He is perhaps right, however: even Pericles compared the empire to a tyranny (Thuc. 2. 63. 2–3). The rigidity which Cleon recommends in dealing with the Mytileneans contrasts with the moderation and flexibility commended by Diodotus (esp. 3. 46. 4), but even Diodotus assures his hearers that neither οἶκτος nor ἐπιείκεια have any part in the policy he recommends (3. 48. 1). No appeals are made to the nobler Athenian ideals of encomia, because the reality of Athens' relationship with Mytilene, as Thucydides' characters see it, is incompatible with them. Diodotus' emphasis on intellect and flexibility, rather than strict deserts, and Cleon's concern with justice and punishment are at best distorted forms of Athenian ideology stripped of its more attractive bits by the self-interest necessary for the maintenance of the empire. How far this is Thucydides' version of the truth about the empire and how far he was recording what was actually said is a problem: I find it hard to believe that few or no appeals to pity were made and that the debate was conducted purely on arguments from self-interest; that said, there were perhaps good reasons for not making too much of the image of the ideal Athens in such a debate.

classified as 'democratic' in that they demand individual judgement of each case, rather than the mere application of rules: Gorgias says that Athens prefers λόγων ὀρθότητα ('right words') to νόμου ἀκριβείας ('strictly accurate laws') and τὸ πρᾶον ἐπιεικές ('kind reasonableness') to τοῦ αὐθάδους δικαίου ('stubborn justice') and Isocrates that philosophy has made Athenians kind (πρᾶοι).[123] We have come full circle to the ideal Athens of the *Eumenides* with which the chapter began. The heroic *prostates* for all oppressed Greeks must by definition be the strongest and most just state in Greece (Isoc. 4. 41, 12. 164), voluntarily fighting on her own for justice as the lone policeman of the Aegean.[124] Fighting for justice necessitates giving due punishment to the wicked, which is normally the prerogative of the gods, and 'punishing the bad' (κακοὺς κολάζειν) is a favourite description of the Athenian mission.[125] The Athenians are uniquely placed to determine the nature of just action, both because of their innate intellectual endowment and because of the support of the gods. Gorgias sums up Athenian action in his inimitable way: θεράποντες μὲν τῶν ἀδίκως δυστυχούντων, κολασταὶ δὲ τῶν ἀδίκως εὐτυχούντων . . . ὑβρισταὶ εἰς τοὺς ὑβριστάς, κόσμιοι εἰς τοὺς κοσμίους ('helpers of those unjustly wronged; punishers of those unjustly fortunate . . . violent towards the violent; orderly towards the orderly').[126] In tragedy, Theseus will be shown as just such a character. Agents of divine justice need have no fear of punishment themselves; such a proposition is attractive to any individual, but especially useful for a powerful city in dealing with its relations with others.

[123] Isoc. 4. 47; cf. Ziolkowski 1981: 102. οἶκτος is a praiseworthy characteristic of tragic heroes (e.g. S. *Aj.* 121–6), and a particular attribute of Theseus and Athens. See de Romilly 1979: 97–112. On the superiority of τὸ ἐπιεικές to τὸ δίκαιον cf. Arist. *NE* 1137ª31–38ª3.

[124] Compare Andoc. 3. 28; Pl. *Mx.* 244e; Lys. 2. 12–13; Isoc. 4. 53; Dem. *Lept.* 3. For Theseus the volunteer, see Isoc. 10. 25 and esp. Ch. 4.

[125] E. *Supp.* 341; cf. Lys. 2. 16, 19; Dem. 60. 11; Pl. *Mx.* 240d–e, 241c; Isoc. 12. 47; Hyperid. 5: Schroeder 1914: 31 cites Ζεὺς κολαστής ('Zeus the punisher', A. *Pers.* 827) in this connection. Isoc. 4. 101 describes the massacre at Melos as 'severe punishment', excusable in wartime; see also Thuc. 6. 87. 3.

[126] For Athens as helper of the wronged: Thuc. 2. 37. 3, 41. 5; Lys. 2. 13, 14, 22; Pl. *Mx.* 240d, 244e; Isoc. 4. 41, 47, 52–3; 8. 136–44; Hyperid. 6. 5. Pretended criticism of the Athenians' excessive fondness for looking after the oppressed is found at E. *Hcld.* 150–77 and *Supp.* 576–7; Isoc. 4. 53, Andoc. 3. 28 and esp. Pl. *Mx.* 244e–245a; compare the genuine criticisms of Cleon, above, n. 122.

2.5 THUCYDIDES AND THE IDEAL ATHENS

An obvious objection to this sketch of some currents in mainstream Athenian ideology, whose influence on the portrayal of Theseus in tragedy is explored in the next chapters, is that much of Thucydides' view of Athens is very different from that of later encomia and tragedy. There is a marked discrepancy between the unattractive portrait of the empire which Thucydides paints in parts of the *History* and the picture of Athens' benevolent civilizing mission which appears to a large extent in Pericles' *epitaphios*, the Theseus tragedies and fourth-century oratory. It is shocking to read the last three hundred lines of Euripides' *Heracles*, in which Theseus appears as representative of Athenian humanity, and then the roughly contemporary Melian dialogues, and shocking to move from Pericles' funeral oration to his last speech in which he openly describes the empire as being 'like a tyranny', or other passages which acknowledge that Athens' allies hate their ruler.[127]

The two images of Athens, as civilizer and as tyrant are contained in the same book, some twenty chapters apart from one another;[128] and the juxtaposition of the two recurs in other parts of the *History*. Apart from Pericles' *epitaphios* speech, only in the Athenians' speech in book 1 does Thucydides present the idealized image of Athens which is so common in other sources, and this speech is notable for its mixture of idealism and realism, so that the civilizer and the tyrant coexist awkwardly. In fact, the idealizing passages which connect Athens' services in the Persian Wars with the possession of the empire are decidedly undermined. The topos 'we got into the ships' is a standard justification for the possession of the empire (as Lys. 2. 30), but the way that it is repeated rather tritely here (1. 73. 4, 74. 2, 74. 4) suggests that such glories are somewhat faded. Twice, the Athenians themselves go so far as to deny that their altruism on behalf of Greece can justify their present actions. At 5. 89 (cf. 105), the Athenians, contemplating the massacre of the Melians, say that they will use no ὀνόματα καλά ('nice talk') concerning the justice of their claims, merely the law of the stronger,

---

[127] Tyranny, Thuc. 2. 63. 2; cf. Ar. *Eq.* 1111–14, 1330, 1333; *Vesp.* 620. Hatred of Athens, Thuc. 2. 8. 4, 11. 2, 3. 37. 1, 4. 79. 2, 85, 108. 4, 5. 11. 1, 6. 83. 4, cf. 87. 2, 8. 48. 6, 64. 5.

[128] For the close and complementary relation between the two speeches, see Hornblower 1991: 332; Loraux 1986: 191.

since justice is meaningless where the imbalance of power is so huge. A similarly stark view is taken by Euphemus the Athenian at Camarina (6. 83. 2): οὐ καλλιεπούμεθα ὡς ... τὸν βάρβαρον μόνοι καθελόντες εἰκότως ἄρχομεν ('we will not give lovely speeches about how we alone destroyed the barbarian and deserve to rule'), although, even more strikingly than the Athenians in their first speech, he mingles his picture of an empire based on the fear and self-interest that a tyrant feels (6. 85. 1) with traditional topoi concerning Athens' services to Greece in the Persian wars and 'helping friends' (82–83. 4).[129] Such speeches are not renunciations of the claims of Athens to others' gratitude: they are rather admissions that Athens' power is such that the city can and will do what it likes anyway, and that the justifications which we find implicit in the speech of the Athenians in book one, in the funeral oration and, I suggest, in the mainstream of fifth-century Greek thought, are therefore irrelevant.[130] The importance of the law of the stronger in human nature runs right through the *History* from the Archaeology on, and is already stated by the Athenians at 1. 76. 2–77; even in the funeral speech, the power of Athens is central, and duty and responsibility are not mentioned.[131] At Thuc. 1. 76. 3–77. 5, the Athenians claim that they deserve credit for some attempt to treat their allies justly when they could simply use their full power against them. This is a kind of travesty of the tragedians' Athens, as represented by Theseus, who is stronger than all the rest, but prefers to act according to the dictates of mercy and justice, rather than relying on mere power. In the Athenians' speech, the noble image of the just conqueror staying his hand has become something rather different and less attractive.[132] Even at Melos,

[129] Cf. Raubitschek 1973: 36.

[130] Andrewes 1970: 161; de Romilly 1963: 247; Palmer 1992: 65: already at 1. 73. 2 τὰ παλαιά are ignored, and at 4. 19. 2, the Athenians reject Spartan appeals to ἐπιείκεια, the attribute typical of Athens in the encomia. Not only Athens' past is rejected: see Thuc. 3. 54. 3 with Grene 1965: 52–3 and cf. 1. 82. 1, 2. 65. 12, 8. 18, 47. Thucydides seems to take the unusual view that the past is no longer valid as model or justification for behaviour in the present in an era which saw the destruction of many of the old certainties. Walker 1995: 196–9 suggests that even the benefits of the Thesean synoikism, unquestioningly accepted by mainstream tradition, are challenged by Thucydides.

[131] Gomme 1956: 126. The law of the stronger is a widespread belief throughout the work: 3. 10. 1, 11. 1, 4. 92. 4, 5. 89, 111. 4. It is connected with the idea of fear: 6. 82. 3, 87. 1–2. See also Andrewes 1970: 184–6, cf. 1960: 6; Farrar 1988: 11–12.

[132] See also Palmer 1992: 55–6.

the Athenians say they will not destroy the island if the Melians see sense, and that their proposals are moderate (μέτρια; Thuc. 5. 111. 4): this is perhaps the most striking instance of the perversion of the ideals of the encomia. In the idealized picture of Athens' mission, the power of the city is a concrete sign of its excellence, but it is all too possible for the exercise of power, and power alone, to be thought excellent in itself and necessary as a proof of the continuing splendour of the city.[133]

Around the 440s there is a change in terminology on inscriptions from 'the alliance' (ἡ ξυμμαχίς) to αἱ πόλεις ὁπόσων Ἀθηναῖοι κρατοῦσι ('the cities which the Athenians rule'),[134] and words such as 'empire' and 'subjects' are used by Thucydides' Athenians even in the 'Periclean' books.[135] Power, mastery and all the material and other benefits that ruling brought are thoroughly attractive,[136] as long as mastership of Greece can be shown to have been acquired justly by human effort and divine will as a reward for innate ἀρετή. Just because it is a reward for, and proof of, Athenian virtue, the empire of the Athenians can never remain as it is, but must always expand. In this lie the seeds of its corruption, because unceasing expansion arouses hostility from others, and eventually Athenian freedom comes to depend on ruling others to avoid being ruled by the enemies of Athenian expansion.[137] The freedom to rule is attractive, so that being ruled must by definition be resented, and the objects of Athenian rule will naturally wish to rebel.[138] The acquisition of the empire begins as a glorious enterprise, underlining and extending Athenian worth, but in Thucydides, by virtue of the hatred felt by those ruled, it turns into a mastery motivated by fear, and the empire takes on a momentum of its own in order to keep ahead of its enemies (cf. 5. 91, 95).[139] The speeches of the

[133] Thuc. 2. 41. 2, 64. 3; cf. Loraux 1986: 84f.

[134] Meiggs 1972: 152–71; also de Romilly 1963: 47 n. 4 ; Loraux 1986: 84.

[135] e.g. Thuc. 1. 77. 2 and 5; 144. 1; 2. 36. 2; 63. 1; 64. 3.

[136] Cf. Strauss 1994: 106 who cites recent work on the importance of the self-mastered, aggressive masculine body as a cultural symbol at Athens.

[137] Even in the *epitaphios* speech: Thuc. 2. 36. 1–4; but also 1. 38. 2, 3. 45. 6, 6. 82. 3, 83, 7. 56. 2, 8. 68. 4; cf. Hdt. 1. 210: Palmer 1992: 23; Ober 1994: 108.

[138] Farrar 1988: 7–9; cf. Forrest 1975: 26: Thuc. 1. 77. 5, 2. 64. 5, 3. 46. 5; Ar. *Eq.* 1114f.; Plut. *Per.* 12. 2; [Xen.] *Ath.Pol.* 1. 14.

[139] See especially Macleod 1974: 58–9 and 1978: 66–72, who shows also how Cleon's arguments at the Mytilenean debate reflect some inherent contradictions about the empire as a whole (cf. Hornblower 1991: 421 ff.; Palmer 1992: 61 f.). Cleon argues both that it was unjust of the Mytileneans to revolt and that it was natural—

Athenians in book 1 and that of Euphemus in 6 are especially effective for their mingling of the ideal and the hard-headed (1. 76. 2, 6. 83. 1); the fatal transition from worthiness to rule to necessity of ruling through fear is already found at 1. 75 and is seen to particularly striking effect at 2. 63. 1–2: τῆς τε πόλεως ὑμᾶς εἰκὸς τῷ τιμωμένῳ ἀπὸ τοῦ ἄρχειν, ᾧπερ ἅπαντες ἀγάλλεσθε βοηθεῖν, καὶ μὴ φεύγειν τοὺς πόνους ἢ μηδὲ τὰς τιμὰς διώκειν . . . οὐδ' ἐκστῆναι ἔτι ὑμῖν ἔστιν [sc. of the ἀρχή], εἴ τις καὶ τόδε ἐν τῷ παρόντι δεδιὼς ἀπραγμοσύνῃ ἀνδραγαθίζεται· ὡς τυραννίδα γὰρ ἤδη ἔχετε αὐτήν . . . ('you may reasonably be expected to support the dignity which the state has attained through the empire, in which you take pride, and you should not shrink from its burdens unless you refuse its honours as well . . . nor is it possible to back out, even if any of you through fear in the present wants to play the part of an honest, unambitious man. For what you have is like a tyranny . . . ').

Imperialism is by its nature ambiguous. Where one state is more powerful than another, so that the imbalance of power brings benefits, of a material or less tangible kind, to the stronger from the weaker, the benefits gained by the stronger state tend to be minimized, and the services of the stronger to the weaker are correspondingly emphasized. This is particularly true in Athens' case, because of the competitive nature of Greek friendship, and in addition no Greek city could feel entirely comfortable with the idea of pure aggression and expansion devoid of any justification.[140] The image of the disinterested helper of those who cannot help themselves is an understandably attractive filter through which the powerful may look at power relations,[141] and for an idealized city, helping oppressed friends and offering civilization is unambiguously right in moral terms, whereas ruling is potentially problematic unless it is made into worthiness to rule.[142] Thucydides'

---

thus Athens is somehow both a tyrant city whose actions cause revolt, but also a hegemonist who treats ungrateful allies fairly. Lack of space prevents full discussion, but the echoes of Pericles' speeches in those of Cleon have long been noted (compare 2. 63. 2 with 3. 37. 2, 40. 4; 1. 140 with 3. 38. 1). Cleon is associated with the 'bad' Athens, and Pericles, largely with the 'good' Athens, with some overlap between the two in his last speech. Is this Thucydides' attempt to deal with his sense that the Athenian empire is deeply ambiguous, so that its retention is glorious and also immoral (cf. Andrewes 1970: 186; Loraux 1986: 290)?

[140] Andrewes 1970: 164.

[141] Fergusson 1913: 2; de Romilly 1963: 18–36; Hobson 1938: 201, and chapters two and three *passim*.

[142] Cf. Loraux 1986: 84–5, 88.

account of the empire is exceptional in its tendency to ignore any such justifications of Athenian power.

Why is there such a discrepancy between the image of Athens in encomia, embodied in the Theseus of tragedy and Thucydides' insights on imperial power? Thucydides was, of course, often keen to contradict popular opinion,[143] and his attitude to what I suggest should be seen as mainstream Athenian ideology may be revealed when he describes the ἀληθεστάτην πρόφασιν, ἀφανεστάτην δὲ λόγῳ ('the truest, and least talked-about reason', 1. 23. 6) of the Peloponnesian War, that the Athenians were getting too powerful. This formulation cannot be literally true,[144] and it may instead be symptomatic of his desire to strip the empire of all its ideological justification to bring out what he takes to be the true nature of Athenian power. His account would therefore become a corrective to, and a conscious attempt to distance himself from, conventional Athenian ideology which he saw as irrelevant, given the realities of Athenian power.[145]

Much of Thucydides' history has an emblematic quality: Pericles' *epitaphios* is followed immediately by the plague, and the Athenian arrogance at Melos, by disaster at Sicily; this suggests that Thucydides was influenced, perhaps unconsciously, by the pervasive tragic pattern of hubris and nemesis.[146] Devices such as referring to 'the speech of the Athenians' distance the reader from individuals, and the frequency of the thematic connections between different speeches may imply that Thucydides is deliberately presenting abstract principles of the theory of the war and the empire, rather than what exactly was said by an individual.[147] One has the

---

[143] See e.g. 1. 20–2, 6. 54; Andrewes 1970: 186; also Walters 1981 on Thucydides' exceptional concern for what he saw as the truth.

[144] Andrewes 1959: 225; de Romilly 1963: 18–36.

[145] A fuller discussion of this view is given by Strasburger 1968; see also Loraux 1986: 288–95. This interpretation is compatible with Thucydides' summary of his technique with the speeches (1. 22. 1), if we assume that what he writes differed considerably from what was actually said because he wished to reach what he saw as the real truth which lurked under conventional ideology: this is surely the case at Melos, if not at the Mytilenean debate as well (de Romilly 1963: 398; Andrewes 1970: 182 f.). τὰ δέοντα ('the essential points') in this instance may mean what Thucydides thought the speakers *really* meant: cf. Hudson-Williams 1950: 162; de Ste. Croix 1954: 2.

[146] de Romilly 1963: 322–36; Strasburger 1968: 527–9, n. 82; cf. Hornblower 1989: 41–4, 173; Macleod 1974: 53.

[147] de Romilly 1963: 242; Dover 1970: 396–9; Rusten 1989: 15–17. For a balanced appraisal of the speeches, see Hornblower 1989: 45–72, esp. 63–6.

impression that he is giving examples of the kinds of thing which happen in wars in line with certain theoretical principles which he holds, particularly those regarding human nature.[148] This is almost certainly the case with Melos, whose fate has become emblematic of the terrifying possibilities that open up once justice and mercy have become optional, but it is the logical extreme of tendencies which run through the work from the beginning.[149] It has been suggested that Thucydides was suppressing certain aspects of the Melian campaign which could have been used as justifications of their actions by the Athenians, in order to emphasize the cruelty and irresponsibility of the Athenian empire by this stage. The combination of the climate of the Peloponnesian war and traditional ideology would surely have been sufficient to create justifications for Athenian action, and Melos' stand could have been categorized as wrong-doing which needed punishment.[150] Although Melos was small and powerless and there was no reason why the Athenians should have done what they did, it would hardly be the first time in history that irrational fear and self-interest were made to justify cruelty: in fact Herodotus' expansionist Persians at 7. 11. 2–3 give not dissimilar justifications for invading Greece.[151] Although Athenian action at Melos is the polar opposite of Theseus' benign, and wholly moral, interventions on behalf of justice, these two poles are nonetheless at either end of the same scale. The infringements of the allies' autonomy which were so greatly resented, and which were abolished under the second confederacy were, in fact, just the kind of action which Athens could call 'helping one's friends,' or 'punishing the wicked'.[152] The punishments of the wicked by Theseus or other Athenian representatives made a naturally attractive framework into which to fit much contemporary Athenian action. Even though most Athenians would have enjoyed the thought of their city's power, worked in the assembly and on

[148] Compare his comments, 1. 76. 3; 3. 39. 4; 40. 1; 45. 1; 3. 82. 2.

[149] Cf. especially de Romilly 1963: 296 ff.

[150] At Thuc. 5. 89. 1 the Athenians refer to the possibility that the Melians have done wrong, although they regard it as irrelevant in the circumstances: cf. Ar. *Av.* 186; Isoc. 4. 101. On possible omissions by Thucydides, see Andrewes 1960, revised in 1970: 157–8.

[151] Raaflaub 1987: 228, 234; see also Cogan 1981: 89–99; Hobson 1938: 209–10.

[152] Isocrates tries to minimize Athens' mistakes, but his list agrees with Thucydides. Massacres: 4. 100, 12. 62. Interference: Thuc. 1. 77. 1; 12. 66, 4. 113; cf. 4. 107.

the battlefield to retain it, and could perhaps even have allowed on occasion that it was as great as the power of a tyrant, it is very doubtful that the majority of them would have been able to think that its possession was actually unjust. Ideological justifications, buttressed by what Athenians saw in the theatre, or heard at the *epitaphioi*, created a far more attractive way of looking at an empire which contributed to the well-being of all Athenians, materially and in less tangible ways.[153] It is convenient to see what is beneficial as part of the natural order and as a justly deserved reward.

Thucydides' cynicism and desire to expose the falsehood of popular ideology should therefore not be used as an indication of what the average Athenian generally felt about the empire. Citizens from other cities did attend both the funeral speeches and tragedy: they were perhaps influenced by what they heard, although, in the case of metics living in the city, the influence of the *epitaphioi* or tragedy should not be considered in isolation from many other factors. However, since all the historical stories important to encomia set Athens against other places, I assume that these images were more immediately aimed at those whose superiority they assert.[154] The view of Athens given by the encomia is characteristic of, and contributes to, the self-definition of Athens, and it is meant for non-Athenians to a much lesser extent. The Theseus myth itself has little essential importance for the Ionian allies: the myths of Ion and Athens as the mother city of Ionia had a more obvious function in this respect.[155] Even so, many allies came to Athens, and, surrounded by Athenian prosperity, would hear Athenian encomia of the virtues of Athens. In the emotion and excitement generated at the theatre and at the *epitaphioi* it would not be surprising if a little of the more idealistic view of Athens' power had sometimes influenced allied perceptions of the empire.[156] In the next three chapters, we will see the ideal Athens in action.

---

[153] Universal gain from the empire: Forrest 1975: 22–3; Harding 1981; Hornblower 1989: 165–6; M. I. Finley 1978, esp. 122–4. See also Kiernan 1969, esp. 58f., 230f. on the various ways in which the British Empire benefited all classes.

[154] Foreigners at *epitaphioi*: Thuc. 2. 36. 4; Dem. 60. 13; at the Dionysia, Ar. *Ach.* 505f. See also Loraux 1986: 75–9.

[155] Loraux 1986: 84; Meiggs 1972: 292–5, 305, and note *GHI*, no. 69, which requires the allies to bring cow and panoply to the Panathenaea 'like colonists'.

[156] Cf. Strasburger 1968: 502–3; Loraux 1986: 131; Starr 1962: 331. Socrates says that he is γενναιότερος and σεμνότερος ('nobler and more worthier of respect') in the

eyes of non-Athenians after an *epitaphios* speech (Pl. *Mx.* 235a–b). Of possible relevance also is the fact that Bacchylides 17, though written for the Ceans (17. 130), celebrates the triumph of an Athenian over Minos, who is said to be the ancestor of the Ceans at Bacch. 1. 113. How the allies felt about the empire is a notoriously difficult question: de Ste. Croix 1954 believes that it was only the oligarchs in the allied cites who were really hostile to it; *contra* Bradeen 1960; see also Quinn 1964; Finley 1978. Perhaps also relevant is Václav Havel's observation on living in a totalitarian system, that sheer force of habit among those oppressed by the system kept it running, so that they were its creators and perpetuators as well as its victims (quoted in M. T. Griffin 1991: 23–4).

3

Theseus and the *Suppliants*

3.1 INTRODUCTION

In Euripides' *Suppliants*, most explicitly of all the tragedies in which he appears, Theseus is presented as the representative of the city of Athens and as the mouthpiece for certain modes of thought and behaviour which belong to the idealized Athens of the encomia discussed in the previous chapter. After the failure of Polynices' expedition against Thebes, in which the Seven against Thebes fell before the city walls, the Theban victors refused to allow their bodies to be buried, or to be returned to the Argives for burial. Thus the Argive king, Adrastus, comes to Theseus at the start of the play and asks him to help him retrieve them. Although at first Theseus refuses to do so, on the grounds that Adrastus' expedition was grounded in his ill-counsel and impiety (*Supp.* 110–249), his mother Aethra persuades him to change his mind by reminding him of his duty as an Athenian (*Supp.* 297–364). At this point, a herald from Thebes arrives: their encounter comprises a debate concerning the respective merits of tyranny and democracy (399–462), followed by an exposition of the rights and wrongs surrounding the burial of the dead (*Supp.* 465–563). Theseus is not cowed by the herald's insistence that he should not interfere in what is not his business, and fulfils his promise to Adrastus by going off to fight the Thebans for the return of the dead. After anxious speculation from the chorus over the outcome of his expedition (*Supp.* 598–633), a messenger returns from the battlefield with the good news that Theseus has won the battle. After he returns with the corpses, he invites the Argive king to recite a funeral oration over them; then their pyres are kindled (*Supp.* 798–954). Suddenly, the grief-stricken wife of the dead Capaneus appears, and in spite of her wretched father's entreaties, flings herself to her death onto her husband's pyre (*Supp.* 990–1113). The sons of the dead then return, bearing urns containing their ashes and vow revenge upon the Thebans (*Supp.* 1114–65). Finally, as Adrastus and Theseus are about to bid each other farewell, Athena appears to make Adrastus swear an oath of allegiance to Theseus and to prophesy that the revenge of the sons of the dead on the Thebans will be successful (*Supp.* 1116–234).

The interest of the first half of the play lies in the moral complexities surrounding the Thebans' refusal to bury the dead. The Argive expedition was impious, but so is the Thebans' refusal to bury their enemies, and Theseus must negotiate between their conflicting claims. This type of moral ambivalence is a familiar and enjoyable component of tragedy, and Theseus will rise to similar challenges of decision in other plays. However, the play also contains deeper dislocations which do not fit so easily into the familiar and satisfying form of tragic ambivalence, and even contradictions within itself.[1] Recent criticism has emphasized the function of tragedy as an arena in which established attitudes, values and beliefs of the city may be questioned or subverted,[2] and the *Suppliants* might seem particularly amenable to a complex, ironic reading of this kind, because of its inherent contradictions and plurality of moods and forms. Perhaps the most baffling element of the play is its treatment of the Argive leaders: although their original expedition is condemned, by the time of Adrastus' funeral oration they are praised as model citizens whose splendid qualities enabled them to die gloriously.[3] Second, in spite of the numerous passages in the play which strongly condemn all wars,[4] Theseus himself fights against the Thebans, and although he retrieves the bodies of the Argives for burial, the battle is bloody and hardly leads to happiness or relief for the Argive mothers or Evadne. Ambiguity even surrounds Theseus' position at Athens, since although he is a king, he also claims to be the champion of democracy there. Finally, Athena's epiphany at the end of the play (ll. 1183 ff.) is especially awkward, since she is keen to stir the young Epigonoi to take

---

[1] Well set out by Gamble 1970, esp. 385; see also Fitton 1961 and Greenwood 1953.

[2] See Goldhill 1987: 74–6, 1991: 174.

[3] Amphiaraus' fate is particularly remarkable: at ll. 500–1, the ground swallows him up as a punishment, but at ll. 925–7 Theseus regards this as the gods' eulogy of a 'noble son' (γενναῖον τόκον).

[4] Kitto 1939: 222–3, notes the importance of the pleas for an end to war made by Theseus, the herald and Adrastus who represent three very different perspectives: see esp. ll. 484–5, 745–50.

revenge for what the Thebans had done to their fathers, in spite of the fact that their fathers' original expedition against Thebes had not been divinely sanctioned. By so doing, the goddess ensures that there will be yet more suffering in the future.

The hypothesis of the *Suppliants* describes it quite simply as an 'encomium of Athens', and it contains many motifs familiar from the *epitaphios* speeches and other encomia of Athens, but the contradictions which surround them might be held to turn their ostensible praise of Athenian democracy and military vigour into an ironic dissection of the beliefs of imperial Athens, in which Euripides shows such beliefs to be futile, even dangerous. However, although the play encompasses a variety of moods and forms, its prevailing mood is one of intense misery, and while it is not impossible that Euripides could have mingled a portrayal of acute suffering with dispassionate and ironical comment on the reasons for that suffering, it is hard to imagine an audience swinging easily between emotional feeling stirred by the intense lamentations of the suppliant women of Argos and an intellectual understanding of the causes of their plight which would diminish their sympathy for them. It is especially difficult to view the figure of pious, old Aethra, at whose instigation Theseus takes on the Argive cause, through the distorting lens of irony. Above all, although tragedy is an art form that can question the established values of the city and explore the implications and contradictions behind concepts that are seen as self-evident in normal life, it is notable that usually these questions are removed from an Athenian setting. The critical attitudes to the city that are permissible in comedy are not necessarily permissible in tragedy (cf. Ar. *Ach.* 505 f.). The frosty reception given to Phrynichus' *Capture of Miletus* for 'reminding the Athenians of their own troubles'[5] may indicate that some measure of detachment from the city of Athens was necessary for any tragedian presenting a play to the Athenians. Indeed, the figure of Theseus himself could apparently not be accepted as a representative of Athens without some modification,[6] and it may be that in tragedy too, it was easier for an audience to confront certain questions at some distance, and where the past history of Athens, rather than of Thebes or Argos, was offered to them, then certain

---

[5] Hdt. 6. 21: cf. Heath 1987: 66–7.
[6] See §§ 1.3.2–1.3.4, 6.3 and 6.5.

automatic constraints were laid on what could be offered.[7]
Although Theseus and Athens have a central role in the action of
the *Suppliants*, it is not their own suffering in which they are
involved; their part in the play comprises the solution of a problem,
not the experience of a tragic destiny.

The recovery of the bodies of the Seven against Thebes, like the
protection of the children of Heracles from Eurystheus which
Euripides had dramatized a few years earlier, was a standard example
of the piety and military prowess of the idealized Athens of encomiastic literature. Both myths were familiar to Herodotus, and the
story of the Argive suppliants had already been dramatized by
Aeschylus in his *Eleusinioi*,[8] but there is an important difference
between the Aeschylean and Euripidean versions. Aeschylus'
Theseus is able to recover the bodies by persuasion, but Euripides'
hero has to use force. Euripides contrasts persuasion and violence
throughout his play, and although his Theseus is ultimately compelled to fight the Thebans in order to accomplish the burial, it is
evident that his battle is necessary, rather than desirable, and verbal
means would be morally superior as a means of resolving conflict.
It is probable that Euripides was consciously working against
Aeschylus' version of the story in which Theseus' words were
enough to force the Thebans to bury the bodies; one might guess
that the elder playwright had been more optimistic about the effi-
cacy of πειθώ. However, the more violent version of the story was
not Euripides' invention; the Athenians fight the Thebans already
in Herodotus, and the 'Euripidean' version is so dominant in the
rest of our sources that it is hard to believe that it was not popular
before the *Suppliants*.[9] It is not possible to determine which
version is the earlier: encomia of Athens consistently portray a city
pre-eminent both in war and words, and whether civilized behaviour is re-established by Athenian persuasion or by Athenian arms,
the resulting assertion of Athenian superiority is the same. Nor is

---

[7] Hall 1989: 213–14 points out that noble barbarians in tragedy can sometimes
criticize Greek cruelty, but never Athenian cruelty.

[8] Hdt. 9. 27. 3; Plut. *Thes.* 29. 4–5; for the *Eleusinioi* and its antecedents, see §7.3.
The story is portrayed on only two vases, both datable after Aeschylus' play and
before Euripides': *ARV*[2] 612,1 (*LIMC* 3. 1, 805 no. 3, with older literature), of
450/40 and a cup by the Codrus painter of 440/30 (Para. 472; *LIMC*, ibid., no. 4)
with Berger 1968: 63–4, 125–36, pl. 19.

[9] The 'Aeschylean' version only appears in Isoc. 12. 168–71 and Paus. 1. 39. 2:
Isocrates himself uses the violent version in the *Panegyricus*.

there any danger that Athens will appear aggressive even when using force against Thebes: both Euripides and the accounts which agree with his 'violent' version comment with disapproval on the intransigence of the Thebans which made a battle necessary.[10] The 'Euripidean' version is found more commonly in the *epitaphioi* than the 'Aeschylean' version because it is a more appropriate paradigm of Athenian action when honouring those who have died fighting for a good cause: in the same way, the triumph of Athenian virtue by force may also have been more appropriate for a play performed in the middle of a war.

3.2 EURIPIDES AND THE BATTLE OF DELIUM

Dates ranging from 424 to 416 have been suggested for the *Suppliants*,[11] but all of them are based only on supposed correspondences between the events and attitudes of the play and Thucydides' account of interstate relations in Greece within these years. The metre of the play is potentially a less subjective indication of its date, and its metrical characteristics date it either to the period 428–422[12] or that of 424–420.[13] It is therefore probable that the play was performed after the campaign of Delium in November 424,[14] in which Athens suffered a heavy defeat at Boeotian hands, and was then refused the return of her dead on the grounds that the Athenians had profaned the temple there by using it as a fortification. That Euripides should have chosen to dramatize a myth in which the Thebans refused to return the bodies of their Argive enemies after they had refused to return the bodies of the Athenian dead to Athens, raises some interesting questions about the relationship between history and tragedy in Athenian society.

Because Greek tragedy tends to retell myths in the context of the preoccupations of fifth-century Athens, many different mixtures of the directly contemporary and the purely mythical are possible, and there is a whole range of possible relations (not necessarily constant in the course of a play) between two extremes, first, of what is simply appropriate or necessary within the myth that is being

---

[10] Thus I disagree with Walters 1980: 10–13, who thinks that the violent version was invented to justify the aggressive imperialism of the later 5th cent.

[11] See Collard 1975: 8–9.   [12] Collard 1975: 10–12.

[13] Cropp and Fick 1985: 23.

[14] Thuc. 4. 89–101 and D.S. 12. 69–70: see Gomme 1956: 558.

dramatized, and second, of what may primarily remind the audience of the everyday conditions of their lives. It is possible to find explicit praise of Athens which sits uneasily in its context: for example, at *Troades* 207 and 218, in the midst of bewailing their imminent enslavement to the Greeks, the women hope to be sent to Athens; this brief but inappropriate brightening, influenced by patriotic sentiment, notably detracts from what should be unrelieved despair.[15] Immediately after this, however, they express fear of Sparta, and this is more natural in the context of the play, since the structure of the myth gives them good reason to be afraid of being sent there. It must also be supposed, however, that hostility to Sparta would be especially resonant for an audience, most of whom would have their own experiences of Sparta as an enemy. Just as the *epitaphios* speeches link the behaviour of Athenians in past history with that of those recently dead to construct a mode of behaviour that is 'typically' Athenian, so in the *Troades*, although the relationship between past and present is much more complex,[16] the chorus's fear of Sparta is likely to seem right and reasonable to the majority (at least) of the audience; contemporary attitudes are reinforced by the presentation of the past whose presentation is itself determined by the attitudes of the presenter and his audience.

The treatment of Thebes and Argos by Euripides' *Suppliants* exhibits a similar relationship between the mythical and the contemporary. The primary references are appropriate within the existing structure of the myth, which determines the Theban refusal to bury the Argives; but contemporary observers will see broad similarities between myth and contemporary history which fit some of their preconceptions of what is 'typical' behaviour. Adrastus' complaints of Sparta's cruelty and selfishness at *Supp.* 187–8 are appropriate to the play, but can be detached neither from the context of the Archidamian war, nor from the image of Sparta which emerges from some of the *epitaphios* speeches. The element

---

[15] Cf. Biehl 1989: 151.

[16] The complexity is achieved by the mythical setting, distanced from the audience both by time and place: the sufferings of Trojan women, rather than the glories of the Athenian past, as in the *epitaphioi*, are presented to the Athenian audience, and although the Trojan women express fear of Athens' enemy Sparta, the mythical and literary antecedents of the play intervene so that it does not simply reflect the attitudes of the contemporary audience: Helen is more than just a typical representative of Sparta, and Odysseus, not a Spartan, performs the act of supreme cruelty on Astyanax.

of Athenian patriotism in the *Suppliants* and other plays in which Theseus represents his city is similarly poised between the mythical and the contemporary. Tragedies such as the *Heracles* and *Oedipus Coloneus* are so entirely moulded by Athenian ideology that any praise of Athens is completely necessary in the context of the story, but it can hardly be detached from contemporary feeling. In the *Suppliants*, the praise of Athens is more prominent than in the other two plays, and its explicit patriotism makes it a good introduction to plays whose patriotism lies at a deeper level.

If there is meant to be a more explicit link between the play and history, so that Euripides would be commenting (unusually directly for a tragedian) on the Athenian experience at Delium,[17] we might expect to find details in it which can only be explained as references to contemporary events, rather than those which straddle the dramatic and the contemporary. It is very doubtful whether they can be found. The description of the battle in the play does not correspond particularly closely to the material details given by Thucydides and Diodorus,[18] and its general pessimism is also no indication that it was written in a time of deep despair as a reaction to the battle of Delium. One might as easily argue that Euripides would have borne Phrynichus' experience in mind and have made an effort not to remind the Athenians of past failure.[19]

The resemblances between myth and history in this case depend not on specific details but on broader generalities,[20] concerned with violation and retaliation. The initial violation in the *Suppliants* is the expedition of the Argives against Thebes, which is regarded unambiguously as an impious action which should never have taken place (ll. 219–31). The initial violation in history is the

[17] See esp. Goossens 1932.

[18] In Thucydides 4. 96, Athens overcomes the Theban left wing, but is beaten by the right; in Euripides, Athens' left wing is overcome and their right beats the Thebans. However, Thucydides says that Thebes' cavalry was decisive in the defeat, but no mention of cavalry is made by Euripides. The battle divisions of left, right and centre are hardly unusual. The reference to παραβάται at l. 679 might just as well parallel *Il*. 23. 123 as D.S. 12. 70's παραβάται. Since Wilamowitz, editors have compared Athens' rejection of Sparta's peace proposals after Pylos (Thuc. 4. 17. 4) with Argos' rejection of Eteocles' peace proposals (*Supp*. 739–44). However, the tragic context, in which arrogance must be punished, and the emphasis laid on the uncertainty of human prosperity in the play provide a more immediate context for his words; besides, it is not certain that such proposals were invented by Euripides: cf. Zuntz 1955: 60.

[19] Cf. Delebecque 1951: 205; see also Heath 1989: 5.

[20] See especially Zuntz 1955: 62.

fortification of the temple of Delium by the Athenians after the battle, which was said to flout the νόμιμα τῶν Ἑλλήνων ('laws of the Greeks': Thuc. 4. 97). These violations both incur reprisals which are seen as more serious than the initial acts of aggression. In the *Suppliants*, the Thebans refuse to give back the bodies of the dead Argives; similarly after Delium, the Thebans refuse to return the bodies of the dead Athenians. Thus both situations involve a violation of panhellenic burial customs by Thebes, where the other side is not entirely blameless; but that in the *Suppliants* is determined by the structure of a tale which was already a familiar part of Athenian history as told by the funeral orations long before 424. Thebes' conduct at Delium might have recalled Theban conduct in the myth, but this is not to say that Euripides was using the story to comment primarily on recent history. In fact, the differences between myth and history are more significant than the similarities. In the *Suppliants*, both Argos and Thebes have unequivocally done wrong and Athens is the pious arbitrator between them, but at Delium, there is no such arbitrator, and Athens' conduct is more questionable.[21] Although Thebes has wronged both Argos in the play, and Athens in history, Euripides' emphasis on the impiety of the Argives makes it impossible for an Athenian audience to identify themselves with the Argives, rather than with the representative of their city who proves himself superior to both cities. The Athens of the play is not the real city of 424 but the idealized Athens of the *epitaphioi*.

In the *Suppliants*, Athens forces Thebes to conform to Greek law, by beating the Theban army in battle, while in Athenian history, Thebes reclaims Delium from Athens, and then voluntarily returns the bodies (Thuc. 4. 101). Athens' part in history is not nearly as glamorous as the part assigned to the city in myth; and this discrepancy illuminates Athenian attitudes towards Athens more than attitudes to Thebes at any time. Questions of the nature of duty to the gods and the laws of Greece, on which the comparison between the tragedy and history depends, are concepts central to the whole genre of tragedy. The right of the dead to burial was an important moral issue at least from the *Iliad* on, and the conflicting moral principles attendant on burial of enemies is such a

---

[21] Thuc. 4. 98. 7 may suggest that Athens felt some unease about what she had done: she claims self-defence as a motive, which may be a slightly dubious self-justification: Kuiper 1923: 112–13. See also below.

fertile theme for tragedians that no special explanation need be given either for the dramatization of the story by Aeschylus or that by Euripides fifty years later.[22] It is vital for Athens that she should be the defender of panhellenic law and champion of the defenceless against all oppressors: while this self-portrait may have been especially appealing in the aftermath of Delium, there is no period in Attic history in which it would not have been appealing.

Froma Zeitlin has made some very interesting suggestions about the way that Thebes, and to a lesser extent, Argos, is always an anti-Athens, the opposite of the idealized Athens.[23] While she is certainly right that the settings of tragedy are significant, and that some types of story are not suitable for presentation as part of Athenian 'history',[24] her argument is somewhat undermined by excessive systematization, and a failure to consider the myths as independent structures, existing in the common culture of Greece outside Athenian ideology.[25] Where Athenian behaviour is explicitly compared with that of another city, Athens must naturally shine in comparison, but there is no fixed contrast between Athens and Thebes as such. The myth of the *Heraclidae* demands that Argos must be the city whose impious behaviour is set against Athens' righteous conduct towards suppliants, while *OC* 919f. explicitly dissociates Creon from the righteous ways of the city of Thebes. As in the *epitaphioi*, Athens must be uniquely virtuous, and where the city is involved in an action with moral consequences, the Athenians, or Athens' representative, must behave in an exemplary manner and better than the rest. One result of this is that other cities are shown to their disadvantage. Thebes and Argos tend to get a 'bad' reputation in comparison with Athens because they are the cities who are prominent in the ancient myths which the Attic tragedians preferred to dramatize,[26] but it is the portrayal

---

[22] Zuntz 1955: 4; de Romilly 1979: 30; see also Parker 1983: 42–8 on the burial of enemy dead in tragedy. Compare the themes of Sophocles' *Ajax* and *Antigone*, and for further discussion, see Ch. 7 below.

[23] Zeitlin 1986. For Argos in tragedy, cf. Said 1993.

[24] Compare Isoc. 12. 121–4 who condemns Thebes as a city of incest and parricide; also Nepos *Epaminond.* 15. 6.

[25] While it may well be true that events like those of *Oedipus Tyrannus* could not have been shown as Athenian events, it is hard to believe that an audience watching the *Oedipus* would have seen its events primarily as examples of what happens in a city which is not Athens, as she implies. Objections to Zeitlin are also made by Easterling 1989.

[26] See also Grube 1941: 39; Frey 1947: 43.

of Athens as the best of the Greek cities which is fixed, rather than that of the other cities, which tend to become instruments in Athenian self-definition in tragedies in which they are set against Athens.

The *Suppliants* dramatizes a story which is popular in funeral orations, and so it may not be surprising that the treatment of Athens in the play so closely resembles the city's idealized treatment in the *epitaphioi*. The preference for the idealized is made especially clear at the end of the play. At *Supp.* 1187 ff., Athens and Argos make an alliance which is comprehensible in terms of the events of the play, and, since an alliance was made between Argos and Athens in 421 (and renewed in 416), it is likely that the alliance of the play is also intended to link the myth with contemporary politics for the audience, whether that alliance was in prospect or had recently been concluded.[27] However, although the language of Euripides' treaty strongly resembles that of historical treaties,[28] its actual terms differ significantly from those of the treaty of 421. Under Euripides' treaty, the Argives must give entirely one-sided benefits to Athens, as though Athens had conquered them.[29] Neither this treaty, nor the insistence throughout most of the play on Adrastus' impiety, need indicate anti-Argive bias on Euripides' part:[30] we are instead in the world of the *epitaphioi* and encomia of Athens in which—as in Aeschylus' *Eumenides* (esp. 762 ff.)—such a unilateral treaty is the city's just reward for courage and intelligence in helping a suppliant whose claims were ambiguous. If Adrastus had done nothing wrong, so that his claims on Theseus were absolutely unquestionable, Theseus' wisdom and piety in helping him would not be outstanding.[31] Adrastus is king of Argos, and Argos figures prominently in the play because the established myth dictated that this should be so; but at least in the first half of the play, the focus is on the intelligence and humanity of Athens in

[27] *IG* I² 86 and Thuc. 5. 47: see Collard 1975: 10–11; Delebecque 1951: 217–21. 421 is often taken as the lower limit for the dating of the play, but the historical alliance cannot be used to date the play very exactly: 458's *Eumenides* refers to an Athenian–Argive alliance three years after its historical counterpart.

[28] See Collard 1975: 412–13.   [29] Zuntz 1955: 75.

[30] As, rather surprisingly, Zuntz 1955: 91, who suggests that Athenian irritation at Argive neutrality in the Archidamian War led Euripides to view Argos coldly; see also Goossens 1932: 9.

[31] Cf. Collard 1975: 132. The complexities of Adrastus' case in the *Suppliants* may be contrasted with that of Heracles' children in the *Heraclidae*, where there can be no suspense as to whether Demophon will help them or not.

seeing through moral ambiguity to the higher good. This is a highly
political play, but it does not retell recent political history.

3.3 THESEUS AS DEMOCRAT AND KING

As was seen in the previous chapter, the democratic constitution is
of central importance in Athens' idealized image of Athens, and it
is emphasized that only under such a political system could Athens
have reached the pre-eminence she has acquired. The *Suppliants* is
full of allusions to the virtues of democracy, but many of them are
in the mouth of a monarch. Theseus is the king of Athens (l. 123),
and also the bringer of democracy to Athens (ll. 352–3, 404–5) and
its champion against the Theban herald (ll. 399–597). The contradiction is summed up by Theseus himself:

> δόξαι δὲ χρῄζω καὶ πόλει πάσῃ τόδε
> δόξει δ' ἐμοῦ θέλοντος· ἀλλὰ τοῦ λόγου
> προσδοὺς ἔχοιμ' ἂν δῆμον εὐμενέστερον.

('I want the agreement of the whole city also; it will agree if I want it, but
if I have a reason, then the people will be better-disposed': *Supp.* 349–51,
cf. *Supp.* 394.)

One might well think that Euripides had some special purpose in
portraying Theseus' position in such a blatantly contradictory
manner, and comparisons have been made between the fictional
democrat king and Pericles, whose Athens was described by
Thucydides as λόγῳ μὲν δημοκρατία, ἔργῳ δὲ ὑπὸ τοῦ πρώτου
ἀνδρὸς ἀρχή.[32] Was Euripides using his drama to comment on contemporary politics, casting an ironic eye on the discrepancy
between theories of democracy and its reality?[33] To understand
Theseus' position in the *Suppliants*, it is necessary to consider some
of the traditions which influenced it.

By the fifth century, two distinct accounts of Theseus' constitutional position seem to have been formulated, although the only
explicit contemporary statement that we have is given by Thuc. 2.
15. 1–2. In connection with the move from the countryside into the
city, ordered by Pericles at the start of the war, he tells us that
Theseus, 'intelligent and powerful' (γενόμενος μετὰ τοῦ ξυνετοῦ

---

[32] 'In theory, a democracy, but actually rule by one man': Thuc. 2. 65. 9–10. But
this is a personal judgement, made as much as twenty years later: Gomme 1956: 196.
[33] As e.g. Norwood 1953: 131 f.; Fitton 1961, *passim*; Vellacott 1975: 28.

καὶ δυνατός), united the cities of Attica, which had previously had their own town halls (πρυτανεῖα) and officials (ἄρχοντας) and a measure of local independence, so that they now had to use one council chamber (βουλευτήριον) and town hall. This does not necessarily suggest that Thucydides himself thought of Theseus as a democrat.[34] The mere existence of a *bouleuterion* and *prytaneion*, on whose nature Thucydides does not elaborate, is not enough to indicate that he believed that Theseus had anything to do with a democracy such as is described at *Supp.* 352f. or 404f. Even epic societies had their popular assemblies, and Thucydides' Theseus sounds more like a king who had absolute power to unite the Attic cities under him: the tradition is similar in the Aristotelian *Athenaion Politeia* which says that the constitution diverged only a little from monarchy in Theseus' time.[35] The synoikism of Attica makes Theseus into the *heros ktistes* (founder-hero) of the autochthonous Athenian race, and the origins of the tradition are probably early and antedate the democracy.[36] From the evidence gathered in Chapter 1, however, it seems that there was another tradition, traceable back at least as far as Antiphon, in which Theseus' synoikism was connected with the establishment of democracy and led to his banishment by the aristocrats whose powers had been diminished by his actions.[37] Indeed, the synoikism itself, from being originally an expression of national unity, acquires an ideological colouring as it comes to represent another aspect of democratic Athens' civilization. Unity in one city is set against the bad old days of living in scattered villages, as backward, undemocratic Sparta continued to do in the fifth century.[38]

It is probable that the democratic Theseus was not solely a later creation of the fourth century,[39] but earlier traditions that he was a king of Athens are never entirely forgotten. Neither Herodotus nor Thucydides seemed to have believed that Theseus founded the democracy, and even a writer as late as Pausanias (1. 3. 3) denies

---

[34] *Contra* Podlecki 1975–6, esp. 24.

[35] *Ath.Pol.* 41. 2. See Davie 1982: 30; Wade-Gery 1931: 8. Cf. also Plut. *Thes.* 25. 2.

[36] Cf. Sarkady 1969.   [37] Plut. *Thes.* 32; ΣAr. *Plut.* 627a with §1.3.2 n. 44.

[38] Compare Thuc. 1. 10. 2 with Isoc. 10. 35. By coming together into cities, we avoid 'living like animals' (θηριώδως ζῆν): Isoc. 15. 254: also Walker 1995: 196f. on Theseus as civilizing synoikist.

[39] So Podlecki 1975–6; Loraux 1986: 66; *contra* Norwood 1953: 134–42. See also the discussions of di Benedetto 1971: 179–80 and Calame 1990: 412–15.

that he could have done so. Isocrates is particularly instructive for his efforts to combine essentially incompatible traditions concerning Athens' greatest hero and the constitutional system that was regarded as uniquely Athenian. In the *Panathenaicus*, Theseus ruled Athens until he went off on a life of self-sacrifice for Athens and Greece, leaving the administration of the state to others, whom Isocrates credits with the actual foundation of democracy. In the *Helen*, there is an even more awkward attempt to reconcile the two traditions: Theseus gives up the kingship, but takes it back at the people's request.[40] Dem. 60. 28 compromises by having Theseus invent equal speech (*ἰσηγορία*), one of the watchwords of the democracy. In Plutarch *Theseus* 25, Theseus is the founder of democracy, but by 35. 2–3, he appears as an absolute ruler.[41] Long after the fifth century therefore, people were still aware that a king of Athens in the heroic age must have had nothing to do with a political system which was founded much later. However, on an ideological plane, democracy and Athens were inextricably linked. Democratic government is one of the key distinctions between barbarian and Greek in Athenian tragedy, and where the possession of a democratic constitution is used to mark the difference between Athens and other Greek cities, it is another means by which Athens portrayed herself as 'super-Greek'. It is implied that the best, and only truly Greek, form of government is democracy—invented by Athens—because it represents freedom, as opposed to the slavery which is typical of barbarians.[42]

On the one hand it is unthinkable that Athens could be anything other than a democracy: Isocrates claims that Athens had had democracy for a thousand years, from Theseus to Peisistratus.[43]

---

[40] Isoc. 12. 128–9; Isoc. 10. 36; similarly, Dem. 69. 75. Walker 1995: 145–6 rightly notes that the stories in which Theseus hands over power to the people also portray the constitutional change as an entirely peaceful, unproblematic story of a king making the people his royal heirs: other versions of the foundation of democracy (Paus. 4. 5. 10 and Lys. 2. 18), which do not ascribe it to Theseus, make it into a more violent affair.

[41] Cf. Davie 1982: 29.

[42] Cf. E. *Hcld.* 423–4. Tyranny and oligarchy are often regarded more or less as identical: de Romilly 1979: 106–9. Athens also had an interest in promoting democracy throughout the empire, and Hall 1989: 2 notes that 'One function of [tragedy] is . . . to provide cultural authorisation for the democracy and the inter-state alliances.' See also Hall 1989: 16, 57–60.

[43] 12. 148. Longevity of constitution is, of course, a virtue (cf. Lys. 33. 7), connected with the Athenian autochthony discussed above.

On the other hand, the Athens of the heroic age, when kingship was universal, was the Athens of her greatest hero. An uneasy link is therefore made between the two. Both conceptions, of Theseus the good king, the antithesis of the tyrant,[44] and of Athens as a democracy, are an essential part of Athens' glowing self-image. The moral dimension of the constitution is especially conspicuous in the *Suppliants*: in the debate between Theseus and the Theban herald, and subsequently, when Theseus gives a practical demonstration of the principles he states to the herald, a clear link is made between the νόμοι upheld by a democracy, not by a tyranny (430–2), and the universal νόμος of god and man upheld by Theseus alone.

When Theseus is portrayed in tragedy, further difficulties regarding his constitutional status arise from the conventions of tragic stagecraft, which do not allow for a realistic representation of democratic decision-making; the king must instead represent the democracy, by stating its wishes and actions to the audience. To a twentieth-century audience, this might look as though the king or representative of the city was hypocritical in his protestations of democracy, but we should not assume that a fifth-century audience would have seen Euripides' Theseus as a leader deliberately 'manipulating the people'.[45] When Theseus says (ll. 352–3), καὶ γὰρ κατέστησ' αὐτὸν ἐς μοναρχίαν | ἐλευθερώσας τήνδ' ἰσόψηφον πόλιν ('for I have made the land one single kingdom, freeing the city where all have an equal vote'), it is a simple statement of fact, and it is to Theseus' and Athens' credit that they recognize the superiority of democracy. There certainly is a contradiction between what he says and the apparent truth, but it is an inherent contradiction which must always have existed, ever since the respective rises of Theseus and the democratic ideal, both of which were vital components of Athenian ideas about Athens. Similarly ll. 349–51, quoted above, can be interpreted as a sign of Theseus' concern for the democracy and the importance of the people's wishes.[46] The individual figure of Theseus, then, is representative of the spirit of the idealized democratic Athens as a whole, and the play maintains a consistent and very close identification between

---

[44] See Podlecki 1986: 79.

[45] So Gamble 1970: 400; see also Fitton 1961, for whom Theseus is merely a cynical politician.

[46] Collard 1975: 207.

Theseus and his city.[47] In fact, in this play, and arguably in all the others with the exception of the Hippolytus plays, Theseus is more of a symbol of Athens than an individualized tragic character.[48] Any technical problems concerning Theseus as king of a democracy fade if he is seen as a personification of the ideal democratic city.

In any case, the democratization of the mythical polis is a natural result of the thought patterns of the period, and it is unlikely that the tragedians could have cast their good kings in 'realistic' authoritarian roles.[49] A brief comparison of the representation of Theseus with those of Pelasgus in Aeschylus' *Suppliants* and Demophon in the *Heraclidae* will confirm the suggestion that what moderns have seen as problematic is, in fact, the result of tragic convention and fifth-century thought-patterns. The position of Pelasgus in Aeschylus is nearly as ambiguous as that of Theseus. Not only does the chorus tell him, ll. 370–5, σύ τοι πόλις, σὺ δὲ τὸ δάμιον,[50] but— more decisively—he himself stresses his absolute power at ll. 252, 255, 259 and 398f.;[51] A. *Supp.* 398f. suggests that Pelasgus does have full personal authority as king, but because he is a good king, he prefers the decision to be made democratically.[52] In both tragedies (E. *Supp.* 354–5; A. *Supp.* 516–23), the suppliant is led off to a meeting with the people, and although Aeschylus gives the people's decision more prominence than does Euripides,[53] this is partly to do with the nature of the problem faced by Pelasgus. Like Athena in the *Eumenides*, the decision he faces is too important for him to take it by himself, and the wisdom of the people must be enlisted.[54] In Euripides, however, Aethra's exchange with her son is a substitute for debate in the assembly, and once she has persuaded him that the bodies must be buried, any further debate on

---

[47] e.g. ll. 27–8, 293, 382 and especially l. 576, πράσσειν σὺ πόλλ᾿ εἴωθας ἥ τε σὴ πόλις ('you're always interfering, you and that city of yours'): see also below.

[48] Cf. Collard 1975: 30.   [49] Podlecki 1986: 77–8.

[50] 'You are the city, you are the people'—but their view of the matter is, of course, that of barbarians who know no better: Hall 1989: 193.

[51] Podlecki 1986: 83–5.

[52] Koster 1942: 199 thinks that Pelasgus is more diffident than Theseus in his dealings with the δῆμος at l. 485—κατ᾿ ἀρχῆς γὰρ φιλαίτιος λεώς ('the people tend to blame their leaders')—but this is surely rhetoric designed to heighten the tension of the decision.

[53] Were democratic processes less of a novelty by the 420s?

[54] Podlecki 1986: 84 sees Pelasgus as a smooth demagogue who uses persuasion and rhetoric to lead his people (523, 615f.), but *Supp.* 365ff. stresses that he cannot make the decision by himself: compare A. *Eum.* 470–2. See also Bengl 1929: 24–30.

the subject would be inappropriate; thus the emphasis on the assembly's actual decision is diminished.[55] Naturally they will support Theseus, because his decision represents what is morally right. Thus there is no fundamental distinction between the monarch-democrats of Aeschylus and Euripides, given the different structures and preoccupations of their plays.

As for Demophon in the *Heraclidae*, he is described as τύραννος, that is, a fully powerful king, yet of a free land[56] and ll. 423–4 define his position further: οὐ γὰρ τυραννίδ᾽ ὥστε βαρβάρων ἔχω | ἀλλ᾽ ἢν δίκαια δρῶ, δίκαια πείσομαι ('I do not have a tyranny, like the barbarians, but if I do what is just I will be treated justly'). The relationship between Demophon and his Athenian chorus resembles that between Theseus and his chorus in *Oedipus Coloneus*, in which Theseus represents the higher authority, but the chorus are allowed a measure of independent action. The virtuous and brave chorus of the *Heraclidae* take the lead in defending the suppliants against Copreus, but Demophon remains their leader, and as soon as he appears, it is he who decides that the suppliants should be helped (*Hcld.* 236–49, 335–43). At the end of the play, when Demophon is absent, the chorus are again able to take control: at ll. 961–75 they set Athenian ways of clemency against Alcmena's vengefulness by telling her that killing Eurystheus is displeasing both to the leaders of this land (l. 964) and to this land (l. 968). As in the *Suppliants*, the 'leaders' and the city are so closely associated that it is not possible to make any significant distinction between them.[57] In the *Heraclidae*, the popular vote to confirm the king's decision is omitted altogether, but the active role of the chorus, and the ambiguities of terminology do give the impression that heroic Athens enjoys the freedom of speech and action so lauded by Thucydides' Pericles as an essential part of the democracy. There are fewer overt difficulties in Demophon's position than that of Theseus in the *Suppliants*, because he does not explicitly state that he is king of a democracy; but in the light of the conventions and patterns of thought which seem to lie behind many retellings of

[55] Paduano 1966: 201: *contra* Fitton 1960: 432 f.

[56] γῆν . . . ἐλευθέραν: *Hcld.* 113, cf. 61–2, 262, and 387. Although his position could be interpreted as distinctly contradictory, his treatment by Euripides is not noticeably ironic.

[57] Cf. *Hcld.* 34–6. It is often stressed (esp. ll. 320–8) that Demophon is like his father in moral excellence, and presumably his constitutional position is imagined to be the same.

ancient stories in a fifth-century context, it is rather unlikely that Euripides' portrayal of Theseus is intended as an ironic comment on contemporary politics.

The resemblance between Athens under Theseus and Athens under Pericles as described by Thucydides should not be pressed too far, and the specific equation of Pericles with Theseus is illusory. It is purely a product of apparent correspondences between Theseus' position in the *Suppliants* and Thucydides' view of Pericles which modern critics have developed.[58] The king-democrat of tragedy arises not from contemporary political models, but from a mixture of tragic conventions and the traditions concerning Theseus, Athens and democracy.[59] As far as we know, no contemporary source ever calls Pericles a latter-day Theseus. The comic poets prefer to call him Zeus or Heracles and his enemies, the new Peisistratus.[60] If his supporters called him the new Theseus, it is extraordinary that Plutarch does not record it. Both types of identification point to the vastness of Pericles' ambitions, and criticize his dominance by means of comic exaggeration. Even an

[58] Giles 1890: 95–8 made an early equation between the two, and between other characters in the play and 5th-cent. politicians. The theory was expanded fully by Goossens 1932; also 1962: 436–40. Although the more extreme parts of Goossens's equations (e.g. 1932: 12–15) are currently ignored, the Pericles–Theseus equation has been more readily accepted: see Lesky 1956: 177; di Benedetto 1971: 180; Podlecki 1975–6. Calame 1990: 415–17 is rightly sceptical of all theories that any Athenian politician ever portrayed himself as a 'new Theseus': see also §1.7. The equation of Cimon and Theseus has also won many supporters, notably Barron 1980, who suggests that the audience of Bacchylides 18 was intended, by means of various subtle clues, to realize that the poem's portrait of Theseus was really a portrait of Cimon: constraints of space preclude a detailed refutation of his theory here, but I will just comment that the one-to-one correspondence between myth and political reality that Barron posits is absolutely unique in 5th-cent. literature, and rests on the dubious assumption that certain details in the poem could only be explicable as references to Cimon and his sons. As I will show elsewhere, this is not so.

[59] Podlecki 1975–6 lays emphasis on the forms by which Theseus is addressed in the play. He is never called τύραννος or βασιλεύς (king), but ἄναξ (lord), στρατηλάτης and στρατηγός (general), this last being Pericles' official title. However, Theseus could hardly be called τύραννος, in view of his indignant reply to the herald at ll. 404–5, where his interpretation of the word τύραννος is determined by the opposition between the behaviour of Athens the democracy and that of other places which are not democracies; ἄναξ is too common a title for much significance to be attached to it, and στρατηλάτης and στρατηγός are simply appropriate for a king who leads a military expedition against Thebes; the same titles are used for the Argive military leaders (*Supp.* 102, 162).

[60] Plut. *Per.* 7. Only Cratinus' *Drapetides* may equate Pericles and Theseus, and this is uncertain: see below, Tanner 1916.

admirer such as Thucydides stresses this dominance, and it is precisely this that Theseus the democratic king does not, and cannot,
have.

The only ancient evidence for such an idea is the allegation that
Phidias represented himself and Pericles on the shield of Athena
Parthenos as fighters against the Amazons.[61] The story does not
seem utterly implausible until one considers the enormity of representing two mortals in the company of gods and heroes in the temple
of the patron goddess of Athens. It is hard to believe that Phidias
could have done this without the consent of the democracy, and
harder to believe that the democracy would have given its consent,
if the prevailing reluctance to portray contemporary or recent-his-
torical figures in public art at Athens is any indication of common
preferences.[62] If later copies of the shield are any guide, it was very
difficult securely to identify individuals on it,[63] and one may well
ask whether most Athenians, gazing up at the splendid work, would
have troubled to make individual identifications. Even if the story
is true, it is not serious evidence that Theseus was regarded as the
prototype of Pericles.

3.4 THESEUS AND THE *SUPPLIANTS*

The play is opened by Theseus' mother Aethra at the temple of
Demeter at Eleusis, where she is performing a sacrifice modelled on
the Eleusinian festival of the Proerosia.[64] This pious act makes it
clear that she is a woman who knows her duty towards the gods;[65]

---

[61] Plut. *Per.* 31. 4; Dio. Chrys. *Or.* 12. 6; but these late sources may derive from
a single post-classical source: Stadter 1989: 294.

[62] Deonna 1920: 292–3, 299; Harrison 1966: 108–9. Significantly, Athenaeus
XII. 533 says that the tyrant Peisistratus gave his own features to Dionysus.

[63] To Harrison's bibliography of works relating to the shield, 107, add Hölscher
and Simon 1976, and see also the ambitious attempt to identify every figure on the
shield, including Theseus and his family, in Harrison 1981, esp. 294–311. There is,
however, no agreement among scholars as to which figure on the shield is meant to
be Theseus.

[64] ll. 28 f. See Deubner 1932: 68; Parke 1977: 72–5. An inscription of *c*.422 or earlier (*GHI* 73, 217–23), records an attempt, sanctioned by Delphi, to revive the collection of first fruits for Demeter from the cities of the empire, and even from other
Greek cities: cf. Isoc. 4. 31. This was probably an Athenian bid for hegemony using
religious means. Aethra's offering may, therefore, have recalled to the audience contemporary Athenian aspirations in Greece, as well as more general beliefs about
Eleusis and Athens as the home of civilization.

[65] Compare her immediate judgement on the Thebans, that they are 'dishonouring the laws of the gods' (νόμιμ' ἀτίζοντες θεῶν, l. 19).

at l. 3 she identifies herself as Theseus' mother, at l. 4 , as Pittheus' daughter, and thus as the daughter of a man of proverbially outstanding wisdom. She is also married to Aegeus (ll. 5–7): this is the only version of the myth in which she is his lawful wife,[66] and the combination of her status, origins and innate piety establishes her credentials as a woman who deserves respect, and Theseus will not be able to dismiss her subsequent appeals on behalf of the suppliants. At *Supp.* 18 f. she reveals the identity of the chorus: they are old, as she herself is; but whereas they have lost their noble children (γενναίων τέκνων | ἄπαιδες, ll. 12–13), she is the mother of the living, glorious Theseus.[67] Their similarity in age[68] combined with the contrast between the fates of the Seven and that of Theseus means that Aethra cannot be detached from their sufferings: both she and they are very aware of this, unlike her son when he first encounters them.[69] The mixture of similarity and difference between them stimulates pity in Aethra, and their status as suppliants adds further urgency to their claims.[70]

Pity is a recurrent theme in tragedy, because it is aroused by the realization that human prosperity is fragile, and that it is therefore necessary to feel a common fellowship with human beings in a universe potentially hostile to everyone.[71] To feel pity towards someone else is to recognize one's own vulnerability and the essential limitation of all human beings.[72] Flexibility and a certain tolerance are a part of this, and pity is one manifestation of the moderate approach to life, avoiding the extreme of hubris, which was so commended in Greek morality.[73] The idea of 'acting according to the

[66] Collard 1975: 106. In fact, the version of Theseus' birth assumed here is strikingly at variance with older (less flattering) forms of the story: see above, Ch. 1.

[67] What Aethra acknowledges is reiterated by the Chorus: ἱκετεύω σε, γεραιά, | γεραιῶν ἐκ στομάτων ('I supplicate you, old woman, with my ancient mouth', l. 42); and ἔτεκες καὶ σύ ποτ' ὦ πότνια ('for you also are a mother, lady', l. 55).

[68] Similarly, at 282–3 the Chorus appeal to Theseus to help them by means of his fellowship in age with their dead sons. See also §5.4 on this theme in *Oedipus Coloneus*.

[69] Gamble 1970: 386–8.

[70] At *Supp.* 34–5, Aethra 'pities and honours' their plight and status (οἰκτίρουσα . . . σέβουσα: cf. l. 68, οἰκτρὰ δὲ πάσχουσ' ἱκετεύω ('in my pitiable suffering, I supplicate you'): Adrastus will also appeal to οἶκτος at 168, but Theseus is unmoved.

[71] Cf. esp. S. *Aj.* 121–3: ἐποικτίρω δέ νιν | . . . | οὐδὲν τὸ τούτου μᾶλλον ἢ τοὐμὸν σκοπῶν ('I pity him, not considering his fate any more than mine').

[72] Hence it is not a divine attribute: Heath 1987: 52; see also Dodds 1974: 12.

[73] Explicitly, first in Theognis 335 πάντων μέσ' ἄριστα ('the middle is best of all'); implicitly in pronouncements such as μηδὲν ἄγαν ('nothing too much'). The principle is most developed by Aristotle. See Grossmann 1950: 12–13.

mean' can also be subsumed under the ἐπιείκεια which was regarded as indigenous to Athens, and it is not surprising that the ability to feel pity was also classified by Athens as especially Athenian.[74] As will become clear in this, and subsequent chapters, Theseus as the representative Athenian is normally characterized in tragedy by his ability to be moved by others' suffering and by his moderate approach to life.[75]

The ability to respond to persuasion demands a similar sort of flexibility, and it too is claimed by Athens as a typically Athenian characteristic.[76] To be true to Athenian principles of pity for the unfortunate, Theseus must be amenable to persuasion, even though he is initially opposed to helping the suppliants. Words and civilization are structurally opposed to violence, barbarity and bestiality,[77] and if Theseus is to uphold Greek (and Athenian) civilization, νόμος and δίκη, all of which are prominent themes later in the play, it is essential that he should eventually be persuaded to change his mind. In this he and his city are superior to the Thebans, who will only respond to force, in spite of Theseus' attempts to avoid using violence against them by trying to persuade them to return the Argive dead.[78] When they will not respond to

---

[74] Pity as Athenian: Thuc. 3. 39. 2; Dem. 24. 171; Plut. *Mor.* 790c; Plin. *HN* 35. 69; Macleod 1983: 74 ff. with other references; Stevens 1944. Paus. 1. 17. 1 says that only the Athenians have an altar of Pity, but he is influenced by the claims of the idealized Athens: there was one in the Asclepion at Epidaurus (*IG* IV² 1. 1282). Although Apollod. 3. 7. 1 says that it was to the altar of pity that Adrastus came to ask for Theseus' help, there is no definite literary attestation for the altar itself before D.S. 13. 22. 7: so Wycherley 1954 against H. A. Thompson 1952. It may be a later name for the old altar of the twelve gods, which had *de facto* become an altar of pity: Crosby 1949, esp. 102. This altar was decorated with various reliefs, including one of Theseus apparently being rescued by Heracles from the underworld while Peirithous looks sadly on: *LIMC* 5. 1, 182, no. 3518; for a full discussion, see Goetze 1938, esp. 207–20. The rescue of Theseus, who did not deserve such a fate, is certainly an appropriate subject for an altar of pity (*pace* Zuntz 1953, esp. 83, n. 40). If pity is a necessity in the uncertainties of human existence, and Athens is pre-eminent in pity, this is another way in which the idealized Athens is a kind of super-human state: cf. above §2.4.

[75] As especially at S. *OC* 566–7: ἔξοιδ' ἀνὴρ ὢν χὤτι τῆς ἐς αὔριον | οὐδὲν πλέον μοι σοῦ μέτεστιν ἡμέρας ('I know that because I am a man, I have no greater share in the next day than you').

[76] For their association in a different context, cf. Thuc. 3. 37. 1, 40. 1.

[77] See Buxton 1982; cf. Hall 1989: 199–200. Theseus himself defines the difference between the animal and the human as the possession of, or lack of, σύνεσις and νόγοι (ll. 202–4). See also §2.4.

[78] *Supp.* 347, 560 and 749. In the *Heraclidae* (esp. 266) Demophon is also forced to use violence where he would rather use words.

non-violence, Theseus is forced to bring the full power of Athens upon them, and he is right to do so, because the demands of justice must be met: an Athens with good intentions but no military strength would be unable to carry out the commands of the gods and the unwritten laws.[79]

In the early part of the play, the role of the ideal Athens is divided between Theseus the young man and Aethra the old woman, each of whom exemplifies parts of the Athenian ideal.[80] Aethra, as a woman, may represent the Athenian ability to feel pity and Theseus, Athenian intellect.[81] Theseus must learn, by means of his mother's persuasion, to feel fellowship with the suffering women, whose grief is expressed in the *parodos*, and thus to combine emotion and intellect in order to possess all the virtues as befits an (ideal) Athenian. His initial harshness to Adrastus and the women will be a shock after the acute distress of the chorus, whose *parodos* reiterates themes already voiced by Aethra, such as their old age (l. 42); their pitiable childlessness, as opposed to Aethra's fortune in her son (εὐτεκνία, ll. 66, 67); and the hope that Theseus can be persuaded to help them.[82] They also stress that they are suppliants (ll. 42, 67) and that their claims are just, since Thebes is behaving barbarously,[83] although they also admit that they are sacrilegiously interrupting Aethra's sacrifice (l. 63). Their threatening presence at the sacrifice may reflect the inherently disturbing aspect of suppliants in general.[84] Athens, however, has a reputation for taking risks and accepting suppliants, and it is therefore shocking when Theseus refuses to help them: this is quite un-Athenian.[85]

Adrastus begs Theseus to help him, while admitting, under questioning, that he has made mistakes in the past. He begins his

---

[79] Cf. Loraux 1986: 73.   [80] Zürcher 1947: 161 n. 18: cf. Zuntz 1955: 10.
[81] Burian 1985: 130; cf. Shaw 1982: 10.
[82] The juxtaposition and assonance of εὐ-τεκνία δυστυχίαν emphasizes the difference between them (cf. ll. 955–6). Again, the uncertainty of human life is appealed to in the plea for pity (ll. 46, 68). Even Theseus admits that they are in a bad way (ll. 95 f., 104).
[83] Note the harshness of *Supp.* 46; cf. 282–3.
[84] See above and Collard 1975: 5: compare the dire warnings given by Adrastus at ll. 259–62. At *OC* 887 f. Theseus is called away from a sacrifice to save Oedipus from Creon: this is an example of true (Athenian) piety, and the Theseus of the *Suppliants* must learn something similar.
[85] Mastronarde 1987: 203. The story of the help given by the Athenians to Argos was such a familiar part of Athenian history in the *epitaphioi* that the audience may not have been expecting this response from the national hero.

plea by addressing Theseus as καλλίνικε ('glorious in triumph'), an epithet more commonly used of Heracles, whose use here may reflect Athenian conceptions of Theseus as the Athenian Heracles. At first, Theseus is fairly neutral to him, asking him what he desires, and allowing that his request is for what is holy (ὅσια).[86] Adrastus explains that the Thebans refuse to return the bodies of his men to him because εὐτυχοῦντες οὐκ ἐπίστανται φέρειν ('they do not know how to handle their good fortune'). The uncertainty of life, in which the happiest circumstances can be instantaneously changed to the direst misery, is a recurring theme in the play.[87] At this moment good fortune has made the Thebans arrogant and inflexible: they feel no sympathy for Adrastus because they cannot imagine that their own prosperity may only be transient. The opposite of the arrogance shown by Thebes is the consciousness of human instability exhibited by Aethra, which leads to a sense of fellowship with other human beings, essential for human survival in a tragic and unstable universe.[88] Theseus must be brought to think as Aethra does, because in denying his help, he is in fact behaving like an inflexible Theban. As an Athenian citizen-hero, rather than a 'Sophoclean' tragic hero, he is able to change his mind gracefully.

Theseus' cross-examination of Adrastus makes it very clear that his present plight is the result of extremely poor judgement. Apollo commanded him to give his daughters to a lion and a boar: Adrastus took this as a recommendation of Tydeus, a shedder of kindred blood (αἷμα ξυγγενές), and Polynices, who was under Oedipus' curse, as sons-in-law, because they fought like beasts (ll. 124ff.). This description, along with the omission by Euripides of the traditional detail, that the animals refer to the designs on the breastplates of the two warriors, inculpates Adrastus for foolish and hasty behaviour.[89] He is further to blame for having been led astray by

[86] l. 123: Paduano 1966: 200. The consideration that Thebes is violating the laws of gods and man will ultimately sway Theseus to help the suppliants, and to look beyond Argos' failings.

[87] See e.g. *Supp.* 175-9: on the theme see Cannatà Fera 1986: 258-9.

[88] At Thuc. 5. 90, the Melians use the 'reversal of fortune' argument to the implacable and confident Athenians who discount it, along with any attendant feelings of pity. Here especially, a huge gap has been opened up between Athenian theory and practice.

[89] Lesky 1956: 176. Walker 1995: 153 is, I think, wrong in saying that Adrastus merely 'suffered an inexplicable blow of fortune'.

the clamour of the young men[90] so that he ignored Amphiaraus' omens (l. 155).

Theseus' trenchant, but merciless, judgement on Adrastus' actions is εὐψυχίαν ἔσπευσας ἀντ' εὐβουλίας:[91] εὐψυχία, as Theseus' later actions will show, is important, but εὐβουλία (which is much harder to acquire) is more important. Only Theseus, and Athens, can combine the two satisfactorily. The youthful Theseus (*Supp.* 190, 580) is the antithesis of those young men who led Adrastus astray,[92] and as a sensible, peace-loving young man, he is a kind of contradiction in terms, analogous to the Athenian 'aristocratic democracy' of the *epitaphioi*, in which it is claimed that Athens itself is a remarkable contradiction in terms because the city possesses every kind of virtue, even those which were traditionally opposed to one another.[93] Although most young men may lack εὐψυχία so that they desire war, Euripides' Theseus is not zealous for war at all: he hopes that λόγοι will be sufficient, and only uses βία as a last resort. However, he also knows that some wars have to be fought against the forces of tyranny and injustice, and when war is made unavoidable, because of Theban intransigence, Theseus will prove the total superiority of Athens in deed, as well as word.

Adrastus pleads with Theseus to act in an 'Athenian' manner at ll. 163–92. He appeals to pity (esp. ll. 168, 179, 190) rather than intellectual proofs as reasons why he should help the Argives, but these are the right appeals for a city like Athens. Because Theseus is an Athenian, he *should* feel pity in preference to the claims of strict justice or prudence.[94] Although at this moment Adrastus cannot hold Theseus' attention, because Theseus (wrongly) considers his cause alien to him, pity for his mother's distress will make Theseus listen to her and come to see that no cause concerning injustice can ever be alien to Athens. Adrastus' immediate appeals to Theseus are, in fact, echoed quite closely by Aethra later in the play. He reminds Theseus of Athens' professed ideology of helping

---

[90] As ll. 229, 738, where the young are seen as eager warmongers. The bellicosity of the young is a commonplace in extant Greek literature: compare Thuc. 2. 8. 1 and 6. 13. 1; also de Romilly 1968: 168–9.

[91] 'You were more concerned with bravery than good counsel', *Supp.* 161; and for the antithesis, cf. Thuc. 1. 121. 4, 6. 72. 4.

[92] Rightly Shaw 1982: 5, against Fitton 1961: 433–4.   [93] See Ch. 2.

[94] Cf. *Hcld.* 170ff.; and, in rather different contexts, Nicias, Thuc. 6. 13. 2 and Alcibiades, 6. 18. 2.

the oppressed, and says, more or less, that Athens should help simply by virtue of being Athens:

> πόλις δὲ σὴ
> μόνη δύναιτ' ἂν τόνδ' ὑποστῆναι πόνον.
> τά τ' οἰκτρὰ γὰρ δέδορκε . . .

('Only your city could undertake this labour: for it feels pity . . . ': E. *Supp.* 188–90.)

Aethra too will encourage Theseus to take up Adrastus' cause by reminding him of the past reputation of his city.[95] Adrastus points out that human prosperity is always precarious; and the theme will be reiterated by Aethra at l. 329 f. Thus at l. 166 he refers to himself as πολιὸς ἀνὴρ τύραννος εὐδαίμων πάρος ('an old man, formerly a fortunate king') and ll. 176–9 make more explicit what is implied at l. 166, that Theseus' good fortune may prove to be just as transitory as his proved to be. Theseus should help Adrastus because he is a human being and equally subject to the uncertainties of human existence, but also because he is an Athenian.[96] For Adrastus, for Theseus to refuse the suppliants is to be false to the past record of his city; similarly, his later reproach to Theseus, at l. 255, that he did not seek him as a punisher (κολαστής), is an implicit appeal to him to be true to Athens' reputation for punishing the wicked,[97] rather than those, like himself, who do not deserve it.

In encomia of Athens, it is common for the city to be portrayed as an impartial upholder of justice, but by refusing Adrastus, Theseus exhibits the wrong kind of impartiality: his response is governed strictly by intellect and a narrow conception of justice—τὸ δικαίον rather than τὸ ἐπιεικές. A true Athenian should prefer τὸ πρᾶον ἐπιεικές ('kind reasonableness') to τοῦ αὐθάδους δικαίου ('stubborn justice') (Gorgias, fr. 6). He says that since Adrastus has acted impiously, and culpably so in the context of the divine bene-

---

[95] ll. 305 ff. Athens' unique philanthropy—often implicitly contrasted with Sparta's selfish ways—is a favourite topos of the *epitaphios* speech (cf. Ch. 2); the idea that *only* Athens is capable of helping distressed suppliants is also stressed in the *Heraclidae*, 151, 191–7, 305 ff. and 329–32; also *OC* 260 ff.: cf. Loraux 1986: 148.

[96] As in the *Heracles* and *Oedipus Coloneus*, Theseus is Aegeus' son, not Poseidon's: ll. 655, cf. 647. For the chorus's appeals to kinship at *Supp.* 263–64, cf. E. *Hcld.* 207 and A. *Supp.* 15–22, 274–6. Hermocrates at Thuc. 6. 77. 1 regards cynically the use made of similar arguments by the Athenians in their foreign relations.

[97] As *Supp.* 339–40; see also §2.4.

ficence which Theseus affirms in answer to his entreaties (ll.
195–249), he cannot help him. Although his pious and optimistic
profession of the goodness of the gods is not the whole truth, as will
be more explicitly shown in the rest of the play,[98] at this point, he
says confidently that the gods have amply provided for us, particularly in the field of reason, so that our misfortunes are the result of
our impiety for thinking we know better—witness Adrastus.[99]
Since he has failed in reason, and therefore in piety, by mingling
'the unjust with the just' (ἄδικα with δικαία) and not finding
'friends blessed by fortune' (εὐδαιμονοῦντας . . . φίλους), Theseus
believes that by helping him he would fail in the same way.[100]

There are obvious similarities between *Supp*. 195 ff. and
Prometheus 442–506, *Antigone* 332–83 and *Protagoras* 320c–22d[101]
and they place Theseus firmly in a 'modernist' tradition, asserting
an optimistic view of human progress against the traditional pessimistic view that humans have fallen from an earlier perfection.[102]
In these accounts, the gods are assigned varying degrees of responsibility for human progress, but naturally in the *Suppliants* their
part is emphasized so that it is not just human reason which is
responsible for man's progress, but the gods who gave him that reason (l. 203). As we saw earlier, to achieve complete virtue, the
Athenians must ascribe progress both to man's ingenuity, so that
human intelligence can surmount human vulnerability to superhuman forces, but also to the gods themselves.[103] Thus in this speech,
Theseus is both a 'modernist' and a 'conservative' because he is
representing all possible principles of virtue (just as the *epitaphioi*
often ascribe every virtuous quality to Athens). The parallels from
Aeschylus, Sophocles and Plato all discuss man's early days as a

---

[98] Mastronarde 1987: 203.

[99] *Supp*. 216–37, cf. 504–10, where the herald accuses Theseus himself of flout-
ing divine will in helping the Argives.

[100] W. D. Smith 1966: 158.

[101] See Collard 1975: 160–6 and Bengl 1929: 9–11.

[102] Mastronarde 1987: 202. For the traditional view, see esp. Hes. *WD* 109 ff.
Ideas of human progress are influenced by natural philosophy: see Xenophanes fr.
18; also Democritus 5; Gorgias 30 DK, with Guthrie 1957: 82–90. Belief in divine
providence is usually thought to have originated from Diogenes of Apollonia, who
believed that all things were controlled by some kind of divine thought: Jaeger 1947:
167–71. Theseus' use of such ideas, although in a more traditionally anthropomor-
phized form, mark him as a modern thinker.

[103] Compare Isoc. 4. 32–8 and Pl. *Mx*. 237d–238b (Athens gave the gods to other
men!), both of which blur the distinction between the part of the gods and the part
of humans in human progress.

prelude to the moral development which makes possible life in political communities.[104] Theseus only discusses man's early days, but he reopens questions of politics and morality in his constitutional debate with the Theban herald where it is implied that only the democracy of Athens has achieved full human potential in reason and piety; this earlier admonitory speech by Theseus may imply something similar.[105]

After discussing divine benevolence in general, Theseus turns his attack fully on Adrastus by blaming him for his arrogance concerning the oracle which the gods gave him (ll. 217–18, cf. 159). Adrastus' interpretation of the oracle was evidently mistaken, and his inflexibility in interpreting it may be intended as especially culpable,[106] but neither the reproving Theseus, nor anyone else, gives any explanation of what he should have done.[107] He is more straightforwardly blameworthy in having been led astray by the bellicose young men to attack Thebes, because the transgression is on a simpler, human plane. Although it is suggested by the play, especially in its treatment of Theseus and Athens, that the world is well-ordered provided man conforms to the rational laws by which it is ordered,[108] the exact nature of these divine laws is never specified. Conacher[109] has suggested that Euripides intended to attack religious belief in general, and oracles in particular, by showing that even when one does follow them, disaster can result. If this is really the case, then Theseus' whole speech of ll. 195 ff. is based on an entirely false perception, and what he says and does elsewhere in the play would certainly be undermined. However, this is surely too simple an interpretation, because of the emphasis laid on the

---

[104] See Guthrie 1969: iii. 62.

[105] *Supp.* 195–213 includes material which, like the praise of democracy later in the play, is common in encomia of Athens: for example, the wisdom and language that distinguish us from the beasts which are fundamental to human existence, and the intelligence which has enabled humans to master the land so as to provide food for themselves, and the sea for trade: see Ch. 2 for these themes in Athenian ideology. The encomia tend to make what is vital for human life and human progress Athenian in origin: the enumeration of divine blessings by the representative of Athens also implies that such blessings are native to Athens, but not to Adrastus' city.

[106] As implied by θεσφάτοις Φοίβου ζυγείς ('yoked to Phoebus' oracles', l. 220): Scaliger's ὡς δόντων θεῶν ('as though the gods gave them', accepted by Diggle for L's ὡς ζώντων θεῶν, ('as though the gods were living') may also suggest such an interpretation.

[107] Paduano 1966: 229; Gamble 1970: 398.   [108] Zuntz 1955: 7.

[109] Conacher 1956, esp. 14–21.

bestiality of the fight between Tydeus and Polynices, which indicates that whatever Adrastus should have done, his decision to take
them as sons-in-law was obviously an error of judgement. Adrastus
has erred both on a human and a divine plane; Theseus will therefore criticize him on both planes before giving examples of conduct
that is correct both in human terms and in divine terms.

The optimistic conception of human progress and relations
between the divine and the human is brought into doubt later by
Theseus himself at *Supp.* 549 ff. where he laments the wretched-
ness of human existence. τρυφᾷ δ' ὁ δαίμων ('the god is capricious')
of l. 552 must surely recall 214's ἆρ' οὐ τρυφῶμεν ('are we not
capricious'), and it contradicts Theseus' earlier assertion of pure
divine beneficence. An explanation is to be found in the change of
context: previously, Theseus was concerned to assert Athenian
piety against Adrastus' impiety, but now, so as to show his distaste
for using force against Thebes, he must condemn the cruelty of
human life which leads to Theban cruelty and the necessity of
undertaking the battle. However, this, combined with the mysterious oracle whose true interpretation we never learn, the sufferings
of Adrastus and others and Athena's enigmatic appearance at the
end of the play, does create an ambivalence about the divine in the
universe.[110] Theseus and Adrastus are human beings who live in an
uncertain world, where the gods' purposes are often unclear and
often surprising. Human knowledge is imperfect in the face of
divine purposes: Theseus may censure Adrastus, but he gives him
no idea of what he should have done. This is part of the paradoxical nature of Euripides' treatment of the Argive king.[111] It is common in tragedy for Athens to accept suppliants who have
committed crimes, but who are also in a sense innocent of them,
usually because they have been in some way impelled to do them by
forces beyond their control. Here, Adrastus' mistake is regarded as
entirely his own folly, lacking any mitigating factor of divine
involvement,[112] and although Theseus does grant their inalienable
rights as human beings to the Argive mothers, who are untainted

---

[110] Cf. Paduano 1966: 235.   [111] Paduano 1966: 207.

[112] Apollo forced Orestes to kill his mother, but then protected him, but in the
Suppliants, the gods give no immediate help: Paduano 1966: 228; Zuntz 1955: 5.
Above all compare *OC* 252–3: οὐ γὰρ ἴδοις ἂν ἀθρῶν βροτὸν ὅστις ἄν | εἰ θεὸς ἄγοι
| ἐκφυγεῖν δύναιτο ('even if you searched hard, you could not find any human being
who could escape if a god was impelling him'); cf. also E. *Hipp.* 1433–4.

by the impiety of the expedition, his attitude to their king remains
stern and detached (*Supp.* 334, 513, 591): only later in the play does
he unbend to him as Argive impiety fades out of focus.[113] A final
paradoxical twist is given by Athena's approval of the desire of the
Epigonoi for revenge for the defeat of their fathers by Thebes, even
though this defeat was previously regarded as a just reward for
Adrastus' impiety and bad counsel. At l. 1226, we learn that this
time the gods are with the expedition, so that it will succeed; but
why this should be so remains a mystery.

This peculiarly contradictory treatment of Argos and Adrastus is
a product partly of a tragic view of the human world, and partly of
Euripides' patriotism. Theseus' piety and wisdom must be set
against their opposites in Adrastus, and rewarded, but the world of
the *Suppliants* is essentially tragic, and human beings cannot rely
on mercy or guidance from the gods. Within the framework of
tragic uncertainty, however, certain principles are made clear:
Thebes' disregard for the laws of burial is unequivocally wrong,
and Theseus' realization that the burial of the dead is a more
important consideration than their failings when alive is clearly
right; and, because it is right, it is also beneficial to Athens.[114] For
Theseus and his city, alone of all the other agents in the play, there
is a measure of unambiguous happiness resulting from right action,
which is action according to principles which are classified as
uniquely Athenian.

Almost as soon as he has rejected Adrastus' supplication,
Theseus begins to feel the first stirrings of pity for the bereft mothers; the very sight of their grief is enough to counter his logically
just argument against their king.[115] The turning point comes as
Aethra asks Theseus (*Supp.* 293) if she may speak what is σοί τε καὶ
πόλει καλόν;[116] and Theseus shows a proper desire to learn wisdom, and due respect for his parent.[117] Aethra now states the
orthodox Athenian ideal. In the very act of speaking out she exemplifies ideal Athenian πολυπραγμοσύνη: at l. 305, she says that she
would have stayed silent (ἡσύχως) if Theseus were not making a

---

[113] Grube 1941: 232.   [114] Paduano 1966: 201.

[115] *Supp.* 288: Zuntz 1955: 10.

[116] 'Right for you and the city': note again how closely Theseus is identified with
his city.

[117] Along with duty to friends and to the gods, a cardinal 'unwritten law' of
Greece: Isoc. 1. 16, cf. Hes. *WD* 327–34.

mistake; and she epitomizes the principles of the Athenian democratic system in which, as opposed to a tyranny, it is possible, indeed
imperative, for anyone to offer the best counsel for the city.[118]
First, she warns him that he is dishonouring what is sacred (τὰ τῶν
θεῶν): Adrastus may have done wrong, but refusing to help him is
not equivalent to doing right. The second reason why Theseus
should help them is that it is a matter of his own honour, because
he is bound to help the oppressed, and these women are being
oppressed by violent men (ἄνδρες βιαίοι) who, moreover, are con-
founding the laws of Greece (l. 311). This consideration does not
seem ignoble[119] and certainly would not appear so to an Athenian
audience: it is simply an explicit recognition of the exceptional reputation of Athens, and of the uniqueness of Athens' ability to har-
monize reputation with achievement.[120] Theseus and Athens are so
closely linked in this play that his honour is Athens' honour.[121]

Such sentiments would scarcely be out of place in an *epitaphios*
speech, and Aethra continues with a common topos of Athenian
ideological speeches, that other cities taunt Athens for being foolish (ἄβουλος) in helping the weak, but they do not have the insight
to see that a city like Athens is only strengthened by the tremen-
dous efforts it makes on behalf of the defenceless: ἐν . . . τοῖς
πόνοισιν αὔξεται (*Supp.* 323).[122] Her enemies are those who 'look
darkly', the inactive ones (ἥσυχοι) who, being cautious
(εὐλαβούμεναι), would refuse to help the wretched. Athens must

---

[118] Cf. *Supp.* 438 ff. Those who take no part in public business in Athens are considered ἀχρεῖοι (note ἀχρεῖον at *Supp.* 299), rather than ἀπράγμονες: Thuc. 2. 40. 2.

[119] *Pace* Gamble 1970: 402 and Fitton 1961: 435; on Greek ideas about human
motives, cf. Dover 1974: 224.

[120] Compare *Hcld.* 242 ff.; S. *OC* 258 ff.; E. *HF* 1334–5, with Bond 1981: 396; also
E. *Supp.* 316–19 with Thuc. 2. 41. 3, 42. 2; *TGrF* 4 730c.

[121] As 293 above, 315, 382 and esp. 339–40: πολλὰ γὰρ δράσας καλὰ | ἔθος τόδ'
εἰς Ἕλληνας ἐξεδειξάμην | ἀεὶ κολαστὴς τῶν κακῶν καθεστάναι ('For I have done
many glorious deeds and shown that my nature is always to punish the bad').
Theseus the κολαστής particularly recalls Hyperides 3. 12: ἡ πόλις ἡμῶν διατελεῖ
τοὺς μὲν κακοὺς κολάζουσα, τοῖς δὲ δικαίοις β[οηθοῦσα ('our city is always punishing the bad and helping the just'). For the close identification between Theseus'
virtue and that of his city, cf. *Hcld.* 94 and compare Heracles to Theseus in
Peirithous, fr. 7: σαυτῷ τε] Θησεῦ τῇ τ' Ἀθηναίων πόλει | πρέποντ' ἔλεξας
('Theseus, you have spoken worthily of yourself and your city').

[122] 'It is made great by its labours'. This is a dearly held principle of the Athenian
empire: on the πόνοι that lead to glory, see Ch. 2. It is also stated explicitly at S. *OC*
261, and above all, by Copreus in his appraisal of Athenian behaviour at *Hcld.*
162–78. It is a paradox typical of the idealized Athens that only this city can grow
strong by helping the weak.

not act as her enemies do.[123] Σωφροσύνη ('moderation') and
εὐλάβεια ('caution') are both words which can be used to describe
Spartan, or conservative inaction, as opposed to Athenian vigour in
the service of justice.[124] In this context, therefore, they have a distinctly pejorative tone, while it is asserted that Athenian
πολυπραγμοσύνη is the only way of upholding the laws of gods and
men.

Theseus is bound not to refuse this new challenge, because his
reputation, and that of Athens, depends on accepting the suppliant
women: Aethra's appeals persuade him that they must be helped.
Although he still insists on Adrastus' culpability (l. 334f.), the
combination of the continued condemnation with the offer of help
shows that Theseus and his city have the outstanding intelligence
to see beyond narrower cases of right and wrong to the principles
which they should hold dear in line with universal justice. All
Greeks should uphold such laws, but only Theseus and Athens can
in fact do so. The play will go on to emphasize the panhellenic status of the law Theseus must uphold (Lys. 2. 9, Isoc. 4. 55, 12. 169),
and in the *Suppliants* Theseus himself is a hero of panhellenic status (339–40, cf. 163, 277). Such a portrayal is influenced both by
the Athenian desire to glorify Theseus as a Heracles figure and by
her ideological claims as the pre-eminent defender of Greek civilization. The last words of this speech of acceptance uphold its
principles once more, as Theseus expresses a preference for words
instead of violence,[125] and acknowledges the importance of acting
with the gods' favour (ll. 347–9): he ends his decision, as he began,
with an exemplary avowal of affection and duty to his mother (ll.
359–64).

The importance of this scene lies above all in Theseus' change of
mind.[126] The ideas which he rejects in favour of Aethra's principles

[123] For Sparta as 'dark' (*Supp.* 324), cf. Thuc. 1. 70: also de Romilly 1963: 77;
Walker 1995: 152.

[124] See J. H. Finley 1938: 45 on σωφροσύνη as ἀπραγμοσύνη by any other name.
Similarly in Euripides' *Heracles*, εὐλάβεια demands that Lycus should slaughter
Heracles' defenceless family (*HF* 166). Cleon's demands for the massacre of the
Mytileneans, and Athens' conduct at Melos (esp. Thuc. 5. 107), are arguably ex-
amples of this εὐλάβεια, even though it was 'un-Athenian' in ideological terms.

[125] As at *Supp.* 385–7, where his offer of friendship to Thebes is aggressively
refused. Note, however, *Supp.* 389–92; his troops are at the ready if necessary, just
as Athena has Zeus' thunderbolt to hand if her persuasive skills are to have no effect
on the Erinyes at A. *Eum.* 826–31.

[126] Demophon is similarly, but less spectacularly, biddable at *Hcld.* 271–2.

are strikingly recapitulated by the non-Athenian, non-democratic
herald. At l. 472 the herald tells Theseus that he has no business
with Argos (cf. *Hcld.* 472), which is what Theseus told Aethra at l.
291. At ll. 496–7 the herald says that the impiety of the Argives
debars them from anyone's help, the view expounded at length by
Theseus earlier in the play.[127] There is also a similarity between the
herald's φρονεῖν ἄμεινον ἐξαύχει Διός ('boast that you surpass Zeus
in wisdom', *Supp.* 504) and Theseus' allegation that Adrastus is
one of those who think they are 'wiser than the gods' (δαιμόνων
σοφώτεροι, l. 218).[128] Theseus alone has the wisdom and flexibility
to change from non-Athenian to Athenian behaviour. The emphasis Euripides lays on the process by which he comes to change his
mind effectively highlights correct Greek principles of action,
while simultaneously suggesting that the ability to live up to such
principles is exclusively Athenian. The principles of ideal Athenian
πολυπραγμοσύνη are presented to the audience and its rightness is
reaffirmed.

The herald expresses a strong aversion to war at *Supp.* 481–8,
and in the context of the manifold suffering that war is shown to
bring, it has been suggested that Euripides intended to criticize
Athens' enthusiasm for military action,[129] especially given the
herald's condemnation of wars between Greeks (484–5) and
Adrastus' heartfelt condemnation of the πόνοι of war, recommend-
ing instead a policy of laying slaughter φόνους aside, being 'peaceful among the peaceful' (ἥσυχοι μεθ' ἡσύχων, 949 ff.) which might
have been intended to strike a chord in the hearts of a war-weary
audience.[130] However, all the suffering in the play, both before and
after Theseus' intervention, results from Adrastus' expedition,
while in contrast the just war of Theseus brings unalloyed glory to
his city (l. 779): his military prowess is glorified by the messenger,
and his undertaking causes no suffering to Athens.[131] War, then, is
terrible, but the ἡσυχία recommended by the herald, and at first
espoused by Theseus, is shown not to be right; at least, not for

---

[127] *Supp.* 195 ff.; although there is a hint that Theseus still has this opinion of
Adrastus at l. 513.

[128] As also Walker 1995: 159.   [129] As Fitton 1961: 435–6.

[130] See also Boegehold 1982.

[131] τοὺς θεοὺς ἔχειν ὅσοι | δίκην σέβονται. ταῦτα γὰρ ξυνόνθ' ὁμοῦ | νίκην
δίδωσιν ('having gods who honour justice; for where they are, they give victory',
594–6). The δίκη/νίκη jingle sums up a central portion of Athenian ideology.

Athens.[132] Only Athenian πολυπραγμοσύνη, because it includes
Athenian wisdom and compassion, can uphold the laws of god and
man. In spite of its recognition of the horrors of war, the *Suppliants*
is not a pacifist play.

When he explains to the herald why he cannot allow the Thebans
to maltreat the bodies of the Argives further (*Supp.* 513–63,
answering 465–510), Theseus repeats once more some of the arguments that his mother used earlier in the play: he uses the τιμή
argument, and says that he will not allow Creon to be his master or
that of Athens: again, king and city are closely identified (ll.
518–20). In accord with his honour, he must uphold panhellenic
law in seeking to bury the Argives (cf. 311, 561 and 670). The sur-
render of the enemy dead for burial was a mark of civilization and
humanity at least from Homer's day;[133] the opposite of this humanity is the arrogant barbarity and cowardice of which Theseus (like
his mother earlier) contemptuously accuses the Thebans.[134] When
Theseus says that the Argives have suffered enough by their inglo-
rious deaths and should now be given burial (ll. 528 f.), he shows a
proper sense of civilized moderation,[135] and at 549 f. he makes the
most explicit statement of the reversals of fortune and human
fragility which necessitate the moderation which he is urging upon
the implacable Theban: γνόντας οὖν χρεὼν τάδε | ἀδικουμένους τε
μέτρια μὴ θυμῷ φέρειν.[136] In the battle later in the play, Theseus
will put the principle of μέτρια ... φέρειν (l. 556), which comprises
the pity and ἐπιείκεια native to Athens, into practice: to the admiration and surprise of the messenger, he refuses to sack Thebes—
οὐ γὰρ ὡς πέρσων πόλιν | μολεῖν ἔφασκεν ('for he said that he did
not come to sack the city', ll. 724–5); after the battle, he washes and
tends the dead, exciting Adrastus' amazement at his willingness to
perform such a humble and unpleasant task. The messenger's τί δ'

---

[132] As *Supp.* 509; compare 472 ff. with Aethra's scornful words of 324 ff.

[133] Hom. *Il.* 24, esp. 39–54; S. *Aj.* 1317 ff. Outraging dead enemies' bodies is considered not Greek by Pausanias in Hdt. 9. 78. 9; see also §7.3.

[134] *Supp.* 543–8. Argument from self-defence can often have a rather dim moral
colouring in tragedy, just as terms such εὐλάβεια can be pejorative in Athenian
democratic ideology: see my remarks on Aethra's speech above, and compare also
Hcld. 1006–8, *Tro.* 749 ff. as well as *HF* 165.

[135] Lys. 2. 7–8 says that 'the Athenians' took a similar view of the Argives' case;
cf. also Odysseus, S. *Aj.* 1344–5, 1347.

[136] 'Knowing this, we should respond moderately, not with anger, when
wronged', *Supp.* 555 f., cf. S. *OC* 566. Adrastus, on the other hand, rejected
Eteocles' μέτρια (l. 740).

αἰσχρὸν ἀνθρώποισι τἀλλήλων κακά ('what is shameful to men
about others' troubles?', l. 768) sums up the humanity and moderation of Athens which Theseus offers as a principle to the herald at
ll. 555–6.[137] He will reject it; the Argive messenger and Adrastus
will support it, but their amazement at Theseus' conduct in the battle
highlights the fact that Theseus' moral sense is unique among the
characters of this play.

Athenian virtue operates effectively both on a secular and a religious plane. Some commentators[138] hold that the play sets up an
opposition between religious and secular law, and that Theseus'
motives are only in conformity with the latter. The sufferings of the
Argives do seem to be a particularly terrible punishment from the
gods for Adrastus' mistakes, and they contradict the ideals of moderation exemplified by Theseus. However, Euripides' *Suppliants* is
hardly exceptional in contrasting divine cruelty and human compassion,[139] and although divine principles differ from human principles, men must still respect the gods and act as they decree (as far
as they can know what they do decree). This is what Theseus does,
and he is rewarded for it. Piety is a part of good counsel: Adrastus
has failed in both, but the Athenian king succeeds. The whole point
of Theseus' mission is that it is demanded by higher claims of justice which are themselves sanctioned by the gods: Aethra assures
Theseus of this at l. 328; and Theseus' assertions at ll. 348 and 594
that the gods will support even the use of force to uphold right are
borne out by subsequent events. There is no distinction between
secular law and divine law for man: both are subsumed under
νόμος, and cannot be separated. The burial of the dead is described
as νόμιμα Ἑλλάδος ('the laws of Greece', l. 312), Πανελλήνων
νόμον ('panhellenic law', ll. 26 and 671) and νόμος παλαιὸς
δαιμόνων ('the ancient law of the gods', l. 563). The principle is
therefore religious and secular, and Thebes is violating what
Athens, to be true to the principles of the city, must preserve.[140]

The nature of νόμος lies behind the play's focus on themes such
as constitutional forms and citizenship, which critics have often
condemned as irrelevant or interpolated.[141] The first of what

[137] Grube 1941: 236; cf. Loraux 1986: 80; Walker 1995: 164.
[138] Especially Conacher 1956: 15–21.
[139] Compare, for example, the contrast between Athena and Odysseus at the start
of Sophocles' *Ajax*.
[140] Parker 1983: 170; Zuntz 1955: 10–11.
[141] For example, Kovacs 1982: 34–5.

appear to be diversions comes at ll. 238–45, in which Theseus cat-
egorizes the citizens as greedy rich, needy poor, who are apt to be
stirred up by demagogues, and those in the middle, who keep the
constitutional order. The context of the classification is the rebuke
of Adrastus' stupidity in following the young men's desire for war,
but its precise relevance is none too clear, because it is hard to associate the bellicose young men of Argos directly with either the rich
or the poor. However, it is clear that Theseus is casting doubts on
Adrastus' wisdom as a leader,[142] and that by 'mixing the just with the
unjust' he has failed in the ideal of following τὸ μέσον ('the middle
way'). Theseus' unflattering characterizations of rich and poor
sound like mere commonplaces, and what he commends is vague
and uncontroversial: τὸ μέσον itself is a term of general approval,
since the middle is, by definition, not extreme. The explicit com-
mendation of τὸ μέσον by Theseus is a sign of rectitude, which is
conversely defined by Adrastus' extremism;[143] and it is also related
to Theseus' conduct in the play generally, as the upholder of ideals
of tolerance and flexibility. It is certainly a mistake to interpret the
lines as a kind of political manifesto supporting the middle classes
of Athens, the farmers who lived outside the city who tended
towards ἀπραγμοσύνη.[144] Quite apart from the essential vagueness
of terms such as τὸ μέσον, the first half of the play is a vigorous
defence of Athenian ideals of 'interference'.

It is strongly implied by the *Suppliants* that Theseus and Athens
are as they are because of the democratic constitution, and that
Thebes' conduct is the product of a tyranny.[145] Again, we are in the
world of the idealized Athens and some of its normal assump-
tions.[146] When the herald and Theseus debate the relative merits of
tyranny and democracy (*Supp.* 399–462), they use the language of
contemporary politics and political thought, and the speeches contain many commonplaces of the oligarchy–democracy debate:[147]

[142] Contrast Theseus' sense of responsibility to his people at *Supp.* 247.

[143] Collard 1975: 29; de Romilly 1987, and for a similar use of μέσος, see Dover 1957: 233.

[144] As Carter 1986: 91–3; also Walker 1995: 150. See also Goossens 1962: 429–33; Bengl 1929: 13–17. Koster 1942: 196, suggests that Theseus' democracy depends on the middle classes: this is, again, much too specific.

[145] Cf. ll. 384, 399. Zuntz 1955: 8; Paduano 1966: 212–13. In a similar vein, Isoc. 7. 20 connects Athens' kindness (πρᾳότης) with its openness (κοινότης).

[146] Loraux 1986: 64.

[147] Grube 1941: 236; de Romilly 1987: 7. Thuc. 3. 82. 1 notes that there was a strong polarization between democracies and oligarchies in the war. W. D. Smith

Theseus' picture of the tyrant as murderous, paranoid and sexually rapacious (ll. 442–55) is a stereotype born of democratic orthodoxy.[148] Similarly, *Supp.* 417–22's claim, that the people are incompetent as governors, seems to be a standard criticism of democracy[149] which is fully answered by Thucydides' Pericles (Thuc. 2. 37. 2, 40. 2) and partially by Theseus himself (438).[150] Again, Thucydides' Pericles emphasizes the importance of the 'unwritten laws' (ἄγραπτοι νόμοι) to the democracy, and it is precisely these laws which the Theseus of the *Suppliants* protects.[151] Democracy's concern for νόμος also extends to what is written; Theseus points out that written laws are an essential part of the democracy and equality which states ruled by tyrants lack (ll. 429–38). Such laws are, in fact, a particularly good example of the democratic preference for human intelligence over the superhuman, because they can help to counter the uncertainties of human existence. If fate, or the gods refuse just dealings, at least there is the possibility of getting justice from others by means of human laws (*Supp.* 430 ff.). In short, νόμος in all its forms is best protected by democracy.[152] Freedom is also native to democracy,[153] and the combination of νόμος with freedom leads, by implication, to the active πολυπραγμοσύνη which protects Greek civilization.

The encounter between Theseus and the herald concludes with a short passage in stichomythia in which Athenian πολυπραγμοσύνη is given a final airing before Theseus departs to uphold the laws of gods and men. Once again, he states the Athenian mission, so familiar from the *epitaphioi*, of punishing those who are wicked, and those alone,[154] to which the herald replies, πράσσειν σὺ πόλλ'

1966: 169 remarks on the difference in terminologies used by the two men. Theseus' 'people' (δῆμος, l. 406) is the herald's 'rabble' (ὄχλος, 411); his 'rich' (πλοῦτος, l. 407) is the herald's ἀμείνων ('superior', l. 423); see also Walker 1995: 155–7.

[148] Compare *Supp.* 442–55 with Hdt. 3. 80. 3 ff. and 5. 92.

[149] Hdt. 3. 81. 2 and [Xen.] *Ath.Pol.* 1. 7–8: see J. H. Finley 1938: 41–3 and Bengl 1929: 31 ff.

[150] I differ from some critics (Grube 1941: 234; Fitton 1961: 433; Vellacott 1975: 30) in seeing no irony in the fact that Theseus does not fully defend the democracy from the herald's charges: what the Theban says is instantly discredited by his identity as a messenger from a state run by a tyrant, and since the criticisms of democracy he expresses are entirely standard, Euripides might expect that the audience would automatically have countered them with standard defences.

[151] Thuc. 2. 37. 3: cf. Finley 1938: 36–7.   [152] Paduano 1966: 213.

[153] *Supp.* 404, cf. Thuc. 2. 36. 1 and *Hcld.* 198. Also Zuntz 1955: 18–20.

[154] Note the vocabulary of πολυπραγμοσύνη at 573: πολλοὺς ἔτλην δὴ χἀτέροις ἄλλους πόνους ('I dared to do many other deeds for others also': Diggle's text); and cf. §2.4, for Athens as the punisher of the bad.

εἴωθας ἤ τε σὴ πόλις ('you're always interfering, you and that city of yours'). Theseus' reply—τοιγὰρ πονοῦσα πολλὰ πόλλ' εὐδαιμονεῖ ('yes, by its hard work it achieves great happiness', l. 577)—will be amply justified by subsequent events and in the context of Theseus' comprehensive display of moderation and intelligence, the Herald's criticisms of Athens, the democracy and Theseus' alleged 'meddlesomeness' are fully negated.

This interpretation of the play, as a celebration of the 'Athenian way of life', does not do full justice to its complexities, because it underestimates its inherent pessimism and ambivalence. The *Suppliants* is in many ways an encomium of Athens, but it is also a tragedy. The Athenian ideal is obviously un-tragic, and if the play is to escape the charge of facile patriotism, the Athenian ideal cannot be a perfect panacea for human ills in an uncertain, tragic world. The lamentations of the latter half of the play will therefore provide a contrast and corrective to the comparatively optimistic first half, and gradually, the focus will shift away from Theseus and Athens as Euripides brings in other themes which are somewhat separate from the role assigned to Theseus in the play.[155] In the second half of the play, Theseus will achieve what he set out to do, bringing glory to Athens, but naturally the act, although right in itself, cannot remove the sufferings of the mothers of the dead.[156] Hence, after Theseus' confident decision of 581–97, the two semi-choruses express contrasting points of view of the gods.[157] They do not trust divine goodness: διάφορα πολλὰ θεῶν βροτοῖσιν εἰσορῶ, ('I see many changes in the behaviour of the gods to men', *Supp.* 612) says the more fearful semi-chorus, but the more optimistic one says, δίκα δίκαν δ' ἐκάλεσε ('justice has called to justice', *Supp.* 614). This formulation is very reminiscent of Aeschylus,[158] and it would be interesting to know whether any of this recalls the *Eleusinioi*, and whether Euripides intended to question an Aeschylean vision that justice and rationality could emerge from

---

[155] Cf. Paduano 1966: 214. Because they are separate, they do not necessarily reflect on Theseus' actions so that the suffering of this part of the play is his 'fault'.

[156] So *Supp.* 778–85: cf. Paduano 1966: 203 f.; see also W. D. Smith 1966: 153.

[157] The equivalent passages, at E. *Held.* 748–83 and S. *OC* 1044–95 are more overtly optimistic. Note again the preference for words against violence at ll. 602–4.

[158] e.g. *Cho.* 311–14. Zuntz 1955: 11, compares also *Supp.* 798–837 with the *kommoi* of *Pers.* 852–906 and *Sept.* 832–74, both of which also contrast achievement and loss.

feud and suffering.[159] Even if this were so, however, the ideal of Athens would remain intact.

At this moment in the play, it appears that the gods do look after the deserving, as the messenger appears with glad news of the Athenian army: the messenger contrasts the outcome of their divinely favoured expedition with that of the Argives (l. 644) and no mention is made of any Athenian casualties. This is Theseus' finest hour. He is contrasted with Creon (ll. 669–75), in offering a bloodless way of honouring panhellenic law.[160] When Creon refuses, Theseus proves himself militarily pre-eminent as well in a vigorous and bloody *aristeia* (l. 714 f.).[161] There is no irony in this: Creon is getting only what he deserves, as is made very clear at l. 724, and although Creon has to be taught a lesson, Theseus will not take revenge as far as he has the military power to do, and he refuses to sack Thebes itself. We may compare the Theseus of *OC* 907, who will do no more than drive Creon out of Attica, using his νόμοι.[162]

This account of the battle leads Adrastus to break the silence of several hundred lines, to lament man's foolishness and the hubris which leads to wars. He implicitly contrasts the Argive conduct in refusing μέτρια, with Theseus' moderation.[163] Athens, unlike Thebes or Argos, helps the oppressed but exacts no more punishment than is strictly necessary. To some extent, Adrastus is morally redeemed by this speech which marks the end of his suffering, so that he can be made worthy to pronounce the funeral orations over the dead at *Supp.* 857 ff.[164] Even so, the text does not actually say that Adrastus has been changed by his experiences; he already knows at l. 156 that he has made terrible mistakes, so that we cannot really say that he has attained fresh knowledge. The difference in moral stature between Theseus and Adrastus is, in any case, maintained at *Supp.* 762–8, in which Adrastus' attitude to tending

---

[159] Fitton 1961: 444–5.

[160] At *Hcld.* 813, Eurystheus is too cowardly even to face Demophon.

[161] *Supp.* 716–17 recalls *Il.* 14. 496–8, and 20. 481–3: the Homeric reminiscence helps further to dignify the exploit.

[162] On a less sophisticated level, compare too Theseus' treatment of his enemies on the Saronic Gulf. *Contra* Walker 1995: 162.

[163] Adrastus' judgement on the foolishness of war should be related to Argos and Thebes, each of whom has now suffered for hubris.

[164] Collard 1975: 30–1. Theseus himself allows that suffering for one's mistakes must be finite: ll. 528–30, 549–52: see above.

the mutilated dead is less enlightened than that of Theseus,[165] and both in his tending of the bodies and his desire to spare the feelings of the Argive mothers by not letting them see the hideously disfigured bodies of their sons (941 ff.), Theseus remains superior to Adrastus in humanity and wisdom. Theseus' enlightened πολυπραγμοσύνη is especially striking in this part of the play. He decides that the Argives have suffered enough (*Supp.* 528 ff.), he fights for them and brings the bodies back so that they can be given the proper burial rites; by so doing, he rehabilitates them, just as he helps to rehabilitate Adrastus morally by encouraging him to make the funeral speech (*Supp.* 838 ff.), and he arranges for the burning of the bodies. The Argives are just passive 'clients', as, of course, the imperial Athenians preferred that their allies should be.[166]

Up to this point, the Argive expedition has been strongly condemned, but in the funeral oration pronounced over the dead, the Argive leaders suddenly become paragons of courage and virtue.[167] Theseus himself admires their gallantry, and their upbringing is commended, even though it was such an upbringing which led them to make the failed attack on Thebes which he denounced earlier. In the midst of a performance of a play like this, which is composed of self-contained episodes which are not always closely connected with one another,[168] this change of opinion might strike one as a little less extreme, but the contradictions seem rather glaring. Even so, the fact that Theseus himself, who is consistently endowed with all the Athenian virtues, and set against various characters who lack them, can endorse a favourable view of Amphiaraus and Polynices (ll. 925–8), would suggest that, in spite of the difficulty of relating this part of the play to what has gone before, Euripides was not satirizing the funeral oration or casting doubt on the wisdom of the battle against Thebes.[169] In fact the audience is impelled to feel pity for the Argives largely because Theseus, in his moderation and wisdom has accepted them, so that they are no longer impious men who have met a just punishment,

---

[165] *Supp.* 812 and esp. 942–5. This may be Aeschylean: see also *TGrF* 3 53a and §7.3 below. For this 'enlightenment', compare Theseus at *HF* 1400.

[166] Loraux 1986: 81.

[167] For the textual difficulties in this section of the play, see Collard 1972; Grube 1941: 237–8; Mastronarde 1979: 116–17.

[168] This is especially true of the Evadne episode, which has no connection with what precedes or follows it: Heath 1989: 5–8, 153–5.

[169] As argued by W. D. Smith 1966: 161 ff.; Conacher 1956: 24.

but the dead of the polis of Argos.[170] In the context of a funeral oration, the dead must be an educational example to the audience of
the oration,[171] and in a play with so many affinities to the *epitaphios*
speech, it is appropriate that *epitaphios* form takes over at this
moment. Some critics[172] connect the description of the Seven as
outstanding in courage (διαπρεπεῖς εὐψυχίᾳ) with Theseus' criticism of Adrastus as having preferred εὐψυχία to εὐβουλία, and
Supp. 911 ff. which commends teaching εὐανδρία to the young,
with the desire for revenge by the sons of the Seven, so that the
learning of the lesson of εὐψυχία by the Epigonoi actually makes the
cycle of revenge and suffering continue, and the values attached to
εὐψυχία are questioned. However, even if εὐψυχία does specifically
refer to military prowess here,[173] the play has shown beyond a
doubt that it is sometimes essential if νόμος is to be upheld against
the violent. Moreover, Athena herself promises that the revenge of
the Epigonoi, like Theseus' expedition, will be successful. Her reasons for endorsing the revenge may be mysterious in human terms,
but Euripides' intention, as far as Athenian action goes, is not
proven to be in the least ironical.

As the accent of the play begins to fall on purely tragic events,
Athens and Theseus become less important. Suddenly Capaneus'
wife Evadne appears, so distressed at her husband's death that she
flings herself onto his funeral pyre.[174] Euripides paints a particularly bleak view of the delusion and violence that have accompanied
Adrastus' war, and its effects are shown particularly clearly in
Evadne's old father's desolate speech at ll. 1080 ff.[175] At ll. 1015
and 1055, Evadne describes herself as glorious, and at 1059

[170] Note especially the moderate Capaneus (ll. 861–71); Eteoclus, who was poor
but held in high esteem (871–80); Hippomedon who gave his body for the city (l.
887, cf. Thuc. 1. 70. 6); and Parthenopaeus the perfect metic (889–95). Aeschylus'
mighty heroes have become citizens exhibiting qualities important for a community.

[171] Cf. Loraux 1986: 48. The power of the *epitaphios* to transform a bad man into
a good one is noted (disapprovingly) by Socrates and even Pericles: Pl. *Mx.* 234a and
Thuc. 2. 42. 3.

[172] Notably Burian 1985: 148–9; cf. Fitton 1961: 438 f. and W. D. Smith 1966:
166 ff.

[173] At E. *El.* 367 the word has a very general meaning, and such a meaning would
be appropriate here in view of the praise of various community virtues at *Supp.*
857–908.

[174] See Radt in *TGrF* 3, 134, on the possibility that she appeared in Aeschylus'
Argeiai; also Lloyd-Jones 1957: 527.

[175] Burian 1985: 134, suggests that a contrast is intended between Theseus and
his mother and Evadne and her father.

deludedly calls herself 'victorious' (καλλίνικος), as Theseus is in reality (l. 113). All she achieves by her foolish and tragic sacrifice is more suffering,[176] in contrast with Theseus' intelligent and just self-sacrifice in helping the suppliants. Her death is also very different from that of Macaria in the *Heraclidae*, who dies to save Athens, and exemplifies the right (Athenian) sort of individualism, like that of the citizen-dead whose courage is honoured in the *epitaphioi*.[177]

The lamentation intensifies at *Supp.* 1114, with the pathetic entrance of the Epigonoi to greet their grandmothers, mourning their fathers' ashes.[178] At l. 1143, the children express the desire to take revenge on Thebes: if we leave the text of l. 1144 as it stands in the manuscripts—εἰ γὰρ γένοιτο, τέκνον—the mothers themselves endorse the idea of revenge at 1145 ('may this happen, my child'), only to abhor the thought of the continuing cycle at 1148f.[179] If the mothers are ambivalent, partly wanting revenge for their sons' deaths but partly fearing more suffering, this would suit the general ethos of the play. The Athenian ideal of moderation is fine, but it is not enough to stop the human nature which desires more revenge.

It would seem as though the action of the play has run its course, and we move from lamentation to aetiology as Theseus and his grateful client (*Supp.* 1176–9) share a 'gentleman's agreement' to honour each other's cities, but suddenly Athena appears, after the human action of the play has been completed, to tell Theseus to exact an oath from Adrastus not to attack Athens,[180] and to seal this pact by dedicating at Delphi a knife and a tripod given to Theseus once by Heracles. She also endorses a further round of wars by reassuring the Epigonoi that they will sack Thebes 'with the gods' help'. At S. *OC* 650 and E. *Med.* 733, the need for oaths is con-

---

[176] Koster 1942: 172. She perverts terms such as σοφία (l. 1053) and ἀρετή (l. 1063).

[177] *Hcld.* 503–8: Fitton 1961: 452–3. One could not imagine an Athenian playwright presenting an Athenian Evadne to his audience.

[178] For the parallels between 1126 and A. *Ag.* 441, see Smith 1966: 166.

[179] Diggle gives the line to the Epigonoi in order to preserve an exact responsion between the parts in the strophic amoebaea, and assumes that τέκνον is a corruption, but see Collard 1975: 393–4, who argues convincingly against this; also di Benedetto 1961: 303–6.

[180] Collard 1981: 33–4, says of the *Suppliants*: ' . . . the gods' role is small or nonexistent . . . It is said that Euripides here uses myth to illustrate man's greater freedom to determine and act for himself, for better or worse. If so, the limits of that freedom are made clear.'

demned as indicating a lack of trust,[181] and this, combined with Athena's encouragement of fresh bloodshed, and the gods' somewhat baffling treatment of Adrastus at the start of the play, might be taken as a profound criticism of Athena which would reflect adversely on Theseus' ready obedience to what she says.[182]

Much of the play is deeply pessimistic, and its apparent contradictions do create an impression of a universe which belies the optimism of Theseus' credo at *Supp.* 195 ff. None the less, for a leader such as Theseus, such optimism is not wholly unjustified, because of his exceptional piety and reason. Athens has upheld the laws of heaven (*Supp.* 1204) and it is therefore appropriate for the patron goddess of Theseus to intervene to secure Argos' special gratitude. Whether the aetiology of the dagger and tripod is Euripides' invention or not,[183] the idea of a visible sign of the lasting friendship between Argos and Athens both brings the audience back from the tragic events on stage to historical reality, and also, by linking past and present, it should reaffirm their faith in the ideas of Athenian action which are standard in Athenian accounts of Athens and which have been shown to work here. πολυπραγμοσύνη brings eternal reward from Argos,[184] and in Athena's insistence on formal acknowledgement of the gratitude of Argos we return to the vindication of Athenian activity, and the patriotic strand of the play which dominated the first half of the *Suppliants* before its more tragic second half.[185] Athena gives no explanation as to why the Argives must fight on—although their success is at least assured—but after all, this has nothing to do with Athens: the treaty made between the two cities is purely for Athens' benefit, and does not commit the city to any further help of Argos (*Supp.* 1214, 1223).

Athena is not a malevolent deity: it is most unlikely that she would have appeared thus to an Athenian audience watching a play whose themes are so overtly connected with Athens. She simply makes sure that all will be well for Athens, while carrying on her own more enigmatic purposes as far as places which are not Athens are concerned. None the less, divinity in the play as a whole is

---

[181] Cf. Paduano 1966: 220.

[182] *Supp.* 1228–30: Gamble 1970: 404; Shaw 1982: 18.

[183] Collard 1975: 407 takes it as entirely imaginary, against Zuntz 1955: 77–8.

[184] As A. *Eum.* 762 ff., E. *Hcld.* 312–15. See also §2.4 on the 'risk–reward' topos.

[185] Zuntz 1955: 78; Shaw 1982: 17.

portrayed in a decidedly enigmatic manner.[186] Human nobility and
care for other humans is often set against divine detachment, and
sometimes cruelty, by Euripides. Theseus possesses all the
Athenian virtues and upholds the laws of god and man; by so doing,
he ensures the eternal glory and security of his city. The Argives
failed to uphold such laws, and are therefore bereft of happiness,
but the suppliant mothers are essentially blameless, and did not
deserve the sufferings Adrastus' mistake has inflicted on them, and
Theseus cannot stop their sufferings. Euripides' *Suppliants* fully
endorses the Athenian ideal, but it also shows the workings of an
impenetrable universe.

[186] As often in Euripides, and in authors going back to Homer: J. Griffin 1980:
168–72; Lefkowitz 1989.

4

Theseus and Heracles

4.1 INTRODUCTION

Myths evolve and develop out of the needs of the society that tells them: a myth that has no interest for its audience will die, and thus narrators of myths will always 'customize' their material, according to what is required of it at a particular moment. Euripides' *Heracles* is an especially instructive example of how historical place and time can influence the retelling of an established myth. What we know of the myth of Heracles' madness before, and after, Euripides' play, strongly suggests that his version of the story differs from the more common one in three major respects: he invents the character of the tyrant Lycus; he inverts the traditional order of the labours and the madness, so that the labours are no longer directly connected with the madness; and—most importantly—he introduces Theseus into the myth to offer Heracles honour and a home at Athens, and (by implication) a place to die.[1] Euripides' account seems to have contained too many novelties for it to have influenced later Greek versions, and the introduction of Theseus into a story which originally has no place for him must be a product of a specifically Athenian perspective. Like the Theseus of Euripides' *Suppliants*, the Theseus of the *Heracles* exhibits many of the qualities deemed essentially Athenian by Athenian encomia of Athens.[2]

The structure of the *Heracles* is extremely unusual, since it falls into three main sections, corresponding to the three major innovations made by Euripides. Lines 1–184 concern the wicked tyrant

---

[1] For discussion of these innovations, see especially Wilamowitz 1895: 109–13; Kamerbeek 1966; Bond 1981: xxviii–xxx.

[2] As with the *Suppliants*, the political perspective of the *Heracles* is too 'mainstream' for it to be securely assigned to any particular date in the Peloponnesian War. Its metrical features ought to place it in the penultimate decade of the 5th cent.: see Bond: xxx–xxxii, who suggests 416 or 414; Cropp and Fick 1985: 23 allow a range from 420 to 416. It is, of course, possible that this ideal Theseus was presented to the Athenians around the time of the massacre of the Melians.

Lycus, who has taken advantage of Heracles' absence to make himself the sole ruler of Thebes. When the play opens, we learn that he has determined to annihilate all of Heracles' remaining family (father, wife and three young children) to establish his position once and for all. No help from friends or from the gods seems forthcoming.[3] Just when they are preparing to meet their death, Heracles arrives from Hades, just in time to save them and, as the chorus believes, just in time to vindicate the justice of the gods (ll. 772–80); in ll. 815–1162 we see that the chorus's faith is horribly misplaced, as Heracles is sent mad by Hera and kills his children and wife: finally, the mood of the play changes yet again as Theseus appears (l. 1163), and for the rest of it, he is with the broken Heracles, comforting him and trying to persuade him to carry on living in spite of what he has done. This scene, above all others, is essential to the unity and 'meaning' of the play.[4] In this last part of the play, apart from one disputed comment at 1311–12, the chorus has no speaking role, and their silence concentrates the attention of the audience all the more strongly on the dialogue between Heracles and Theseus.[5] The play is built around the contrast between the chorus's triumphant affirmation of divine justice at 813–14—εἰ τὸ δίκαιον | θεοῖς ἔτ᾽ ἀρέσκει ('if justice still pleases the gods')—and the entrance of Hera's agents immediately after,[6] and this dialogue must, in some sense, be a commentary on the events of the play as a whole. Because of Hera, Heracles has killed his beloved family, and sees no way to end his shame but suicide (ll. 1146–52); but, at that very moment Theseus comes to foil his plans of suicide (ἐμποδών μοι θανασίμων βουλευμάτων, l. 1153). For the Athenian king, suicide is not a proper answer to Heracles' problems, because of the way he views Heracles and the gods: he offers him the only consolation he can, of a home and honour at Athens. The last section of the play, in the context of what has gone before,

---

[3] Noted particularly by Heracles' old father Amphitryon at ll. 218–28 (ingratitude of Thebes) and 338–47 (injustice of Zeus).

[4] Cf. Ehrenberg 1946: 161.

[5] Wilamowitz 1895: 126. The manuscripts assign 1311–12 to Theseus, but Bond, after Camper, to the chorus, because Theseus has already assigned the responsibility to Hera at l. 1189. A comment by the chorus here would certainly accord with tragic convention, but as Schwinge 1972: 162–3 rightly notes, the intensity of the relations between Theseus and Heracles would be increased by a deviation from convention.

[6] Bond 1981: p. xxi.

leads us to consider the nature of these gods who can inflict harm
on a man such as Heracles, and ultimately to consider the man who
saves him; Theseus, whose kindness seems to be opposed to the
gods' cruelty.

4.2 EURIPIDES' INNOVATIONS IN THE MYTH OF HERACLES' MADNESS

4.2.1 *Lycus*

The appearances of Lycus[7] and Theseus frame the action of the
play, and they stand at opposite ends of the scale of kingly behaviour. Theseus is a model of generosity and piety, while Lycus is a
stock tyrant; violent, impious in his disregard for the suppliant status of Heracles' family, and cowardly. In order to make sure of his
position as tyrant, he will kill all of Heracles' defenceless family,
and styles his intention to do so as εὐλάβεια ('caution'), not, as it
really is, ἀναίδεια ('shamelessness', ll. 165–6), Lycus' behaviour is
on a moral level with that of the tyrannically ruled Thebans in the
Suppliants, where such 'caution' is condemned as unworthy of
Greeks by the heroic, risk-taking Athenians.[8] His cynical, sophistic attempts to denigrate Heracles' bravery (ll. 151–64) when compared with his own cowardice and delight in tyranny[9] make him
especially detestable. Like the Thebans in the earlier play, Lycus is
ignorant of the laws of god and men, and his behaviour, like theirs,
is a background against which the virtue of Theseus can shine out
all the more strongly.

Amphitryon describes Lycus' behaviour as ἀμαθία (l. 172) and
flings a similar reproach at Zeus at l. 347: ἀμαθής τις εἶ θεός ἢ
δίκαιος οὐκ ἔφυς ('you are either a stupid sort of god, or you are
unjust by nature'). For Theseus later in the play, Heracles' decision

---

[7] An invented character (at ll. 38, 54, 567, he is called καινός), although Euripides
makes him the son of the Lycus whose place in Theban mythology is secure: see
Bond 1981: 69, 71. Theseus has two adversaries of the same name: his father's
brother, who was driven out of Attica by Aegeus (Hdt. 1. 173, cf. 7. 92), and who is
portrayed as Theseus' enemy on *ARV*² 257,11; and the Lycus who secured his banishment: ΣAr. *Plut.* 627b; ΣAristid. 2. 241,9, p. 688D, cf. §1.3.3.

[8] *Supp.* 324–5; cf. 543–8. For the anti-democratic associations of εὐλάβεια, cf.
Bond 1981: 111–12. Fear (cf. ll. 42–3) and insecurity are also typical of tyrants in
democratic thought: Hdt. 3. 80. 4, 5. 92. 7.

[9] He describes himself without any hesitation as their δεσπότης and Heracles'
family as his slaves (ll. 141–2 and 251, cf. 274, 277–8, 567).

to commit suicide is ἀμαθία (l. 1254). Moral conduct in this play, and more generally in Greek thought, is viewed in intellectualized terms,[10] and the theme of ἀμαθία, 'moral ignorance', along with what are its opposites, justice and gratitude, runs right through the play.[11] Lycus is a prime example of unjust behaviour and ἀμαθία, and on a human plane, he behaves as Hera does on a divine level.[12] A human being's power to inflict suffering, however, is limited by the power of other humans, whereas a goddess can inflict suffering with impunity. Lycus is ἀμαθής, and Theseus its opposite, and he will lead Heracles away from the ἀμαθία of the decision to commit suicide which the ἀμαθία of divinity has brought upon him.

4.2.2 *The Reversal of the Order of the Madness and the Infanticide*

The madness of Heracles was known to the author of the *Cypria*, and to Stesichorus and Panyassis (Paus. 9. 11. 2) and also Pherecydes (*FGrH* 3 F14), and it is likely that some of the seventh- and sixth-century epics with a Heraclean theme included the story.[13] All the surviving later accounts of Heracles' labours places them after the madness; and if this is the chronology of some, at least, of the pre-Euripidean sources, the unanimity of later sources against the Euripidean chronology would easily be explained.[14] It is possible that the labours were Heracles' atonement for the infanticide in at least one account, though our extant sources do not explicitly say so, and a madness–labours chronology would also remove the difficulty admitted by *HF* 827–9, in which Euripides has to explain why Hera only decides to attack Heracles after she

[10] Cf. Denniston 1954: 65 and esp. 85, where he translated it as 'lack of finer feeling', both intellectual and moral; see also Bond 1981: 145, on *HF* 347.

[11] In Thucydides, ἀμαθία is an anti-Athenian attribute: Cleon is said to prefer ἀμαθία μετὰ σωφροσύνης ('ignorance with prudence', 3. 37. 2) to the intelligence which is usually held to be characteristic of Athens, just as he condemns the οἶκτος (37. 1) which is also quintessentially Athenian. Again, at 2. 40. 3, Pericles describes others' courage as mere ἀμαθία, while Athens' courage is a product of intelligence (cf. 2. 62. 5).

[12] Arrowsmith in Grene and Lattimore 1969: 274. Chalk 1962: 16–17 suggests that Lycus is the embodiment of the violence latent in Heracles which causes the infanticide. Violence is, however, a typical characteristic of tyrants, and as a theme it has no wider relevance to the play.

[13] See M. Davies 1989: 31 and Jouan 1966: 381–3. For discussion of variants of the story, see Wilamowitz 1895: 81–8. For illustrations of the madness and infanticide in the 5th cent., see Vollkommer 1988: 61–2.

[14] *FGrH* 90 F13; Apollod. 2. 4. 12–15. 12; D.S. 4. 10. 6–28. Bond 1981: p. xxix; Matthews 1974: 89 f., 111–14.

has allowed him to complete his labours. The reversal of the traditional chronology is theatrically most effective. It produces in a play a striking disunity, contradicts the normal causal relationship between desert and reward; and creates a contrast between divine justice and human friendship. At the height of his strength and youth, Heracles has even symbolically conquered death by bringing Cerberus up from the underworld,[15] but although he conquers the greatest evil for mankind, his fall will bring him so far from that previous triumph that he will wish, instead, to kill himself (*HF* 1146–53).

In this play, Heracles kills his wife as well as the children, but later tradition says that he gave Megara to his friend and helper Iolaus in case he killed any more of their offspring.[16] In Euripides' story, Theseus takes over Iolaus' role to some extent,[17] but marriage to Megara would detract from the intense relationship between the two in the last scene of the play, where it is explicitly characterized as that of father and son, and also saved and saviour. Reference to Megara's future with Theseus would also distract attention from Heracles' future at Athens: it is therefore dramaturgically convenient for Megara to be killed with the children.[18] The inclusion of Theseus in the myth reveals an exclusively Athenian perspective. For Athens, no other hero except Theseus could have the wisdom and heroic stature to be a successful source of comfort to the greatest panhellenic hero of all.[19]

4.2.3 *Tradition and Innovation: The Introduction of Theseus*

Theseus' arrival at l. 1169 seems very surprising, and it is only on a subsequent reading of the play that we realize that his arrival is not

---

[15] In wider mythological tradition, his marriage to Hebe is also related to the conquest of death: Hom. *Od.* 11. 602–4; Hes. *Thg.* 950–9, fr. 25. 26 ff.

[16] D.S. 4. 31; Apollod. 2. 6. 1. For Iolaus as Heracles' assistant in his labours, see Vollkommer 1989: 1–19. He even helps him with Cerberus: *LIMC* 5. 1, 89–91, nos. 2585, 2592, 2594 and 2607. Although Peirithous is to Theseus what Iolaus is to Heracles, he is rarely portrayed as his assistant in art, except in the labours of the Amazons and the Centaurs, whom even Theseus could not subdue entirely on his own. Indeed, in Athenian accounts of the abduction of Kore, far from assisting Theseus, he gets him into trouble (cf. §1.3.2)!

[17] Though well established in the legend, the figure of Iolaus would have little resonance for an Athenian audience.

[18] Euripides has resisted any temptation to include such a marriage as an aetiological vindication of Athens' claims to the town of Megara.

[19] See Tarkow 1977: 31.

totally unexpected, because Heracles has already told Amphitryon that his return had been delayed by rescuing the Athenian king from the underworld (l. 619). At l. 613 we learn that Heracles had been initiated into the Eleusinian mysteries,[20] and he seems to ascribe his success with Cerberus to his Eleusinian initiation. Already, therefore, though unobtrusively, by means of the civilizing power of Eleusis, Athens has helped the great civilizer and benefactor of mankind.[21] This brief reference hints at the theme which dominates the last scene: Athens alone is able to help Greece's greatest hero. Although the emphasis in the *Heracles* on Theseus as the embodiment of Athenian values is less explicit than in the *Suppliants*, his portrayal, as will be shown, is none the less strongly influenced at a deeper level by Athenian ideas of what Athens' representative must be.

If pre-Euripidean tradition put the murders before the labours, Theseus' role in the aftermath of the madness will not antedate Euripides' play.[22] The offer of a home in Athens, where Heracles is apparently to die,[23] must be Euripides' invention, since it clearly cannot be reconciled either with the tradition of his death on a pyre on Mt. Oeta, or with that of his apotheosis, both of which were current long before the composition of this play.[24] No known source locates the burial of Heracles in Attica, and Euripides himself is silent as to its whereabouts.[25] This is not surprising: no city could ever lay exclusive claim to the grave of the one truly panhellenic hero, and although his greatness made the fostering of close links with Theseus highly desirable, Heracles remained essentially a foreigner for Athens. The story does not appear in extant fourth-century *epitaphioi*, and the fact that not even the Athenians, for

[20] The tradition was probably already current in a sixth century Heraclean Catabasis (Lloyd-Jones 1967 and cf. §1.3.2); for the initiation in art, see Brommer 1984: 18–19. A fighter against death and a civilizer such as Heracles would be a particularly worthy initiate. In Plut. *Thes.* 30, Theseus himself initiates Heracles; Triptolemus does so in Xen. *Hell.* 6. 3. 6. He also appears on the Parthenon with the Eleusinian goddesses: Harrison 1967: 43–5.

[21] 'Out of love for gods and men' ($\theta\epsilon o\phi\iota\lambda\hat{\omega}s$ and $\phi\iota\lambda\alpha\nu\theta\rho\omega\pi\omega s$), Athens shared the mysteries with all: Isoc. 4. 28–9.

[22] Bond 1981: p. xxx; Kamerbeek 1966: 3.

[23] *HF* 1331–3; Athens will also offer Oedipus a place to die in *Oedipus Coloneus*.

[24] Wilamowitz 1895: 71, 110; Easterling 1982: 9–10, 15–19. For the popularity of the apotheosis of Heracles in mid-6th-cent. Athens, see also Boardman 1972 and 1975.

[25] Compare Sophocles' mixture of vagueness and precision concerning Oedipus' grave in Attica: Jebb 1900: p. xxiii.

whom Euripides' account would have had unique significance, took it up is a clear indication of just how innovatory his version of the story is. In his *Heraclidae* which was written at least a decade earlier, there is no reference to it: in contrast, the help given by Athens to the Heraclidae is one of the standard examples of Athenian virtue found in the *epitaphioi*. Theseus' help to Heracles is perhaps a kind of derivation from the established story of the help given to his children; an extravagant extension, but not an implausible one.

At ll. 1327–33 of the *Heracles*, Theseus offers Heracles all the enclosures (τεμένη) that had been given to him for saving Athens from the Minotaur. According to Philochorus, however, Theseus handed most of them over to Heracles, but kept four for himself. Although the historian may simply be 'correcting' the playwright, without necessarily referring to tradition beyond Euripides, since Euripides could hardly have made his open-handed, open-minded Theseus deny Heracles any of the precincts, it would be possible that Euripides was adapting, to Theseus' credit, an existing 'official' aetiological tradition, intended to explain why Attica had so many shrines of Heracles and so few of Theseus, according to which Theseus had given Heracles most of the τεμένη which he once had, to thank him for rescuing him.[26] On the other hand, Athenian literature tends to portray Theseus as a self-sufficient hero who helps others, because he is the representative of a city which helps others,[27] thereby obtaining their gratitude which, as Chapter 2 has demonstrated, is a position vastly preferable to that of accepting help from others. It is therefore unlikely that Euripides could have been using a very widespread Athenian tradition, just because such a tradition would be a permanent memorial of the weakness of Theseus. In the context of the play, of course, with its emphasis on human and divine ingratitude for services rendered, Theseus' gratitude to Heracles must certainly be stressed, but such gratitude was probably not suitable for emphasis in traditions influenced by Athenian ideology. Interestingly, the *Heracles*, unlike the

---

[26] For discussions of the sparseness of shrines to Theseus, see Wilamowitz 1895: 110; Jacoby 1954: 307, commenting on *FGrH* 328 F18, followed by Bond 1981: p. xxx; Walker 1995: 20–1. For the locations of the four precincts, see Jacoby, 309. Webster 1967: 191 connects *HF* 1331 ff. with an extension of the Theseion in the late 5th cent., discussed by Thompson 1966b: 46–7.

[27] See my remarks on Theseus and Ariadne and the *Peirithous* §§7.5.1, 7.6.2: note also *ARV*² 1086,1, *LIMC* 5. 1, s.v. 'Heracles' 3516, on which Heracles watches Theseus raise himself from the floor of Hades, rather than having to help him.

Eumenides, Suppliants or *Oedipus Coloneus*, lays little emphasis on the benefits that Athens will receive from the reception of Heracles:[28] here, the topos of Athenian altruism takes over, and also leads our attention away from any debt owed by Theseus to Heracles. The debt is mentioned and admitted, only to be overlaid with an emphasis more flattering to Athens, and thus it is effectively suppressed.

4.3 HERACLES AND THESEUS

The story of the rescue from the underworld was a subject of literature and art at least from the early sixth century.[29] The consistent association of Theseus and Heracles on Athenian public architecture even in the fifth century, a long time after Theseus had been built up as a hero to match Heracles, indicates that the Athenians never stopped needing to equate the deeds of their national hero with those of Greece's greatest hero.[30] Indeed, for Isocrates (10. 23), the greatest praise that Theseus can have is that his deeds match those of Heracles. At the end of the *Heracles* Theseus will even be asked to share Heracles' unique triumph over death, by helping him with Cerberus,[31] but long before the *Heracles*, Athens was keen to associate Theseus with Heracles and to draw parallels between them, often so that they work to Theseus' advantage and, in an interesting piece of symbolism, the panhellenic hero is outstripped by the hero of a city which was trying to achieve panhellenic domination. Heracles' encounter with the Cretan bull is often portrayed as more of a struggle than that of Theseus with its Marathonian counterpart,[32] and similarly, while Theseus the clever young hero must always represent the Athenian perception

---

[28] Though the theme is not entirely absent: cf. *HF* 1334–5.

[29] See §§1.3.2, 7.6.2. There is no mention of Peirithous in the *Heracles*, nor any reference to the reasons for Theseus' being in the underworld. Peirithous is irrelevant to Euripides' needs; and since it is also Peirithous who tends to take the blame for any impiety in the journey to Hades, he is best omitted.

[30] Above all, on the Athenian Treasury at Delphi and the Hephaesteion, but also on the temple of Zeus at Olympia, where Heracles is dominant, Theseus is still given a part: Apollo stands behind him as he fights the forces of disorder symbolized by the Centaurs: see Paus. 5. 10. 6 and Ashmole and Yalouris 1967: 17–22. Theseus is also one of Heracles' allies against the Amazons both on the statue of Zeus and on his footstool: Paus. 5. 11. 4, 11. 7.

[31] *HF* 1386, and see my remarks on the *Peirithous*, §7.6.2.

[32] Shefton 1962: 344–53.

of Athens as the versatile city which can do everything easily,[33] the
metopes at Olympia portray a Heracles whose exhaustion after having killed the lion is very noticeable. However, Heracles' prestige
was so great throughout Greece that he had to have a unique connection with Athens: thus he is an Eleusinian initiate; and the
Marathonians claimed that they were the first to regard him as a
god.[34] Because of this, and because of his peculiar nature, it is
worth saying a few words on Heracles as he appears before
Euripides' play.

Heracles has a bestial side, but he is also a most mighty champion
of humanity and human civilization, and both aspects of him are
part of one and the same quality; that of superhuman strength,[35]
which can be exercised either in excess and violence or in civilizing
deeds.[36] He never loses his essential violence, and even Pindar can
portray the violent and greedy Heracles of the parallel tradition.[37]
Generally, however, Pindar portrays the Heracles whose labours
are beneficial to mankind. For example, his first Nemean ode
describes Heracles' triumph over the serpents sent by Hera and
prophesies immortality to him as a reward for the slaughter of 'lawless beasts' (θῆρας ἀϊδροδίκας, *Nem.* 1. 63) by land and sea. He
even sets the boundaries of the Greek world[38] and is also a great
athlete.[39] In both of these roles as culture hero, he is a model for

[33] Compare esp. Thuc. 2. 40. 1, and the references to Athenian ἁβρότης at Bacch.
18. 1 and E. *Med.* 830: above, §2.4. Even so, it was Heracles, not Theseus, on whom
one called as a saviour at Athens.

[34] Paus. 1. 15. 3, 32. 4. cf. Isoc. 5. 33; D.S. 4. 39. 1. *Il.* 395 and 8. 362ff. know him
as a combatant with death, which may be connected with his immortality. We know
only of actions of Heracles the hero, not of Heracles the god, and he can only have
achieved divine status at a late date: M. L. West 1966: 417; Boardman 1972.
Whether or not the Marathonians' claim is actually true, the belief was evidently a
source of pride to them.

[35] Galinsky 1972: 3, and cf. §1.2. Heracles is an extreme example of tendencies
typical of Greek heroes.

[36] Already at Hes. *Thg.* 526–31: Heracles kills the eagle torturing Prometheus, the
benefactor of mankind; in the *Shield of Heracles*, he kills Cycnus, a wicked violator
of hospitality like those killed by Theseus. But he also fights the gods (*Il.* 5. 393–404,
cf. Hes. *Thg.* 314, *Il.* 15. 25, Panyassis 21D), and gets drunk like the Centaurs
(Panyassis, frr. 12–14D, with Matthews 1974: 74–8).

[37] Fr. 168 Sn., and probably the much-disputed fr. 169. See Pavese 1967: 47–88
(full bibliography at 52 n. 4): Gentili 1977: 299–305.

[38] The pillars of Heracles: Pind. *Ol.* 3. 44, *Nem.* 3. 21 and *Isthm.* 4. 12. His further-
flung exploits could be used as examples for the early Greek colonists: Bowra 1961: 89.

[39] Founder of the Olympic games, *Ol.* 2. 3, 3. 11, 6. 68 and 10. 44. *Nem.* 10. 53,
11. 27: Morgan 1990: 220–3. The hypothesis to Pindar's Isthmian Odes makes
Theseus the founder of the Isthmian games.

Greek aristocracy all over Greece. Similarly, in fifth-century
Athens, the portrayal of Theseus is influenced by Athenian ideas
about Athens to become a sort of role model for the democracy.
Athens' interest in the rescue of Heracles by Theseus is therefore
important for what it indicates about Athenian self-assertion in the
fifth century.

Theseus never attains the subhuman depths or superhuman
heights of Heracles, and the immortality which Heracles receives
indicates the essential difference between the two. Any monstrousness which Theseus once had is lost as Athens takes him up and
refines him, whereas Heracles never loses his monstrousness.[40]
Because he is both a godlike figure and also bestial, he is not very
easy to incorporate in tragedy, and the monstrous, excessive
Heracles of satyr play or comedy predominates in Attic drama.[41]
As a god and saviour figure, Heracles cannot be tragic because the
gods themselves are not tragic.[42] In this, Theseus is similar to
Heracles: like him, he is usually not a tragic hero in the normal
sense of the term, because he has to be a kind of saviour figure.
However, Heracles' bestial side is much more marked than that of
Theseus, and because Theseus is a more completely humanized
figure than Heracles,[43] it is easier to fit him into a genre which deals
with the civil and domestic questions of life in the polis.[44]

Yet Heracles is the subject of this play, and it is very striking that
Euripides has completely rid him of the 'outsize', un-human qualities, which are fundamental to Heracles in earlier tradition, except
in so far as his exceptional strength has enabled him to perform
exceptional feats. Already at l. 20 we are told that he has civilized
the earth, clearing it of wild beasts, and the claim is recapitulated

---

[40] Cf. §1.2. Although Heracles himself becomes a more peaceful hero after *c*.450:
Vollkommer 1989: 92 f.

[41] He is known to have appeared in ten satyr plays, and up to twelve more, and he
appeared in at least thirty-two comedies: Vollkommer 1989: 67–78. His two sides
are not always distinct: in the *Syleus*, he is both the benefactor of man and a hero of
monstrous appetites, and a similar duality is to be found in the *Alcestis*. But this
again is very different from Theseus. See also §7.1.1 on the rarity of Theseus'
appearances in comedy.

[42] Silk 1985: 1–6; Ehrenberg 1946: 164.

[43] Note also Isoc. 10. 24; Heracles' deeds were more famous and impressive, but
Theseus', more *useful* [because smaller and on a more human scale?] for Greece and
Athens. A fully human, 'Thesean' Heracles is to be found in Bacchylides 5, of which
ll. 89–92 may be compared with S. *OC* 564: Foley 1985: 177–8. His words to
Meleager at ll. 160–4 are not unlike Theseus' advice to Heracles in the *HF*.

[44] Foley 1985: 171, and compare Silk 1985: 1–12.

with great effect in the mouth of Madness herself: ἄβατον δὲ χώραν καὶ θάλασσαν ἀγρίαν | ἐξημερώσας ('having cleared the impassable land and the wild sea', ll. 851–2). We have already seen the importance in Athenian ideology of claims to the power of civilization, and Bond aptly compares Thuc. 2. 41. 4 on the Athenians' achievement with this passage: πᾶσαν μὲν θάλασσαν καὶ γῆν ἐσβατὸν τῇ ἡμετέρᾳ τόλμῃ καταναγκάσαντες γενέσθαι ('by our daring, making every land and sea accessible').[45] By rescuing the great civilizer from suicide, Theseus will be upholding Athens' reputation as the civilizing city.

Both the civilizing aspect of the labours and their panhellenic scope[46] are stressed in the play, especially in the important choral ode which enumerates them. The Nemean lion is 'terrible' (δεινός, l. 363) and the hydra 'murderous' (πολύφονος, l. 420); he kills the 'race of the wild Centaurs' (ἀγρίων | Κενταύρων . . . γένναν) which made cultivation of Thessaly impossible (ll. 364–74).[47] The hind (ll. 375–9) was another ravager of crops, in marked contrast to the peaceful creature described by Pindar *Ol.* 3. 25 ff. and elsewhere;[48] Diomedes' horses (ll. 379–86) are man-eaters, reversing, like the Cyclops, the civilized order by eating human beings; and Cycnus offends against hospitality (l. 391). He was even able to hold up the houses of the gods for Atlas (ll. 402–7). Only Geryon is not explicitly characterized as a danger to men, and even he was physically monstrous (l. 423). It is this mighty benefactor whose deeds Theseus—and Theseus alone—will not forget. By his intelligence and persuasive ability he will make Heracles agree to live on for the potential benefit of mankind, and of Athens (ll. 334–5), and thus the representative of Athens becomes the saviour of the greatest saviour of humanity in Greek tradition.

---

[45] Bond 1981: p. xxvii. Compare the Athenians' conversion of an untamed land (χθόνα ἀνήμερον) into a tame one (ἡμερωμένην): A. *Eum.* 13–14; cf. *HF* 30, ἐξημερῶσαι.

[46] Notable also on the Heracles metopes at Olympia *c.*460: Holloway 1967; Bond 1981: 154. For a general account of the literary and artistic tradition relating to the labours see especially Brommer 1953 and 1984.

[47] Theseus and Peirithous also fought the Centaurs, but here the glory is Heracles' alone, just as Iolaus is not mentioned in connection with the Hydra. Only in connection with the band of Amazons (another exploit shared by Theseus) does Heracles share glory with others.

[48] So Brommer 1953: 20.

4.4 THESEUS AND HERACLES: DEBTS REPAID

When Heracles returns from Hades, his family greets him rapturously, describing him as 'no less than Zeus Saviour' (ll. 621–2), and at this moment, when he has returned from the dead, having triumphed over humanity's greatest enemy, just in time to save his family, it is an understandable, if an unusually bold, claim.[49] At this moment of the play, Heracles is simultaneously a supreme civilizing hero and supremely human. His humanity is exhibited to a surprising degree in the remarkable rejection of all his superhuman labours in favour of the preservation of his family (ll. 562–82), but, since the labours have already been accomplished successfully, there is no need to condemn him for rejecting them now:[50] it is rather the case that Euripides has created a unique Heracles, combining his traditional role as superhuman (without any of the accompanying excesses) with the capacity for ordinary human affection. The two are not fully compatible, as is evident from ll. 632–3: although οὐκ ἀναίνομαι | θεράπευμα τέκνων· πάντα τ' ἀνθρώπων ἴσα ('I do not scorn looking after my children; in all things men are equal') expresses a 'democratic' way of life which might have commended him to many in the audience,[51] it sits oddly in the mouth of the great superhuman. Indeed, subsequent events in the play will make Heracles equal to the least fortunate of human beings, and will prove the incompatibility of his superhuman deeds with his essentially human, and vulnerable, nature, in the eyes of Hera. His devotion to his family here will make her intervention seem all the crueller, and it also underlines the difference between Heracles the human father (like his human father Amphitryon) and his distant, apparently indifferent divine father Zeus: and it is to Heracles the man that Theseus will appeal when he comes to save him with the purely human comforts of Athens.

[49] There is no suggestion that Heracles must deserve punishment for the apparent hubris of Megara's claim (as Sheppard 1916: 77–8). Although Heracles' position is, indeed, too high for the jealous Hera's liking (ll. 841–2), any exalted human being runs the risk of incurring divine jealousy: Hdt. 1. 32. 1. Rather, it resembles other indictments of the gods' unconcern in the play, especially ll. 339–47. See also l. 1191, where Amphitryon complains that Heracles once fought the giants to help the gods, implying that the gods have ungratefully abandoned him now.

[50] As Foley 1985: 190.

[51] Bond 1981: 223–4 on ll. 633–6 compares what Theseus says at E. *Supp.* 406–8 and 429–34; see also Foley 1985: 189.

In the first half of the play, then, Euripides consistently idealizes Heracles as a humanized saviour and culture hero, so that when the madness comes, he may fall from the heights to the depths, and Theseus alone will come to save him from those depths. Many scholars have not been able to bear an apparently motiveless peripeteia,[52] and it is true that Heracles' fate seems much harder to accept than that, say, of Hippolytus, whose rejection of Aphrodite at the start of the play is at best unwise.[53] Euripides himself draws attention to the injustice of Heracles' downfall by making Lyssa, of all gods, reluctant to inflict suffering on the benefactor of gods and man (ll. 845–54); but for Hera, such services are simply irrelevant.[54] His existence as Zeus' son, combined with the successful accomplishment of the labours, is ample reason for the hatred of such a deity in the context of the play's frightening view of the relationship between gods and man.[55] At the end of the *Hippolytus*, we see that the gap between god and man which Hippolytus had thought that he had narrowed by his devotion to Artemis remains, after all, a huge chasm,[56] and a similar effect is produced in the *Heracles*. Although Heracles' family describes him as 'no less than Zeus', Lyssa stresses that he is merely a mortal at Hera's mercy. The middle section of the play, in which it seems as though traditionally comforting views of a theodicy are being upheld,[57] makes the apparent truth about the gods in the last section all the more

---

[52] Hence, most famously, Wilamowitz's theory (1895: 128–32), that Heracles is mad before he actually goes mad. He later abandoned the theory—Wilamowitz 1926—but later scholars have used variants of it: e.g. Kamerbeek 1966: 14. Burnett 1971: 157–82 makes an interesting, if ultimately unconvincing, reading concerning the theodicy of this play. Chalk 1962: 16 and also Barlow 1982 suggest that Heracles' violence is meant to parallel Lycus'; but Lycus is a violent tyrant who fully deserves violent revenge, and we are not meant to pity him. Heracles' revenge against such an enemy is not excessive in Greek heroic terms, but rather another expression of the 'help friends/harm enemies' ethic which run through this play and wider Greek ethics.

[53] Cf. Stinton 1975: 249–52.

[54] Compare her implacable attitude to Hector, *Il.* 24. 56–63, which contrasts Zeus' awareness of his obligations to him.

[55] Rightly, on this point, Zürcher 1947: 102; Rivier 1975: 17 f. His return from the underworld, from which no human being should return, is the greatest challenge to divine authority, and, like Lycus, Hera and her ministers feel they must inflict force on those who are a threat to their authority: so esp. ll. 841–2.

[56] Compare *Hipp.* 1437–41 with l. 19.

[57] Cf. Foley 1985: 165, with ll. 739, 757–61, where the relief of the Chorus at being able to return to traditional ideas about divine justice is especially evident (see also Bond 1981: 260–1), and 772–80.

disconcerting. Heracles 'deserves' his downfall in divine terms, but not in human ones, as Theseus, the representative of the human and humane in the play, will argue. At l. 1189, his immediate judgement on the scene is that it is all Hera's doing:[58] his assertion has an air of finality, as if no more need be said. The gods[59] are, quite simply, just in their sense, not the human sense. Instead, Theseus will offer Heracles human remedies for his distress, based on the enduring obligations of gratitude and concern for fellow human beings.[60]

In spite of the brief preparation for his arrival at l. 619, Theseus' appearance is a great surprise.[61] The parallels between the entrances of Heracles and Theseus are instructive for the underlying differences between them. Line 525's ἔα, followed by a string of questions, is paralleled by *HF* 1172–5, but whereas Heracles merely questions uncomprehendingly, Theseus is intelligent enough to explain the situation to himself.[62] Both characters arrive in the nick of time to prevent disaster, but whereas Heracles' homecoming is joyous as he comes in his traditional role as a saviour figure, the joy of the rescue of his family will be short-lived as disaster comes from an unexpected source. Theseus' arrival is not joyous, because the tragedy has already happened, but he will stop further catastrophe, by preventing Heracles from killing himself; by his friendship he will prove to be the true saviour and provide lasting benefit to Heracles and to the Greek world. Theseus' arrival is motivated by gratitude to a friend and is totally voluntary.[63] He comes as soon as he hears the rumour that Heracles needs help. Speed is obviously important if one is to give effective help to one's friends, and Theseus' swift arrival recalls the idealized image of

[58] *Pace* Silk 1985: 16 and Drexler 1943: 338, who deny that Hera's anger is sufficiently stressed in the text. See ll. 20, 829, 831 and 840 (which emphasize Iris' close liaison with Hera), 1303, 1393.

[59] Although the blame is put on Hera, no deity except Lyssa condemns Heracles' unjust fate: divine silence concerning her apparent cruelty to Heracles recalls Artemis' explanation of why she could not save Hippolytus (*Hipp.* 1327–30).

[60] Cf. Lefkowitz 1989: 79; see also Dover 1974: 156.

[61] Like that of Iris and Lyssa, and even more than that of Heracles. Normally gods come on at the end of a play, human characters in the middle, but this order is reversed in the *Heracles*: Halleran 1985: 88–90.

[62] Schwinge 1972: 137–8; Bond 1981: 364. Porter 1987: 86–112, makes some illuminating remarks on the verbal parallels between both passages, although some are more convincing than others.

[63] Compare Theseus the volunteer, Plut. *Thes.* 17. 2, *Comp.Thes.* 1. 2. By contrast, Heracles is forced to do his deeds (*HF* 20).

imperial Athens in Thucydides (2. 39. 4), where Pericles compares the spontaneous excellence of the Athenian people with the Spartans' habitual slowness and selfishness.[64]

Theseus came as a military ally, σύμμαχον φέρων δόρυ ('bearing an allied spear', l. 1165), but when he learns that the time for such military assistance is long past, he will be Heracles' ally in his misfortune instead. From 1202ff., the συν- compounds are notable: συναλγῶν ('sharing your pain', *HF* 1202); σύν γε σοὶ ('with you', l. 1220) and συμπλεῖν ('sharing the voyage', l. 1225) all mark Theseus' determination to experience Heracles' bad fortune with him as once he enjoyed his help at the height of his powers.[65] This is the first time that reciprocity is in question for Heracles, and Theseus' tact in helping him is notable.[66] At 1236, Theseus tells him ἐγὼ δὲ πάσχων εὖ τοτ' οἰκτίρω σε νῦν ('I fared well and now I pity you'). This is the pity which is a part of Athenian ἐπιείκεια, the opposite of inflexibility and hubris, and which derives from intelligent awareness of one's own vulnerability. It was an essential attribute of Athens already in the *Suppliants*, and it will be seen again in the *Oedipus Coloneus*. Theseus' feelings lead the way for those of the audience, showing them how an Athenian treats the defeated and suffering: once more Theseus exemplifies the spirit of πολυπραγμοσύνη in its most glorious form. The chorus itself uses the vocabulary of ideal πολυπραγμοσύνη when condemning the tyrant Lycus: πράσσω πόλλ' ἐγώ ('am I interfering?') by helping my friends, they ask indignantly at l. 266;[67] but although they agree with Theseus on the rightness of helping friends in distress, unlike Theseus they lack the strength to provide active support. Hospitality, active help, and the confidence to help friends even at the risk of personal cost are all facets of the idealized image of Athens. τήν τε γὰρ πόλιν κοινὴν παρέχομεν ('we have an open city', Thuc. 2. 39. 1, cf. 40. 2); and only Athens gives 'the most secure

[64] Compare Isoc. 12. 170, who says that the Athenian people went to help Adrastus, 'without delay', at his request.

[65] Vickers 1973: 86; Walker 1995: 132 n. 57: cf. esp. καὶ γάρ ποτ' εὐτύχησ' (*HF* 1221) and 1223–5.

[66] Gregory 1977: 271. Note the euphemistic ἐφ' ἑτέραισι συμφοραῖς ('in different fortunes') of l. 1238. Walker 1995: 133 comments that Theseus' behaviour belongs to 'the code of a city of equal hoplites, where the *aristeia* performed by a noble warrior to further his own glory is replaced by the mutual protection of the phalanx, where each man's shield defends his neighbor'.

[67] And, as at *Supp.* 576–7, they use it in a context in which 'interfering' could only be commendable, thus vindicating πολυπραγμοσύνη.

refuge' (ἀσφαλεστάτην καταφυγήν) to the unfortunate because philosophy has taught the city to distinguish between misfortunes culpably incurred 'through ignorance' (δι' ἀμαθίαν) and those in
which the sufferer cannot be blamed for his suffering (ἐξ ἀνάγκης:
Isoc. 4. 47).

Theseus' first reaction to the horror of what Heracles has done is
one of conventional piety—εὔφημα φώνει[68]—but at once he understands the situation and ascribes responsibility for the disaster not
to the essentially guiltless Heracles, but to Hera (l. 1189).
Gradually, he will convince Heracles that his infanticide is no reason for him to remove himself from the rest of mankind. Heracles'
gradual return to human society is underlined by the stage directions implicit in Theseus' words. Amphitryon encourages Heracles
to unveil his head (ll. 1159 and 1202–3), but it is Theseus who
finally gets him to do so at l. 1226,[69] recalling Heracles' instructions
to his family to remove their mourning outfits at ll. 562–4. At l.
1394, he makes Heracles rise from the ground, encouraging him to
stop his lamentations, and at ll. 1398 and 1402, he gives him his
hand in support, just as Heracles did for Megara and his children at
625 f. Again, the parallels between the two sets of actions bring out
the reality of the comfort represented by Theseus and his city.
These parallels culminate in the striking repetition and reversal of
the image of Heracles the father tugging his children along as
though they were boats (ἐφολκίδες) at l. 632: by l. 1424, Heracles
himself needs to be borne along by his son and saviour.[70] Thanks
to Theseus' tact, and also his persistent persuasion,[71] Heracles will
go on living. Although some critics[72] have doubted the importance
of Theseus' role because nothing of what he actually argues is
explicitly accepted by Heracles as a valid reason for carrying on living, Heracles himself says that Theseus has arrived in time to prevent his suicide (l. 1153); and although the decision he makes to live
on is impelled by fear of being called a coward (l. 1348), it is

---

[68] 'Be silent!': *HF* 1185. On the order of the lines, see Bond 1981: 368.

[69] Porter 1987: 97.

[70] Halleran 1985: 91–2, and especially Barlow 1986: 108. See also 106–7 on the
yoke imagery in the play and its connections with the theme of friendship: the
imagery of ll. 454–5 and 1375–6 culminates in the ζεῦγος φίλιον ('friendly yoke') of
Heracles and Theseus at l. 1304.

[71] In the *Eumenides*, esp. l. 881, Athena's verbal persistence, avoiding physical
coercion, is also notable.

[72] e.g. Wilamowitz 1895: 126: *contra* Schwinge 1972: 164 f.

Theseus' persistent persuasion that has brought him to what is, in effect, a return to his former courage, if in straitened circumstances. Heracles' moral stature would, in any case, greatly be diminished for us if he were to accept that he was not guilty of killing his children, even though objectively, and as Theseus sees it, the infanticide is not his fault. To say 'the gods made me do it and I am not to blame' is unacceptable: to say 'the gods made you do it and you are not to blame' is possible.[73]

If Heracles is an ideal when he goes off to kill Lycus, Theseus will gain the highest honour for himself and his city by persuading him to come and live at Athens.[74] The cases of Oedipus and Orestes provide some parallel. Objectively speaking, Oedipus has committed parricide and incest, yet Theseus accepts that at a different level, Oedipus is innocent and deserves a home at Athens. Oedipus' fate was caused by the mysterious wishes of the gods, and Theseus exemplifies the wisest and best behaviour possible for a human being by simply showing compassion to him. By so doing, Theseus both maintains and enhances his reputation and also wins active benefits for his city by daring to take the apparently polluted suppliant into his city. The complexity of Orestes' case, and the rewards gained by Athens for wisdom and daring in judging it, have already been discussed; but it is worth noting in addition the difference in divine involvement between Euripides and Aeschylus. In the *Eumenides*, the gods, primarily Athena, take a far more active concern for human misfortune than do those of the *Heracles*, who are at most indifferent, and at worst, thoroughly cruel.[75] The *Heracles* has some features of a suppliant play: in the normal structure of such a play (such as the *Eumenides*), distressed suppliants come to a city, usually Athens, asking to be taken in, and the city's representatives must decide whether to risk the dangers posed to the people by accepting them: in the *Heracles*, the king of Athens actually comes to the distressed suppliant and offers him

---

[73] Compare the end of the *Choephori*, where the chorus (like Theseus in the *HF*) tries to reassure Orestes that he has done right, but Orestes (like Heracles in the *HF*) must accept full responsibility and guilt, to preserve his moral stature. As in the *Oresteia*, questions of responsibility, guilt and punishment attendant on that guilt are bound up with the will of the gods. The conflict between human responsibility for action and divine encouragement to do what might lead to punishment is endemic to the Greek theological system.

[74] So Chalk 1962: 15.

[75] Foley 1985: 165–7, comparing the *Oresteia* with the *Heracles*.

his protection. In Athenian ideology, it is only the daring city of Athens which has the courage and the strength voluntarily to incorporate among its citizens such potential dangers.[76] An invincible city has no need for εὐλάβεια.

In the way that he appears suddenly and takes command of the situation, Theseus is like a *deus ex machina*,[77] but whereas a real *deus* can provide an insight into divine motivation which is meant to explain tragic events to those who have suffered, even if it cannot exactly comfort them,[78] he remains rooted in the purely human world, and though he represents the very best of all human virtues, the human comfort which he provides is by definition limited. Although his discussions with Heracles play an important part in elucidating the themes of the earlier parts of the play, he cannot offer him anything other than advice to endure and the comforts of human fellowship, which are little enough compared with what a god might do, though helpful in view of what a god has done. As in the *Suppliants*, he represents (Athenian) humanity, and therefore, as we will see, also its limitations, but whereas in the *Suppliants* he withdraws from the Argives' tragedy after he has helped them, in the *Heracles*, he must stay with Heracles, and his limitations in the context of the world of the play are more clearly exposed. In the *Hippolytus*, Artemis can prophesy Hippolytus' future honours directly to him because she is a goddess, but Theseus' promises to Heracles that he will be worshipped at Athens must necessarily be rather vague (ll. 1331–3). It is fitting that the human hero should concentrate more on the honours to be gained by Heracles while he still lives at Athens (ll. 1325–31). The apotheosis of Heracles and his marriage to Hebe was a long-standing part of his tradition, and Burnett suggests that the play hints at this tradition at ll. 1151, 1240 and 1295–8, along with the emphasis on youth in the ode of 637 ff.; but it is not necessary to interpret these lines as a reference to action outside the play. It would be rather jarring for Heracles to take his place among the Olympians after what we are told about their dealings with him, and the overriding impression that the play gives is rather that a home in 'god-built Athens' is a kind of substitute for

[76] Foley 1985: 193: Aegeus does the same in the *Medea*, with potentially disastrous results, but in the *Aegeus*, however, Athens is able to withstand even Medea, and Athens is not permanently harmed by the open-door policy which Athenian writers loved to contrast with Spartan secrecy.

[77] Cf. Norwood 1953: 21; Silk 1985: 16.   [78] Cf. Lloyd-Jones 1983: 155.

apotheosis.[79] This is in keeping with the general ethos of the play. The ending is very far from a happy one, but the bleak view of the gods' relations with humans is offset by the promise of the possibility of affection and gratitude between human beings.[80]

The ingratitude of those who were supposed to be Heracles' friends is a dominant theme of the first part of the play,[81] and verbal links contrast the ungrateful Thebans and gods with Theseus. At l. 226, Amphitryon complains that no repayment (ἀμοιβάς) for Heracles' services is forthcoming from Thebes, and the same word is used by Theseus on his entry to explain why he has come to Thebes (l. 1169). Indeed, all of Greece except Athens has failed Heracles' family.[82] Alone of gods and man, Theseus has a moral sense of obligation to a benefactor, and the contrast between his gratitude and everyone else's ingratitude runs through the last scene, right up to Heracles' final judgement on his position at ll. 1425–6: ὅστις δὲ πλοῦτον ἢ σθένος μᾶλλον φίλων | ἀγαθῶν πεπᾶσθαι βούλεται, κακῶς φρονεῖ.[83] That Theseus is characterized in this way as soon as he appears immediately fixes his moral status in the play, because of the fundamental importance in Greek thought of the obligation of helping one's friends.[84] By rescuing Theseus from Hades, Heracles put Theseus in his debt, but in the *Heracles*, Theseus is able to return the benefit given to him by his friend by doing Heracles an even greater service, thus righting the balance of services rendered in Athens' favour: this is particularly appealing for an Athenian audience if I am right that Athens was uneasy about the idea of the rescue from Hades of the hero who normally exemplified Athenian piety and competence. By helping Heracles, he upholds the ethical ideals which fifth-century Athens perceived as particularly Athenian but which were also universally

[79] Cf. Arrowsmith 1969: 269; Tarkow 1977: 31 against Burnett 1971: 182.

[80] See also Foley 1985: 20, who has some interesting comments on the substitution of the city for the gods as saviours of human beings in Euripides.

[81] See ll. 84, 217–29, esp. 551, 555–9 and 561, 568, 762–80, 1334–9, 1403–4, 1425–6. Particularly effective in underlining divine ingratitude is Lyssa's reluctance to harm a man who has helped the gods: ll. 852–3.

[82] *HF* 222–6 with Drexler 1943: 322. In the *Heraclidae* (esp. 189–94), only Athens will help Heracles' children: cf. *Supp.* 187–8. See also Ch. 2 on the importance of Athens' unique stand against the Persians and the uniqueness of Athens in general.

[83] 'Whoever prefers wealth or strength to noble friends is foolish': Sheppard 1916: 73–8.

[84] See §2.4; Dover 1974: 180–4; Blundell 1989: 26–59; Adkins 1966.

admitted to be important in Greece as a whole. Unlike the Thebans and the gods, Theseus does not suffer from ἀμαθία: once again, Athens is portrayed as the most ethical city in Greece. We have already seen how the obligations attendant on so-called friendship could be used to justify an aggressive Athenian foreign policy, and the *Suppliants* is fairly explicit in commending vigorous Athenian activity beyond the borders of Attica. The action of the *Heracles* is influenced by similar factors, but at a deeper level: at first glance, the play is not nearly as explicitly patriotic as the *Suppliants*, but a close reading of the text reveals certain Athenian topoi which appear in both plays, and which can be related to an underlying ideology of a wider general scope.

Successful friendship necessitates a degree of strength.[85] At *HF* 55, Amphitryon distinguishes between two types of friends; the insincere (οὐ σαφεῖς) and the weak (ἀδύνατοι), which must include the decrepit chorus, whose loyalty to Heracles and his family is unquestionable, but who are unable to help them in their danger, as they themselves admit, ll. 312–14, 436–41, cf. 247–52, 275–8. In spite of his love for, and pride in his son (ll. 37, 46, 97), Amphitryon is himself old and incapable at the start of the play: at l. 42, he describes himself as 'useless' (ἀχρεῖος) and at 228, as 'feeble' (ἀσθενής).[86] Heracles is performing the labours on Amphitryon's behalf (*HF* 17–21), and in one sense Amphitryon's weakness is 'ingratitude' to his son for what Heracles is doing for him. It is significant that impotence and ingratitude are regarded as much the same as one another in the play, given the tendency in Athenian ideology for all intervention to be regarded as a benefit given by Athens to friends who cannot cope by themselves. Thus in this play, Theseus alone, as king of the strong city of Athens, is willing and able to offer active assistance to weaker friends.

In Greek literature, men are consistently portrayed as utterly inferior to the gods except insofar as they, unlike the gods, are capable of forgiveness, loyalty and true concern for the sufferings of their fellow humans.[87] Heracles' choice of Amphitryon instead of

---

[85] Cf. Chs. 2, 3 and 5. In other circumstances, this facet of the 'help friends' ethic can be used, for example, to justify the maintenance of a powerful Athenian navy.

[86] Bond 1981: 73 notes that ἀχρεῖος is commonly used of a citizen who is useless for any social purpose, citing Pericles' equation of the ἀπράγμων with the ἀχρεῖος (Thuc. 2. 40. 2).

[87] Cf. especially Lefkowitz 1989.

Zeus as a father (ll. 1264–5) marks the end of a series of ambiguities concerning Heracles' parentage, as Heracles consciously chooses what is human in preference to what is divine.[88] In the same way, Theseus treats Heracles as a human friend who is not immune to the possibility of divinely-caused misfortune, rather than as a semi-divine hero.[89] As in the *Suppliants* and *Oedipus Coloneus*, Theseus himself is Aegeus' son, not Poseidon's, and Amphitryon's first address to him—ὦ τὸν ἐλαιοφόρον ὄχθον ἔχων <ἄναξ> ('O lord of the olive-bearing hill')—identifies him closely with the polis of Athens.[90]

Certain currents of contemporary Athenian thought are notice-able in what Heracles and Theseus have to say to one another. Like Pylades in *Orestes* 792–4, Theseus values human friendship above the risk of incurring pollution. He unveils Heracles to the light, saving him from death as once Heracles saved him from Hades (ll. 1222–5), but Heracles thinks that Theseus will run the risk of being polluted thereby (l. 1233).[91] The question of pollution is reopened at the end of the play at l. 1399f., very strikingly, as Theseus pro-claims that he does not object even to being smeared with the chil-dren's blood.[92] The argument used by Theseus to show that he has no fear of pollution—οὐ μιαίνεις θνητὸς ὢν τὰ τῶν θεῶν (l. 1232)— is at first glance surprising because of its sophistic flavour,[93] and because it so strongly recalls Creon's argument justifying Antigone's imprisonment (S. *Ant.* 1043). The contexts of the two arguments are, however, entirely different. Creon is trying to jus-tify a crime against the gods; Theseus, to rescue Heracles from feel-ings of shame, guilt, and isolation from humanity which are attendant on pollution.[94] Like the later argument of Theseus at ll. 1314–21, it is a far from perfect argument, but in the context of

[88] *HF* 1–3, 339–47, 353–4, 501, 696, 798–804, 826 (with Bond). Note also *HF* 1113, where Amphitryon reaffirms his relationship with his son, in contrast to the silence of Zeus.

[89] *HF* 1195, 1232, 1248: cf. Silk 1985: 13–16; Gregory 1977: 270.

[90] *HF* 1178; cf. S. *OC* 17, 717; E. *Ion* 480–3.

[91] For pollution by sight alone, compare, for example, E. *El.* 1195 and *Hipp.* 946; by touch, S. *OC* 1132; see Bond 1981: 354, on 1155f. On pollution in general, see Parker 1983.

[92] οὐκ ἀναίνομαι of 1400 compares with οὐκ ἀναίνομαι of 632.

[93] 'As a mortal, you cannot pollute what belongs to the gods'; see e.g. Kerferd 1981: 164–71.

[94] Parker 1983: 109–11.

Hera's dealings with Heracles, it is the best that can be managed.[95] Theseus' argument is not impious: on the level of ritual, he still accepts the idea of pollution, and must purify Heracles at Athens (*HF* 1325), because he cannot stay at Thebes (l. 1322).[96] The argument is, however, essentially rationalistic,[97] and in a sense it treats the more mysterious aspects of the gods as irrelevant to human experience. One should not assume that this comparative disregard for pollution is part of a general trend in Athenian society,[98] because so fundamentally disturbing a notion as pollution is bound to create conflicting but coexisting attitudes towards dealing with it. However, Theseus' arguments may well have been classified by a contemporary audience as those of enlightened opinion,[99] since the rationalistic approach to matters which traditionally had a purely religious importance is a particular feature of fifth-century scientific writing.[100] Moreover, the *Heracles* can be fitted into a dramatic pattern whose outlines are already seen in the *Eumenides* of 458, and subsequently in the *Oedipus Coloneus*, and even in the *Medea*. The plays show Athens as the only city ready to accept people who are polluted by crimes committed in their own cities.[101] Thuc. 2. 37. 2 says that Athens especially obeys those laws 'that help the unjustly treated' (ἐπ' ὠφελίᾳ τῶν ἀδικουμένων): Orestes, Heracles, Oedipus and even Medea could all be described as 'unjustly treated'. It is unlikely that the Athenian dramatists would portray their city as doing what was ethically or religiously suspect, and it is likely too that the 'school of Hellas' would wish to see itself as enlightened, though also pious. Theseus may therefore represent

---

[95] *HF* 1232 has a faint echo of l. 341, another passage contrasting unfavourably divine and human morality.

[96] See Parker 1983: 310 and Macdowell 1963: 118–20. Exile was the penalty for unintentional homicide in Draco's law.

[97] Bond 1981: 359–60; Foley 1985: 162. Compare also the remarks of ch. 2 regarding the importance placed by Pericles on the mastering of superhuman forces by human intelligence.

[98] See Dodds 1951: 36–7.

[99] He is perhaps slightly more 'enlightened' than Sophocles' Theseus, who does not offer to touch Oedipus (*OC* 1132–4): Parker 1983: 309–10.

[100] For example, the Hippocratic *On the Sacred Disease*, chs. 4, 21. See Guthrie 1969: iii. 55–84, on the influence of natural philosophy on traditional views of religion and Farrar 1988: 38.

[101] Similarly, in the *Suppliants*, Adrastus is accepted by Athens in spite of past mistakes, although he is, of course, not literally polluted.

an outlook which was recognizably that of Athenian progressive, democratic thought to an Athenian audience.[102]

While he agrees with Heracles that his sufferings are greater than anyone else's, Theseus exhibits a mixture of conventional piety[103] and rationalism by refusing to accept that suicide is the proper action for Heracles. His suicide will achieve nothing: it will merely be a gesture of defiance towards the gods, who will not be swayed by such futile gestures,[104] presumably because they are too powerful to concern themselves with such things. Theseus' view of the gods is respectful, and he accepts that they have the power to punish man for impiety (*HF* 1243–4). Indeed, Heracles criticizes the gods far more directly than Theseus does, particularly in his great speech of 1255 ff. Theseus' attitude to Hera's action is one of simple acceptance, but he shows no real interest in understanding why she should have done as she did, and concentrates almost exclusively on what can be done on a human plane to help his friend. His arguments as to why Heracles should continue to live are almost all based on ethical, rather than religious, grounds;[105] and one has the impression, that while the divine is not exactly irrelevant to Theseus, his interest lies in Heracles the man, and in human reasons for Heracles to carry on living, rather than reasons based on the nature of gods whose ways need not resemble human ways. Human courage, as expected of a man like Heracles, is to accept and endure, and to live on for the benefit of humanity, maintaining his reputation for outstanding help to his fellow men.[106] That the 'easily-living gods' are different from human beings is an idea at least as old as the *Iliad*;[107] although Euripides' gods in this play are

---

[102] Tarkow 1977: 32 is surely wrong to assume that an Athenian audience would have thought that Theseus was rash to accept Heracles immediately, recalling Aegeus' acceptance of Medea, who nearly killed his son. Athens alone of all the Greek cities is strong enough to absorb and turn to the city's benefit anyone who comes to the city.

[103] *HF* 1244, cf. S. *Aj.* 361–2.

[104] *Hf* 1241 prefigures 1254's accusation of ἀμαθία. I am not sure that the lacuna after 1241 accepted by Bond (after W. Schmid and Broadhead) is necessary.

[105] Note especially the exchange at ll. 1253–4: cf. James 1969: 15.

[106] See *HF* 1227 and esp. 1248—εἴρηκας ἐπιτυχόντος ἀνθρώπου λόγους ('You have spoken like an ordinary man'). There are parallels between Theseus' advice to Heracles and Amphitryon's optimism against Megara's pessimism at *HF* 90–106, cf. 275–318: Chalk 1962: 9; Gregory 1977: 262 and Heath 1987: 161.

[107] e.g. *Il.* 2. 110–18, and see J. Griffin 1980: 167–72, and Heath 1987: 51. Although Matthiesen 1979: 148–52 suggests that a more optimistic view of the gods' justice was a part of Athenian democratic thought about the gods (as E. *Supp.*

rather less attractive than those of Homer, the Hera who strikes Heracles down is not that far removed from the Hera of *Il.* 4. 51–4, who trades the destruction of three of her cities for revenge on Troy.

Suicide itself was not regarded in Greece with particular horror, especially in cases of acute shame,[108] but whereas in four plays of Sophocles there are five suicides (cf. *OT* 1368), in the whole of Euripides, only Phaedra, Jocasta and Evadne die thus, and more than once his characters condemn suicide as an answer to their problems.[109] As with the case of pollution, it would be unwise to be dogmatic about whether this is Euripidean or indicative of wider trends; and from a dramatic point of view, the suicide of Heracles may have been too great an innovation in the myth for the audience to have accepted it. Even so, it may be that suicide was not generally commended in democratic Athens, and was rather viewed as the act of an individualistic hero, incompatible with a more collective mentality.[110] Responding to misfortune by committing suicide is essentially an anti-social, inflexible response to the unexpectedness of human events. As we saw in the *Suppliants*, flexibility is an Athenian characteristic, and one essential for human happiness in an uncertain world.[111] In Sophocles especially, the hero's intransigence often precipitates the tragic events, and both in Sophocles and Aeschylus, characters rarely change their minds: when they do, the change tends to be regarded as something imposed from outside, often by a god, rather than a willing decision.[112] For the Euripidean hero, however, a change is possible, even if not easy (*HF* 1357), under the persuasion of Theseus in his role as substitute *deus ex machina*.

198ff.), this is only really true in accounts of divine dealings with the virtuous city of Athens. At Thuc. 5. 105. 2, the gods are assumed to act according to the law of the stronger.

[108] Demosthenes, who killed himself after the Athenian disaster at Sicily, had his name on the commemorative stele; Nicias, who surrendered, did not (Paus. 1. 29. 12).

[109] At *Or.* 415, Menelaus says μὴ θάνατον εἴπῃς. τοῦτο μὲν γὰρ οὐ σοφόν ('Do not speak of death; it is not sensible:') see also E. fr. 1070.

[110] De Romilly 1968: 135; Dover 1974: 167–9. Cf. also Bond's (1981: 402) excellent note on *HF* 1347ff.: 'It requires an effort to remember that Euripides' plays were written for an audience who spent much of their lives on military service. In hoplite fighting cowardice is particularly anti-social.'

[111] De Romilly 1968: 118ff. and 131.   [112] Knox 1966: 231–74.

It would be an exaggeration to think that this 'enlightened' Theseus was directly criticizing the older heroic ethos as embodied in Ajax's suicide, and setting up a different kind of heroic ἀρετή.[113] Ajax never doubted that killing the Atreidae was right, and kills himself for shame at his failure and loss of honour. To change would be to lose face in front of a human enemy,[114] but Heracles' enemy is Hera. Although she caused him to kill his children shamefully, this is clearly not a loss of ἀρετή in the same sense as that of Ajax. The two worlds of these tragedies are differentiated from one another most of all by their treatment of friendship. There is a much stronger emphasis on the value of human affection (φιλία) in the *Heracles* than in the *Ajax*.[115] Sophocles uses Ajax's aporetic 'where can I go?' questions to emphasize his desolation, but in Euripides such questions (*HF* 1282–90) are answered by an invitation to Athens.[116] For Ajax, even human affection is not to be trusted because of the changeability of the world,[117] but for Heracles, the changeability of the world can be borne because of his friendship with Theseus.

Suicide would be the right course of action if Heracles' was a case of culpable shame, but as it is, only by living and enduring, can he act heroically, as befits his past life.[118] Theseus strongly asserts the values of life in a human community over the uncertainties and cruelties that come from the gods, and in his attempts to persuade Heracles to live on, he concentrates on his responsibility to other human beings who need him as the gods do not need him. Thus it is that he addresses Heracles at l. 1250 as ὁ πολλὰ δὴ τλάς ('much-enduring'), calling him εὐεργέτης βροτοῖσι καὶ μέγας φίλος ('great friend and benefactor of humanity'), and at l. 1254, he reminds him of his responsibilities to Greece at large. Theseus the Athenian has the intellect to look beyond Heracles the infanticide, and by following τὸ ἐπιεικές rather than τὸ δίκαιον, recognizes greatness even when it is temporarily overshadowed.[119] Such intelligence is

---

[113] Furley 1986: 110; *contra* Zürcher 1947: 106. *HF* 106 and 1227 do, however, set up a different idea of heroic conduct from S. *Aj.* 479–80.

[114] James 1969: 10f.

[115] ll. 57–9, 1425–6: the word φιλία and its compounds appear over sixty times in the *HF*, compared with thirty in the *Ajax*: B. Simon 1978: 131 n. 19. See also Stanford 1983: 38–40 on φιλία and its objects.

[116] De Romilly 1980.   [117] S. *Aj.* 678–83, 1359–61; see James 1969: 18.

[118] De Romilly 1980: 10: Heracles accepts this at *HF* 1351.

[119] Chalk 1962: 13.

beneficial to Heracles, to Athens, in the reputation she will earn from the rest of Greece (*HF* 1334–5), and to Greece.

Although Heracles cannot expressly say that Theseus has persuaded him to live, and must regard his whole life with disgust, enumerating his labours very differently from their earlier enumeration by the chorus (ll. 1255–80, cf. 347–435), already at l. 1306 he describes himself as 'the foremost man in Greece' (ἄνδρ' Ἑλλάδος τὸν πρῶτον) and not guilty (αἴτιος, l. 1310), which is how Theseus views him, and puts some of the blame on Hera, as Theseus does. Thus there is an active link between what Theseus says and Heracles' eventual acceptance of life, which is symbolized by his picking up his bow at l. 1385. This is like the old Heracles, the man of endurance who cannot endure the charge of cowardice (l. 1348).[120] Although Heracles has superficially lost the glorious position which was once his, and must now depend on Theseus, Theseus is not exalted at his expense. Theseus' greatness is as a model of human nobility and intelligence, but, as Heracles points out at *HF* 1249, he is ἐκτὸς . . . συμφορᾶς ('not involved in the suffering'). Heracles' nobility and endurance in the face of such suffering leaves his heroism unchallenged by Theseus', whose heroism is confined to intelligence, kindness and positive action on the human plane.

It seems clear that some lines of the play have been lost after l. 1312. It is impossible to say how much has been lost, but it is not necessary to assume that Heracles' subsequent change of mind is motivated by what Theseus said here, given Heracles' more self-assertive tone already at 1302 ff.[121] The general sense of what is missing is perhaps most plausibly supplied by Drexler,[122] who suggests that before παραινέσαιμ' ἂν μᾶλλον ἢ πάσχειν κακῶς ('I would advise you . . . rather than to suffer'), one should expect a conditional clause setting forth an alternative; and the most likely alternative to πάσχειν κακῶς would seem to be death. Thus the burden of Theseus' speech might be: 'if you alone had suffered, I would advise you to die rather than to suffer, but, as it is, no mor-

---

[120] Furley 1986: 109. There is no sign that he has found an essentially different, non-violent kind of ἀρετή: Bond 1981: p. xxii against Wilamowitz 1895: 129. Nor has he lost his essential ἀρετή: Stinton 1975, citing Thuc. 2. 52. 5, against Adkins 1966: 209. It is indicative of the cruelty of the world of the *Heracles* that human ἀρετή can only amount to endurance in the face of unbelievable suffering.

[121] As Pohlenz 1954: 125.

[122] Drexler 1943: 333 n. 21, with Schwinge 1972: 163. See also Bond 1981: 392.

tal or god is unassailed by fortune.' It is, however, clear that the (mis)deeds of the gods—adultery, mistreatment of parents—which Theseus goes on to list are hardly misfortunes like those of Heracles.[123] An obvious parallel is the sophistry of the nurse to Phaedra at *Hippolytus* 443–61, where she appeals to the ways of the gods to justify what is not justifiable for Phaedra.[124]

Like the pollution argument above, this is a flawed argument, because it is human and exclusively rational, and one has the impression that Theseus is discussing divine behaviour purely to comfort Heracles, rather than presenting a serious argument with theological implications: he is more concerned with alleviating his friend's distress, using any arguments he can, than with a theodicy. His previous argument depended on the view that Heracles' threats of suicide would not interest the gods—that is, that the gods cannot be assumed to be like human beings; but now, in his attempts to persuade Heracles, he suggests that humans can only follow divine example, even though such examples as he gives are at odds with normal human morality. What is a slightly confused theology arises from Theseus' goodwill towards Heracles, and also from a sense that the gods are essentially mysterious and cannot be relied on. What is implied in Theseus' earlier dialogue with Heracles (l. 1242), that the gods cannot be assumed to be like men, is borne out by the rest of the play. The human friendship of Theseus and Heracles is all the more sure and stable in comparison. Although the representative of Athens may not, and cannot, have all the right answers, he has the right character to salvage whatever can be salvaged.[125]

Theseus is on solider ground at ll. 1322–31 when he offers human remedies for Heracles' distress. The main remedy is the city of Athens, for which he will leave Thebes. In Athens, Theseus the powerful king will have the ability to purify him, and the power of human φιλία exemplified by Theseus will get Heracles' splendour in a form more human, predictable, and beneficial than anything that the gods have sent.[126] A visible and lasting memorial of Heracles will be the enclosures generously given to him by

---

[123] Grube 1941: 58. They rather add to the unlovely impression of the gods which we get from this play: ἐκηλίδωσαν ('stained') of l. 1318 is a very condemnatory word.

[124] Compare also the comic but disturbing results of such a line of thought taken to its logical extreme by Pheidippides in the *Clouds*.

[125] Cf. Tarkow 1977: 30.   [126] Foley 1985: 165; Vickers 1973: 229.

Theseus. These enclosures were originally the gift of the twice seven to their saviour Theseus, and now Theseus the saviour passes them on to someone else in need of his help. In this part of the speech, Theseus, his city and his citizens are all one[127] and the hint of Heracles' cult conveyed by the words τεμένη ('enclosures', l. 1329) and λάϊνοισί τ' ἐξογκώμασιν ('stone monuments', l. 1332) recalls the speech of a normal *deus ex machina*.

Heracles' immediate response is to refute Theseus' attempts to comfort him, denying that the gods are capable of the crimes which Theseus ascribes to them: δεῖται γὰρ ὁ θεός, εἴπερ ἔστ' ὀρθῶς θεός, | οὐδενός· ἀοιδῶν οἵδε δύστηνοι λόγοι ('the god, if he is truly a god, needs nothing: these are wretched tales of poets'). If ll. 1340–6 in conjunction with ll. 1307–8 are taken literally, they make nonsense of the whole of the story, including that of Heracles' divine birth;[128] but l. 1315 is echoed so closely by l. 1346, and ll. 1316–18 by 1341–2 that it is reasonable to take 1341 ff. purely as an *ad hominem* reply to Theseus,[129] in which he denies that the gods could possibly behave like this, and clings instead to a more comforting view of them. His argument is all the more pathetic because we have just seen the agents of a goddess very different from the autonomous deity who needs nothing:[130] Hera does, in fact, need her revenge over Heracles, and both before 1341 ff., and after it (l. 1393), Heracles seems to accept this. σοφωτέρους γὰρ χρὴ βροτῶν εἶναι θεούς (E. *Hipp.* 120); ὀργὰς πρέπει θεοὺς οὐχ ὁμοιοῦσθαι βροτοῖς (E. *Ba.* 1348); gods should be wiser than men, gods should never behave as badly as humans can. χρή, πρέπει and εἴπερ ἔστ' ὀρθῶς θεός express some doubt over this proposition, but also a pious hope that it is true. We know it is not.[131] It would be an unusual human religion which fully accepted the idea that there are beings more powerful than we are whose actions are entirely unpredictable. We want the gods to be like us, but better and just according to our understanding of the term. Often the workings of the gods can be interpreted to suit human ideas of justice, but in Heracles' case, this is not so, and therefore the whole notion of

---

[127] Tarkow 1977: 27.

[128] Ehrenberg 1946: 162; Brown 1978. A milder form of the idea is in Conacher 1967: 88–90.

[129] Bond 1981: 399; Heath 1987: 61.   [130] Knox 1966: 327.

[131] Stinton 1976: 83; Silk 1985: 16. A good parallel is Hecuba's profession of faith in the gods' goodness at *Tro.* 969 ff.; see also *IT* 380 ff., *El.* 75 ff., *IA* 793 ff.

divine justice comes into question. Heracles states that real gods simply cannot at all be like the beings we have seen on stage because such deities are too dreadful to contemplate. The spectators of the tragedy, however, see a difference between these gods and human beings who care for one another. The view of the gods expounded by Heracles at 1341 ff. is entirely belied by the rest of the play: Theseus and Athens are his only sure hope.

Thus it is that in spite of what he says at 1341 ff., Heracles decides to live.[132] He refuses to incur the charge of cowardice (δειλία), which is essentially very like ἀμαθία (cf. ll. 1349–50, 1227–8). He will endure[133] and though he is crying as he has never cried before (l. 1353), he will bravely accept Theseus' offer of a home in Athens. Theseus' services to Heracles do not end there, as Heracles must make one last request: ἔν μοί τι, Θησεῦ, σύγκαμν᾽· ἀγρίου κυνὸς | κόμιστρ᾽ ἐς Ἄργος συγκατάστησον μολών ('Help me with one thing, Theseus; go to Argos and arrange my reward for conveying the wild dog', ll. 1386–7).[134] Although such a request should be interpreted primarily in the context of Heracles' own weakness and desire not to be left alone with the knowledge of what he has done, at a secondary level, the request enables Heracles' greatest labour, the symbolic triumph over death, to be shared with Theseus.[135] Theseus' impious journey to the underworld with Peirithous in early myth seems very far away indeed.

By the final stichomythia, Theseus is clearly in command, dispensing imperatives and advice, as Heracles' adopted son, friend and guide, and both Heracles and Amphitryon praise him, and Athens, warmly (*HF* 1404–5).[136] There is a painful contrast between the earlier part of the play, in which Heracles is a devoted husband, father and son, and this ending, where Heracles' only surviving relative is his old father, still as powerless to improve the situation as he had been when Lycus was in control.[137] Words and stage action combine to make a most moving picture: it is, however, marred for a modern audience by the rather unedifying exchange at

---

[132] Influenced by Theseus, although the impression gained is that it is Heracles' independent choice: Drexler 1943: 334; Schwinge 1972: 176.

[133] βίοτον is preferred by Bond 1981: 402–3, but θάνατον is the manuscript reading: whichever is accepted, the meaning is the same: Schwinge 1972: 173 with older literature.

[134] For a slightly different translation, see Bond 1981 on *HF* 1387.

[135] See also §7.6.2.   [136] Compare Adrastus' attitude in the *Suppliants*.

[137] See also Bond 1981: 415–16 on the parallels between the two scenes.

ll. 1410–16, which slightly detracts from Theseus' humanity towards Heracles. This may just be a matter of modern taste,[138] and in any case, it is a partial resumption of earlier themes of the scene. At l. 1248, Theseus reminds Heracles that he is a great hero who should not be bowed by misfortune, to which Heracles' response is σὺ δ᾽ ἐκτὸς ὤν γε συμφορᾶς με νουθετεῖς ('you, who are not involved in the suffering, rebuke me'), followed by a miserable catalogue of reasons why his life is not worth living. At 1410f., when needled by Theseus, again Heracles reminds Theseus that his suffering is exceptional, but by this time he has recovered enough of his heroic pride to remind Theseus of what he did for him once: Theseus has the grace immediately to acknowledge this at l. 1416;[139] and the gulf in heroism between the pair is retained.

In spite of the emphasis on the comforts of human friendship, the ending of the *Heracles* is not happy: Heracles is a broken man, and the very real problems of the theodicy are not remotely resolved. Whereas Aeschylus' *Eumenides* shows that the gods can be benign to those who deserve it by their wisdom, no such promises are made by the end of Euripides' play. Human goodness as exemplified by Theseus and Athens is a marvellous thing, but, given the world in which it operates, its value is limited. The same is true of Euripides' *Suppliants* and Sophocles' *Oedipus Coloneus*. It would therefore be misleading to think of such tragedies as Athenian 'propaganda': unlike the encomia of Athens which we find in the *epitaphioi*, they do not exclude complexity, uncertainty and suffering. At the same time, however, to ignore the strong undercurrent of Athenian ideology in the *Heracles* would be to fail to grasp an important facet of the tragedy. Although it may seem a rather paradoxical assertion in the light of the emphasis placed on the role of Theseus in this chapter, the *Heracles* is not, in fact, a play primarily about Athens, but rather a play about divinity and humanity. For the reasons which we have seen, Heracles cannot kill himself when he realizes that he has killed his children, but nor can he cheer *himself* by putting the blame for the infanticide on Hera. Someone else must therefore be introduced to save Heracles from an unjust death. For the Athenian Euripides, who could scarcely

---

[138] Bond 1981: 417–18, suggests that the exchange would go better between *HF* 1253 and 1254, but cites E. *El.* 508–46, and H. *Od.* 24. 235 ff. as parallels for his kind of 'callousness' (pp. 411–12).

[139] *HF* 1416. Compare a milder expression of the same point at S. *OC* 592–4.

have avoided being influenced by Athens' self-perception, the only possible candidate for such a role was Theseus. Naturally, in a tragic world like that of the *Heracles*, we can have no happy ending, but intelligence and humaneness can help to alleviate suffering to some extent. Athens, as exemplified by Theseus, makes the very best of a thoroughly imperfect world.

5

Theseus at Colonus

5.1 INTRODUCTION

The previous chapter traced the influence of Athenian ideals on Euripides' reinvention of the myth of Heracles' madness. Theseus' encounter with Heracles is almost certainly Euripides' own extension of older traditions of Athenian hospitality to distressed suppliants, so as to include Greece's greatest hero in the list of clients of Athens. In *Oedipus at Colonus*, Sophocles takes the process of Athenian reinvention even further. Although Oedipus, like Heracles, is a well-established figure in Greek mythology, he has no close or early connections with Attica, and the help Athens gives to him has no roots in mainstream Greek tradition.[1] Sophocles' account may instead be seen as a kind of local variant of the Oedipus story, whose primary interest is for Athenians. Moreover, Oedipus is a figure whose appalling crimes had perhaps previously made any help or resolution of his sufferings unthinkable. The daring of Sophocles in suggesting that he could be welcomed into the city is akin to the daring of Athens in the face of danger that is emphasized in the Athenian encomia. The mythological expansionism which claims for Athens a share in non-Athenian myths, and even resolution of their problems by a virtuous representative of the city is, perhaps, akin to Athenian territorial expansionism and its justification in terms of the justice and τόλμα of Athens (cf. Thuc. 2. 41. 4).

---

[1] Although Dem. 18. 186 includes the help given to Oedipus among the many benefits given by Athens to Thebes (entirely against the spirit of Sophocles' play), neither of the two receptions is included in the encomiasts' canon of the glorious deeds of Athens.

5.2 FROM THEBES TO ATHENS: OEDIPUS' DEATH
BEFORE SOPHOCLES[2]

Although it is clear that Oedipus died at Thebes in the earliest versions of the story,[3] exile is an obvious response to the crimes of incest and parricide which put Oedipus far beyond the boundaries of normal social relations,[4] and it would be surprising if there were no traditions in which he was exiled before *Oedipus Coloneus*.[5] Indeed, Sophocles' earlier Oedipus play is rather ambiguous concerning his eventual fate.[6] We are told more than once that Laius' killer must be punished with exile,[7] and at the end of the play he begs again and again to be expelled from Thebes (*OT* 1340ff. 1410ff., 1436, 1449ff. and 1517; cf. *OT* 420–2, 1026, esp. 1086–93, and 1290). Although at this point it is more dramatically effective that Creon should not immediately grant Oedipus his wish, so that his fate may remain horribly uncertain, as early as *OT* 454–6, Teiresias had already prophesied the very scene which greets us at the start of the *Coloneus*:

> τυφλὸς γὰρ ἐκ δεδορκότος
> καὶ πτωχὸς ἀντὶ πλουσίου ξένην ἔπι
> σκήπτρῳ προδεικνὺς γαῖαν ἐμπορεύσεται.

('Blind, no longer seeing, and a beggar instead of a rich man, he will journey in a strange land, showing the way forward with his staff.')

Sophocles offers exile as one of the destinies possible for Oedipus, at least, and it is quite likely that he was not the first writer to imagine such a fate for him.

[2] For accounts of the Oedipus myth, see Robert 1915; T. von Wilamowitz, 1917: 313–76; Deubner 1942: 39–43; Valgiglio 1963. 20ff. and 153–71; Kirsten 1973; Edmunds 1981; Bremmer 1987: 4–8.

[3] *Il.* 23. 679 with *Σ*; *Od.* 11. 271–80; *Thebaid* 2–3; also Paus. 1. 28. 7 and no. 131 in *Papiri Greci e Latini*, ii. 51–2. See also Parsons 1977: 7–36, esp. 20; March 1987: 131.

[4] Cf. Parker 1983: 104–43, esp. 113f., 387; Macdowell 1963: 120–5.

[5] Thus it would be possible that Pind. *Pyth.* 4. 263 (*c*.462 BC) refers to Oedipus' exile: Edmunds 1981: 224–5 with older literature: Braswell 1988: 362 denies it but gives no specific reason for doing so. Deubner 1942: 41–2 suggested that the source behind Androtion's account of Oedipus' last days in Attica (*FGrH* 324 F62) was Aeschylus' *Oedipus*, because it differs from Sophocles' account; however, the discrepancies between the two accounts are minor, and at most Androtion may be combining an earlier tradition in which Oedipus was buried in Boeotia (cf. *FGrH* 382 F2) and Sophocles: Valgiglio 1963: 27; Robert 1915: 1–9; Bremmer 1987: 49; on Androtion's account, see now also Harding 1994: 192.

[6] Cf. Taplin 1978: 45–6; see also M. Davies 1982.

[7] By the oracle, *OT* 96–8, 100, and Oedipus himself, ll. 236, 308f., 816ff.

Euripides' *Phoenissae* of 409 BC explicitly refers, not only to Oedipus' exile, but also to his reception at Colonus (*Phoen.* 1690, 1703–7). The play has certainly suffered at the hands of at least one interpolator, but a case can be made for accepting the exile, if not the reception at Colonus, as Euripides' own conclusion to the Oedipus story, rather than that of a later interpolator. First, Euripides has deliberately kept his Oedipus alive through his sons' civil wars, and it is likely that he did so, either with some existing tradition in mind,[8] or so as to set the crowning misery of exile on the old man's life. Second, the exile is a recurring motif throughout the last 150 lines of the play: such references are perfectly well integrated into their context, so that it would seem legitimate to doubt whether every single reference to an exile could be spurious.[9] The main point of importance is that as soon as he is turned out of Thebes, Oedipus is a potential candidate for Athenian assistance, with a view to Athens' own credit and benefit: the framework, so familiar by now, of Athens' never-failing help to the wretched will be imposed on the Oedipus story to bring it to a uniquely Athenian conclusion.

5.3 COLONUS, CULT AND HISTORY

It is unlikely that Sophocles could have invented the physical details of a grove at Colonus, and thus probable enough that he did not invent the cult of the Eumenides there, either: it seems to have been associated with a rift in the ground there which was believed to connect with the underworld.[10] As for Oedipus' links with the Erinyes, his crimes are precisely those in which they had an interest;[11] thus a special association between Oedipus and the Erinyes would be intelligible even on a theoretical level, and there is some

---

[8] Conacher 1967: 94.

[9] E. *Phoen.* 1584–94, 1619–26, 1644, 1663–79, 1710, 1723: Kitto 1939: 105. The specific references to Colonus have with more reason been suspected: Fraenkel 1963; Reeve 1972: 468. For an exhaustive discussion of the problem, see Müller-Goldingen 1985: 255–6, who decides in their favour: see, however, n. 17 below.

[10] Physical conditions are similar on the Areopagus where the Eumenides were also worshipped, and where Oedipus' grave was also located: Paus. 1. 28. 7; Val.Max. 5. 3. 3. The location on the Areopagus probably post-dates that of Colonus: Kirsten 1973: 22, cf. Kearns 1989: 50, 208–9.

[11] For Oedipus and the Erinyes, see *Od.* 11. 271–80; *Thebaid* 2. 8; Pind. *Ol.* 2. 31–42; A. *Sept.* 69–70, 975–7; E. *Phoen.* 624; Euphorion ap. *ΣOC* 681. See also Brown 1984: 260; Edmunds 1981: 222–3; Blundell 1990: 11, 92.

evidence, though it is admittedly rather scrappy, to suggest that they were linked in cult before Sophocles.[12] At Athens (or rather the idealized Athens of encomia), the Erinyes have a special kind of significance: known as the Eumenides or Semnae,[13] they pursue criminals, as the Erinyes traditionally did, but they do so as part of the Athenian polis, which allows for degrees of guilt, the importance of intention, and the importance of flexibility to temper the violence of straight retribution.[14] Because it was wished upon him by higher powers and entirely unintentional, Oedipus' parricide and incest is a particularly suitable case for Athens to consider in tragedy.

Colonus itself is sacred to Theseus' divine father Poseidon (himself called σεμνός, l. 55), and the rift in the ground which is associated with the Eumenides must also be identified with the way down to the underworld used by Theseus and Peirithous.[15] It is therefore quite probable that there was a particular association between Theseus and Colonus before Sophocles; by Pausanias' day, a *heroon* of Peirithous and Theseus and Oedipus and Adrastus was situated at Colonus (Paus. 1. 30. 4). Adrastus' connection with this *heroon* surely antedates that of Oedipus, and may go back even to the *Theseid*:[16] perhaps the story of Adrastus' supplication had some influence on the later story of Oedipus' own reception.

At *OC* 616–23 and 1524–37 Oedipus warns Theseus of war between Thebes and Athens in the future: although these prophecies are vague in themselves, they are sometimes held to recall the defeat suffered by Agis and a large troop of Boeotian cavalry near the Academy, near Colonus, in 407.[17] ΣOC 57 quotes an oracle referring to an attack of the Boeotians on Colonus (Βοιωτοὶ δ᾽

---

[12] Hdt. 4. 149. 2; probably at Sicyon: ΣE. *Phoen.* 26 and Paus. 2. 11. 4, with Bethe 1895: 67–74; perhaps Cithaeron, according to [Plut.] *de fluv.* 2. 3. In general, Edmunds 1981: 225–9; cf. Robert 1915: 21.

[13] Paus. 1. 28. 6. As the Semnae, cf. *OC* 41, 55, 90.

[14] Jebb 1900: p. xxvii; Kirkwood 1986: 108.

[15] Compare ll. 56–8 with ll. 1590–4. See also Jebb 1900: p. xxxvi, 245–6.

[16] The story of Adrastus' flight from Thebes, after his army's failed attempt to take it—clearly the starting point for the reception at Eleusis—was already in the *Thebaid*, and Jacoby, 1954: 442–8, esp. 444, suggests that an Eleusinian story, or even the *Theseid*, recounted the story of his reception and the burial of his dead: see also §7.3.

[17] D.S. 13. 72–3. 2. ΣAristid. 3. 188 Lenz-Behr (Dindorf, iii. 560) mentions an Athenian defeat of Thebes gained with Oedipus' assistance, but gives no date for it. If Diodorus' dating is right, the battle will post-date the *Phoenissae*: this might suggest that the references to Colonus were inserted by a later hand (cf. n. 9 above).

ἵπποιο ποτιστείχουσι Κολωνόν | ἔνθα λίθος τρικάρανος ἔχει καὶ
χάλκεος οὐδός), which seems to hint at the defeat of Thebes by
Athens. The references to an Athenian defeat of Thebans at
Colonus might possibly be independent of traditions deriving from
Sophocles, since there is no mention of Oedipus in either the
oracle or Diodorus, and the historical details that Diodorus gives
do not entirely conform to what is said in the play. It would therefore be conceivable that Sophocles was expanding and exploring a
story of Oedipus in Attica which had been invented to explain
Athens' recent victory over Thebes.[18] However, the emphasis laid
by the play on the protection of Attica by Oedipus would be equally
intelligible as a general reassurance in the context of a long-
protracted war, without reference to existing tradition. The 'risk
and reward' motif, which influences Theseus' actions so frequently, usually demands that the Athenians receive some sort of
benefit from the suppliants they have helped, and ideological tendencies, at least as much as history or cult as such, lie behind
Sophocles' play. Even if many constituent elements of the story of
the *Oedipus Coloneus* were not invented by Sophocles, his form of
the story conforms to a well established pattern of 'reception of a
suppliant by Athens', and will not antedate the late fifth century.

5.4 THESEUS AND OEDIPUS

The play begins as Oedipus and Antigone have found their way
unknowingly into the grove of the Eumenides at Colonos Hippios
in Attica. Their intrusion into the sacred ground is a source of
alarm, first to a local man who meets them, and then to his fellows
(the chorus); Oedipus, however, knows, thanks to an oracle given
to him by Apollo (85 ff.), that he has reached the place where he will
die and that he can offer Athens his protection after his death. He
is persuaded to move out of the grove by the chorus on condition
that they will not drive him forth (176), but their promise is
revoked when they discover his identity (229 f.). The two Theban
exiles appeal for mercy (237 ff., 258 ff.) so that the chorus are torn

---

[18] As, tentatively, Kearns 1989: 51, 209. But though the emphasis laid by the *OC*
on the secrecy of the tomb is in itself no guarantee that the burial in Attica was
Sophocles' invention (Méautis 1940: 23), no evidence for Oedipus' death in Attica
is definitely independent of Sophocles: see Aristid. 3. 188; Paus. 1. 28. 7 (cf. Paus.
1. 30. 4); Val.Max. 5. 3. 3.

between pity for their misery and fear of the indelible pollution clinging to Oedipus. Thus they decide to summon Theseus, their king, to adjudicate. Meanwhile Ismene arrives from Thebes to warn her father that his two sons are preparing to fight each other for the kingship of Thebes. Whichever of them has Oedipus on his side will be victorious, and thus Creon is coming to try to bring him back to Thebes: however, Ismene goes on to admit that the Thebans are too frightened of his pollution to allow him back into their city, and he must remain on the borders of Theban territory even when he is buried (360–407). Angered by their selfishness, Oedipus swears that they will never get his help (408 ff.). After a painful interlude in which the chorus ask Oedipus about his past with a mixture of fascination and repulsion that distresses the old man (510–50), Theseus appears and, without asking him anything further, welcomes him into the city and promises him his protection (551 ff.); in return, Oedipus promises that his body will protect Athens after he is dead, and the chorus mark his reception into their community with a magnificent ode in praise of Colonus (668 ff.). Now Creon arrives, and when his cajoling fails to move Oedipus to come with him, he resorts to violence, abducting Oedipus' two daughters and laying hands on Oedipus; but Theseus comes to the rescue and sends Creon off ignominiously. Finally Polynices comes to try to persuade Oedipus to support him against his brother; the old man is adamant and sends his son away. This is the last of Oedipus' confrontations with those whom he left behind in Thebes. The play draws to a close as he understands that the end of his life is near and, with only Theseus as a companion, leaves the stage for a mysterious death. His daughters can only lament the loss of their father, while Theseus respectfully accepts the strange old man's strange destiny.

When we first see old, blind, destitute Oedipus, his fortunes are at their lowest, but beneath the feeble exterior (emphasized, ll. 20, 81, 146, 207), there is power at the disposal of the city with the wisdom to look beyond his weakness, pollution and hideous appearance. As soon as Oedipus learns from the man of Colonus that he is in the grove of the Eumenides (ll. 39–43), his whole demeanour changes, and he states positively that the grove is where he belongs, to the man's alarm (ll. 44–5) and the chorus's horror in their *parodos* (118 ff.). For the pious dwellers of Colonus, who are ordinary human beings, the grove is a source of fear and awe and an inviolable place, but Oedipus has walked into it without ill-effects, as Apollo once prophesied that he would. Oedipus was always different from other people, and thus it is appropriate that whereas ordinary human beings try to avoid the Erinyes, Oedipus goes to meet them.[19] Right from the beginning of the play, he is marked as strange and special, by his blindness and his relations with the Erinyes, and his strangeness is further defined by the subsidiary characters in the play, including Theseus.

From the very start of the play, Oedipus knows that he will one day have the power of a hero to help his friends and harm his enemies after his death.[20] Although his power is all in the future, and in Colonus he is a feeble suppliant, he consistently reveals a closer acquaintance with the purposes of the gods and the future than is usual for a suppliant, and he has a certainty, even an inflexibility, which the other humans lack.[21] Even at his weakest moments, he is associated with divinity, in the form of Apollo's oracles, by which he knows his destiny and that of Thebes (*OC* 46, 791). He is a strange mixture of strength and vulnerability caused both by his old age and by the appalling pollution that his acts have incurred.[22] Of all the suppliants that Athens has welcomed so far, Oedipus is undoubtedly the strangest, so that his reception is the ultimate test for Athenian wisdom and courage because he is potentially the most threatening suppliant imaginable.[23] Any city faced with the decision of whether or not to receive a suppliant runs a double risk of incurring war if it does, and the risk of offending the gods if it does not. With Oedipus, the danger is even threefold: Athens runs a risk of incurring war with Thebes by taking Oedipus in, and of suffering divine displeasure by taking into the city someone whose

---

[19] Rosenmeyer 1952: 107.

[20] He cannot be a hero in the full religious sense until he is dead, but he has heroic potential, and knows that he has it: cf. Linforth 1951: 99; Easterling 1967: 1. For the view that Oedipus is heroized earlier in the play see Winnington Ingram 1954: 16, cf. 1980: 255; Gellie 1972: 162; cf. Bowra 1944: 307.

[21] e.g. ll. 45, 74, 84–95, 287–8, and esp. 616–23.

[22] Apollo and his oracles lie behind both: cf. *OC* 969–77.

[23] Kirkwood 1986: 104 suggests that Sophocles intended to distinguish between Colonus, where values traditionally Athenian, such as *epieikeia*, could still be found, and Athens itself, whose imperial status was incompatible with such qualities. However, the prominence of Theseus and the constant references to Athens, especially at l. 260, where Oedipus reminds the chorus that they should live up to values which are standard in imperial encomia make this a difficult reading and suggest instead that Colonus is meant to represent the whole Athenian polis. See also the discussion of the Colonus ode at the end of this chapter.

actions have made him the most polluted of men, whatever his intentions had been, as well as the risk of divine displeasure if the claims of a suppliant are not honoured.

A central motif in the Athenian image of the ideal Athens is that the city will always take risks, and be rewarded for so doing. In many Athenian stories of Athenian action—notably in Aeschylus' *Eumenides*, but also in Euripides' *Suppliants* and *Heracles*—the reward for risk is that risk itself, neutralized by the power or courage of Athens to surmount it, so that it is no longer a danger to Athens, but a means of protecting the city. Such a worthy and unusual reward emphasizes the worth of the city and its exceptional nature.[24] Oedipus is strange and terrifying, but his eventual acceptance by the Athenian community, after initial fear, will render him beneficial to that community; though he is from a city which will become hostile to Athens, he will reward Athens with lasting security and protection against Theban enmity.[25] In his frightening aspect, combined with the ability to reward respect and acceptance by the community with protection for the community, he resembles the Erinyes, who were welcomed into Aeschylus' Athens as Eumenides over fifty years earlier. In Aeschylus' *Eumenides*, the virtue and courage of Athens turned the potentially dangerous powers of the Erinyes to keeping Athens safe: they have retained this function in Sophocles,[26] and it may be that Sophocles had Aeschylus' play in mind as a background for the reception of Oedipus.

Thus, when the *xenos* of Colonus distinguishes between the name of 'Eumenides' given by the local people, and the other names by which the Eumenides are known elsewhere (*OC* 42),[27] his

---

[24] This is also striking in stories in which enemies of Athens change their allegiance, such as Eurystheus in the *Heraclidae*, or the Amazon who fights on Theseus' side: see Kearns 1989: 47–56. Respect given to an enemy also has a particular potency. Visser 1982: 426 rightly notes that honour is always more gratifying when it is offered in spite of normal feelings, such as when an enemy acknowledges the worth of another enemy.

[25] This is, of course, not the main theme of the play; but as a subsidiary theme it is worth exploring.

[26] *OC* 458 calls them δημοῦχοι, a word used of the chorus itself at *OC* 1087, cf. 1348.

[27] 'Eumenides' is, however, also attested as a name at Sicyon: Paus. 2. 11. 4. For other names which indicate a more purely frightening conception of the Erinyes, see Wüst 1956: 86–91; Brown 1984: 276–81, but his arguments that Erinyes and Eumenides are essentially different from one another are not convincing.

words hint that Colonus (like Athens itself in Aeschylus) is a place which has had the wisdom to incorporate even frightening beings such as the Erinyes so that they are turned to her benefit, and they help to set the scene for the welcome of another potentially harmful being into the community. Oedipus is in some respects a kind of ally and agent of the Erinyes, as well as a being like them, both kind and terrifying.[28] Through his curse,[29] punishment is exacted, but through his blessing, Athens is rewarded. Both Oedipus and the Erinyes are terrible, the antithesis of civilization; but they are also special and divine and it is Athens alone who understands the paradoxical necessity of finding a place for what is terrible but special and divine within her civilized polis.[30] She will be amply rewarded, both by Oedipus' favour which will keep the city immune from defeat, and by the gods for clear sight and piety.[31]

Oedipus is a strange figure; human, but set apart from normal human experience.[32] Theseus is his opposite in many ways; his humanity saves Oedipus and also throws the old man's strangeness further into relief. Like the Theseus of the *Suppliants* and of the *Heracles*, he, and the ideals which he embodies, represent the best of humanity, but he is fundamentally limited in power and knowledge. Like the Theseus of the earlier plays, he is no *deus ex machina*, since he has no power or knowledge beyond what might be expected of a wise human king; he can mitigate suffering, but he cannot explain it. Active in helping his fellow human beings, obedient in his services to the gods, Theseus—once again—represents perfect human virtue. However, virtue in a less perfect form is found in the chorus of Coloneans. That such virtue is native to Attica is emphasized also by the consistent evocation of the landscape of Colonus throughout the play.

[28] The connection of Oedipus with the Eumenides is forcefully denied by Linforth 1951: 94, but one should remember the possibility that Oedipus has a connection in cult with the Erinyes. Verbal and visual links are made between Oedipus and the Eumenides throughout the play: Jebb 1900: 45, with Winnington-Ingram 1980: 268; Segal 1981: 375–6; they are both 'terrible' (δεινός, 141, 84); they are his allies, and explicitly associated with Athens: e.g. *OC* 106–7, 457; note also *OC* 621 and 631 which mentions Oedipus' 'kindness' (εὐμένεια).

[29] Note esp.*OC* 1375–6, τοιάσδ' ἀρὰς ... νῦν τ' ἀνακαλοῦμαι ξυμμάχους ('such curses do I now invoke as allies'): Ἀραί is another name for the Erinyes (A. *Eum.* 417).

[30] So Whitman 1951: 157; Segal 1981: 374–6.

[31] On a more normal, human plane, Oedipus also resembles Orestes, whose deliverance at Athens brought a reward to the Athenians: cf. Gellie 1972: 161.

[32] Cf. Jebb 1900: p. xxii; Festugière 1973.

There is a revealing structural parallel between the beginning of the *Coloneus* and that of Euripides' *Suppliants*, in which the role of the ideal Athens was shared between Aethra and Theseus, and the proper, Athenian way to behave was highlighted by Theseus' change of mind after Aethra had reminded him of Athenian ideals and Athens' reputation. A similar pattern can be seen in the *Oedipus Coloneus*, in which the chorus and Theseus are used by Sophocles in slightly different ways to highlight the principles of the ideal Athens. Just as Theseus was initially disinclined to help Adrastus because he had been foolish and impious, so Oedipus is potentially a serious threat to the purity of the state, and the chorus has first to react to him in the 'wrong' way, by instantly rejecting him when they discover who he is, in spite of their earlier promises (*OC* 224 ff., cf. 176). The right behaviour of perfect acceptance is then exemplified by Theseus. In both plays, the act of acceptance is made to seem all the more remarkable by the prelude of rejection.

As in the *Suppliants*, the representatives of Athens are brought to change their minds from a rigid lack of sympathy to a more merciful attitude, by appeals to human fellowship, made by Antigone,[33] and to Athens' past reputation, made by Oedipus (*OC* 258–91): though these appeals are separate, they are connected with one another at a deeper level. The chorus acknowledge the force of both arguments: immediately they assure Antigone that they do feel pity for Oedipus, but that the claims of piety are too strong for them to be able to accept him unquestioningly (*OC* 254–7; cf. 461). In answer to these appeals to piety, Oedipus makes an impassioned statement of what Athenian ideals should be (*OC* 258–65, 282–5; cf. 1125 f.), and of his essential innocence (*OC* 265–74), reminding the chorus of how they should behave as Athenians; once again, the standard values of the *epitaphioi* are set forth and will be reaffirmed as right. Thus he states that Athens is 'most god-fearing' and unique in compassion for the oppressed and power to help them, and reproaches the Coloneans with the charge that they fear 'just a name' (*OC* 265–6). Such a charge recalls Theseus' reproach of cowardice to the Thebans at *Suppliants* 542–8: courage is sometimes a

---

[33] *OC* 237–53, esp. 252 f.: οὐ γὰρ ἴδοις ἂν ἀθρῶν βροτὸν ὅστις ἄν | εἰ θεος ἄγοι | ἐκφύγειν δύναιτο ('even if you looked hard, you could not find any human being who could escape if a god was dealing with him'), words which are equally apt for Orestes in the *Eumenides* or Heracles in the *Heracles*, both of whom are given sanctuary by Athenians who recognize their underlying innocence. See also below.

part of piety, and since courage is a quintessentially Athenian characteristic, so is genuine piety, which will be set against its counter-
feit in Creon later in the play.

Although fear of the gods and compassion are also quintessentially Athenian qualities, as the chorus itself recognizes, it will take
the wisdom of Theseus to settle their apparently conflicting claims
(*OC* 293–4). The men of Colonus are by nature pious, compas-
sionate and honourable, and only the exceptional nature of
Oedipus' circumstances leads them temporarily astray. By the
same token, it is only the exceptional wisdom of Theseus which can
accept Oedipus at once, but once the chorus is persuaded by
Theseus' acceptance, their loyalty to Oedipus is more or less
unswerving.[34] In the subsequent adventures of Oedipus at Colonus
we see the loyalty of Athens to friends and the power of Athens to
defend these friends.[35]

The chorus also represent Theseus during his absence: more
than any other Sophoclean chorus they take part in dialogues,[36] and
they are the guardians of the land who welcome Oedipus and
receive Creon when he comes.[37] At *OC* 47–8 and 78–80, Colonus
seems to have some form of local democracy, although it is clear
from 66–9 that Theseus is the king, and only when the Coloneans
decide that Oedipus' case is too difficult for their judgement alone
is he summoned (*OC* 288; cf. 831, 1348). They represent the
Athenian democracy when Theseus is absent, while Theseus himself represents the finest qualities of the democracy when he is present.[38] There is, of course, a technical conflict between democratic
Athens and the monarchy of Theseus, but as in other tragedies, the
conflict arises partly from dramatic conventions. It is dramatically
effective to have the chorus' ambivalent response to Oedipus
capped by Theseus' total and commanding acceptance. Although
this makes Theseus appear to be a more traditional ruler than was

---

[34] See esp. *OC* 629–30, and in general the Creon scene.

[35] The reference to the 'ever-faithful pledges' ($\pi i \sigma \tau$' $\dot{a} \epsilon \grave{\iota}$ $\xi \upsilon \nu \theta \acute{\eta} \mu a \tau a$) of Theseus
and Peirithous (*OC* 1593) is another minor example of Theseus' capacity for human
affection ($\phi \iota \lambda i a$) and loyalty. As in other fifth-century Athenian sources, the mission
of the pair to Hades is characterized as a sign of their mutual loyalty, rather than a
dangerously impious exploit.

[36] Burton 1980: 264–5; Gardiner 1987: 109.

[37] *OC* 145, 728, 831 and 871: also the whole of the Colonus ode.

[38] As in the *Suppliants*, Theseus is linked with Athens, at 309, 553, 1124–5, 1496
and 1553, where Oedipus' last words bless Theseus and Athens: cf. Jebb 1900: 57.

the Theseus of the *Suppliants*, his role is partly determined by the need to emphasize the potential dangers attached to accepting Oedipus, and Athens' daring in so doing.[39]

Sophocles alters the conventions of the suppliant play, in which suppliants must overcome a king's unwillingness to help them; whereas the Danaids have to threaten suicide before Pelasgus will accept them, Theseus never lets matters go so far.[40] All fear of Oedipus' pollution is put into the mouths of the chorus, and all warning of war between Creon and Athens is given by Oedipus (*OC* 653–6, cf. 579–80). Theseus is left as the epitome of Athenian kindness and daring, by accepting Oedipus straightaway: although Oedipus is bringing benefits to Athens, Theseus accepts him before he knows this. Unlike a normal king in a suppliant play, he asks no questions of his suppliant,[41] and the repetition of ἀκούων at 551–4 stresses that Theseus knows all about Oedipus' past and refuses to hurt him with any more questions now. Moreover, physical contact is normally essential for a supplication to be successful. The polluted Oedipus can only make a verbal supplication (cf. 1130ff.), but even so, Theseus does not take advantage of this loophole to reject him.[42] In his calm acceptance, he contrasts with the chorus (*OC* 204–6, 510–48), but both responses to Oedipus are necessary; the chorus's because it underlines the risk which Athens is taking by accepting a man like Oedipus into the state; Theseus' unquestioning acceptance because it demonstrates the highest form of Athenian virtue.[43]

---

[39] See also Frey 1947: 62–4. I doubt the claim of Walker 1995: 171–2 that Sophocles is 'undermining' the myth of the eternal democratic constitution at Athens, nor do I detect any 'resentment' in the chorus's attitude to Theseus and Athens (Walker, 1995: 175). Deme and city, demesman and king, are united, but their unity is slightly obscured by the stylized allocation of different facets of the 'typical Athens' to chorus and king.

[40] Cf. Reinhardt 1979: 195, 207–8; Burian 1974: 409. Euripides' *Heracles* also plays with the conventions of the suppliant play with a very similar aim of glorifying the uniqueness of Athenian compassion: above, §4.4.

[41] Contrast *Supp.* 115ff. and even *HF* 1178ff., although, as with Oedipus, Theseus will have no doubts about actually receiving him at Athens: see Burian 1974: 414–17.

[42] Walker 1995: 185–6.

[43] Lesky 1952: 100. Gardiner 1987: 112–13, is too dogmatic on this point. Lines 510–50 remind the audience of Oedipus' horrific acts, but they also circumvent the need for any more questioning by Theseus, and add to the impression that he wishes to avoid causing the old man any more pain.

Theseus' attitude to Oedipus on first meeting him is a part of a world view which can be classified both as specifically human and (in the terms of the encomiasts of Athens) as specifically Athenian. This is made most explicit at *OC* 567–8: ἔξοιδ᾽ ἀνὴρ ὢν χὤτι τῆς ἐς αὔριον | οὐδὲν πλέον μοι σοῦ μέτεστιν ἡμέρας ('I know that because I am a man, I have no greater share in the next day than you'). This is the world view which comprises an awareness of human fragility and the flexibility to feel pity for other human beings in the midst of one's own prosperity.[44] We have already explored the importance of pity as a characteristic of Athens and its connections with the moderate conduct which was so prized in Greek ethics as essentially appropriate to human beings, though not to gods. The expression of human fellowship through pity stimulated by mutual suffering leads Theseus to draw a comparison between himself and Oedipus at ll. 562–5. He, like Oedipus has suffered—ἐπαιδεύθην ξένος | ὥσπερ σύ.[46] Although both Oedipus and Theseus were not brought up in their native land, Theseus' Trozenian childhood holds no record of any misery like that of Oedipus. Theseus' next attempt to ally himself with Oedipus' sufferings—χὠς εἰς πλεῖστ᾽ ἀνὴρ ἐπὶ ξένης | ἤθλησα κινδυνεύματ᾽ ἐν τὠμῷ κάρᾳ ('In exile I suffered as many dangers as a man could on my person')—might hint at Medea's attempt to kill him, but must primarily refer to his Isthmian exploits, which brought him glory, not pollution and ignominy, as Oedipus' exploits did. Thus Theseus' comparison is in fact entirely inexact,[47] but its purpose is to show his humanity and fellowship with an unfortunate man, and to save him from the distress of further explanations of his past. This is the right way to behave to others; the perversion of the idea

[44] With the themes of Theseus' speech at *OC* 560–8, compare E. *HF* 1236 and *Supp.* 768, τί δ᾽ αἰσχρὸν ἀνθρώποισι τἀλλήλων κακά ('what is shameful to men about others' troubles?'); also Odysseus, S. *Aj.* 121–6, where, for once, the motif is not used to glorify Athens.

[45] Compare my remarks above on the chorus' acceptance of Antigone's appeals to human fellowship. See also Wasserstein 1969: 197–200, who distinguishes the human characters (of Odysseus and Theseus) and the divine or heroic (of Athena, Ajax and Oedipus), in the *Ajax* and *OC*. Although both plays are pessimistic concerning human destiny, they are optimistic concerning the potentialities of human nature.

[46] 'I was brought up as a foreigner, as you were.' On the passage see especially Lesky 1952: 100–5.

[47] The real similarity between them—parricide—is, of course, avoided: see §1.3.4.

of fellowship in suffering will be seen in Creon's and Polynices' mouths later in the play.

The theme of connection between human beings in a precarious world is further underlined in the play by the use of the word γενναῖος ('noble') to describe both Theseus and Oedipus: at l. 76, the man of Colonus describes Oedipus as γενναῖος . . . πλὴν τοῦ δαίμονος ('noble . . . except for his fate', cf. *OC* 8). In this, the man of Colonus shows some of the Athenian insight which is possessed in complete measure by Theseus, whose own γενναῖον is acknowledged by Oedipus at l. 569 (cf. also *OC* 1637): it takes one to know one.[48] Though the two are different in status and character, they are equals, because they are human. Theseus is a happy king today, and Oedipus a blind beggar, but yesterday Oedipus was a happy king.[49] In his speech of welcome to Oedipus and his acceptance of his responsibility to the suppliant, which is part of duty both to god and man, Theseus recognizes this and he will be rewarded for so doing.

It is, of course, slightly paradoxical that Theseus should appeal to the essential similarity between himself and Oedipus, since one of the functions of Theseus in the play is to be a background of perfect humanity and moderation against which the heroic inflexibility of Oedipus can be set. A great gulf is fixed between the noble human king, who stands outside the tragic aspect of the play, and the tragic hero whose world view is far from the moderation of Theseus. At l. 592, Theseus chides Oedipus for unbending hostility towards Thebes—ὦ μῶρε,[50] θυμὸς δ᾽ ἐν κακοῖς οὐ ξύμφορον ('Fool, having a temper in troubles is not helpful')—which receives a sharp rejoinder from Oedipus, and Theseus apologizes. This exchange is highly characteristic of both men: Theseus is a noble king, but he does not, and cannot, have the tragic experience and knowledge that Oedipus has, as he himself will recognize.[51] This

---

[48] Walker 1995: 188. For other significant repetitions in the play, see Easterling 1973: 30–1.

[49] The famous third stasimon of the *OC* is a general expression of such sentiments: at l. 1239, the chorus expresses its fellowship with Oedipus. Compare my remarks on the relationship between Aethra and the Argive mothers, §3.4. Gellie 1972: 197, suggests that contemporary events influenced this kind of sentiment of common human endurance in the face of the arbitrary, but the idea is much older: see, e.g. Hom. *Il.* 24. 525 ff.; Archilochus 128W.

[50] Knox 1957: 18 notes that μῶρος is a particularly sharp word of condemnation in the vocabulary of the Oedipus of *Oedipus Tyrannus* (*OT* 433, 540).

[51] Cf. Winnington-Ingram 1980: 273–4.

exchange resembles Heracles' sharp rejoinder to Theseus' exhorta-
tions, followed by Theseus' apology at the end of the *Heracles* (ll.
1415–16). In both of these dialogues, we see the difference between
Theseus and the tragic hero, but also the flexibility and wisdom of
Theseus which make him apologize. *OC* 592 forms virtually a single
argument with Antigone's plea of 1197ff., γνώσει κακοῦ | θυμοῦ
τελευτὴν ὡς κακὴ προσγίγνεται,[52] and this flexibility which both
Antigone and Theseus possess is the antithesis of the all-
embracing, 'heroic' θυμός of Oedipus. Oedipus will eventually
curse his sons, and neither Theseus nor Antigone will attempt to
instruct him not to do so. His sufferings have put him beyond normal human behaviour, and, like a hero, he can be implacable without fear of the nemesis which attends human hubris. Polynices has
committed a terrible crime in not looking after his father,[53] and
Oedipus is simply the instrument of his punishment.

The superficial similarities between Theseus' reception of
Oedipus, and Oedipus' reception of his son underline the profound
differences between them. Theseus the good Athenian is bound to
accept the claims of all suppliants because his is essentially the
moderate, human view, but Oedipus is a different sort of character.
Although he eventually consents to see Polynices, apparently out of
affection for Antigone rather than because he accepts the validity of
his claims on him as a suppliant,[54] he cannot feel anything other
than rage towards him. Polynices is a more pitiable figure than
Creon, but he is still stubborn, refusing to halt a course of action
which he knows will be disastrous,[55] and hypocritical in his pleas
for a forgiveness which all too obviously derives from his desire for
the kingship of Thebes, rather than any real change of heart concerning his father's sufferings. At 1278, 1292 and 1335–7, he compares his pitiable status with Oedipus'; but this is an abuse of the
human fellowship whose proper workings we saw in Theseus'

[52] 'You will know what an evil end comes from an evil temper': cf. Winnington-
Ingram 1954: 17–18.

[53] Loss of citizenship rights was the punishment in Attic law for a son who
neglected his father: Jebb 1900: 213. The conduct of Oedipus' heartless sons is mea-
sured against that of his loving daughters (esp. *OC* 337–55): the sons acted as they
did ἐκ θεῶν του κἀξ ἀλειτηροῦ φρενός ('because of some god and their own
accursed hearts', *OC* 371–2'), and there is no reason for Oedipus to forgive conduct
which has broken bonds which should be sacred.

[54] *OC* 1204–5, in spite of Theseus' appeal to Polynices' suppliant status
(1179–80).

[55] *OC* 1418ff. with Diller 1950: 27.

reception of Oedipus. Oedipus' anger is repulsive in comparison
with Theseus' reasoned moderation and by his curse, he will cause
his daughter's death, but his curse is a product of his own uniquely
appalling experiences and he could not behave differently.[56]
Theseus and Antigone—and the audience—are right to pity
Polynices, but Theseus remains essentially outside Oedipus'
tragedy.

Theseus' two brief attempts to advise Oedipus (*OC* 592,
1175–80) mark Theseus as a wise, moderate human king: the
awareness of human uncertainty and vulnerability which allowed
him first to accept Oedipus also leads him to urge such moderation
upon the old man. Oedipus is, however, beyond any advice that
Theseus can give him, and in most of the play, it is he who is
Theseus' instructor. Gods are distinguished from men partly by
the possession of real, certain knowledge. Oedipus' knowledge of
the future is limited, but he knows much more than any of the other
characters in the play, even his eventual place and manner of
death.[57] Old and blind, like Teiresias himself, he knows the oracles,[58] and must explain to Theseus and his people how they can
obtain the benefits of the eternal protection which he knows that he
can give them. In his role as Theseus' instructor, the differences
between Oedipus and the representative of Athenian humanity are
particularly notable: Oedipus warns Theseus that nothing human
is safe from the ravages of time[59] and that there will one day be war
between Thebes and Athens. At l. 624, however, he breaks off,
because these are τἀκίνητ' ἔπη ('words that should be kept secret');
Theseus is not allowed to know everything that Oedipus knows
from the god, and Oedipus' sudden silence emphasizes the difference between himself and Theseus. By the end of the play, however, Theseus' unique nobility will have earned him the right to

[56] Winnington-Ingram 1954: 17–18: compare Easterling 1967: 7–9; Walker 1995:
187.

[57] Cf. Diller 1950: 5; Whitman 1951: 152, although he exaggerates Oedipus'
divine qualities.

[58] *OC* 84–95, cf. 450–4; 616–23, 791–3. Shields 1961 notes that there are ten distinct references to sight and blindness in *OC* 1–42 alone. As in the *OT*, sight symbolism is used to emphasize the inferiority of physical vision to intellectual insight:
cf. Buxton 1980, esp. 26 f.

[59] *OC* 607–13. His gift, however, of protection to Athens will be that of a hero,
and therefore it will transcend the shifts of human fortune (*OC* 1518–19).

know more of the mysteries which Oedipus knows even than his daughters, even if this knowledge is only partial.[60]

Theseus cannot conceive that there could be future wars between Athens and Thebes because his knowledge is more limited than that of Oedipus,[61] and he seems entirely unconcerned about the possibility of war with Thebes caused by the reception of Oedipus (*OC* 652–67). Such calmness is partly a result of his (justifiable) confidence in Athens' ability to cope with any threat, but it also adds to the impression that Oedipus has a knowledge of the future which Theseus lacks, and that he must be instructed by the older, wiser man.[62] At the end of the play particularly, from 1500 onwards, as his connection with the gods becomes more obvious, Oedipus is in control and Theseus obeys him unquestioningly, but even in the early part of the play, when Oedipus is physically at his weakest, his presence is still commanding. Thus, although Theseus is, as usual, the representative of a pious and powerful state, and Oedipus a feeble outcast, there are ways in which he is the suppliant's inferior. The meeting between Theseus and Oedipus is less one of helpless suppliant and omnipotent king, than one of equals, where σωτηρία is, for once, quite explicitly exchanged for σωτηρία.[63] At least on the surface, his relationship with the heroic Oedipus is rather different from that with the human Adrastus in the *Suppliants*. In both plays, however, Theseus is absolutely dominant and his suppliant much more passive, where military prowess is needed (*OC* 1019–35).

The character of Theseus' relations with Oedipus is determined on the one hand by the inherent strangeness of Oedipus, and on the other, by the portrayal of Theseus as the highest representative of human, and Athenian, potential. In the *Oedipus Coloneus*, as in the other Theseus plays which have been discussed, Theseus is always the son of Aegeus rather than Poseidon (ll. 69, 550, 940, 1518 and 1538, cf. 297); although Poseidon is a presence in the play (*OC* 55, 888–9), as befits the setting of Colonus, there is no indication that Theseus has any closer association with him than anyone else does. Sophocles' Theseus and men of Colonus particularly honour the

---

[60] *OC* 1526–9: Whitman 1951: 169.

[61] *OC* 606; compare his curious questions to Oedipus, ll. 579–88.

[62] Compare also Theseus' deference to Oedipus, *OC* 1150–3.

[63] Burian 1974: 415. I say 'explicitly', because underlying the apparent altruism of Athens towards her 'friends' in distress, there is always a covert expectation that those friends owe their rescuer something in return.

gods, and their piety is one of the reasons for Athens' greatness. The piety of Athens is a dominant theme of the play, lasting from the very first words of the *xenos*, through the chorus's anger at the violation of the grove and their horror of one polluted, which is then altered by instruction from Theseus' superior vision, through their devotion to ritual (468 f.) right down to the final ode honour-ing the divine purpose, and Theseus' piety in the face of the mys-tery at *OC* 1654–5. Although the gods' role in Oedipus' sufferings is not ignored, the problems of the theodicy which lie behind Oedipus' fate are not thoroughly discussed; the same was true of Euripides' *Heracles* and *Suppliants*. The Greeks always hoped that the gods would be just and merciful to them, but did not rely on such hopes, and remained essentially agnostic about divine justice and mercy:[64] none the less, human beings themselves must honour those rules which the gods have laid down for them. Pitying, and welcoming, a suppliant, is a part of this, but it takes the particular intelligence and courage of Theseus to see beyond Oedipus' more threatening aspect so as to uphold the highest laws of the gods and also of humanity.

We are not allowed to forget what Athenian acceptance entails: at *OC* 1480–5, the chorus briefly interpret the thunder that heralds Oedipus' departure as a sign of Zeus' displeasure at his reception at Colonus,[65] and despite his pleas of innocence, Oedipus himself knows that he cannot escape the unique pollution which clings to him. At 1130–6 he wishes to touch Theseus, but then shrinks back; and Theseus, unlike the Theseus of the *Heracles*, makes no attempt to touch him.[66] Although the humane Theseus accepts Oedipus into his city, he seems to avoid any explicit statement vindicating Oedipus' ritual purity, perhaps because Oedipus' status is so com-plicated.[67] Although it is evident that the reception of Oedipus is morally right, his innocence could not be uncontroversial, and its treatment in the play sheds yet more light on the idealized Athenian perception of 'the Athenian way of life'. As in Aeschylus' *Eumenides* and Euripides' *Heracles*, *Oedipus Coloneus* considers

---

[64] Cf. Dover 1974: 156. See also Whitman 1951: 202.

[65] Cf. 1463 ff., esp. 1482. Ronnet 1969: 278 n. 1, is wrong to think that Theseus has nothing to lose by accepting Oedipus.

[66] Whitman 1951: 207 makes too much of ll. 639–40 as an indication that Theseus discounts Oedipus' inescapable pollution.

[67] Cf. Linforth 1951: 153. Compare too the 'human' (and limited) outlook of the Theseus of the *Heracles*.

questions of moral responsibility in an Athenian setting. The cases of Oedipus, Heracles and Orestes are all characterised by ambiguity: Orestes was forced to kill his mother and could not deny it (*Eum.* 588), but the issue is clearly not a simple one of crime and punishment. In the *Heracles*, Heracles did kill his family, but this was not what he wished to do. In the *Oedipus Coloneus* Oedipus himself denies that he could truly have been guilty of parricide and incest, and again, questions of intent and compulsion are vital.[68] At *OC* 267, he describes himself as πεπονθότ[α] . . . μᾶλλον ἢ δεδρακότα ('having suffered more than done'), and thereafter insists that both the parricide and incest were inevitable,[69] because of what had been ordained by the oracle, and then the human circumstances which enabled the oracle to be fulfilled: such deeds were therefore not intentional, but 'unwilling' (ἄκων).[70] When logically analysed, some of these claims may seem a little strained, and the use of divine compulsion as a way of disclaiming all responsibility would hardly pass muster in an Athenian court.[71] We are, however, not in a court, but in a play whose setting in the idealized Athens exercises a powerful underlying influence on some of its themes. Oedipus' crimes were appalling, yet his intent was entirely innocent, and dilemmas of intent and result by their very nature demand the flexibility of τὸ ἐπιεικές rather than the strict logic of τὸ δίκαιον. The reception of Oedipus may thus be seen as the ultimate test for the supreme ἐπιείκεια of Athens.[72] As in the *Oresteia*, Athens is the place where humanity has the final judging sanction after divinity has acted according to its laws. It takes the magnanimity of a Theseus to understand Oedipus' essential innocence without question.[73] As Oedipus himself says of Theseus and Athens (1125–7):

[68] Note also his insistence on intent at *OC* 498–9: Jebb 1900: p. xxii. For a detailed discussion of the question, see also T. Gould 1965, esp. 373.

[69] He claims that he was forced to marry Jocasta: ll. 525–6. The marriage is, of course, harder to defend as unintentional, and is minimized, compared with the parricide, which is treated by Oedipus as self-defence: Gellie 1972: 163.

[70] *OC* 266–74; 510–48, where the exchange at l. 539—Cho. ἔρεξας Oed. οὐκ ἔρεξα ('you did it . . . I did not do it')—is striking; 963–99.

[71] Rosenmeyer 1952: 96–7; see also Parker 1983: 317.

[72] Since Draco, a distinction was made in Athenian law between voluntary and involuntary homicide: for the distinction between intent and result, see also (e.g.) Sim. 4. 18–20D; Soph. fr. 665; *Trach.* 727; and esp. Ar. *NE* 1135ᵃ10ff. Thuc. 2. 39. 1 and Isoc. 4. 41, 47, which were cited as a commentary on the reception of Heracles at Athens, could be cited equally appropriately as a comment on the reception of Oedipus.

[73] Cf. Parker 1983: 317–18; Jebb 1900: p. xxiii.

τὸ γ' εὐσεβὲς
μόνοις παρ' ὑμῖν ηὗρον ἀνθρώπων ἐγὼ
καὶ τοὐπιεικὲς καὶ τὸ μὴ ψευδοστομεῖν

('only with you have I found piety and flexibility and telling the truth'.)

Nothing very profound can be deduced from the play about contemporary attitudes to guilt and pollution, partly because of the ambivalent nature of pollution, and partly because of the dominant ideological component which underlies the reception of Oedipus by Athens. Belief in pollution can live side by side with a more rationalistic attitude: even when we complain about bad luck, we often have a sneaking suspicion that we have brought it on ourselves, and as for Oedipus' defence that the gods made him do it, the victim was not necessarily exonerated thereby, since suffering might be regarded as a punishment for wrongdoing.[74] Even so, it is probably true to say that Theseus represents advanced opinion, partly because, as with the *Heracles*, it is unlikely that the tragedians would wish to portray Athens behaving impiously, and also because Oedipus' problem particularly deserves the wisdom and flexibility which we have come to see as inherently Athenian in Athenian democratic eyes. Unlike the Theseus of the *Heracles*, Theseus does not touch the polluted man when given the opportunity but this may simply be Sophocles' personal preference.[75] There is, in fact, one quite separate indication that Theseus is particularly enlightened.[76] At *OC* 887, he rushes to rescue Oedipus' daughters at the call of the chorus, leaving a sacrifice to Poseidon unfinished. For dramaturgical reasons, Theseus has to be nearby, but he does not have to be in the middle of a sacrifice. In having him leave the sacrifice, Sophocles has portrayed him as a 'typical' Athenian; although he is impeccably pious, piety includes the intelligence to weigh up different claims, and the immediate needs of a suppliant must outweigh ritual. The speed of his response is also emphasized, and speedy assistance of friends is another proud boast of Athens.[77] We may contrast this 'typically' Athenian behaviour with that of the Spartans, who would not help at Marathon for religious reasons (Hdt. 6. 106).

[74] Dover 1974: 149–50.
[75] Contrast *OC* 1130ff. with E. *HF* 1400, cf. 1230ff. Lesky 1952: 104 suggests that Sophocles is deliberately opposing Euripides.
[76] Whitman 1951: 165, although it is denied by Ehrenberg 1954: 52.
[77] *OC* 890, 897, 904; cf. §2. 4.

Nearer home, the obvious contrast to Theseus is Creon, who stands on a form of piety, in spite of being entirely devoid of true piety or humanity. Creon is the opposite both of his brother-in-law, in pretending to be harmless when he is not,[78] and also—and much more strikingly—he is the antithesis of Theseus. The contrast of Creon and Theseus provides us with the clearest example of the opposition between Athenian and non-Athenian, because Sophocles takes care to dissociate Creon from Thebes: Theseus tells him at l. 911 that his conduct is a disgrace to his country, and the point is made explicit at *OC* 919: καίτοι σε Θῆβαί γ᾽ οὐκ ἐπαίδευσαν κακόν.[79] Athenian values are celebrated in their positive aspect in Theseus, and inverted in Creon, but in this inversion, they are not Theban values as such, but rather, anti-Athenian values, the antithesis of what Athens is held to represent.[80]

The first difference between anti-Athenian Man and Athenian Man lies in their attitude towards Oedipus. We have known before Creon's arrival that the Thebans need Oedipus' body, even though their form of piety has made him stateless and will prevent him even now from having a proper home in Thebes. Creon has, however, taken care to cloak his real intentions in forms of speech which are 'Athenian' in all but their sincerity,[81] and the similarity between Creon's forms of words and those of Theseus and Oedipus emphasize the real difference between them. Thus, in his initial attempt to win Oedipus, he speaks respectfully to the Coloneans, telling them not to be afraid,[82] and falsely denies that he has come with violence in mind (*OC* 732). He appeals to Athens' reputation, as did the genuinely deserving suppliant Oedipus, and to democracy,[83] although

---

[78] Compare the admonition of the chorus to Oedipus at 185–7 ὅ τι καὶ πόλις | τέτροφεν ἄφιλον ἀποστυγεῖν | καὶ τὸ φίλον σέβεσθαι ('hate what the city holds hateful and respect what is dear to it', cf. 171–2): Oedipus does do this (cf. 12–13), and Creon does not, as Theseus points out at 924–8.

[79] 'And yet Thebes did not educate you to be evil.' Compare the chorus's summary: ὡς ἀφ᾽ ὧν μὲν εἶ, | φαίνῃ δίκαιος, δρῶν δ᾽ ἐφευρίσκῃ κακά ('To judge from your origins, you seem to be just, but you are caught doing what is wrong', *OC* 937–8).

[80] Compare my criticism of Zeitlin 1986, §3.2.

[81] Cf. Reinhardt 1979: 210–11.

[82] *OC* 731: as did Oedipus when his identity was revealed, l. 223.

[83] Athens' reputation: πρὸς πόλιν δ᾽ ἐπίσταμαι | σθένουσαν ἥκων, εἴ τιν᾽ Ἑλλάδος, μέγα ('I know that I have come to a city great in strength, if any in Greece is', ll. 733–4) and compare 941–9; note also εὐγενεῖς ('well-born'), l. 728. Polynices accuses his father and sister of flattering others (ἄλλους δὲ θωπεύοντες, l. 1336), but Creon, not Oedipus, is guilty of flattery (as l. 1003). Appeals to democracy: *OC* 737–8, 741–2, cf. 947–9 (appeal to the authority of the Areopagus).

it is clear that Thebes is a tyranny (as he lets slip, l. 851), the kind of corrupt place where sons are more interested in gaining power than in their father's well-being (*OC* 419, 448–9). The pity for suffering and human fellowship whose genuine expression we saw in Theseus is also perverted by Creon, who claims fellowship in old age with Oedipus, and pretends pity for Oedipus' wretched condition which he himself has caused.[84]

Neither Oedipus nor the chorus is moved by such spurious appeals, and when at last Theseus appears as the κακῶν κολαστής to bring the military strength of Athens to bear on anti-Athenian hypocrisy and oppression, the contrasts between Athens and anti-Athens are brought out even more strongly. Creon has behaved like a typical tyrant, violently breaking the law of gods, as well as men, by outraging suppliants.[85] Theseus upholds the laws which Creon ignores, both in his words of *OC* 913–16 and 924–9, and in his actions: again we see the combination of excellence in word and deed on which Athens prided itself. Creon himself appeals to this combination at *OC* 939–40, but word and action are not in harmony in him: his words respect Athens, while his deeds insult her (ll. 917–18); and whereas he misuses words as a cloak for his violence (βία, ll. 916, 922), Theseus will see through his behaviour, and match violence justly with violence. Thus, at *OC* 939 ff., as in his earlier speech to the chorus, Creon tries once more to appeal to the reputation of Athens: in the mouth of a sincere man, such appeals cannot be dismissed, but Creon is both insincere[86] and completely antithetical to Athenian values. He appeals to the famous piety and wisdom of the council of the Areopagus, which ought not to let a polluted man such as Oedipus stay in the city, but he misunderstands true, Athenian piety.[87] Athenian piety is the daring, active piety of πολυπραγμοσύνη and the ἐπιείκεια which accepts Oedipus' essential innocence, but the only piety which Creon knows is the selfish, cowardly piety of ἡσυχία and εὐλάβεια, which will accept Oedipus only in so far as the oracles say that he

---

[84] *OC* 735, 740–52: for fellowship in old age, compare the chorus's genuine expression, 1239 and cf. Blundell 1989: 242.

[85] *OC* 922–3: compare my remarks on democracy and law, §§3.4 and 2.4; see also Vidal-Naquet 1988: 338.

[86] Oedipus did not curse Creon until after his daughters had been kidnapped, in spite of what Creon says at *OC* 951–3.

[87] Vidal-Naquet 1988: 336–7. Oedipus understands it and has benefited from it: *OC* 1003–9.

will be useful to Thebes. At l. 590, Theseus had suggested that it
would be more honourable for Oedipus to return to Thebes, in
spite of what he is offering Athens: Creon, in contrast, thinks only
of gain.[88]

Strength, success and ability are important parts of the Athenian
code: an Athens who practised justice but was militarily weak
would be useless. Athens looks after suppliants, not only because it
is right, but because Athens can, and already has a reputation for so
doing.[89] In the *Coloneus*, Theseus exemplifies Athenian pride in
Athens as a city of action, courage and the self-sufficiency which
can cope with any emergency.[90] After Oedipus has been accepted
as a friend, the protection of Theseus extends to his daughters. In
Creon's attempted abduction of Antigone and Ismene, the chorus
exemplifies part of the Athenian ideal, just as they did in the original reception of Oedipus, while the advent of Theseus shows us
that ideal in its full form. Thus the strength of the chorus alone is
not sufficient to chasten Creon, because they are old and weak, so
that they must eventually call on Theseus and younger men to save
the day (*OC* 884–6, cf. 862). They are, however, far less feeble
against forceful wrongdoers than similar choruses in the
Agamemnon or the *Heracles*; they put up a good verbal fight against
Creon, as a sign of their absolute loyalty to Oedipus (*OC* 824–40,
856–62, 875–83), and even lay hands on him (*OC* 856). When
called, Theseus comes to help his friends at once: at l. 894, as soon
as he has heard what has happened, he issues instructions, as befits
a man of confident action, mindful of his duty and reputation (ll.
902–3), and the full military strength of Athens will chasten Creon
effectively. Even though the chorus can have no part in the battle,
their enthusiasm for justice, and confidence in Theseus and his
army,[91] creates the dramatic illusion that they are active partici-
pants in the exploit. Theseus' modesty both regarding his eventual

[88] Blundell 1990: 96; Whitman 1951: 205, 207, aptly compares Odysseus' attitude
to Philoctetes.

[89] *OC* 258–65, and even more explicitly, E. *Supp.* 323–5: compare the previous
three chapters, *passim*.

[90] Thus at *OC* 649–54 Theseus disdains oaths and ignores Oedipus' timid warnings.

[91] *OC* 1054–5, cf. 1065–6: see Reinhardt 1979: 215. ἐγρεμάχης ('arousing battle'), used of Theseus, l. 1054, is elsewhere associated with Athena (see *Hom. hymn
Dem.* with Richardson 1979: 291). Note also αὐτάρκει ... βοᾷ ('with a self-confident
shout') of *OC* 1057, and compare my remarks on Athenian self-sufficiency, above,
Ch. 2.

victory (ll. 1143–4),[92] and in his stern, but fair treatment of Creon (ll. 905–8), in which he uses the *lex talionis* purely to rectify injustice,[93] may also be interpreted as another aspect of the moderate Athenian world view: the victorious Theseus of the *Suppliants* was equally restrained. We have seen Athens at her very best both in times of emergency and in eventual victory: again, the best of πολυπραγμοσύνη is exhibited to an Athenian audience.

The loyalty of Theseus and the chorus to their friend continues after his death. When Antigone and Ismene lament their unknown future, the chorus suggest that they should not go home: Athens could give them a home, but the remaining offspring of the tragic house of Labdacus are too closely bound to Thebes and their unhappy destiny there to accept such an offer.[94] At *OC* 1750ff., Theseus offers his daughters comfort in accord with the charge laid on him by Oedipus at 1631–5, but he can do little for them, apart from offering sympathy, and warning them gently but firmly that they must not return to their father's grave because it is forbidden by divine law. As usual, Theseus accepts divine commands, and his powers do not extend beyond purely human remedies for distress; he can only continue to act in the best interests of Athens (*OC* 1764–7).

Athenian Man gets his reward for his loyalty and the risks taken on Oedipus' behalf in Oedipus' final promise of blessings for Athens for all time.[95] Theseus' virtue in receiving Oedipus is all of a piece with past Athenian piety. The connection between divine good will towards Athens for past piety, and divine benevolence in the future is made particularly explicit in the chorus's song to Colonus. The Colonus ode represents the glories of peace in Athens, just as the battle ode of 1044–95 represents Athens'

---

[92] A lengthy speech from Theseus at this point would, in any case, be dramatically inappropriate: the next episode must start immediately.

[93] Blundell 1989: 250. Compare Theseus at E. *Supp.* 724–5, and even his exploits on his journey around the Saronic Gulf, in which he merely does to his enemies what they did to others.

[94] *OC* 1735–50. Contrast the invitation to Athens which Euripides' Heracles accepts.

[95] *OC* 1555, εὐτυχεῖς ἀεί ('fortunate always'), even though the conditions of human life are generally uncertain: μόνοις οὐ γίγνεται | θεοῖσι γῆρας οὐδὲ κατθανεῖν ποτε, | τὰ δ' ἄλλα συγχεῖ πάνθ' ὁ παγκρατὴς χρόνος ('To the gods alone do neither old age or death ever come; all-subduing time throws everything else into confusion', *OC* 607–8).

military glories.[96] In both, Colonus represents a kind of miniature Athens and exemplifies many of the characteristics regarded as especially Athenian in encomia of Athens. Thus Colonus is highly numinous;[97] Dionysus and Aphrodite live there, as do the Two Goddesses and the Muses, who have an ideological significance as deities of Athenian civilization.[98] It is exceptionally beautiful, both in sight and sound.[99] It is also extremely fertile, and the emphasis on abundance and continuity symbolizes a confidence that the gods will not let Athens be destroyed in the future, just as the city has survived in the past.[100] The olive in particular symbolizes everlasting Athenian civilization:[101] the civilization of Athens is unique, and the olive is said to grow best in Athens, not Asia or the Peloponnese (694 ff.); it is ἀχείρωτον ('unconquerable'), αὐτοποιόν, | ἐγχέων φόβημα δαΐων ('self-creating, an object of fear to enemy spears', 698–9), like Athens' indefatigable and self-sufficient strength.[102] It is also παιδοτρόφον, nourishing the young children who will grow up as the next generation of that strength.[103] Although Athena and Poseidon were portrayed on the west metopes of the Parthenon as rivals for the possession of Athens, here they work harmoniously for the good of Athens; the gift of

[96] Burian 1974: 421.
[97] Also emphasized at the start of the play: 7–10, 39 ff., 44–54, 84 ff., 126 and 153 ff. In no other play are so many gods mentioned: Bröcker 1971: 48.
[98] Prometheus is mentioned at 56 (and see Σ56) and Eleusis, at 683, 1044–53. For Aphrodite and the Muses at Athens (691–3), compare E. *Med.* 831, 838 and Paus. 1. 30, whose list of gods worshipped around the Academy largely agrees with that of Sophocles. E. *Med.* 824–65 is another hymn in praise of Athens, but it focuses rather less on the role of the gods in Athenian civilization, emphasizing human wisdom above divine provision.
[99] Colours: 669, 673–4, 685, 693, 701; sound: 671–2, cf. 18, and see Jebb 1900: p. xii–xiii, n. 2. Its loveliness almost recalls Homer's description of Olympus at *Od.* 6. 43 ff., which also resembles E. *Med.* 839–40. See Page 1958: 132.
[100] ll. 672, 676, 681 ff., 685 ff., 691 and esp. 700 ff., cf. 16–18. The Eumenides promised fertility of all kinds to Athens: A. *Eum.* 938–48.
[101] Jebb 1900: 84, notes the connection of the olives with the Eumenides' kindness to Athens (cf. A. *Eum.* 907): see also Detienne 1970, and compare E. *HF* 1170.
[102] Athena's olive grew again the day after the Persians burnt the Acropolis: Hdt. 8. 55.
[103] Cf. l. 727, τὸ τῆσδε χώρας οὐ γεγήρακε σθένος ('the strength of the land has not grown old'); cf. also *OC* 917 ff. Characteristic of the tyrant is that he fears the young (E. *Supp.* 447–9), and perhaps the fertility of Athens is contrasted with the abnormal family of Oedipus. The Cephissus is ὠκυτόκος ('swiftly fertilizing', l. 689).

each is equally important.[104] Poseidon is particularly important as the tamer of the horse (l. 715); the horse is a symbol of energy and fertility, and its taming represents civilization.[105] Relations between god and Athenian man are at their closest in this ode, and all these advantages possessed by Colonus and Attica are the gift of the gods in return for Athenian piety, past and future. Athenian piety has now helped Oedipus, and he, in turn, will keep Athens safe for ever.[106]

It is sometimes asserted that the *Oedipus Coloneus* is a lament for Athens: emphasis has been laid on alleged undertones of mourning in the Colonus ode, and Theseus is held to be the Periclean leader missed by Athens.[107] The play is the latest tragedy that we possess, and we know how the Peloponnesian War ended; but it is hard to believe that Sophocles was really writing Athens' death lament in 406. The references in the play thought to have contemporary significance fit the context of the myth quite satisfactorily, and in what he says about Thebes, Sophocles takes care to distance himself from the contemporary. None the less, it is a fitting accident of preservation that the latest extant Athenian tragedy should reinvent the ideal Athens for the very last time and in so many different aspects. Sometimes explicitly, sometimes by implication, Sophocles portrays Athens as the upholder of civilized human values, in the persons of the chorus, and most of all in the person of Theseus.

---

[104] Cf. 1070–3. There is probably a pun on χαλινός, (l. 713) both as bridle and anchor, which recalls the story of the first ship, built by Athena and dedicated to Poseidon: Stinton 1976*b*. This is another minor example of the unity of opposites at Athens.

[105] Jebb 1900: 122; McDevitt 1972.   [106] Cf. Segal 1981: 377.

[107] As Knox 1963: 143, 155. Both the nightingale and the narcissus are associated with death in Greek thought, but in the context of this ode, they must also be important examples of the beauties of Colonus (Gellie 1972: 294 n. 18). In any case, hints at death are appropriate for Oedipus, who knows that he must die at Colonus. At most, they might signify an interlink of death and life (present in the emphasis on fertility and continuity), so that Colonus would be a kind of microcosm of human experience: cf. McDevitt 1972: 231–4, who rightly points out that life and fertility ultimately predominate over any darker elements in the ode.

6

Theseus of Trozen: Euripides' *Hippolytus* and its Predecessors

6.1 INTRODUCTION

Euripides' *Hippolytus* of 428 BC is the earliest extant play in which Theseus appears, and its Theseus is strikingly different from the hero of the plays considered in previous chapters: the only other tragedy which treated him similarly was Euripides' other version of the Hippolytus story. The presentation of Theseus in the *Hippolytus* is unique in that he is no longer the wise democrat, receiver of suppliants and champion of the oppressed, but a foolish and violent father who will not listen to pleas for clemency or even for a less hasty judgement; a father whose curses condemn his son to an agonizing and undeserved death. Although consistent characterization from play to play was no concern of the Greek tragedians, the unusually unflattering portrayal of a hero who normally personifies an idealized image of Athens for Athenians invites comment, especially as this play won Euripides one of his very few first prizes, and the favourable critical reaction to the play of 428 contrasts with the disgust felt by the audience at Euripides' earlier version of the Hippolytus story.[1] If, as I have argued through earlier chapters, it is true that the Theseus of tragedies other than the *Hippolytus* is so closely associated with Athens that he reaffirms the beliefs and national identity of the audience by what he says and does, then the high esteem of the Athenian judges for a play in which their ancestor and role model killed his blameless son demands exploration. Since the Theseus of the *Hippolytus* cannot

[1] See below. I assume that the *Hippolytus Kalyptomenos* is earlier than the extant play, although the *Vita Euripidis* seems to base its chronology of the two plays purely on conjecture: as Cropp and Fick 1985: 69–70 note, the *Kalyptomenos* could, in theory, have been performed after the *Stephanephoros*. However, the extant *Hippolytus* contains some small oddities of setting and plot which are most easily explicable on the assumption that Euripides was deliberately writing against an earlier version of the story: see below.

be an example of, or a model for, typical Athenian conduct, there is a clear contradiction between the function of Theseus in tragedy considered so far and this Theseus, which may seem to undermine some of the conclusions reached in previous chapters.

The *Suppliants, Heracles* and *Oedipus Coloneus* largely reproduce conventional pictures of the ideal Athens without any distortion, so it is not difficult for their audiences to accept them as 'what really happened'. Because such plays reaffirm standard beliefs, the audience need not distance themselves at all from what is being offered to them. However, there is no need to suppose that an audience always accepts everything presented to them with the same measure of belief and identification with what is happening on stage: where a play presents events which cannot simply reaffirm the audience's beliefs, the audience can distance themselves from it in various ways,[2] and Euripides himself has taken care to allow the Athenian audience to distance themselves from this portrayal of Theseus. In the plays which have been discussed in earlier chapters, Theseus personifies the essence of the idealized Athens, so that in him, the audience can recognize themselves and imagine a glorious continuity between his past and their present.[3] By contrast, the Theseus of the *Hippolytus*, as will become clear, is entirely dissociated from the fifth-century Athenian imperial sentiments which have been so important in defining him up until now. This Theseus is simply a different character from the Theseus of the plays we have seen so far. Even so, it can never be certain that a portrayal of Theseus as he must appear in the *Hippolytus* was utterly uncontroversial. Euripides, who had a reputation for handling risky subject matter, may have been the first Athenian playwright to dramatize the Hippolytus story;[4] and a story which was acceptable in 428, and earlier, in the first *Hippolytus*, may not have been so subsequently, as the Peloponnesian War dragged on and Athens' national heroes were particularly needed as unproblematic inspirational models for Athenian pride and action.[5]

---

[2] See Taplin 1986: 164f.; Easterling 1985: 2. Vernant 1988: 34 notes a continually shifting tension in tragedy between past and present: this ambiguity will also enable the audience to distance itself from the truth of the tragedy where necessary.

[3] Compare the function of the historical examples in funeral speeches.

[4] There is no evidence for dating Sophocles' *Phaedra*: I follow conventional modern opinion (e.g. Barrett 1964: 12) in placing it between Euripides' two Hippolytus plays.

[5] Strauss 1993: 108 (cf. Neils 1987: 129) notes the comparative absence of

As we saw in the first chapter, there are other stories, such as the desertion of Ariadne, the abduction of Helen and the descent to the underworld, in which Theseus is not the democrat-hero of fifth-century tragedy: these stories date from before the democracy and from a time when it was not necessary that Theseus should be a moral example of, or for, Athenian behaviour. Such traditions were naturally less popular in public art than those in which Theseus was simply portrayed as a civilizer, but they could not be expunged from his story. Since myth can be so easily reinvented, however, Athenian writers reinvent those myths concerning Theseus to make them more pleasing to an Athenian ear: thus Athena told Theseus to leave Ariadne; Theseus may have abducted Helen, but he did not lay hands on her; and he went on the trip to abduct Persephone purely out of loyalty to a friend. In the same way the characterization of Theseus in the second *Hippolytus* may be read less as a retelling of a story in which Theseus was morally to blame than as a reinvention of a plot already dramatized by Euripides which 'rehabilitates' him (and also Phaedra) as far as it can. Euripides' *Hippolytus* is therefore best understood against its mythical and literary backgrounds which comprise both the myth as it came down to Euripides, and the conventions which surround the dramatization of such a story.[6]

Theseus from public buildings during Pericles' period of ascendancy, and suggests that the hero was out of favour because of his Cimonian associations. In general, the Periclean buildings show a preference for group action rather than that of individual heroes, as is fitting for a democracy, so that aversion to Theseus as such may not explain his relative neglect at this time, and the Theseus cycle is popular enough to adorn the temple of Poseidon at Sunium, *c.*430–420: Neils 1987: 129, 140; Boardman 1985: 247–52. However, if Theseus was temporarily less important as a national representative at this time for any reason, this would also make such a portrayal easier for an Athenian audience to bear.

[6] Walker 1995: 113 f. also discusses the differences between this Theseus and the democrat hero of other plays, but I very much doubt his conclusion (125) that 'Euripides has constructed a tragedy based on the double nature of Theseus as both a hero king and a model Athenian. For the tragedy to reach a stable denouement, the hero king must be exorcized and we are left with a good citizen and family man.' The Theseus of the *Hippolytus* is a typical hero king, but he is not a model Athenian. Euripides does his best to remove him from Athens and to make acceptable a story that—as, perhaps, in the earlier *Hippolytus*—was potentially offensive to Athenian sensibilities. At the end of the play, the hero king may be exorcized, but 'good citizen and family man' is an odd description of the broken, tragic figure who has lost his son and wife.

6.2 THE MYTH BEFORE THE FIFTH CENTURY

The story of Phaedra in its full form was known to the painter Polygnotus, who included it in his mythological compendium on the Lesche of the Cnidians, in the mid-fifth century.[7] She is placed in the same part of the picture as Ariadne and Procris, and the painter is probably recalling the association between the three that exists in *Odyssey* 11. 321: Φαίδρην τε Πρόκριν τε ἴδον, καλήν τ' Ἀριάδνην ('I saw Phaedra and Procris and lovely Ariadne'). Ariadne and Procris are both associated with Attica and known for unhappy love affairs, and if, as is probable, the story of Phaedra and Hippolytus antedates the fifth century, the poet of the Odyssean catalogue may have felt it appropriate to classify her with the other two here because there were some similarities in their stories.[8] However, even if some account of Phaedra's unhappy love for Hippolytus was known to this poet, the passage itself is unlikely to be older than the sixth century.[9]

According to the author of the *Theseid*, Theseus was attacked by the Amazons at his marriage to Phaedra, and Antiope, the Amazon who was his previous wife, was killed. The story seems to be designed to link two traditions about the marriages of Theseus; that he married an Amazon and that he married Phaedra (Plut. *Thes.* 28. 2). Phaedra has no demonstrable importance in Greek mythology beyond her role as Hippolytus' seductive stepmother, and tradition is unanimous that Theseus was his father.[10] This is the only known narrative concerning the three, and it is complete in itself, having very little organic connection with the rest of the narrative of

[7] Paus. 10. 29. 3: her portrayal on a swing, grasping the rope on either side of her is apparently a tasteful way of alluding to her death by hanging. For the story in art, see *LIMC* 5. 1, s.v. 'Hippolytus', 445–64. The story is popular in 4th-cent. Italy, but Theseus' role in the story is represented very rarely, and where he does appear, it is always in composite scenes with Phaedra, Hippolytus and the Nurse, which correspond to no known literary version of the tale: see *LIMC* 5. 1 nos. 68–71 and 96–9.

[8] Procris' inclusion in the line makes it impossible to decide whether this poet envisaged Phaedra as well as Ariadne as a daughter of Minos, although Procris herself had a Cretan connection (Apollod. 3. 15. 1): see Herter 1940: 277–8; Séchan 1911: 108–9.

[9] See §1.3.4, and Barrett 1964: 9.

[10] ΣLycophr. 610 tells us that in Mimnermus, Aphrodite made Diomedes' wife Aegiale have many lovers; ἐρασθῆναι δὲ καὶ Ἱππολύτου Κομήτου τοῦ Σθενέλου υἱοῦ ('and she loved Hippolytus Kometes (?), the son of Sthenelus'), but the scholion is corrupt: Barrett 1964: 6 n. 3.

Theseus' life in Attica.[11] It is therefore very probably Trozenian in origin. Theseus' Trozenian roots are never forgotten in spite of his other life at Athens, and Hippolytus, though a minor hero at Athens,[12] is of much greater importance at Trozen: by Pausanias' day, he commanded a large precinct, a priest and annual sacrifices.[13] Plutarch remarks on the remarkable consensus surrounding the details of the story (*Thes.* 28. 2, cf. Paus. 1. 22. 1), and it may be that a tale which was originally Trozenian was already well known by the time of the composition of the *Theseid*, so that the author of the poem was forced to reconcile the story of Theseus and Phaedra with the conflicting tradition in which he married the Amazon.[14] It is a plausible conjecture that the story of Hippolytus became familiar in Attica when interest in Theseus himself was increasing, and around the time when the stories of Theseus' travels around the Saronic Gulf from Trozen were beginning to be of interest at Athens.[15]

The author of the *Naupaktika* knew a sequel in which Hippolytus was resurrected by Asclepius (Apollod. 3. 10. 3). According to Paus. 10. 31. 11 (cf. 4. 2. 1), it was a poem about women, and the information given by these two citations might suggest that the *Naupaktika*, as well as the *Theseid*, knew the full story of Phaedra's attempted seduction and Hippolytus' death.[16] The poem is generally dated to the sixth century,[17] so that Hippolytus' resurrection is evidently not a late invention, but the version of the story in which he dies and is rewarded with a cult has a logical consistency and is likely to be the older version.[18]

---

[11] Phaedra becomes the mother of Demophon and Acamas at Athens after it is no longer appropriate that Theseus' legitimate sons should have an Amazon mother, but the Amazon is their mother as late as Pindar (173–6 Sn.): cf. Herter 1940: 280. She has a grave in Trozen: Paus. 2. 32. 4.

[12] He has a grave mound and a precinct on the south side of the Acropolis (*IGI*² 324. 69; 310. 280) and there is some evidence for another Hippolytus cult somewhere in Attica: *IG*² 190 (Sokolowski 1969: 11A5) with Barrett 1964: 4–5.

[13] Paus. 2. 32. 1: cf. Herter 1940: 273; Barrett 1964: 3–7.

[14] Simonides (ap. Apollod. *Ep.* 1. 16) calls Theseus' Amazon wife Hippolyte rather than Antiope. Perhaps the fame of the Amazon's son influenced the poet's choice of name: Barrett 1964: 9.

[15] Herter 1940: 273–8; Barrett 1964: 3–5; Reckford 1972: 414–16.

[16] Séchan 1911: 106f.   [17] Barrett 1964: 5 n. 6.

[18] Cf. Paus. 2. 32. 1–4: the Trozenians 'will not show' the grave of Hippolytus. Hyg. 2. 14 and Philodemos *peri eusebeias* 131 also mention the resurrection. Three late 5th-cent. or early 4th-cent. reliefs also connect Hippolytus and Asclepius: *LIMC* 5. 1, s.v. 'Hippolytus', nos. 124–6; see also Barrett 1964: 5.

Ironically in the light of Euripides' *Hippolytus*, the cultic connection between Hippolytus and Aphrodite is quite firm, but not
nearly such a firm connection is known between Hippolytus and
Artemis.[19] Both at Athens and at Trozen, his precinct contained a
temple of Aphrodite, and in Trozenian myth and cult, he was associated with unmarried girls, for whom he was a subject of cult songs
and the recipient of their hair when they married.[20] By the time we
first see him he is a fully humanized hero, but his cult was perhaps
originally concerned with turning young girls from virginity to
marriage. It may be that the worship of Hippolytus itself gave rise
to a story shaped by the popular motif of the seduction of a young
man by a predatory married woman which was used to explain why
he was worshipped at Trozen.[21]

6.3 THESEUS' CHARACTER IN THE HIPPOLYTUS MYTH: NECESSITY AND FREEDOM

The Hippolytus story is one of a number of Greek myths in which
a bad married woman tries to seduce a virtuous young man, and on
failing to do so, denounces him to her husband who takes unjust
revenge on him. Euripides' *Hippolytus* plays are not unique in taking this form: his *Stheneboia*, *Phoenix* and probably his *Peleus* are
all based on this essential plot structure.[22] Such a story imposes
instant constraints on the dramatic portrayal of the husband who
believes his wife's false accusation. The structure of the Hippolytus
myth necessitates that Theseus must condemn his son unjustly,
and therefore he must be portrayed as the type of man who would
do so, since the tragedian must always make his characters react in
a plausible way to the particular situation created by the structure
of the plot.[23]

[19] Barrett, 1964: 6 n. 2; Herter 1940: 274–5; Burkert 1979: 111f. Paus. 2. 31. 4
mentions that the temple of Artemis Lycea was said to have been dedicated by
Hippolytus.

[20] E. *Hipp.* 1425ff., cf. 446N²; Paus. 2. 32. 1–4.

[21] Barrett 1964: 6–10; Herter 1940: 273.

[22] These are not the only examples of this kind of story, nor is it confined to Greek
myth: Lattimore 1962; Schmid-Stählin 1929: i. 2, 92 n. 8. Homer *Il.* 6. 160ff. tells
the story of Bellerophon and Proetus' wife Anteia (more commonly known later as
Stheneboia).

[23] Arist. *Poet.* 1449ᵇ41: cf. Heath 1987: 116–17. Lattimore 1962: 5 notes that the
Hippolytus is unique among plays of this type in that its innocent protagonist dies;
this too has a potentially detrimental effect on the portrayal of Theseus.

The structure of the Hippolytus story compels Theseus to appear as a distasteful character. However, the way that the story is told in the second *Hippolytus* imposes other, quite distinct constraints on his actions and character. Aphrodite makes it clear from the outset of the play (*Hipp*. 42–6) that she is going to punish Hippolytus and that Theseus will be involved in that punishment. He has no choice but to act in the way that he does because his role in the play is essentially secondary and instrumental. The play centres on Hippolytus' moral choice, its influence on him and on those around him: it is his choice, not that of Theseus, which is the stimulus of the action, and thus Hippolytus and Phaedra, not Theseus, are the main sources of interest in the play.[24] Theseus only appears half-way through the play after Aphrodite has set up her plan: the audience must expect him to hurt his son because that is the only reason he has been brought onto the stage. Because he must (unknowingly) fulfil the destiny Aphrodite has determined for Hippolytus, he exemplifies the human impotence against divine will that is a major theme of the play, just as the more immediately important characters, Phaedra and Hippolytus, do. If Theseus is inevitably doomed to do what he does, an audience should feel pity as well as horror or disgust at his actions. By the terms of the plot, Theseus has no choice but to act unjustly towards his son, and therefore, though it is shocking, it is less so than if he had 'free will' and performed an act of cruelty which was unexpected.[25] In any case, within the framework of what Theseus is compelled to do, there remains some scope for depicting the specific stages by which he reaches his fatal action, and his reasons for condemning his son can be made to evoke more, or less, sympathy from the audience. Theseus is essentially instrumental in a tragedy in which Hippolytus is punished, but there is still some room for moral judgements on how he becomes instrumental in it. This chapter attempts to show how Euripides manipulates traditional material

[24] For this sort of assessment of Theseus, which is one of the few things that critics of the *Hippolytus* tend to agree on, see Herter 1940: 290–1; Kitto 1939: 207; Norwood 1953: 86–7; Lattimore 1964: 56–60.

[25] By contrast, the 'free will' of his unexpected appearance in the *Heracles* made it seem especially admirable. Parallels can also be made between Theseus in the *Hippolytus* and Creon in the *Antigone*: both are kings, essentially secondary characters, who destroy their families by their own errors of judgement; but Creon is more directly responsible for his tragedy than Theseus is, nor does a divinity explicitly forgive him for what he does. See further below.

and plot structures to provide Theseus with every excuse for what he does in the *Hippolytus Stephanephoros*.[26]

Theseus is distanced from what he does, not only by the surrounding circumstances, but also, and importantly, by the absence in the *Hippolytus* of the links between Theseus and Athens which are vital to an understanding of his role in the plays discussed in earlier chapters. The second *Hippolytus* was set in Trozen, rather than Athens where the earlier *Hippolytus* and Sophocles' *Phaedra* were very probably set.[27] The new setting cannot have been employed purely for the sake of variety, because it involves some awkwardness. Theseus' presence in Trozen is explained as an exile to atone for the murder of the Pallantidae, even though every other version of the myth associates their killing with Theseus' youthful exploits, long before he becomes king of Athens,[28] and normally he never returns to Trozen once he is established at Athens. It is a little surprising that Theseus is king of Trozen while Pittheus is still alive, and certainly awkward that—apparently just so that Euripides can refer to the temple of Aphrodite ἐφ' Ἱππολύτῳ ('next to Hippolytus') at Athens—Hippolytus must be sent to Athens for the mysteries, so that Phaedra can fall in love with him and found the temple (ll. 24–33), only for him to return home again, followed eventually by his father and stepmother.[29] All these oddities would seem to result from the transplanting to Trozen of a story which was previously set in Athens.[30]

Although Euripides could hardly have avoided making Theseus king of Athens as well as Trozen (cf. *Hipp.* 974, 1093 f., 1158), he is never linked with Athens as its representative as he is in all the other extant Theseus plays.[31] Expressions such as 'you and your

[26] In line with my earlier remarks concerning the educational value of tragedy, I assume that it is not mistaken to look for mitigating circumstances in his portrayal. Needless to say, Euripides did not write the second *Hippolytus* with the primary aim of rehabilitating Theseus; but a comparison with the first *Hippolytus* (§6.4) will show that his handling in the two plays is very different.

[27] Herter 1940: 281–2 and especially Barrett 1964: 32–3: but cf. n. 81 below.

[28] The murder of the Pallantidae does not foreshadow Theseus' violence towards his son. They are always the enemies of Theseus and therefore of Athens, and if Euripides had intended a link between Theseus' past and future violence, he could have made it more explicit, as Seneca does: cf. Jeny 1898: 402.

[29] Barrett 1964: 32–4, 159; Zintzen 1960: 16.

[30] Though the story is originally Trozenian, it can be assumed that Athenians had given it an Athenian setting, perhaps in the 6th cent. or before: Barrett 1964: 9–10.

[31] Though Theseus has been described as a typical statesman (Knox 1952: 23), he is a statesman without being the wise king of Athens. Knox bases this view of

city', so common in the *Suppliants*, *Heracles* and *Oedipus Coloneus*
are entirely absent from the *Hippolytus*. In all the other plays that
have been discussed so far, Theseus personifies the idealized imperial Athens. The city which is uniquely god-fearing, which always
takes the wider view beyond merely retributive justice and, above
all, which always feels pity, has a king who will always be swayed
by such considerations and by an appeal to Athens' pre-eminence
in these qualities. The *Hippolytus* could have been a radically disturbing play if, say, in the *agon* scene with his father, Hippolytus
had begged Theseus to show the pity that an Athenian should naturally show and Theseus had explicitly denied that he cared for the
reputation of his city, or that its reputation was false or irrelevant,
or if Hippolytus or Artemis had bitterly referred to the ideals of
Athens at the end of the play.[32] As it is, the city of Athens and its
ideals is excluded from this tale of the power of Aphrodite and one
young man's mistaken belief about the gods, and it is possible to be
touched by it without finding Theseus' role too awkward, because
he has been detached from representing the ideal Athens. It is not
hard to understand why the story was more palatable to the
Athenians as a piece of the history of Trozen—in Peloponnesian
hands at this time[33]—than as what happened in Athens.[34] The
fluidity of Greek myth, in which no version has absolute dominance as the 'right' version, facilitates this shift of emphasis: one
may compare Bacchylides' unflattering portrayal of Minos, the
ancestor of the Ceans (Bacch. 1. 112 f.) in poem 17, in which he is
careful to detach him from any mention of Ceos, so that the Cean
chorus can both rejoice whole-heartedly in Theseus' inspiring
ethical triumph, and also avoid awkward implications concerning
their own origins from such an ancestor.

Theseus partly on 817's cry of outrage, ὦ πόλις ('o, city,') but Barrett 1964: 320
makes out a good case for preferring the alternative reading ὦ τάλας ('o, alas').

[32] Only at 1089 is pity even mentioned, as Theseus, at the extreme climax of his
wrath, tells his son that he feels no pity for him. This is the moment when he is furthest from the idealized city of Athens, but Euripides makes no attempt to emphasize his divergence from the conventional ideal.

[33] Thuc. 2. 56. 5 mentions Athenian raids in Trozen in 430 BC.

[34] Herter 1940: 284; Webster 1967: 71 and especially the more detailed analysis
of Jeny 1989.

6.4 THE EARLIER HIPPOLYTUS PLAYS

The story of Phaedra and Hippolytus was also treated by Seneca in his *Phaedra* and Ovid in *Heroides* 4. Their versions are utterly unlike that of the extant *Hippolytus* and it is always assumed that the lost Phaedra tragedies had some influence on them: the Phaedra of Euripides' first *Hippolytus* was notorious for her blatant display of her passion for Hippolytus,[35] and an outrageous Phaedra naturally had more dramatic appeal for the Latin writers than Euripides' second Phaedra who struggles hopelessly against Aphrodite.[36] Although it is tempting to use Seneca and Ovid to try to 'reconstruct' the earlier plays, only the surviving fragments of Sophocles and Euripides are reliable evidence, and it is certainly not safe to assume that what is in Seneca and Ovid but not the extant *Hippolytus* derives from any lost Greek tragedy.[37] Many of the fragments of the first *Hippolytus* have, however, no obvious relevance for Theseus' role in the plays: the quotations which have come down to us from their inclusion in anthologies naturally tend either to refer to the fascinating Phaedra, or to be too general or sententious to be assigned to particular characters.[38] The question is further confused by the existence of Sophocles' *Phaedra*: even less is known about this play and its relation to later Latin sources than about the earlier *Hippolytus*, although this Phaedra does not seem to have achieved the notoriety that clung to Euripides' first Phaedra. The problems surrounding any reconstruction of Euripides' first *Hippolytus* and Sophocles' *Phaedra* from later sources are innumerable, and most of them are not relevant to the portrayal of Theseus; however, general tendencies in the portrayal of Phaedra and Hippolytus are likely to affect any evaluation of Theseus.[39]

[35] Cf. Ar. *Th.* 497, 547 and 550; *Ran.* 849–50; see also the argument to the second play. Barrett 1964: 12–13.

[36] Herter 1940; Zwierlein 1987: 52.

[37] On the complex relationship between Seneca and his alleged Greek 'models', see Tarrant 1978.

[38] e.g. 441, and 436N², which faintly recalls Theseus' outburst at *Hipp.* 925 ff., but it is too conventional to be significant in establishing anything about the portrayal of Theseus in the earlier *Hippolytus*.

[39] For full commentaries on the fragments, and various attempts at reconstruction, see Mayer 1883: 65 ff.; Séchan 1911; Herter 1940: 287–92; Barrett 1964: 15–45; Webster 1967: 64–76; also Zintzen 1960, who goes the furthest in using the Latin works to reconstruct the lost Greek works, but see Grimal 1964. I shall not comment fully on every fragment of all the lost Hippolytus plays—Barrett 1964, of course,

It can be assumed that the action of the second *Hippolytus* copies that of the earlier play in outline: the first play must have included (as a bare minimum) a scene in which it is revealed that Phaedra is in love with Hippolytus, a scene in which he finds out and condemns her violently, a false accusation of rape by Phaedra, his condemnation by Theseus, the story of the bull from the sea (cf. fr. 442N²), the final revelation of the truth and a prophecy that Hippolytus will be famous in cult (fr. 446N²). It can also be assumed that the second *Hippolytus* did not follow the earlier play much beyond these fundamental requirements of the plot. The later, first prize-winning play came to be regarded as a repentant offering to the Athenians by Euripides after his earlier, shocking play, but it is unlikely that recantation was really his aim in writing another play on the Phaedra theme. A very attractive explanation for why Euripides—unusually—returned to a theme he had already dramatized is that the story offered a particular challenge to his ingenuity and dramatic skill.[40] The myth as it is normally told makes Phaedra guilty and Hippolytus innocent: this must be the picture that most of the Athenian audience would have, especially if they had seen Euripides' earlier play. In his *Medea*, Euripides evened the moral balance a little between an infanticidal mother and a Greek hero; in his *Helen* he would turn the most famous adulteress in Greek into a much misunderstood model of wifely fidelity: in the same way, Euripides reinvented the story of Phaedra and Hippolytus to make the old truths of Phaedra's wickedness and Hippolytus' virtue less obvious than they had been. The sophists were able by their ingenious arguments to reverse the usual certainties of the world, making what would normally be the weaker argument into the stronger: in the second *Hippolytus* Phaedra's traditionally weak *logos* is not turned into the stronger one—it would be impossible—but it is certainly transformed and the Phaedra of the second play is like no other known Phaedra.

Many of the fragments of the first *Hippolytus* are quoted to show Phaedra's shocking lack of inhibition concerning her stepson: it is likely, for example, that he discovered her feelings for him because she propositioned him herself on stage in her desire for him.[41] The

makes the most useful comprehensive collection and commentary—but cite only such fragments as can give an idea of the character of Theseus and how he appears against the background of Phaedra and Hippolytus.

[40] Cf. J. Griffin 1990, esp. 131 f.

[41] As frs. 428, 430 (cf. Sen. *Ph.* 184ff.), 421, 434. See Barrett 1964: 11, 30–1.

later Phaedra must also be in love with her step-son, but in total contrast she struggles against her passion to the utmost until she is betrayed by her well-meaning but misguided nurse. We, however, have known from the outset of the play that her struggles will be useless. In the prologue of the extant *Hippolytus*, Aphrodite agrees that Phaedra is εὐκλεής ('honourable'), but regards her εὐκλεια as quite irrelevant, because the goddess has revenge on her mind and Phaedra is essential to her as an instrument to secure the downfall of a young man who, for all his virtues, has offended against an important power in the universe (E. *Hipp.* 41 ff.). Aphrodite prophesies that disaster is about to hit Theseus' family, and from this moment on, we know that Phaedra is helpless. Even Hippolytus' supporter Artemis understands that Phaedra's position was impossible, describing the false accusation made for the sake of her good reputation as 'a sort of nobility' (*Hipp.* 1300–1); Hippolytus himself says of her, ἐσωφρόνησε δ' οὐκ ἔχουσα σωφρονεῖν ('she did the right thing when she could not do the right thing', *Hipp.* 1034); such phrases aptly demonstrate how difficult it is to make absolute moral judgements concerning this Phaedra. Phaedra must die because Aphrodite must punish Hippolytus, whose foolishness— like Phaedra's doom—is made clear from the outset of the play, as will be discussed below. He is therefore not simply a guiltless recipient of unwanted attention from an uninhibited woman. Although Phaedra's love has exactly the same terrible effect that it has in the first play, the circumstances in which it functions are utterly different, and its origin is rooted very firmly in divine purpose.

It has often been noticed that the plot of the *Hippolytus* could work perfectly well without the element of divine causation, and it is sometimes suggested that Aphrodite and Artemis are simply projections of human psychology.[42] This is surely mistaken: Aphrodite speaks as an offended goddess who wants an absolute revenge, as Greek divinities tend to do. Phaedra has up until now been εὐκλεής. Now Aphrodite has made her fall, and the only intelligible explanation for her sudden change of character is that the goddess of love has, in the way of divinities, sent a cruelly suitable punishment on the young man who has offended her by rejecting love.[43] The divine framing of human action has an inescapable effect on the evaluation of the human action in a play in which there is a

[42] As Lesky 1962: 136 f.   [43] Rightly Heath 1987: 53.

continual shift between divine compulsion and human free will.[44]
Aphrodite creates the love that will lead to disaster, because she has
good reason to do so in her terms, but after carefully setting her plot
up (cf. *Hipp.* 22–3) she can retreat into the background and we
watch purely human choices being played out: the human partici-
pants choose freely in accord with their own characters (as far as
they are aware), and only at the end will another goddess reveal to
Theseus and Hippolytus what Aphrodite has told the audience
from the beginning. The action of the play is unusually equally
divided between four characters[45] and the equal division is fundamental to this version of the play: Aphrodite sets the situation up,
but thence inexorably, the Nurse's well-meaning choice must pre-
cipitate that of Phaedra; and Phaedra's moral choice must lead to
Theseus' choice, which causes Hippolytus' death, the result so
desired by Aphrodite. It is perfectly usual in Greek literature for
the gods to intervene in human life, but their intervention does not
invalidate the influence of human character and motivation: indeed
the gods work through what they know of human character, and for
Aphrodite's plan to work, she must know that Phaedra is especially
concerned that her reputation should be spotless from the outside
(*Hipp.* 401–2) and know that Hippolytus will rigidly adhere to his
principles.[46] The *Hippolytus* is a very traditional tragedy in the way
that the human and the divine are linked together,[47] and, like the
Heracles, it is partly a study in the lack of ἐπιείκεια among the gods.
Euripides' technique in recasting his myth in the *Hippolytus* is similar to that of the *Heracles*, where the play agrees with traditional
myth in having Heracles kill his children in madness, just as the
Hippolytus follows traditional myth in having Phaedra fall in love
with Hippolytus before falsely accusing him, but in both plays, the
element of divine compulsion over human action opens up gaps
between intention, crime and punishment. In the *Heracles* Theseus
is outside the tragedy, and exploits these gaps in order to help his
friend and offer him a future life in Athens. In the *Hippolytus* he is

---

[44] The feeling that all human characters are trapped is emphasized by the preva-
lence in the play of images of impossibility and impotence: walls are feared or
desired as witnesses (*Hipp.* 418, 1070 ff.); Hippolytus wishes that women did not
exist, and that they did not even speak (*Hipp.* 616 ff., 645 ff.); the tablet seems to
'speak' so clearly to Theseus (*Hipp.* 877) but its clarity is false; Theseus wishes that
men could have more than one voice (*Hipp.* 925 ff.): Knox 1952: 16–17.

[45] Cf. Knox 1952: 3 f.   [46] Cf. Knox 1952: 16–17.

[47] Cf. Vernant 1988: 21–2.

a part of the tragedy, and Artemis and Hippolytus can offer him absolution but no real help.

The divine framework of the second *Hippolytus* cannot be separated from the main body of the human action and it affects moral evaluation of it. Fr. 444 of the first *Hippolytus*, ὦ δαῖμον, ὡς οὐκ ἔστ᾽ ἀποστροφὴ βροτοῖς | τῶν ἐμφύτων τε καὶ θεηλάτων κακῶν ('O god, there is no escape for mortals from innate and god-sent evils') suggests that Aphrodite sent Phaedra's love upon her in the earlier play as well,[48] but Aristophanes and the writer of the *Hypothesis* to the extant play both imply that the machinations of the goddess did not in the least exonerate Phaedra from blame. Presumably Phaedra did not exactly try to resist her every inch of the way as she does in the extant *Hippolytus*: the play would have lacked the presentation of a noble but vain struggle of a human being against divine ruthlessness that is uniquely admirable in the second Phaedra, throwing more relief instead on the shocking element of her unnatural love.[49] Not only are the troubles[50] god-sent, however: they are also 'innate' (ἔμφυτα). While the extant *Hippolytus* primarily emphasizes Aphrodite's will as the creator of the tragedy, it has been noticed that Phaedra's Cretan origins are sometimes mentioned at apparently significant moments in it.[51] Allusion to previous plays is not uncommon among the tragedians,[52] and it has been suggested that the references to Crete in the extant *Hippolytus* are meant to recall the prominence given to them—and thus to Phaedra's own nature and personal guilt—in the first *Hippolytus*: thus Aristophanes' complaints (*Ran.* 849–50) about 'Cretan monodies and unholy marriages' would apply to the first *Hippolytus*, as well as to the *Aerope* and the *Cretans*.[53] The

[48] In Sen. *Ph.* 124 ff. Aphrodite's motive for causing Phaedra's love is her hatred of the house of Helios for spying on her affair with Ares. With Barrett 1964: 34–5 (cf. Zintzen 1960: 10, cf. Webster 1967: 74–5), I doubt that the first play opened with a prologue speech by Aphrodite and it is quite probable that Phaedra herself or her nurse spoke it: cf. below, n. 63.

[49] Cf. Reckford 1974: 310–11.

[50] Presumably Phaedra's, not Theseus' (Barrett 1964: 22). Wilamowitz thought that the *Hippolytus* belonged to an *Aegeus, Theseus, Hippolytus* trilogy, but this is unlikely: see §7.4.2.

[51] *Hipp.* 156, 719, 758 ff. and esp. 372: Norwood 1953: 79; Reckford 1974: 319. Also Sen. *Ph.* 85 and esp. 175 f.

[52] See Zielinski 1925: 1–132.

[53] Reckford 1974: 319–28. For the idea that Crete was seen by the Athenians as a pseudo-barbarian place particularly prone to 'non-Athenian' conduct, see §7.1.2.

Cretans is probably to be assigned to the same part of Euripides' career as the first *Hippolytus*;[54] like the Hippolytus story, it concerns a visitation of unnatural love—in this case that of Phaedra's mother Pasiphae for a bull—and presumably with questions of guilt and responsibility. Fragments reveal that Pasiphae makes a shockingly sophistical attempt to absolve herself of any blame whatsoever for the terrible deed: first she blames divinity (4. 9–10); and by 31 ff. she tells Minos that it was completely his fault.[55] Although we have no directly quoted fragments of the first Phaedra's defence, Plutarch says that she too tried to minimize her guilt by complaining of Theseus' infidelities: one might speculate that mother and daughter had some characteristics in common.[56] In fact Phaedra's conduct is connected with that of her mother both by Seneca (*Ph.* 115–28) and Euripides at *Hipp.* 337 ff., where Phaedra recognizes that she is the third in a series of women from the same family who were unlucky or unnatural in love. At E. *Hipp.* 339, she calls Ariadne her 'unlucky sister, the bride of Dionysus': the conjunction of 'bad luck' with Ariadne's status as Dionysus' bride can only refer to the (Attic) version of the story first found in *Odyssey* 11. 325 ff., in which she was killed for betraying Dionysus.[57] Even if Phaedra's passion in the first play was ultimately attributed to divinity, as it was in the later play, the element of blame attached to Phaedra herself and the way she handled her passion was surely much stronger in the first *Hippolytus* than in the second. If Phaedra and the shocking Pasiphae of the *Cretans* were alike in some respects, then the first play may also have stressed the element of deviant 'Cretan sexuality' in Phaedra that was also inherent in her family and that led her to such shameful conduct.

It appears, then, that Phaedra's unwillingness to yield to her passion and her attempts to justify herself were probably prime ingredients of the earlier *Hippolytus*. The revelation of her love to Hippolytus and its rejection were presumably followed by a false accusation of rape to Theseus. Its motivation was probably fear and

---

[54] Cantarella 1963: 105–7.

[55] Reckford 1974: 319–22 on *Cretans* fr. 4. 24 ff. and 31 ff. Presumably Pasiphae's passion was divinely inspired; but her apparent refusal to accept any responsibility (in contrast with Euripides' *Heracles*, for example) is disturbing.

[56] Plut. *Mor.* 27f–28a; cf. Sen. *Ph.* 85 ff.

[57] See § 1.3.3: Barrett 1964: 222–3; Reckford 1974: 323 n. 23. The Ariadne of Euripides' *Theseus* may also have been portrayed as a 'typically' shameless Cretan woman: see §7.5.2.

anger, and it is even possible that she made the charge look more convincing by appearing with deliberately dishevelled hair.[58] In all other accounts Phaedra kills herself only after it is revealed that her accusation was false, and it is probable that these narratives reflect the structure of the earlier play.[59] If so, its Phaedra could have accused Hippolytus directly to Theseus, and it may be argued that he is more worthy of blame in believing Phaedra's accusation when she can be cross-questioned than in believing the evidence provided by his wife's suicide (a natural reaction to rape) and her letter in the second play. Indeed, in the extant *Hippolytus*, Phaedra's essential concern with εὔκλεια and Theseus' love for her make his credulity understandable, but the portrayal of a woman like the Phaedra of the earlier play might make such credulity seem ill-advised and his condemnation of Hippolytus all the more brutal and foolish. Fr. 440, Θησεῦ, παραινῶ σοι τὸ λῷστον, εἰ φρονεῖς· | γυναικὶ πείθου μηδὲ τἀληθῆ κλύων ('Theseus, I give you excellent advice, if you are sensible; do not trust a woman even when you hear the truth [from her]'), must be taken from the section of the play that corresponds to *Hipp.* 856–98.[60]

Fragments 437–8 were assigned by Barrett to a confrontation between Theseus and his son after Phaedra's accusation. Fr. 437, ὁρῶ δὲ τοῖς πολλοῖσιν ἀνθρώποις ἐγὼ | τίκτουσαν ὕβριν τὴν πάροιθ' εὐπραξίαν ('I see previous good fortune giving birth to arrogance in many men'), could be a comment by Theseus on Hippolytus; and 438, ὕβριν τε τίκτει πλοῦτος, οὐ φειδώ, βίου ('wealth engenders arrogance, not a sparing life'), his son's reply. If Hippolytus is implying that Theseus is prone to hubris, accusations of tyranny are perhaps not far behind, and similar accusations are made in the *agon* between Creon and his son in *Antigone* (S. *Ant.* 736–9; cf. *OT* 872). The exchange could easily have been written to present Hippolytus in the best possible light against a thoroughly unsympathetic Theseus. This is not the case in the *agon* of

[58] For Phaedra's anger cf. perhaps fr. 429N. For the faked evidence, see Sen. *Ph.* 731f., 825f.; cf. Apollod. *Ep.* 1. 18–19 with Barrett 1964: 38–9. Also *LIMC* 5. 1, s.v. 'Hippolytus', nos. 97–8. When Seneca's Hippolytus flees from Phaedra's immoral suggestions (*Ph.* 717ff.), he also leaves his sword behind as incriminating evidence. This detail may have come from the first *Hippolytus* but Phaedra's evidence ought to be sufficient to condemn him: Zwierlein 1987: 29.

[59] Barrett 1964: 43–4.

[60] Who says this to him is unknown. The vocative Θησεῦ is used by the chorus at *Hipp.* 798 and 805, and they warn him against too hasty a judgement at *Hipp.* 891, but in Seneca, the chorus is not in Phaedra's confidence.

the second play. However, on the assumption that the second play should present an entirely different account of the story, a confrontation between Theseus and his son is not indispensable to the action of the earlier play,[61] and it is quite possible that this confrontation in the second *Hippolytus* is a substitute for more obviously dramatic encounters between Hippolytus and Phaedra and Theseus and Phaedra in the first play; in fact there are other possible attributions for these two fragments.[62] It is true that the tone of fr. 439,

> φεῦ, φεῦ, τὸ μὴ τὰ πράγματ' ἀνθρώποις ἔχειν
> φωνήν ἵν' ἦσαν μηδὲν οἱ δεινοὶ λέγειν
> νῦν δ' εὐρόοισι στόμασι τἀληθέστατα
> κλέπτουσιν, ὥστε μὴ δοκεῖν ἃ χρὴ δοκεῖν

('Alas, would that deeds of men would have a voice so that those clever at speaking would be nothing! As it is, they hide what is the real truth with glib tongues, so that what ought to be the truth does not seem so.')

resembles that of Theseus' words at E. *Hipp.* 925 ff., but it is too conventional a protest against dishonest speech to be used as proof that the lost *Hippolytus* contained an *agon* between Theseus and his son.

Barrett suggests that ἔγωγέ φημι καὶ νόμον γε μὴ σέβειν | ἐν τοῖσι δεινοῖς τῶν ἀναγκαίων πλέον ('I say that I do not even honour custom more than necessity in a difficult situation', fr. 433) should also be assigned to a confrontation between father and son, and to Theseus, 'not over-nice in the formalities of his punishment'. If so, this Theseus is consciously tyrannical and unjust, but the fragment is normally ascribed to Phaedra and this attribution must remain attractive, even leaving aside the uncertain status of the Theseus–Hippolytus encounter in the first *Hippolytus*. Although Barrett argues against the attribution because 'trans-

---

[61] I am not convinced that Hippolytus must reappear in the play, nor that fr. 440 must suggest 'an interval between Phaidra's accusation and the curse, pointless unless Theseus intends to question Hippolytus in person' (as Barrett 1964: 40–1, cf. 20). In Seneca, Hippolytus flees immediately after Phaedra's proposal; not that this can prove that the earlier *Hippolytus* used the same series of events. Barrett 1964: 42 suggests that Seneca may have been following Sophocles' *Phaedra* here, but see below, n. 86.

[62] See Zintzen 1960: 3, 112; Zwierlein 1987: 38 f.; J. Griffin 1990: 132. For alternative attributions of the lines see Leo, *Seneca*, p. 174, who connects them with *Hipp.* 384 and 409 (cf. Sen. *Ph.* 204 ff.); Snell 1964: 40–1; Webster 1967: 67 f., who connects them with fr. 428's advice to Hippolytus to give up his celibacy.

gressing νόμος is too mild a term for what she does', such an ano-
dyne description of desire for her stepson might be exactly the kind
of thing we should expect from a Phaedra who is keen to minimize
her guilt in what she does: again, a comparison with Pasiphae of the
Cretans might be relevant.

> ὦ λαμπρὸς αἰθὴρ ἡμέρας θ᾽ ἁγνὸν φάος
> ὡς ἡδὺ λεύσσειν τοῖς τε πράσσουσιν καλῶς
> καὶ τοῖσι δυστυχοῦσιν, ὧν πέφυκ᾽ ἐγώ

('O shining air and holy light of day, how lovely it is to see you, both for
those who fare well and the unfortunate, of whom I am one', fr. 443.)

This fragment was once assigned to Theseus on his return from the
underworld, but it is now more usually given to Phaedra, perhaps
in a prologue speech.[63] However, it is relevant to ask at this point
how the first *Hippolytus* treated the relationship of Phaedra and
Theseus in order to make her love for Hippolytus and her proposal
to him dramatically possible. In Sophocles' *Phaedra* he was certainly in the underworld, and, with the exception of the extant
Hippolytus, tradition is unanimous in placing Phaedra's love for
Hippolytus at a time when Theseus was away in Hades. In the surviving play, Euripides takes care to state that Theseus is not in
Hades, but has gone on an unexplained visit to an oracle (θεωρία,
Hipp. 792–3, cf. 280), and this rather ill-motivated explanation for
his absence may indicate that the playwright was working against
the usual tradition which said that Phaedra fell in love with
Hippolytus when Theseus was in the underworld.[64] It is certainly
dramatically convenient, even essential, that he should be absent at
the start of the play.

Ovid's Phaedra says that her husband is more interested in
Peirithous than in his wife, and Seneca may imply something similar.[65] This twist probably originates from Ovidian ingenuity in

---

[63] Barrett 1964: 18 n. 2; Snell 1964: 27; Webster 1967: 66; see also Zintzen 1960:
10.

[64] Herter 1940: 285–6. Barrett 1964: 32 denies this, on the grounds that Phaedra's
proposal is less shocking if Theseus is presumed to be dead, but this is hardly con-
clusive: Sen. *Ph.* 219 ff. shows that his supposed death need not exonerate her from
anything. Once Phaedra justified her feelings for Hippolytus by saying that he
reminded her of the young Theseus: Sen. *Ph.* 646, Heliodor. 1. 10. Does this make
her love more shocking (Snell 1964: 43), or is she trying to pretend that she is being
loyal to her missing husband (Kiso 1973: 28, who refers the motif to Sophocles'
Phaedra)?

[65] Ov. *Her.* 110; also, perhaps, Sen. *Ph.* 225, 244: Mayer 1883: 67–8.

rewriting Greek mythology and it should not be assumed that Theseus and Peirithous were lovers in the first *Hippolytus*. However, Phaedra did try to justify her love for Hippolytus by accusing Theseus of his own transgressions.[66] The purpose of his visit to the underworld was the abduction of Persephone, and earlier sources link this abduction with the abduction of Helen: such traditions would provide ample ammunition for Phaedra against her husband, even if her use of them is undercut by the context of her complaint.[67] If these old stories are the source of her complaints, it must be emphasized that Euripides would have been departing radically from the abnormal Athenian tradition in which the journey to the underworld was viewed as a manifestation of Theseus' exceptional loyalty to Peirithous and the Helen affair was scarcely handled.[68] The second play, on the other hand, emphasizes Theseus' love for Phaedra, both in what he says (*Hipp.* 817 ff., 861–2) and in the words of others.[69] At E. *Hipp.* 152 ff. and 320, it is suggested that Theseus might be unfaithful to Phaedra, but this is rejected as impossible: since the supposition is not essential to the action, Euripides may be glancing back at his earlier play.[70] If the adventure in the underworld had been used to his discredit, his absence on a θεωρία in the second play removes him from any hint of impropriety. In sexual fidelity at least, the second Theseus is demonstrably superior to his earlier incarnation, just as the second Phaedra is superior to the earlier Phaedra. Similarly, while there is no hint in the second play that the death of Theseus' Amazon wife was due to other than natural causes, the two Roman writers say that he killed her; it must remain open whether the motif was in the first *Hippolytus*.[71] Ovid associates Ariadne and Phaedra as victims of Theseus' brutality and the portrait of Theseus is unrelentingly

---

[66] Plut. *Mor.* 27f–28a; cf. Sen. *Ph.* 85 ff. Compare the self-justification of Clytaemnestra to Agamemnon at A. *Ag.* 1440. Kiso 1973: 32 thinks Phaedra's accusation came at the end of the play just before she killed herself, but cf. Webster 1967: 66.

[67] Kalkmann 1882: 36.

[68] But if this presentation of Theseus' exploits would have been too radical even for Euripides, what could these transgressions have been?

[69] Contrast Sen. *Ph.* 92 and Ov. *Her.* 63 ff. and 116. Naturally, the surviving *Hippolytus* does not mention Peirithous.

[70] For the technique, see Zielinski 1925: 68–132.

[71] Zintzen 1960: 31. Heracles killed her in the *Uprising of the Amazons* (Plut. *Thes.* 28. 3).

unfavourable in the Roman writers.[72] It would be surprising if it had been as unflattering in Euripides' earlier play, just because of Theseus' status in Athenian culture, but even the meagre evidence remaining suggests that he was given an actively blameworthy part in the play, and the Roman writers were perhaps expanding what was implicit in Euripides.

After Theseus has cursed his son in response to Phaedra's false allegations,[73] and the curse has had its effect (cf. 442N[2]), Phaedra must have killed herself, either because the truth was revealed or because she feared that it would be revealed.[74] The end of the play was aetiological, announcing the establishment of the cult of Hippolytus, but even if a *deus ex machina*[75] was employed for this purpose, the divinity could not have been responsible for revealing the truth if Phaedra is to kill herself before the play is over,[76] and it is most unlikely that he or she would have forgiven Phaedra for what she did, as Artemis does in the extant play. Seneca omits any cult aetiology and ends as Theseus pieces together Hippolytus' dismembered body and laments his guilt: this is surely his own ending[77] and it must remain uncertain whether Hippolytus was brought on dead or alive, or at all, at the end of Euripides' play.

Much less is known about Theseus in Sophocles' *Phaedra*.[78] The majority of the extant fragments either clearly refer to Phaedra, or are mere commonplaces of tragic diction.[79] It is sometimes thought that his plot is preserved by Asclepiades in *Σ*Hom. *Od.* 11. 321 (=*FGrH* 12 F28), but his normal practice is to recount stories rather than the plots of individual tragedies and it is most unlikely that Sophocles is his only source for the account.[80] This account

---

[72] See Ov. *Her.* 4. 59, 63; Sen. *Ph.* 85, 226, 927.

[73] For the contrasting treatments of the curse in the first and second plays, see §6.5.

[74] In Seneca, she kills herself out of remorse, after a voluntary confession: Barrett 1964: 43–4 ascribes this to Sophocles; see also Kiso 1973: 32.

[75] Probably neither Artemis or Aphrodite: Barrett 1964: 45 n. 2.

[76] Barrett 1964: 45; Zwierlein 1987: 41–4. He suggests that the truth may have been revealed by the Nurse: fr. 428N[2] is often ascribed to her, and the part of the Nurse in Seneca, who tries to dissuade Phaedra from her love, may be modelled on the first *Hippolytus*: Barrett 1964: 36; cf. Webster 1967: 70.

[77] *Contra* Zintzen 1960: 131.

[78] The most detailed reconstruction is that of Kiso 1973; much of it is plausible, but in the state of our evidence it can be no more than this.

[79] Phaedra: 679, 680, 684N[2]. Commonplaces: 677 and 681; also 682, despite the claim of Kiso 1973: 31 that it must be attributed to Theseus: compare, for example, E. *Hipp.* 616ff.

[80] On Asclepiades, Wilamowitz 1875: 181 n. 3; see also Webster 1967: 75–6.

presupposes a Trozenian setting, which may have been taken over
from the second *Hippolytus* (like the foundation of the temple of
Aphrodite in Athens by Phaedra), although the setting is connected
with the detail that Hippolytus was sent to rule Trozen because
Theseus feared that his stepmother Phaedra was plotting against
him, which may be a motif from one of the tragedies.[81]

The hostility that Euripides' Phaedra inspired is missing from
the literary tradition concerning the Sophoclean Phaedra, and it
may be assumed that his Phaedra did not indulge in what so
shocked Euripides' audience. Thus it is probable that she did not
try to justify her misdeeds by setting them against those of
Theseus, and, as in the extant *Hippolytus*, that the approach to
Hippolytus was probably made by an intermediary rather than by
Phaedra herself.[82]

It is absolutely certain that Theseus had been away in Hades:

$$A \; \ddot{\epsilon}\zeta\eta\varsigma \; \ddot{\alpha}\rho' \; o\dot{v}\delta\dot{\epsilon} \; \gamma\hat{\eta}\varsigma \; \ddot{\epsilon}\nu\epsilon\rho\theta' \; \ddot{\omega}\chi ov \; \theta\alpha\nu\dot{\omega}\nu;$$
$$B \; o\dot{v} \; \gamma\dot{\alpha}\rho \; \pi\rho\dot{o} \; \mu o\dot{\iota}\rho\alpha\varsigma \; \dot{\eta} \; \tau\dot{v}\chi\eta \; \beta\iota\dot{\alpha}\zeta\epsilon\tau\alpha\iota$$

('So you are alive, and did not go to die under the earth?' 'Yes; fortune does
not compel [death] before it is fated', fr. 686.)[83]

In Seneca (*Ph.* 838), he has been away for four years, and it is sometimes suggested that if Sophocles' Theseus had also been absent for
so long that he had been given up for dead, his presumed death may
partly have mitigated the charge of adultery against Phaedra.[84] She
must have made a false accusation of rape against Hippolytus, but
perhaps as in the extant play, the preservation of her honour may
have been her main concern, and panic or shame at her husband's
sudden return led her to accuse Hippolytus. Even so, especially if
the Theseus of Euripides' first play was also thought to be in the
underworld, his absence in itself does not absolve her. She would
still be no Penelope, and her love for a stepson would be questionable, although, for what it is worth, the fragments that clearly refer

---

[81] Cf. Paus. 1. 22. 1. It is usually assumed that the scene of Sophocles' play was
Athens: Barrett 1964: 33, who denies that a Trozenian setting was possible, because
of the difficulties Euripides has with it in the second play. A Trozenian setting
would, however, not be incompatible with Theseus' return from the underworld: cf.
Paus. 2. 31. 2.

[82] Barrett 1964: 37; J. Griffin 1990: 130, with ἀπέπτυσεν λόγους ('he rejected the
words', fr. 678); Kiso 1973: 30–1.

[83] Compare the reference to Heracles and Cerberus, 687.

[84] Pearson 1917: 296; Barrett 1964: 12, 32.

to Phaedra's love use terms such as αἰσχρόν ('shameful'), rather than the θράσος and τόλμα ('boldness and daring') associated with the first Phaedra.[85]

Only fr. 683 could conceivably have a bearing on the depiction of Theseus:

> οὐ γάρ ποτ' ἂν γένοιτ' ἂν ἀσφαλὴς πόλις
> ἐν ᾗ τὰ μὲν δίκαια καὶ τὰ σώφρονα
> λάγδην πατεῖται, κωτίλος δ' ἀνὴρ λαβὼν
> πανοῦργα χερσὶν κέντρα κηδεύει πόλιν.[86]

This fragment may come from a confrontation between Theseus and his son: if Phaedra's proposition was made off-stage, an *agon* scene between Theseus and his son is perhaps more necessary for Hippolytus' characterization than it would have been in the earlier play.[87] ἀσφαλής (l. 1) is a word sometimes used by conservative politicians,[88] and it would be conceivable that Sophocles had characterized Theseus as a rigid type of ruler, like Creon in the *Antigone*. Barrett would connect the fragment with the detail preserved in later sources that Hippolytus is king or regent in Trozen.[89] These are obviously mere speculations and are indicative of the severe limitations of our knowledge of this play, although it appears that there was more in common between Sophocles' Phaedra and Euripides' second Phaedra than between Euripides' two Phaedras and although very little can be deduced about Sophocles' Theseus, a more sympathetic Phaedra could imply a more sympathetic Theseus.

6.5 THE PLACE OF THESEUS IN THE SECOND *HIPPOLYTUS*

The role of Theseus in *Hippolytus* cannot be detached from the far more important roles of his wife and son, or from the two divine

---

[85] See fr. 679 and 680, which also refers to 'god-sent' troubles; also perhaps fr. 685, ἀλλ' εἰσὶ μητρὶ παῖδες ἄγκυραι βίου ('but children are the anchors of a mother's life,' cf. E. *Hipp.* 717).

[86] 'For a city could never be secure in which justice and moderation are trampled underfoot, and a flatterer, holding wicked goads in his hands, looks after the city.' See also Kiso, 1973: 30–1, who assigns 677 to the same part of the play.

[87] Kiso 1973: 30.

[88] Cf. S. *Ant.* 162. κέντρα (l. 4) is a word also used in connection with the powers of a demagogue at E. *Supp.* 240, but see Barrett 1964: 25.

[89] Barrett 1964: 35, 33 n. 3: cf. *FGrH* 12 F28 and Paus. I. 22. 1.

powers which precipitate the human action. Since he appears only half-way through the play, it is necessary to give a brief account of events up until the moment of his arrival, concentrating particularly on the nature of Hippolytus, whose tragedy this is, before considering the portrayal of Theseus in the play. Hippolytus' first appearance is set against the background of Aphrodite's explanation of what is fated to happen in the play, and why it must be thus. As every god does, she demands respect from humans because respect is a sign that they recognize the gods' superior power. When men refuse respect, they must expect to be punished (*Hipp.* 5–8, cf. 47–50); Hippolytus must be punished for calling Aphrodite κακίστην δαιμόνων ('worst of goddesses', *Hipp.* 13). She does not object to his closeness to Artemis in itself, but rather, the exclusivity of his choice in which she is allowed no recognition at all (*Hipp.* 20-2). Her striking judgement (*Hipp.* 19) that his association with her is 'a more than mortal companionship' (μείζω βροτείας . . . ὁμιλίας) is unwittingly endorsed by Hippolytus himself as soon as he first appears: the imagery of his first speech at *Hipp.* 73 ff. shows that his life is undeniably beautiful, but it is also narrow and exclusive. He has plucked a garland for Artemis from a lovely pure meadow which is untouched by cattle or by iron[90] and forbidden to all but those 'who have nothing that is taught, but in whose nature virtue in all things has been allotted a place' (ὅσοις διδακτὸν μηδέν, ἀλλ' ἐν τῇ φύσει | τὸ σωφρονεῖν εἴληχεν εἰς τὰ πάντ' ἀεί, *Hipp.* 79–80): the others, the worthless (κακοί)—are debarred from it. Hippolytus is exclusive in the company he keeps and his talk of κακοί, emphasis on the importance of inborn nature and denial that τὸ σωφρονεῖν can be taught would suggest that he is no democrat.[91] Aphrodite has complained about his uniquely exclusive devotion to Artemis, but Hippolytus prides himself on what he sees as his unique closeness to her: μόνῳ γάρ ἐστι τοῦτ' ἐμοὶ γέρας βροτῶν (*Hipp.* 84).[92] It should be emphasized that his life is beautiful and virtuous, but it is too narrow a life to be led by a human being.

This facet of Hippolytus' nature, which is fundamental for an understanding of his subsequent scene with Theseus, and ulti-

[90] Hippolytus' obsession with the 'purity' of the meadow from harmless and natural elements such as cattle is revealing: Barlow 1986: 98–9.

[91] Cf. Gregory 1991: 62–3; Strauss 1993: 168: but Hippolytus' 'oligarchical' views have implications that transcend contemporary politics: cf. Barrett 1964: 173.

[92] 'Only I among mortals have this privilege.' Aphrodite says that Hippolytus '*alone* of all the Trozenians' calls her a hateful goddess (*Hipp.* 12–13).

mately of his fate, is explored in further detail in his dialogue with
the servant who tries in vain to warn him against this narrowness,
which he calls τὸ σεμνόν. As Euripides establishes through a series
of plays on the word (*Hipp.* 94–5, 99, 103), this is essentially a quality fitting for gods, who are powerful and must be worshipped, but
not for human beings, whose limitations in power should impose
moderation and flexibility on them; a theme which has been
explored from a rather different angle in the *Suppliants*, *Heracles*
and *Oedipus Coloneus*. The dialogue centres particularly around the
question of how far men can understand the gods' behaviour and
how far men and gods are alike. Although Hippolytus grants that
both gods and men desire respect (*Hipp.* 91–9; cf. Aphrodite's
words, *Hipp.* 7–8), his mistake is in assuming that ἄλλοισιν ἄλλος
θεῶν τε κἀνθρώπων μέλει ('everyone has favourites, both in men
and gods', *Hipp.* 104). In saying this he is appropriating the privi-
leges of a divinity: Aphrodite and Artemis may have their
favourites among men, it is true, but, as will be made clear, a man
who is at the mercy of all the gods cannot have his favourites among
them. The huge gulf that exists between gods and men is already
apparent to an alert spectator but not to Hippolytus: although he
considers himself uniquely close to Artemis, there is no normal
closeness between them; he cannot even see her, because he is
merely mortal (*Hipp.* 86). Concerned at his rashness, the servant
ends the scene with a prayer to Aphrodite for forgiveness
(συγγνώμη), and touches for the last time on the differences
between divine and human nature, optimistically attributing a
superior morality, as well as power to the gods: σοφωτέρους γὰρ
χρὴ βροτῶν εἶναι θεούς.[93] Forgiveness and good sense, however,
are only compulsory for men;[94] there is no such compulsion on
insulted divinities.

Hippolytus is both a victim and a transgressor. So is Phaedra:
although it is her false accusation which will cause Hippolytus'
death, her attempt to resist Aphrodite's irresistible force brings her
a moral credit that was denied to her in earlier dramatizations.
After some initial scene-setting in which Phaedra's pain and the
helplessness of her friends is presented (*Hipp.* 121–283),

---

[93] 'Gods should be wiser than men', *Hipp.* 120; cf. *HF* 1341 ff.; *Ba.* 1348 and
above, §4.4.

[94] At *Hipp.* 615 Hippolytus himself will reject an appeal to συγγνώμη, thereby
setting in train the false accusation which leads to his death.

Aphrodite's plan begins to work straightaway through human agency as the Nurse is inspired by her goodwill to Phaedra (*Hipp.* 285–8) to make a last and fatal attempt to discover the cause of her troubles. Aphrodite knows her victims: the Nurse knows Phaedra. Thus it is by reminding Phaedra of what she loves—the children to whom she wishes to bequeath honour—that the Nurse shakes her initial resolve to take her love to the grave (*Hipp.* 310), and she worms the truth out of her mistress by appealing to her as a suppliant and thus to her moral sense (*Hipp.* 325–35).[95] Even when her secret has been revealed, Phaedra tries hard to maintain her sense of honour: her great monologue of 373 ff. is full of terms such as αἰδώς ('shame'), τὸ καλόν ('the good') and εὔκλεια ('honourable reputation'), which show how concerned she is with virtuous conduct;[96] she has decided to die so as to keep her moral reputation intact, and sternly condemns those weaker women who give in to their passions (*Hipp.* 406 ff.). The significance of 403 f., ἐμοὶ γὰρ εἴη μήτε λανθάνειν καλὰ | μήτ' αἰσχρὰ δρώσῃ μάρτυρας πολλοὺς ἔχειν ('may I not escape notice when I act honourably, nor have many witnesses when I am doing what is shameful'), the hole in her moral armour, will only become clear later, as it emerges that for her, εὔκλεια is ultimately more to do with appearances than reality (cf. also *Hipp.* 321, 430). Still her resolve resists bombardment from the Nurse almost to the very end of the scene (*Hipp.* 486–9, 498–9, 503–6). The Nurse is morally wrong to urge Phaedra to gratify her love, though intellectually right that Aphrodite is unstoppable (*Hipp.* 443 ff.): Phaedra is destroyed by clinging to human morality against this ungovernable force, which is commendable, but by taking Hippolytus with her, she shows that her moral sense is flawed.[97] Even so, just over 400 lines are taken up

[95] Dodds 1925 links this passage with the notoriously difficult lines concerning good and bad αἰδώς ('shame'), *Hipp.* 373–87. Whatever these two types of αἰδώς are, her concern for them, like her concern for the Nurse's supplication, characterizes her as the kind of woman who thinks about moral conduct: this transformation from her earlier portrayal must make the audience better disposed to her, even though in the end she cannot avoid falsely accusing Hippolytus. See also next note.

[96] In the human world of the *Hippolytus*, even αἰδώς, normally a commendable quality, is problematic: in the same way, the Nurse's loyalty to Phaedra and Theseus' love for his wife, both of which would seem to be commendable, have dire results; indeed, even Hippolytus' pious refusal to break his oath destroys him (cf. Cairns 1993: 320–1).

[97] A parallel is to be found in *HF* 1313 ff., where Heracles considers himself guilty in terms of human morality and Theseus tries to comfort him with arguments very like those used by the Nurse at *Hipp.* 453–7 (cf. also 471–2). In Ch. 4, I suggested

with her struggles, and only when she is at last physically and mentally exhausted does she let the Nurse take control of her (516 ff.):
although we know that she should have continued to resist, it is
hard to condemn her out of hand for succumbing. Because
Euripides has traced every stage in Phaedra's decision-making, bal-
ancing divine necessity with an unusually detailed account of her
progress from untroubled εὔκλεια to the false accusation, the
wickedness of what she eventually does is partly mitigated.

The conjunction of Phaedra's anguish and Hippolytus' violent,
unreflecting condemnation of her and all women is very striking. It
is as though he had always mistrusted her because of his convic-
tions concerning women, and his instantaneous response to her will
be matched by Theseus' immediate condemnation of his son. Both
think of those whom they see as their enemies in absolute terms,
just as Aphrodite's rage against Hippolytus is absolute; but human
perception and human power are not absolute. We have already
seen that Hippolytus' belief that 'gods and men use the same customs' is only partially true, and his dangerously absolute reaction
to Phaedra is another product of this view of the world. If the
Phaedra of the first play had made little effort to restrain herself,
even a very strong reaction of disgust from Hippolytus would have
been unproblematic: this is the reaction of any virtuous tragic hero
in response to an immoral proposal. But because we have seen
Phaedra's struggles and self-hatred, Hippolytus' response by definition seems unsympathetic. Though his outrage is understandable, it is alarmingly lacking in understanding of a situation which
we know to be complex, and in ἐπιείκεια.[98] Although his view of
women is hardly unparalleled in Greek literature,[99] he shows an
extremism which is less common and more disturbing (especially at

that we are meant to see that Theseus' arguments are flawed but the best that any
human can manage in a flawed world. Theseus' argument is well intentioned and
brings good results, but such arguments could easily be misused, as they are here,
by the Nurse: both plays explore the clash of two incompatible worlds of divine and
human.

[98] Note especially the Nurse's appeal to this at *Hipp.* 615.

[99] Already Clytaemnestra in the *Odyssey* (11. 427 ff., 455 ff.) sets the pattern for
the 'typical' woman in her wantonness, deceit and destructive effect on men;
Pandora is the punishment for Prometheus' theft of fire (Hes. *Thg.* 570 ff.);
Semonides complains that they sit at home, using up the resources of the household
and planning trouble (cf. *Hipp.* 630–40). Jason's belief that women are all obsessed
with sex and his wish that men could have children by some other means, at *Med.*
569–75, is particularly close to *Hipp.* 616–27.

Hipp. 645 ff. and 664 ff.). The moral balance favours Hippolytus,
but is not entirely on his side. Euripides handles the moral ambiguity brilliantly. The Nurse tells Hippolytus the mere fact of the
story: because she omits to mention the attendant struggles of the
last 400 lines, he could hardly be expected to give Phaedra the benefit of the doubt, but his hatred of women, and the absolutist character which have brought Aphrodite's hatred on him in the first
place, cause the violent response which will seal his own destruction for her satisfaction.

When he arrives, all Theseus' concern is for his family: he
assumes at once that the sounds of lamentation that greet him must
be for the death of his old father or, even worse, for one of his children (*Hipp.* 794–9): the truth is more awful than he could have
imagined, and he himself notes the wretched contrast between his
joyous homecoming from his θεωρία and what awaits him (*Hipp.*
792, 806 ff.). His piety, family feeling and miserable reaction to the
dreadful surprise mark him initially as pitiable. Both Theseus and
Phaedra are at the other end of the scale from Hippolytus who has
renounced marriage and thus all the emotional attachment
expressed here by Theseus: Hippolytus' closest companion is a
goddess whom he cannot see, and he does not know the human love
that Theseus expressed in his lament. Aphrodite works through
Phaedra's love for her children and Theseus' love for Phaedra to
destroy Hippolytus for his rejection of those forms of love.
Theseus' lament is striking in its passion for a wife and his emotional response to Phaedra's death, like her own expressions of tur-
moil and passion, contrasts with Hippolytus' curt and violent
dismissals of her suffering. Phaedra's death is the worst grief
Theseus can imagine (*Hipp.* 817–18, cf. 822 f.), and he desires death
now that she is dead (*Hipp.* 836 ff.). Particularly remarkable in view
of his normal mythological reputation, is his promise that he will
not marry again (*Hipp.* 860–1). The strength of his grief, like the
irresistibility of Phaedra's divinely-sent passion and her physical
weakness, are an essential explanatory and apologetic framework
for the tragedy that is to come.

When he discovers Phaedra's note which falsely accuses
Hippolytus of rape, his reaction is instant and at the peak of his
anger, he curses his stepson. It is a foolish and appalling act, but, as
with the accusation itself, Euripides has provided enough of the
background to the curse for the audience to understand why he acts

as he does. In this respect, Theseus' treatment of his son in the violence of his grief may be contrasted with the cold-bloodedness of Creon's edicts and blasphemies in *Antigone*; both men meet a similar fate, but Creon is more responsible for his tragedy than Theseus is. Theseus is particularly at fault in cursing his son instantly without inquiring more deeply, in spite of the chorus's warnings, but the facts do look clear: because of Phaedra's past reputation for fidelity and honour, her revelation in the concrete form of a suicide note looks all too convincing, and from a human, limited perspective there is no reason to ask further. Theseus suffers because of his limited human perception and an excessive violence which is not permitted for a human being. The Theseus we have seen up until now is always intensely aware of his humanity and the limitations imposed on him thereby.

Even in the handling of the curse with which he destroys his son, however, the Theseus of the second play is portrayed more sympathetically than the earlier Theseus. In itself, cursing Hippolytus could only ever be a thoroughly dangerous act, typical of the impulsive hero in a rage, and utterly untypical of Theseus as he is normally portrayed. However, in the extant play, as soon as he has uttered the curse at *Hipp.* 888–90, he adds a sentence of exile to it. At 895 ff. he speaks of death at Poseidon's hand or exile as alternatives to one another, but thereafter (*Hipp.* 973, 1048, 1094–7, 1041–4), all the emphasis is on the exile, and the curse fades from view until the messenger returns with the news that Theseus' original prayer has, in fact, been granted. Theseus' reaction to his message is instructive: ὦ θεοί Πόσειδόν θ'· ὡς ἄρ' ἦσθ' ἐμὸς πατὴρ | ὀρθῶς ('O gods and Poseidon, so you really were my father after all', 1169–70). These words suggest that Theseus had not been sure that the curses would work, and hence, having used one at the climax of his heroic rage, added the human sentence of exile, which would have been reversible once the truth had been revealed.

Theseus can only have doubted his divine paternity if he had not used any of the curses before now: this is clearly the first of the three prayers that his father once gave him. In contrast, Seneca's Theseus explicitly says that he is using the third curse (Sen. *Ph.* 944): he knows that it will work, and he has no need of imposing exile on Hippolytus as well. It cannot be proved that Seneca is following the first *Hippolytus* here, but it is at least likely: the scholiast on E. *Hipp.* 46 says that the other two wishes had already been used, in the labyrinth and in Hades, and since he cannot be referring to the extant play, his information may derive from the first *Hippolytus* or Euripides' *Theseus*.[100] It is certain, however, that in the second *Hippolytus*, Theseus used the first of the three prayers granted him by Poseidon to destroy Hippolytus.[101] The terms of the plot mean that Theseus cannot avoid uttering the fateful curse, and the shock for the Athenian public of seeing a father wish his son dead should not be underestimated.[102] Yet the framework which compels him to act blurs the edges of his guilt, so that although he kills his son, there is a sense in which he did not intend to do so.

The resulting *agon* between Theseus and Hippolytus explores once more certain themes that are fundamental to the play: the limitations placed on human perception, and the sense of impotence that this engenders; above all, it shows us once more exactly how Hippolytus is destroyed by the qualities that have caused Aphrodite's unfavourable notice in the first place. She is punishing him for his rigidity towards her, and Theseus, as her instrument, destroys him through his mistrust of his previous conduct and because of the rigid moral sense that makes him unable to break his oath. Hippolytus is right not to break an oath, but paradoxically his rightness destroys him, just as Phaedra's desire for a good reputation and Theseus' love for her, which seem good, can be disastrous, θεῶν διδόντων ('when the gods grant it', *Hipp*. 1434).

There are similarities between Theseus and his son, in the dangerous speed of their reactions,[103] and even in the way they

[100] Kakridis 1928: 24–7 thinks the scholiast was just guessing, because in no other extant tradition does Theseus get out of the labyrinth without Ariadne, or Hades without Heracles, but Attic sentiment might have preferred stories in which Theseus escaped from these dangers without having to call on anyone's help: cf. Barrett 1964: 40. For the *Theseus*, cf. §7.5.2.

[101] Although he still has two prayers (ἀραί) left, one curse cannot be revoked by another: Barrett 1964: 166, 400 against Kakridis 1928: 21 f. Barrett thinks that the curse was certainly intended as the first (see p. 334), but his suggestion that the exile is included just so that Hippolytus will be found driving his horses by the sea is not convincing.

[102] Cf. Vickers 1973: 114; and see now Strauss 1993 on the importance and difficulties of the father–son relationship at Athens. Legally, a father did have the permanent right to remove his son from the house, but there are very few recorded cases of this, and probably public sentiment obstructed too arbitrary a use of the provision: Harrison 1968: 75.

[103] The phrase πόλλ' ἐγὼ χαίρειν λέγω ('I bid a warm farewell to . . . ') is used by Hippolytus at *Hipp*. 113 and by Theseus at *Hipp*. 1058; both men dismiss without further thought what they should not have dismissed. Compare also *Hipp*. 1057 with 1074 f.

approach those whom they perceive to be their enemies: both of them begin by addressing their enemy in generalizations, wishing that human life could be other than it is, before homing in specifically on the enemy (*Hipp.* 616–51; 916–43). More important, however, is Theseus' scornful adoption of words that his son has used as commendations of his life throughout the play: σὺ δὴ θεοῖσιν ὡς περισσός ὢν ἀνηρ | ξύνει ('are you the special one who consorts with the gods?', *Hipp.* 948, cf. 17, 85, 445); σὺ σώφρων καὶ κακῶν ἀκήρατος; ('are you the virtuous one, who is untainted by evil?', *Hipp.* 948–9, cf. 73, 76, 80, 667, 994 f., 1100); θηρεύουσι γὰρ | σεμνοῖς λόγοισιν, αἰσχρὰ μηχανώμενοι ('they hunt with high-flown words, while their plans are shameful', 956–7). It seems as if he has never believed in Hippolytus' rejection of what he considers to be (and what are) normal pursuits for a young man.[104] In fact, what he has apparently long mistrusted in Hippolytus, because it seemed so incredible, is exactly what Aphrodite is punishing; the rejection of the normality of which she is an important part, and Theseus is unwittingly her representative and tool.

The use of legal language and types of argument that would be familiar from the law courts are a notable feature of this *agon* scene. Theseus uses arguments based on probability (*Hipp.* 962–70) to 'prove' Hippolytus' guilt, but his appeal to logical reasoning is brief, and although he uses legal terminology as though this were a proper trial, he perverts forensic practice by relying for the most part on his own false picture of Hippolytus so as to condemn him even before he has made his defence: he appeals to 'witnesses', but one is dead and the other is just a letter.[105] Here, and in his exchange with Hippolytus after his speech for the defence, he most closely resembles the typical tragic tyrant, the sort of ruler who always believes the worst without making proper investigation, and

---

[104] Jeny 1989 suggests that the Trozenian setting helps to explain why Theseus, so long resident in Athens, mistrusts and misunderstands a son whose daily life and long association with Artemis is unfamiliar to him. Thus Euripides can exalt the nobility of Hippolytus' life while partially excusing Theseus' hostility to him.

[105] Lloyd 1992: 46–7; and on the legal vocabulary of the play, cf. 32. *Hipp.* 944–72 are especially full of words of discovery, many of them with a legal flavour: ἐξελέγχεται | πρὸς τῆς θανούσης κάκιστος ὤν ('he has been convicted of utter wickedness by the dead woman', 945); ἐλήφθης ('you have been caught', 955); ἐν τῷδ' ἁλίσκῃ πλεῖστον ('in this, above all, you are found guilty', 959); τί ταῦτα σοῖς ἁμιλλῶμαι λόγοις | νεκροῦ παρόντος μάρτυρος σαφεστάτου; ('why do I contend with words when the corpse is lying there as the clearest witness?', 972).

who relies on violence.[106] And yet Phaedra's writing tablet does seem to be clear evidence: he is not really like violent, unreasoning and blasphemous kings such as Pentheus in the *Bacchae*, or even the Creon of the latter half of the *Antigone*. His reasoning and even his entirely mistaken arguments from probability would in themselves be credible in a normal world in which divinity had not intervened.[107]

Hippolytus' defence against his father's accusations is that he did not rape Phaedra because it is not in his nature to do so. This is the only means of defence open to him, since it is not in his nature to break his oath of silence, but of course, Theseus' accusation turns precisely on the fact that Hippolytus' true nature is very different from what he has always alleged about it, so it is doomed to failure, as Aphrodite, who hates this nature, intends. Like Theseus, he adopts the language of the law courts: in his opening words he contrasts fine speech with the truth, says that he is not used to public speaking and that he must try to defend himself (*Hipp.* 984–9). All of these are commonplaces of forensic oratory; but Hippolytus characteristically mixes these clichés with sketches of himself and his friends based on the same exclusive view of his relations with the world and contempt for those not of his circle that we saw in his first appearance: ἐγὼ δ᾽ ἄκομψος εἰς ὄχλον δοῦναι λόγον | εἰς ἥλικας δὲ κὠλίγους σοφώτερος ('I am not clever at speaking before the masses, and better at speaking before a few of my equals', *Hipp.* 986–7; cf. 996–1001, 1018).[108] This cannot mollify Theseus, who has already jeered at what he sees as the falsity of his alleged virtue (σῶφρον), but Hippolytus has no other language in which to defend himself.[109] There is a huge gap in communication between the two men. Theseus does not understand his son and is clearly in the wrong for not doing so, and yet Hippolytus makes no effort to

[106] Cf. Karsai 1982: 119ff. who notes that the ideal Athenian democracy was supposed to allow for individual peculiarities, such as that of Hippolytus: thus Theseus' perversion of normal legal practice is undemocratic. We are very far from the Theseus of *Suppliants*, *Heracles* or *Oedipus Coloneus*, but the whole world around this Theseus is also entirely different: in other plays, Theseus tends to appear when divinity has done its worst, but here he is in the middle of divine revenge.

[107] Lloyd 1992: 46–7.

[108] Compare *Hipp.* 79–81. Lloyd 1992: 48 notes that although there are examples of criticisms of juries in extant forensic oratory, none comes anywhere near Hippolytus' total disdain for his 'prosecution'.

[109] As also σωφρονέστερος (995, 1100), τὸ σῶφρον (1007) and cf. 1034–5.

understand Theseus either,[110] and it is typical of his nature that he cannot do so. It is possible to feel compassion for both, even though the moral balance obviously favours Hippolytus. At *Hipp.* 1009–20, he adopts arguments from probability (like Theseus at 962–70), in an attempt to prove his innocence by rejecting all the common motives that might have led an ordinary man to commit the crime of which Theseus is accusing him. Again he is trapped, both by Theseus' unjust suspicions, but also by his own nature: the way in which he rejects motives that are understandable to Theseus, and indeed, by any normal young man, such as sex, power and public life,[111] is tactless at best—ἀλλ' ὡς τυραννεῖν ἡδὺ τοῖσι σώφροσιν; ('but because being a tyrant is attractive to anyone with sense?', *Hipp.* 1013)—and can hardly win credence from him because it is mingled with a simple reassertion of the σωφροσύνη in which Theseus disbelieves (*Hipp.* 994–1007).

Perhaps it is because he is so sure of his own righteousness, that he makes no appeals, as one might expect, to pity or to Theseus' reputation for showing it;[112] this is also necessary if I am right that such appeals may be too intimately connected with Athens for Euripides to put them in Hippolytus' mouth, since they must be rejected for the tragedy to take place. Only in the dialogue that runs between them from 1041–89 does Hippolytus come to realize that Theseus does not believe him, and the incomprehension between the two men reaches new heights. Theseus continues to be enraged by Hippolytus' stubborn adherence to what he thinks is a discredited persona, and answers his increasingly desperate questions with a stinging, disdainful literalism (*Hipp.* 1053–5, 1068–9). Every appeal Hippolytus makes to the truth is derided by Theseus as

[110] Cf. Barrett 1964: 348, 351 f. Walker 1995: 120–2 makes some excellent remarks on the use by both men of 'magico-religious' language whose truth cannot be 'doubted nor proved by lesser beings', and which is therefore out of place in a democracy.

[111] The rejection of the universal male experience of political life may be compared with Hippolytus' rejection of the universal human experience of sex: contrast Creon at S. *OT* 587, who also rejects kingship but not public life, as Hippolytus appears to do. Cf. also Cairns 1993: 319–20, who notes that Theseus' echo (948 ff.) of Hippolytus' self-description (73 ff.) shows that this self-description is intimately connected with his later inability to convince his father of his innocence.

[112] Cf. Barrett 1964: 348. Of course he is right to be sure of it; but his trouble is that he is also sure of it in relation to Aphrodite, and this is what destroys him, because of Theseus' sense of his own rightness. Nothing is what it seems to those within this play, and the *agon* provides some prime examples of the limitations of human perception and communication.

humbug and typical of Hippolytus' hypocrisy: the most striking
example of this, and one in which Theseus is utterly wrong is at
1060–4:[113] Hippolytus cries to the gods, asking why he cannot
break his oath, but then reaffirms his decision to keep it. Instead of
seizing on this extraordinary appeal, Theseus takes it as all too typical of Hippolytus—οἴμοι τὸ σεμνὸν, ὥς μ᾽ ἀποκτενεῖ τὸ σόν! ('Ugh,
that high-flown talk of yours will kill me', *Hipp.* 1064; cf. 1045,
1080 f.).

Theseus is utterly wrong to trust his limited perceptions of the
evidence of the tablet, whose 'speech' is unreliable,[114] over his son's
clue here and his oath. He is wrong to act so hastily (*Hipp.* 1051)
and to reject divination (*Hipp.* 1058–9). His final words to
Hippolytus—οὐ γάρ τις οἶκτος σῆς μ᾽ ὑπέρχεται φυγῆς ('I feel no
pity for your exile', *Hipp.* 1089)—show how far behind him he has
left the moderation and sense of human fragility that the Athenian
Theseus exhibits in other plays.[115] Even so, it is interesting that
when the messenger announces what has happened to his son, his
anger has already abated and, apart from a brief reference to the
justice of his fate at 1171, he does not gloat over Hippolytus.
Instead his quiet comment, unlike the boast of a triumphantly
righteous hero is simply: ὦ θεοί Πόσειδόν θ᾽· ὡς ἄρ᾽ ἦσθ᾽ ἐμὸς
πατὴρ | ὀρθῶς, ἀκούσας τῶν ἐμῶν κατευγμάτων ('O gods and
Poseidon, so you really were my father after all and heard my
prayer', 1169–70). Theseus' crime against his son is the work of the
moment but has everlasting effects: any human punishment would
be reversible, but because he enlists a god, he enlists an absolute
power that hurts him, as well as the son he has cursed. Euripides
creates a situation in which, given his love for Phaedra and her previous good character, and his innate suspicion of Hippolytus,
which cannot be allayed by Hippolytus himself, Theseus has every
reason to think that he has been harmed. Hurting one's enemies
was acceptable in Greek popular ethics; anger itself could be
regarded as justifiable in certain circumstances, even for ordinary
people.[116] It is anger, however, which frequently leads heroes into

---

[113] On the passage, cf. Bain 1977: 30–1.

[114] *Hipp.* 1057. He himself accuses Hippolytus of appealing to voiceless witnesses
at 1074 f.!

[115] Compare §3.4 on the connection between οἶκτος and ἐπιείκεια.

[116] Cf. Dover 1974: 181–4; Blundell 1989: 26–59. Aristotle *NE* 1125ᵇ32 ff. says
that it is a moral failing not to show anger where it is necessary.

trouble, because it is inimical to the moderation which is essential for human survival and success, and antithetical to ἐπιείκεια: the angry man will not listen to persuasion. Only divine anger can be unlimited: central to the portrayal of Hippolytus in the play is his mistaken assumption that the gods are like men and men like the gods. Theseus' mistake is not dissimilar in the way that he invokes powers which are beyond human limitation. To be extreme, implacable and unwilling to listen to persuasion is also, in one sense, to be un-Athenian;[117] Hippolytus and Theseus are both guilty of this failing, and though the Theseus of the *Hippolytus* is not the national hero of Athens, in the context of wider trends of Athenian ideological thought, it is striking how many of the heroes who meet a tragic end do so precisely because they are not flexible in the ways which encomia of the ideal Athens set up as typical of the city.

Theseus lacks the wisdom and clear-sighted flexibility of the other portrayals which have been discussed, but even here, his heroic anger abates more quickly than it might have done. The muted tone of his comment on the messenger's speech is extremely striking:

> μίσει μὲν ἀνδρὸς τοῦ πεπονθότος τόδε
> λόγοισιν ἥσθην τοῖσδε· νῦν δ' αἰδούμενος
> θεούς τ' ἐκεινόν θ' οὕνεκ' ἐστὶν ἐξ ἐμοῦ
> οὔθ' ἥδομαι τοῖσδ' οὔτ' ἐπάχθομαι κακοῖς

('out of hatred for the man who suffered this, I was pleased with your words, but now, in reverence for the gods, because he is my son, I am neither happy or sorry at his sufferings', *Hipp.* 1257–60).

Here, although his prayer has been granted, he is curiously humble, and in a surprisingly brief space of time, he has gained a measure of ἐπιείκεια which prevents him from actively rejoicing at the death of one whose crime against him has apparently been avenged by a god (cf. *Hipp.* 1265–7). By contrast, Creon in *Antigone* is forced into an unwilling recantation by those external to him (S. *Ant.* 1096–106). Theseus' words are not utterly removed from the exemplary words of Odysseus in Sophocles' *Ajax* who understands that it is not always right for men to hate their enemies (S. *Aj.* 1344–5, 1347).

---

[117] Theseus and Peitho are connected: Paus. 1. 22. 3.

It is in this mood of comparative calm that Artemis comes as *dea ex machina* and as representative of the beings at whose instigation the tragedy has happened. She makes no initial attempt to spare Theseus and begins by condemning him sternly for what he has done, giving him the 'god's eye view' of events, even though it is too late to do any good and all she does is cause him pain (*Hipp.* 1297). Theseus is to blame for his son's agony, and, especially after the messenger's account of the horrors Hippolytus has endured (*Hipp.* 1173–254, esp. 1205–43) and his own monody (1348–88), the son's essentially undeserved suffering must command far more sympathy than that of the father. Even so, Theseus also suffers, and while the play emphasizes his son's pain and his nobility in keeping his oath to Phaedra, Hippolytus is still as convinced of his rightness as he was at its outset.[118] The ultimate cause of the tragedy—his refusal of Aphrodite—is acknowledged by Hippolytus (*Hipp.* 1401), but he never admits that he may have been at fault in rejecting her. He dies, as absolute in death as in life, and never retracts his hatred for her. In this, he remains true to the exclusivity, the σεμνόν and mistaken idea that human beings have a choice of which gods they worship, that characterized him in the first scene. In fact, Artemis can call Aphrodite 'most hateful' (*Hipp.* 1301) with impunity and agree with Hippolytus that he is truly σώφρων (*Hipp.* 1402, cf. 1419) but, as the play has shown, Hippolytus cannot.[119]

But though Artemis will spare Theseus nothing initially, and lists all his fatal mistakes one by one, dwelling particularly on his haste and foolishness, as soon as she has conveyed to him the full implications of what he has done, she does relent (*Hipp.* 1325 ff.). Divine command or explanation of human events is perfectly common at the end of Greek tragedy: but divinity does not normally absolve human characters from blame for their tragedy, and the judgement of Artemis must be taken very seriously in determining Theseus' final moral status in the play. She explicitly states that where man and god come into conflict, man must lose and there is nothing that can be done (*Hipp.* 1339 f.). Most remarkably, even Phaedra is forgiven as far as she can be (*Hipp.* 1300–6). Because

---

[118] His oath: *Hipp.* 1307 f.; his unbowed sense of his own rightness: *Hipp.* 1363–5, cf. 1242.

[119] At *Hipp.* 1416 Hippolytus tries to overstep the boundaries of what is permissible for human beings, when he wishes that men could curse the gods; Artemis stops him from saying any more.

these gods are in charge of the human world, the play offers no hope
for a more satisfactory future: as is traditional, gods do not frustrate
another god's purposes (*Hipp.* 1328 f.), so that Artemis was unable
to save Hippolytus; such an 'apology' makes the theodicy of *Hipp.*
1339–41 decidedly problematic. While Aphrodite has destroyed a
favourite of Artemis this time, Artemis will destroy Aphrodite's
favourite in memory of Hippolytus. Unlike Hippolytus, Artemis
can vow eternal hatred of Aphrodite, since Aphrodite can hurt her
(cf. 1339) only through him and others. Although she will ensure
that his name lives on in cult (*Hipp.* 1423–30), she cannot save him
now; because she is divine, his invisible 'best friend' cannot comfort Hippolytus physically, cry for him (*Hipp.* 1396) or be present
as he dies (*Hipp.* 1437–8); he is just a mortal. For the human characters, forgiveness and lamentation are the only possibilities:
Theseus will embrace his son (*Hipp.* 1445) and Hippolytus will
accept that his father has also suffered (*Hipp.* 1405, 7, 9). Artemis
finally exercises a beneficial influence on the human scene, as she
commands Hippolytus to forgive his father (*Hipp.* 1432–5, cf. 1442,
1449). Both on the divine and on the human level, Theseus is forgiven, and this is unusual. In his turn, Theseus will acknowledge
his son's own nobility (γενναιότης) and piety (εὐσέβεια) which have
been so important to him.[120] In the bleakness of human existence
there is at least the comfort that human beings can provide for one
another, as Euripides showed even more clearly in the *Heracles*,
where Theseus was removed from the tragic action. The Theseus
who represents Athens in tragedy is wise and moderate and sufficiently detached from others' tragedies to be able to offer them the
comforts of Athenian help. The Theseus of the *Hippolytus* neither
represents Athens nor is he removed from the tragedy. Indeed, he
plays an active part in it, but he, like Hippolytus, is working within
Aphrodite's trap: ἀνθρώποισι δὲ | θεῶν διδόντων εἰκὸς ἐξ-
αμαρτάνειν ('when the gods give it, it is natural that men should go
wrong', *Hipp.* 1433–4).

---

[120] For the order of lines, *Hipp.* 1452–6, see Barrett 1964: 416.

7

Theseus in Fragmentary Tragedy

7.1 INTRODUCTION

7.1.1 *Subject Matter and Choice*

Error and human suffering are central to tragedy: as Phrynichus discovered at the cost of 1,000 drachmas, it is easier for an Athenian audience to look at others' errors than their own (Hdt. 6. 21), and therefore the role of representative of the ideal city, in which Theseus is normally cast in tragedy, fundamentally conflicts with any attempt to make him into a tragic hero like those whose crimes and punishments are judged by Aristotle to be part of the 'best' tragedies (*Poetics* 1453^{a}17 ff.). A hero who embodies Athens must normally be competent and successful, and in the *Hippolytus*, where he is neither—and more like traditional tragic heroes—his connection with the ideal Athens has been cut. Theseus tends to be of secondary dramaturgical importance in tragedy in that his role is usually confined to alleviating the sufferings of others as best he can, carrying on the Athenian mission of helping friends and punishing the wicked. He also appeared in other fifth-century plays of which only fragments now remain: in tragedy, he had roles in the *Eleusinioi* of Aeschylus, the *Aegeus* and *Theseus* of Sophocles, the *Aegeus*, *Theseus* and perhaps the *Alope* of Euripides, and the *Peirithous* of Euripides or Critias, as well as in the first *Hippolytus*; the satyr plays *Cercyon* by Aeschylus and *Skiron* by Euripides presumably alluded to him; he may also have appeared in Cratinus' comedy, *Drapetides*, and possibly Aristophanes' *Polyidus*.[1] Very little indeed can be made of the handful of extant comic and satyric fragments, although the appearance of the champion of exiles in a

---

[1] For a full list of Theseus comedies, see Herter 1973: 1047; cf. 1939: 317, 387, and for texts of the comic fragments, see Kassell and Austin 1983, 1984. I hope elsewhere to discuss the little we do know of the comic and satyric Theseus, giving special emphasis to the problems of Euripides' *Skiron*.

play called 'The Runaways' may be significant. Unlike Heracles, Theseus could not easily be accommodated in literary genres that rely so heavily on deflating heroism or tragic seriousness, and the scarcity of his appearances in comedy and satyr play is not surprising.[2] Although there are many more fragments from tragedies in which Theseus appeared, still our information is sparse and interpretation is very difficult.

None the less, to judge from the scanty information which survives, the role of the Theseus of the fragmentary plays seems to be very similar to that of the Theseus of most extant tragedy. Closest in form to the *Suppliants, Heracles* and *Oedipus Coloneus* are the *Eleusinioi* and the *Peirithous*, in which Theseus represents Athens' power to help the oppressed and Athenian loyalty to friends and clients. The *Aegeus* and *Theseus* plays are ostensibly rather different in structure, because they dramatize stories in which Theseus is for once a central, rather than a secondary character; but they too are closely tied to the Athens of encomiastic literature in affirming the competence and invulnerability of the city, as Theseus successfully overcomes the enemies who would harm him, contrary to justice and the will of the gods.

Out of all the tragedies whose subjects and settings are known, only some nineteen are set in Athens.[3] The sufferings of other people were preferable as spectacles for the Athenian audience, and in any case, material of panhellenic interest, such as the Trojan cycle in which Athens had little part, was always of paramount importance in Athenian literary life. Not all of the tragedies set in Athens concern Theseus, and Thesean subject matter is largely confined to specific episodes in his career. Certain principles behind the selection of such episodes, related to broader currents in Athenian culture, may tentatively be sketched.

7.1.2 *Crete*

The story of Theseus in Crete mixed excitement and pathos with a comprehensive triumph of Athenian right over Cretan might and had obvious dramatic possibilities, but other stories of Minos and

---

[2] Contrast Heracles' numerous appearances in satyr plays (at least 10, and possibly as many as 22) and comedy (32, and possibly 18 more): Vollkommer 1988: 67–75.

[3] Schroeder 1914: 49; Schmid and Stählin 1934: ii. 87–8; see also Radt 1982: 196–7.

Crete also commanded considerable interest among Athenian play-wrights.[4] More than one source notes that Athenian literature paints a consistently unflattering portrait of Minos, in contrast with the respect accorded to him outside Athens.[5] The story of Theseus' triumph over the proto-tyrant of the Aegean was a model for much of the development of the political aspect of the Theseus myth as Athens grew in status in the Greek world from the sixth century on, and it must acquire a special relevance after the Persian wars. In the fifth century, Crete lay outside mainstream Greek politics and cul-ture, and it took no part in the Persian wars (Hdt. 7. 169–70), which were so important in shaping a common Greek identity and espe-cially Athens' role as the leader of Greece. As the oldest enemy of Athens in myth, it can fittingly be portrayed as a place which rep-resents what is foreign, different and antithetical to the virtues which were held to be pre-eminently Athenian. Its very geograph-ical position, much further away from Athens than other tradi-tional mythical enemies, may favour its acquisition, at least for Athenian audiences, of a kind of 'pseudo-barbarian' status.[6] In the Platonic *Minos*, Socrates himself seems to connect the characteri-zation of Minos in tragedy with the Athenian image of Athens, judging it to be a distortion of the truth about the Cretan king which was designed merely to please mass opinion, since he asserts that tragedy is δημοτερπέστατον ('most enjoyable for the people'),

---

[4] Aeschylus wrote a *Kressai*; Sophocles, a *Daedalus*, a *Kamikoi* (if the two are not the same play) and a *Manteis* or *Polyidus* (the additional titles *Kretes* and *Minos* are probably not plays in their own right): Radt 1977: 324, 348. Euripides wrote a *Kretes*, *Kressai* and a *Polyidus*: cf. also adespota 166 and perhaps 255, 419. For a list of plays with Cretan themes see Cantarella 1963: 157–8.

[5] καὶ γὰρ ὁ Μίνως ἀεὶ διετέλει κακῶς ἀκούων καὶ λοιδορούμενος ἐν τοῖς Ἀττικοῖς θεάτροις ('moreover, Minos always has a bad reputation and is con-demned in the Athenian theatres'): Plut. *Thes.* 16. 3; cf. Strabo 10. 4. 8. Liban. *decl.* 1. 177 mentions the shame of Minos in tragedy at the sexual exploits of Pasiphae, and the Minos of tragedy is characterized as ἄγριος, χαλεπός, ἄδικος and ἀπαίδευτος ('violent, cruel, unjust and uneducated') by [Plato] *Minos* 318d–321a. See also Schmid and Stählin 1929: 433. This portrayal of the Cretan king is not con-fined to Athenian tragedy: cf. §1.7 above on Bacchylides 17.

[6] Cf. Bacon 1961: 6–7; *contra* Hall 1989: 169–70. As with Thebes (cf. §3.2) some distinction should be made between the denigration of the literal Crete and praise of Athens effected by an implicit or explicit contrast with a city which symbolizes what is not Athens. It may, however, be significant that Dorian Crete and Dorian Sparta are often associated with one another: see e.g. Hdt. 1. 65; [Pl.] *Minos* 318d–321a, *Crit.* 53e, *Protag.* 342a–344b, *Laws* 626c, 856b; Arist. *Pol.* 1269ᵃ29–1273ᵇ27; Ephorus *FGrH* 70 F118, 148–9, 173–5 with Tigerstedt 1965: 71 and 376 n. 549.

'and in it we get Minos on the rack of verse and avenge ourselves for the tribute he made us pay'.[7]

The stories told of Crete in tragedy portray a very different world from that of the Thesean democracy. Crete is ancient, exotic and rather uncanny. The queen of Crete falls in love with a bull and gives birth to a monstrous creature. Minos is cruel and tyrannical, not only in his treatment of the youths of Athens, but in his attempt to punish the wondrous craftsman Daedalus at the court of the Sicilian king Cocalus and in his behaviour to the seer Polyidus (a story dramatized by all three tragedians). Magic and strange tests are important in such tales: the Polyidus story includes a magic cow that changes colour, divination and the resurrection of Minos' son Glaucus; in the Sicilian story, Minos tricks Daedalus into revealing his identity by challenging him to pass a thread through a spiral shell.[8] Ultimately, however, Minos is never victorious: in the Polyidus story, Polyidus saves himself by successfully resurrecting Glaucus, but avoids passing the secret of divination on to him as Minos wanted him to; Cocalus' daughters save Daedalus from Minos by pouring molten pitch or boiling water on him. Similar patterns shape Bacchylides 17, in which Minos offends against right by molesting the defenceless Eriboia; Theseus stands up to him; he sets Theseus what he hopes will be an impossible challenge, but Theseus confounds all expectations by meeting it and symbolically defeating Minos. Concentration on the tyrannical behaviour of Minos may also help to divert attention from any possible impropriety in Theseus' treatment of the king's daughter Ariadne, and it is surely no accident that the daughter of Minos who is especially well known—even notorious—in Athens is Phaedra whose maternal inheritance caused so much harm to the house of Theseus, not the daughter who was wronged by Theseus.

7.1.3 *Finding Aegeus*

Theseus' journey from Trozen to Athens, where he is reunited with his father, was popular in art from the late sixth century onwards, and the episode was another favourite of Athenian

---

[7] [Pl.] *Min.* 321a. Not only is tragedy δημοτερπέστατον, but also ψυχαγωγικόν ('seductive'), a term of condemnation used of dishonest rhetoric at *Phdr.* 261a and 271c (cf. *Laws* 909b).

[8] Polyidus: Apollod. 2. 3; Hyg. 136. Minos in Sicily: Hdt. 7. 169–70; Apollod. *Epit.* 1. 13–15 and Zenob. 4. 92; cf. D.S. 4. 79. 2; Tztez. *Chil.* 1. 508; ΣHom. *Il.* 2. 145; ΣP. *Nem.* 4. 59; Ov. *Ib.* 289.

dramatists. This is a story of action with a specifically, if not exclusively Athenian appeal: Theseus triumphs first over the adversaries
of the Saronic Gulf, using his strength in the service of virtue to
benefit future travellers along the road, and then over his enemies
at Athens to reassert his place there.[9] Like those of the Athenians
of old whose glorious deeds are paradigms of Athenian action in
encomiastic literature, his courage and competence 'prove' that he
is a true Athenian, and in turn become 'proof' of the courage and
virtue of all Athenians through the ages which will always protect
the city. The most intriguing of all his many enemies on his journey to the throne of Athens was surely Medea.[10] A female, foreign
adversary who could be built up into a frightening figure, she, like
Minos, is an enemy of Athens who particularly captured dramatists' imaginations beyond her role in the Theseus myth,[11] and like
the Cretan king, she is associated with a region beyond mainland
Greece and is known for her uncanny ways. As a sorceress, she is
clever and dangerous, and is particularly destructive of Greek families:[12] the royal house of Athens will be exceptional in overcoming
her. After the Persian Wars an added bonus is provided by the ideological possibilities attached to her name.[13]

The discussion of the *Hippolytus Kalyptomenos* in the previous
chapter showed very clearly that once a tragedy consists of a mere
handful of fragments, it cannot be reconstructed in any detail at all.
None the less, those fragments did yield a Theseus who was strikingly different from the character familiar to extant tragedy, and

---

[9] The emphasis on the bond between father and son as Aegeus recognizes him
as his own and an Athenian may also draw attention away from stories in which
Theseus causes his father's death. Although *ARV*[2] 1269,5 of *c*.430 shows Aegeus
consulting the oracle about having children, and it is mentioned at E. *Med.* 707f.,
5th-cent. Athens must ignore the striking fact that Theseus was a product of
Aegeus' disobedience to the oracle, and that he is punished by meeting death (indirectly) at his son's hands: cf. §1.3.3.

[10] In comparison, the enemies of the Saronic Gulf might have seemed somewhat
one-dimensional, as may also be true of his cousins the Pallantidae who laid claim to
the Athenian throne; but see §7.4.1.

[11] She appears in Sophocles' *Colchides* and *Rhizotomoi*, if not his *Aegeus*; probably in Euripides' *Aegeus*, and certainly in his *Medea* and *Peliades*; *Medea* plays are
also ascribed to Melanthius, a contemporary of Cimon (Plut. *Cim.* 4); Neophron
(*TGrF* 15); Morsimus (*TGrF* 29 F1); cf. adespota 6, 37a, 91, 103, 188c, 296 and 297.

[12] Cf. below, n. 68. Her destructive drugs and magic are important in all known
Medea plays, and the title of Sophocles' *Rhizotomoi* suggests that her magic played
a particularly large role in it.

[13] Hdt. 7. 62: cf. Hall 1989: 35 and §7.4.2.

even from the Theseus of the surviving *Hippolytus*. The other fragmentary Theseus tragedies are also more informative than a cur-
sory glance at the evidence would suggest. The evidence falls into
two categories: first, the fragments of the plays, preserved by later
writers or on papyri, and then more general considerations based
on what is known of the Theseus myth in literature or sometimes
art, and on the structures and themes that are familiar in a Greek
myth or tragedy.[14] A conventional dramatic structure will impose
some easily recognizable constraints on the narrative of a play, so
that Aegeus can recognize his son only when he is just about to
drink Medea's poison, and Theseus must always kill the Minotaur
and leave Crete. A knowledge of dramatic convention and the techniques of individual tragedians will also influence any attempt at
recreating the outline of a play, although there are obvious dangers
in assuming that tragedians always wrote 'to type' or that what
would appear to be a dramatic convention is unbreakable.[15]

7.2 THE MINOR TRAGEDIANS

An 'Ήίθεοι (*Youths*) is ascribed to Thespis, who is traditionally
dated to the second half of the sixth century; since this is also the
title of Bacchylides' seventeenth poem, it is possible that Thespis
treated this famous story. Theseus' fight with the Minotaur is
undoubtedly popular with vase painters at this time. Perhaps a little
later is *Alope* by Choerilus: a play with the same title is also ascribed
to Euripides, and it is probable that both plays concern the
cruelty of Alope's father Cercyon after she became pregnant by
Poseidon.[16] All that is known of it is that Choerilus made Cercyon

---

[14] See especially Lattimore 1964: 18–55. Although the value of art in suggesting
possible reconstructions of the plots of tragedy and satyr play is limited (cf. Séchan
1926: 521 and above, Ch. 6), considerations such as the appearance of a new motif
after a certain date can occasionally shed some light on particular developments in
tragedy.

[15] Similar difficulties apply to Zielinski's suggestion that any author who
reworked a subject treated by a predecessor must have had the earlier work in mind,
and that motifs of the earlier work may turn up in some form in the later work. This
idea was of some help in considering the first *Hippolytus* in the light of the extant
play, and may help in considering Aeschylus' *Eleusinioi* in the light of Euripides'
extant *Suppliants*, but it must be used with caution since it is based on an assumption that tragedians could never have invented anything for themselves: Zielinski
1925: 1–32 and 1931: for criticism, Cataudella 1969: 402–24.

[16] The story is told in full by Hyginus 187, and see Kron 1976: 177–9; Sutton 1974:
114. Pherecydes *FGrH* 3 F147 also mentions Alope. For Euripides' *Alope*, see §7.6.1.

the half-brother of Athens' culture hero Triptolemus,[17] but
Cercyon must have been very different from his virtuous half-
brother, because he has no known role in Athenian mythology
apart from his cruelty to his daughter and the lethal wrestling
matches to which Theseus put an end. Whether or not Theseus
actually appeared in Choerilus, it is likely that he at least alluded to
the triumph of the Athenian hero over the cruel Eleusinian king.
Most importantly, Alope is the mother of Hippothoon who was the
eponym of an Athenian tribe which retained strong Eleusinian
connections, and such a subject is of obvious contemporary significance if the play is near in time to the Cleisthenic tribal reforms.[18]
Equally little of substance is known of treatments of the Theseus
story by the minor tragedians of the later fifth century. Achaeus, a
contemporary of Sophocles and Euripides, wrote a *Theseus* (*TGrF*
20 T1 and F18, 18a) and a *Peirithous* whose content is unknown.[19]
Finally, the *Theseus* of one Hera[clides?], won second prize at 419's
Lenaea (*IG* II² 2319. 73–4).

Late sources (Suda, s.v. Neophron; D.L. 2. 134; Hyp. Eur.
Med.), contend that Euripides borrowed from the *Medea* of
Neophron of Sicyon for his more famous play. Sicyon was well
known as an early centre for tragic poetry and Neophron's obscurity may indicate that he should be dated in the early days of tragic
writing, at the start of the fifth century.[20] There is certainly a very
close relationship between the two plays: in *TGrF* 15 F1, Aegeus
comes to Medea to ask for her help in interpreting the oracle concerning his childlessness (cf. E. *Med.* 663 ff.); F2 is part of a monologue in which Medea addresses her θυμός (cf. E. *Med.* 1056 ff.);
and in F3, Medea prophesies an undignified death for Jason (cf.

---

[17] Paus. 1. 14. 3. Their mother was the daughter of Amphictyon, a king of Athens
in later traditions: Paus. 1. 2. 5; Apollod. 3. 14. 6.

[18] If it is true that Phrynichus was the first to bring women onto the stage, the
play will not be earlier than *c.*510: Snell 1971: 67. In Hyg. 187, Theseus gives Eleusis
to Hippothoon at his request; Istrus (*FGrH* 334 F10) makes Hippothoon the son of
Theseus, not Poseidon; cf. Plut. *Thes.* 29. 1: see also Kron 1976: 179.

[19] The references to Artemis Saronia and a 'sharp-pointed bull' in frs. 18 and 18a
of the *Theseus* are not proof that the subject of the play was Hippolytus, as Latte suggests in Snell 1971: 120. For the Peirithous play of uncertain authorship (adespota
658 Sn.), see below on the *Peirithous* of Euripides or Critias.

[20] See A. Griffin 1982: 162–3, esp. n. 15, although she dates Neophron after
Euripides. E. A. Thompson 1944: 12 f. argues that the author of the *Hypothesis* to
Euripides' play ought to be trusted, since he may have had access to full records of
dramatic performances.

E. *Med.* 1386f.). Medea's only role in Athenian mythology is her failed attempt to destroy the national hero, and if Neophron dramatized her meeting with Aegeus, he ought also to have presupposed her subsequent hostility to his son. In this story, the Athenian ideal of protecting the oppressed exposes the city to danger when hospitality is extended in good faith to someone like Medea who abuses it, but ultimately, the ideal city will never be damaged by enemies like this.[21] It is somewhat surprising, although not impossible to believe, that a Sicyonian playwright of the early fifth century should have treated themes which are so central to the Athenian image of Athens.[22] However, Euripides' *Aegeus* comes to Medea entirely unexpectedly; in Neophron, their encounter is more explicitly motivated, and the suspicion that Neophron was trying to improve on a supposed illogicality in Euripides cannot be banished.[23]

7.3 THE *ELEUSINIOI* OF AESCHYLUS[24]

Only two fragments of Aeschylus' *Eleusinioi* remain, but it is one of the most interesting of the lost Theseus tragedies. Like Euripides' *Suppliants*, the *Eleusinioi* treated the aftermath of Polynices' failed attack on Thebes and told the tale of how the bodies of his army were eventually buried, in spite of opposition from the Thebans. According to the source (Didym. in Dem. 13. 32) which quotes fr. 53a, ὦργα τὸ πρᾶγμα· διεμύδαιν' ἤδη νέκυς ('the time is ripe; the corpse is already rotting'), the line was spoken over the bodies lying in front of the Kadmeia. The putrefaction of the human bodies is perhaps a reproach to the Thebans for their inhumanity in

---

[21] See further below on the *Aegeus* plays of Sophocles and Euripides.

[22] The typically 'Athenian' patterns which run through Bacchylides' dithyramb for the Cean chorus would be some kind of parallel, but only a partial one.

[23] Page 1938: pp. xxx–xxvi; Séchan 1926: 592–4, although their proof of Euripides' priority from stylistic considerations is not decisive: see Thompson 1944: 12f.; von Fritz 1962: 334–6; Michelini 1989; Manuwald 1983: 50–6. In Snell 1971, he is placed before Ion of Chios.

[24] All texts of Aeschylus and Sophocles are Radt's, and of Euripides', Nauck's, unless otherwise stated. Very few attempts at original supplements and emendations or at assigning any of the *incerta* to particular plays have been made, although subjective preconceptions inevitably influence discussions of plays which only exist in outline. The comments attached to each fragment are largely confined to what we can hope to know about the role of Theseus in these plays and, as with the *Hippolytus Kalyptomenos* in Ch. 6, fragments which can reveal little or nothing about Theseus will be omitted without any discussion.

continuing to refuse burial (cf. S. *Ant.* 431; E. *Supp.* 762–9, 944). The only other direct citation is the verb ἀοζήσω.[25]

Plutarch (*Thes.* 29. 4) adds that Aeschylus' Theseus did Adrastus a favour by helping him to recover the bodies of the fallen, not by conquering the Thebans in battle, as Euripides had it, but πείσας καὶ σπεισάμενος ('by persuading and making a treaty with them'); according to Philochorus, this was the first truce for the recovery of the dead. It seems certain that the play explored and ultimately reaffirmed the importance of mercy and restraint in dealing with dead enemies, an obligation which is divinely sanctioned and which should be binding on all Greeks, according to encomia of Athens which consider the Athenian intervention in the burial of the Argives to be an outstanding example of the behaviour of the ideal city.[26] Plutarch's summary suggests that the *Eleusinioi* presented a picture which is very familiar by now, of a Theseus who exemplifies the ideal Athens in his wisdom and strength, and whose innate ἐπιείκεια and persuasive ability will ultimately enable justice to prevail on behalf of his 'client' Argives.

In the plays discussed in earlier chapters, Theseus is the champion of words against force, but has force at his command where necessary. In Euripides' *Suppliants* and Sophocles' *Oedipus at Colonus*, Theseus must regretfully force the Thebans to behave as they should. By contrast in the *Eleusinioi*, the Thebans apparently accept the wisdom of Theseus' words, but one can hardly doubt that he kept the Athenian army in reserve to compel them to act justly if necessary.[27] The play was evidently more optimistic than Euripides' *Suppliants* about the ability of (Athenian) flexibility to counter (Theban) intransigence, but whether persuasion or force is used to effect the burial, the moral triumph of Athens remains a constant feature of the story.[28] The themes of hubris and the disas-

---

[25] Glossed by Hesychius as διακονήσω, ὑπουργήσω ('I will serve'). Could it be from a speech by Theseus offering to bury the dead himself (cf. E. *Supp.* 762 ff., 940)? ἄοζος on a Corcyrean inscription (*IG* IX 1. 976) is no indication that the play can be dated just after Aeschylus' first visit to Sicily: Griffiths 1978: 106–9. Frs. 178, 199, 200, 214, 215 and 241 have also been assigned to the *Eleusinioi*, but for no compelling reasons.

[26] Cf. Lys. 2. 7–11, esp. 9; Isoc. 12. 55, 170, 174; E. *Supp.*, *passim*: see Ch. 3.

[27] For the combination of persuasion backed up by force, compare Athena's tactics at A. *Eum.* 824–9.

[28] To some extent, the Thebans' submission to Theseus mitigates their earlier outrage, and Podlecki 1966: 150–1 thinks that a more favourable view of Thebes is incompatible with the views of his pro-Themistoclean Aeschylus; but even if

ters arising from it are frequently explored by Aeschylus, and in his *Suppliants*, Euripides' Theseus strongly condemns the foolishness of the Argive expedition before he relents and agrees to help Adrastus; but whether Aeschylus' Theseus was eager to help them at once (as in Isoc. 12. 170, in which the burial is also achieved without bloodshed) or had to be coaxed into doing so, as in Euripides, must remain uncertain, and will depend partly on the unanswerable question of what other material the play contained and Theseus' role in it aside from enabling the burial.[29]

The title of the play suggests that its chorus was composed of men of Eleusis. Traditionally, Eleusis was the place where the Argive leaders were buried, while the troops were buried at Eleutherae. This distinction was already made by Euripides' *Suppliants*, and may well have been made by Aeschylus. Any connection between the king of the civilizing city of Athens, and those who dwelt in the centre of Greek spirituality has obvious attractions.[30] The Eleusis–Eleutherae distinction itself points to some sort of compromise between two different versions of the story. Eleutherae in Boeotia is likely to have been the original resting place of the seven,[31] and Athenian claims to their burial depend entirely on the physical existence of tombs at Eleusis. Mylonas excavated eight such tombs, and two of the oldest geometric inhumations, dating from *c*.800 BC, have also been found here. The date

Aeschylus' political beliefs are recoverable from his plays, the Thebans are still the moral inferiors of Theseus, and a story which sets Athenian virtue against another city's failings transcends individual affiliations.

[29] The reconstruction of Mette 1963: 38–43 is too specific to command confidence, but the themes of persuasion and reconciliation after enmity naturally recall the *Eumenides*. It is possible that the *Eleusinioi* formed the culmination of an 'Argive' trilogy, since tragedies with names such as *Epigonoi*, *Argeioi* or *Argeiai* are tantalizing: Gantz 1978: 302–3 and Radt 1985: 116; but the scepticism of Taplin 1977: 195–6, 464 is salutary.

[30] E. *Supp.* 745 ff.; Plut. *Thes.* 29. 4: Jacoby 1955: 442–8 (on *FGrH* 328 F112–13); Collard 1975: 302 n. 759.

[31] Eleutherae defected to Athens probably before the mid-5th-cent. (cf. Meiggs and Lewis 1988: 127 (no. 48, ll. 96–7)), but it retained Boeotian traditions: Chandler 1926: 9–10. The emphasis of the later tragedians on the failure of the Argives to gain burial may reflect the account of the *Thebaid*, but their burial at Thebes did feature in other Theban traditions: van der Kolf 1924: 28 f. Tyrtaeus 12. 8 and Pl. *Phdr.* 269b mention Adrastus' exceptional eloquence: even if it had no effect in the *Thebaid* (Jacoby 1954: 251–2 n. 24 against Welcker 1849: 367, 324), perhaps it secured the burial of his men in these traditions. If so, it is highly characteristic of Athenian πολυπραγμοσύνη in myth-making that Adrastus is demoted from a position of competence in favour of their own hero.

of these may be a *terminus post quem* for the revival of interest in the heroes thought to be in the tombs, and perhaps for the growth of the rival claims of Eleutherae and Eleusis and Thebes and Athens to possessing their bodies.[32]

As far back as the *Iliad*, the precept that revenge on an enemy is acceptable only when he is able to defend himself, and that once he is dead and no longer dangerous, it must cease, is commended as a difficult principle to uphold, but one which a civilized Greek society must uphold.[33] Just as the Greeks appropriated 'civilization' as Greek, Athens tended to appropriate and redefine 'typically Greek' qualities or institutions as 'typically Athenian', and so Theseus comes to take on exploits with a cultural or moral significance which had been previously attributed to the panhellenic culture hero Heracles.[34] According to Plutarch (*Thes.* 29. 4), writers on Heracles claim that it was he who first took up the dead under a truce, and an Oxyrhynchus papyrus asserts: νεκροὺς δ ὑπο[σπόνδους ἀ/ποδοῦναι λέγουσιν πρῶτον | Ἡρ[ακλέα ('they say that Heracles was the first to give back corpses under a treaty'), followed by gaps until l. 24, and then [ἀν]ελέσθαι πρῶτον Θησέα [πρὸς Θηβαίους ('Theseus was the first to take them up from the Thebans', *POxy* 1241 col. iii. 13–28). It may be that the custom was originally ascribed to Heracles, and only later did Athenian pretension transfer it to Theseus in this particular setting. There is, of course, no chronological reason why the story of Theseus' service to the Argives could not have been in the *Theseid*:[35] as soon as Adrastus escapes from Thebes (*Thebaid* fr. 6D), he is a potential candidate for Athenian help.

After Plataea's defection to the Athenians in 519 BC, followed by the Theban attempt to crush the newly established democracy in 506, relations between Athens and Thebes were unfriendly, and even if the burial of Polynices' army did not immediately acquire a political dimension, the subsequent contrast between Athens' defence of Greece and Thebes' collaboration in the Persian wars may have helped to stimulate contemporary interest in a myth in

---

[32] Mylonas 1953; Coldstream 1977: 351; cf. Burkert 1985: 203; Jacoby 1954: 443–5, who dates Eleusinian stories about the Seven to the 7th cent.

[33] Segal 1971: 13–17, 48–56, and note especially Hdt. 9. 79 and Moschion, *TGrF* 97 F6. 30–34 as well as the plots of Sophocles' *Ajax* and *Antigone* and Euripides' *Suppliants*: see also Jacoby 1954: 446–7 (cf. 1944: 42).

[34] See esp. §§1.3.2, 1.4 and 4.3.   [35] Jacoby 1954: 444–8.

which Athens so comprehensively outshone Thebes. This is, of course, the era in which other myths of older origin are turned into 'proofs' of an eternal and unchanging Athenian virtue in the funeral orations.[36] By the late 470s, the Theban Pindar was keen to stress that the Thebans cremated the enemy dead without any hesitation or Athenian intervention, and it is tempting to see his insistence as a riposte to ideological claims of the 470s, although not necessarily to the *Eleusinioi* itself.[37]

The help given by Theseus demands gratitude from its recipients, and if extant tragedy is any guide, it is likely that the *Eleusinioi* would have looked to a future in which relations between Athens and Argos were friendly. The *Eumenides* of 458 BC envisages particularly close relations between the two, and its audience could hardly have failed to think of their historical alliance of 461 as Athens finally broke with Sparta after years of suspicion between the two. The relationship between the *Eleusinioi* and Athenian politics has tempted speculation, but to judge from extant Theseus tragedy, especially Euripides' *Suppliants*, pre-existing mythical structures and the established image of the ideal Athens in conventional Athenian thought are at least as influential in determining the structure of a tragedy as individual events of contemporary politics.[38] Although the mythical alliance may validate current or

---

[36] I date the establishment of the *epitaphios* speech to the 470s: see Ch. 2, p. 34. Hauvette 1898 suggested that the *epitaphios* speech in Euripides' *Suppliants* reflected such a speech in the *Eleusinioi*; see also Zuntz 1955: 13–16. Aeschylus also wrote a *Heraclidae*, but it is not safe to assume that its subject was another of the standard topics of the *epitaphioi*: Herter 1939: 301 n. 285; Radt 1985: 190.

[37] *Ol.* 6. 15 f., *Nem.* 9. 21 of 468 and 474/1 respectively: Jacoby 1954: 445; Farnell 1932, vol. II, 40, 310.

[38] For speculations on the political background to the play, see Hauvette 1898; Jacoby 1954: 445 n. 30; Podlecki 1966: 150–1; Gastaldi 1976. Arguments concerning the relationship of the content of the play to its date have tended to be circular, since there is no real evidence for its date apart from the (lost) content of the play itself, and it is difficult to place it any more accurately than sometime between the early 470s and the late 460s. If we could be sure that Pindar was referring directly to the play (as Podlecki), it would have been produced soon after the Persian wars, before any prospect of an Athenian–Argive alliance. One other possible indication of a date in the 470s for the play is a vase (Athens N.M. 18606), datable just after 470, which shows three pairs of men on three altars: Karusu 1972 suggests that the picture illustrates a scene in the *Eleusinioi*, but the supplication of the Heraclidae is also possible: cf. J. Schmidt 1988: 725, no. 5. On *ARV*² 612,1 warriors ask Athena and a young, vigorous man (probably Theseus) for help: the vase is datable 450/440, so certainly antedates Euripides' *Suppliants* and may illustrate Aeschylus: E. Simon 1963: 54, Jeffery 1965: 51 suggests that the scene was also portrayed on the Stoa Poikile in the 460s.

prospective realities—and it is undoubtedly aetiological in asserting an unbroken line of Athenian power and virtue between the
days of Theseus and the mid-fifth century—it is also Athens' due
reward for risk taken in helping the oppressed much earlier in
Athenian 'history'. Since Theseus achieves a peaceful settlement
with Thebes, there would be no reason why the *Eleusinioi* could not
also have envisaged some kind of pact between Athens and Thebes
as well, and any direct correspondence between myth and politics
would be blurred even more. Like the *Eumenides* which it probably
antedates, the *Eleusinioi* is an unusually early example in tragedy of
the risk and reward pattern which shapes later extant tragedy in
which Theseus plays a part, but which can also be seen in rudi-
mentary form in some of his earlier adventures before the development of tragedy.

7.4 THE AEGEUS PLAYS OF SOPHOCLES AND EURIPIDES

7.4.1 *Sophocles*

Sophocles' *Aegeus* shares with Euripides' homonymous play the
subject of Theseus' journey from Trozenian obscurity to recognition as an Athenian by his father Aegeus. Whereas the Theseus of
most extant drama (and perhaps also the *Eleusinioi*) is essentially a
secondary character, his position in the plot of these plays was presumably more central. They must both have traced the progression
from suspense, caused by Aegeus' ignorance of Theseus' identity,
to relief as the two are reunited. The story of the sword and sandals
left by Aegeus under a rock at Trozen for Theseus to take up when
he reached adulthood and was ready to come to Athens is portrayed
in art as early as the sixth century.[39] Sophocles fr. 19 mentions the
Trozenian river near which Aegeus concealed these tokens (cf.
Paus. 2. 32. 7), and it is likely that they were the means by which the
recognition was effected in both plays. Reference to the canonical
cycle of Theseus' labours could hardly be avoided, and fr. 20—
κέστρᾳ σιδηρᾷ πλευρὰ καὶ κατὰ ῥάχιν | ἤλαυνε παίων ('he struck
and wounded him on the back and sides with his iron hammer')—

---

[39] Sourvinou-Inwood 1971; cf. D.S. 4. 59. 1; Plut. *Thes.* 3. 6, 7. 2; Paus. 1. 27. 8,
2. 23. 7, 32. 9; Apollod. 3. 16. 1, 3. 15. 7; Hyg. 37. 2, *Astr.* 2. 6 etc.

probably refers to the dispatch of Polypemon.[40] It is also pretty certain that Theseus was questioned about his deeds and identity when he first arrived at Athens, and πῶς δῆθ' ὁδουρῶν + ὅμοιος + ἐξέβης λαθών ('how, then, did you come out, escaping the highwaymen's notice?', fr. 22) may come from the same early part of the play as fr. 20.[41] If the recognition between father and son is not to be effected until near the end of the play, then Theseus combines strength in dispatching his enemies on the road to Athens with an Odysseus-like intelligence in not revealing his identity as soon as he arrives. In later sources, Aegeus' childlessness and the designs of the Pallantidae on his kingdom make him uneasy about Theseus' initial arrival: Bacchylides, imagining the reaction of those in Athens to the approach of Theseus, fresh from his Saronic conquests and as yet unknown in his father's city, makes his Aegeus view the young warrior with some trepidation (18. 30). Perhaps Sophocles' Aegeus was similarly concerned.[42]

The longest and most intriguing fragment of the play is 24 (though it is not explicitly ascribed to the *Aegeus*) whose speaker must be Aegeus himself.

> ἐμοὶ μὲν ἀκτὰς ὥρισεν πατὴρ μολεῖν
> πρεσβεῖα νείμας τῆσδε γῆς—Λύκῳ
> τὸν ἀντίπλευρον κῆπον Εὐβοίας νέμει
> Νίσῳ δὲ τὴν ὅμαυλον ἐξαιρεῖ χθόνα
> Σκίρωνος ἀκτῆς· τῆς δὲ γῆς τὸ πρὸς νότον
> ὁ σκληρὸς οὗτος καὶ γίγαντας ἐκτρέφων
> εἴληχε Πάλλας.[43]

This is the earliest literary reference to Aegeus' brothers, but they were not Sophocles' invention, and there is a tradition of hostility

[40] Wilamowitz 1880: 120 n. 35, 225. For the κέστρα, see Pollux 10. 160, and for Polypemon, above, Ch. 1. For the list of the labours in tragedy, cf. E. *Hipp.* 976ff.; E. *Supp.* 316–17; S. fr. 730C.

[41] Sutton 1984: 74. Radt 1977, ad loc., lists the emendations offered for ὅμοιος. Valckenaer's πῶς δῆθ' ὁδουρὸν οἷος ἐξέβης λαθών is an attractive possibility; on the cycle vases, Theseus single-handedly vanquishes all his opponents. Fr. 905 ὃς παρακτίαν | στείχων ἀνημέρωσα κυωδάλων ὁδόν ('I who cleared the road of monsters') almost certainly refers to Theseus (compare A. *Eum.* 14–15), but its provenance is unknown.

[42] For further suggestions concerning the structure of the play, see Post 1922: 13; Pearson 1917: 15–16; Pfeiffer 1949: 227.

[43] 'My father assigned the shore to me, granting me the best parts of the land. He apportioned the garden of Euboea facing it to Lycus and for Nisus picked out the land that borders on Sciron's shore. Pallas, this tough nurturer of giants, obtained the part of the land towards the south.'

between them in which Aegeus is always dominant, as would befit the father of Athens' most famous representative (cf. Apollod. 3. 15. 6; Paus. 1. 5. 4, 39. 4). Already on a vase of *c*.480 (Athens Acropolis Museum 735), Aegeus' brothers, along with Orneus (Menestheus' grandfather) and Minos, all of whom are Theseus' enemies, watch his struggle with the Minotaur, apparently hoping that the creature will get the better of him. Herodotus says that Lycus was expelled by Aegeus and went to Lycia,[44] while traditions of the enmity of Aegeus and Nisus, the eponym of the Megarian harbour of Nisaea, must ultimately originate in the conflict between Megara and Attica over Salamis.[45] The division of Attica was also described by Philochorus (*FGrH* 328 F107) who assigns the land slightly differently: although Nisus gets the Megarid once more, the Atthidographer lays more emphasis on the internal divisions of Attica than does Sophocles, so that Lycus is given the Diacria (cf. *ΣAr. Vesp.* 1223) rather than Euboea as in Sophocles' more ambitious division. Both writers emphasize the dominance among the Pandionids of Aegeus: in Philochorus, he is assigned the land around the city, and Sophocles' description of his share as τὰ πρεσβεῖα ('the best bits') gives him pre-eminence among Pandion's sons. Sophocles' fragment reflects fifth-century Athenian beliefs concerning their relations with neighbouring Greek states: what belongs to Aegeus now will belong to Theseus, the epitome of Athenian virtue, so that its possession by his descendants is clearly justifiable in the eyes of the audience. In 446 BC Euboea, followed by Megara, which had been an Athenian possession since 461 (Thuc. 1. 103. 4), revolted from Athenian control (Thuc. 1. 114. 1), but one can only speculate about a possible relationship between the revolts and this division of Attica.[46]

---

[44] Hdt. 1. 173. 1, 7. 92; compare Medea and Medus at Hdt. 7. 62. One Lycus secured Theseus' ostracism after he set up the democracy (*ΣAr. Plut.* 627a), and Theseus was killed on Skyros by king Lycomedes (Plut. *Cim.* 8); compare also the Lycus who is the enemy of Heracles' family in Euripides' *Heracles*. According to Paus. 10. 25. 8, Aegeus also expelled Peteos, Menestheus' father.

[45] Jacoby 1954: 430–1 suggests that the myth was used as justificatory propaganda for Peisistratus' capture of Nisaea in the 6th cent.

[46] See Meiggs 1972: 177–81. Strabo 9. 1. 6 quotes the Sophoclean fragment to prove the highly controversial claim that Megara was Athenian. Accounts of the division of Attica may reflect conditions before the synoikism, the internal politics of the 560s or even a regionalism which never died out, but—importantly—they are also purely aetiological in the way in which they explain Athens' dominance over Attica and link it reassuringly with the distant past, to make it immutable and right.

Finally the west and south are assigned to Pallas, the 'breeder of giants'. The description of Pallas as σκλῆρος suggests that there was particular hostility between Aegeus and this brother, and the demonstrative οὗτος[47] may imply that he has some particular importance in the play. Later sources tell us that the Pallantids had already plotted against Aegeus before Theseus' arrival, and that later in his career, after he had been recognized by Aegeus, they tried to ambush him.[48] Plutarch gives quite specific geographical locations for the ambush, envisaging a movement on Theseus from Sphettus and Gargettus (cf. *FGrH* 328 F 108), and Sophocles' apportionment of the south to Pallas is compatible with this location. It would be possible that Plutarch and Philochorus were working from Sophocles, or traditions known to him; a relationship with the *Theseid* itself cannot be excluded from consideration.[49]

Later accounts link Theseus' recognition by Aegeus with an attempt by Medea to kill him. Most commonly, he arrives at Athens and is recognized by Aegeus after narrowly escaping being poisoned by her, and then shows his heroism by volunteering to kill the bull which was terrorizing the inhabitants of Marathon.[50] Alternatively, Medea sends him against the bull as soon as he arrives at Athens unrecognized by everyone else, in the hope that it will kill him; when this fails she tries to poison him, but he is recognized by his father just in time. This version is only recorded in literature by Apollod. *Ep.* 1. 5. 6 (cf. Myth.Vat. 1. 48). It is very probable that the conquest of the Marathonian bull featured in Sophocles' *Aegeus*, since fr. 25 refers to rope and binding (κλωστῆρι χειρῶν ὀργάσας κατήνυσε σειραῖα δεσμά), but what of Medea?

[47] Emphatic and indicative of contempt, according to Liddell–Scott–Jones, and also of an object which is, by implication, close to the speaker, if not actually present: Kühner and Gerth 1898: 641.

[48] Plut. *Thes.* 3. 5 and 13; Apollod. *Ep.* 1. 11 and Paus. 1. 22. 2, 28. 10; see also Philochorus *FGrH* 328 F108 (with Jacoby 1954: 431 ff.), whose story is essentially the same as Plutarch's. The description of the Pallantids as giants may refer to their insolent behaviour to Aegeus (Pearson 1917: 20–1), or be intended to align them with monstrous figures such as those overcome by Athena, Heracles and others in the name of true civilization (cf. Apollod. 1. 6. 1).

[49] Cf. Jacoby 1954: 339 n. 5. Sourvinou-Inwood 1979: 55–8 suggests that Pherecydes, whose *Histories* were published by *c*.470 at the latest, was used by Sophocles, and the *Theseid* was almost certainly one of Pherecydes' sources: Jacoby 1947*a*: 31–3 and n. 46.

[50] *Σ*11. 741; Plut. *Thes.* 12. 2–3; Apollod. 1. 9. 8; Paus. 2. 3. 8; D.S. 4. 55. 6; Call. *Hecale* fr. 233Pf.; Dion.Per. 1020–8; Eustath. *Comm.* on Dion.Per. 1017. 20; Ov. *Met.* 7. 404–24.

Apollodorus' story is more dramatic than the more commonly attested version, and it is often conjectured that the mythographer was summarizing the plot of a tragedy, especially as his story has been connected with a group of vases dating from 460/450 onwards, on which an old man stands to the right of Theseus who is mastering a bull, while to the left, a woman, carrying a jug and phiale, hurries away.[51] Which (if either) of Sophocles' or Euripides' Aegeus plays these vases are illustrating is unfortunately impossible to tell in the present state of the evidence.[52] The fragments of Sophocles' *Aegeus* show no trace of Medea or her attempt to poison Theseus after he had successfully dispatched the bull: they are so meagre that it is not necessarily safe to conclude that Sophocles did not include her,[53] but there is more positive evidence to suggest that it was in Euripides' version of the story that she was important. If the reference to Pallas in fr. 24 points to the inclusion of the Pallantidae in the play, however, a plot which comprised their hostility, the recognition of Theseus and the triumph over the bull might seem rather overloaded if Medea is to be included as well. There is no reason why the conquest of the bull, or of the Pallantidae, should not have been the crowning moment of the play after the recognition scene. They were famous enough adversaries of Theseus to have been awarded a prominent place among his triumphs on the mid-fifth century Hephaesteion in the heart of Athens.[54] On a more certain final note, the *Aegeus* was surely a tragedy of action with a 'happy ending', and its Theseus was portrayed as a virtuous and mighty victor, a true-born example of Athenian virtues and as a hero in his own right, rather than the comforter of the suffering of earlier chapters. It is of some interest that it must have been different in tone from the extant plays of Sophocles, and probably neither Aegeus or Theseus resembled the Knoxian 'heroic temper' type of hero.

[51] Before *c*.430 she wears Greek dress, as she often does on vase scenes from the *Peliades*, but her portrayal subsequently as a barbarian woman may have been influenced by the *Medea* of 431: Webster 1965; Kron 1976: 32; Sourvinou-Inwood 1979: 33–4. Shefton 1956: 161, however, denies that the figure is Medea.

[52] For the priority of Euripides' *Aegeus*: Kron 1976: 128; Wilamowitz 1925: 234 ff. For Sophocles: Webster 1965: 520; Sourvinou-Inwood 1979: 56.

[53] *Pace* Pfeiffer 1949: 227; Mayer 1883: 60.

[54] The Hephaesteion may even have portrayed the ambush itself: Thompson 1966a. On occasional representations of Medea and the bull, such as the late fifth century *ARV*[2] 1346,2, another figure appears. Kron 1976: 131 suggests that this is Pallas.

7.4.2 *Euripides*

Wilamowitz first suggested that the *Aegeus, Theseus* and *Hippolytus Kalyptomenos* of Euripides formed a connected trilogy centred on Aegeus' initial crime in begetting Theseus against the gods' will, and the resulting divine retribution, as Theseus causes first his father's death and then that of Hippolytus (cf. Plut. *Thes.* 3. 3–4).[55] Metrical evidence suggests that the *Aegeus* preceded the *Medea*; the parody of the *Theseus* in Aristophanes' *Wasps* makes 422 its *terminus ante quem*,[56] and the first *Hippolytus* must have been produced before 428. Wilamowitz's suggestion cannot be refuted on chronological grounds alone, but it must remain as possible that the *Aegeus* was produced very early in Euripides' career, the *Theseus* rather nearer the time that it was parodied, while the *Hippolytus* may stand somewhere between the two.[57] As in Aeschylus' case, it is unwise to create trilogies purely out of the names of the plays which have survived to us, and above all, although Euripides could create a Theseus who curses his son in a fit of rage, once in an unpopular play and then in a popular play which absolved him (and Phaedra) from guilt as much as it could, it is hard to believe that an Athenian playwright would have built a whole trilogy around the premiss that the birth of the national hero was against the will of the gods.

The arrival of Theseus at Athens, his enemies' dismay, and the reunion with Aegeus must be common to Euripides and Sophocles, and fragments of the Euripidean *Aegeus* which seem to refer to his exploits on the road to Athens and to his unknown identity are extant.[58] There is a little more positive evidence that Medea was his

[55] Wilamowitz 1875: 175, 1880: 483–4, 1891: 42 f.; Mayer 1883: 59; Wüst 1968: 533; *contra* Buchwald 1939: 43 ff. The story itself probably antedates the 5th cent.: see §1.3.2. Walker 1995: 135 comments on the 'atmosphere of the archaic age' about the extant fragments of Euripides' *Aegeus*.

[56] Webster 1965: 519–20; Buchwald 1939: 44.

[57] Cropp and Fick 1985: 70 tentatively date the *Aegeus* between 455 and 430 and the *Theseus* between 455 and 422. The Aegeus scene in the *Medea* is certainly given an added dimension if we can assume that her failed attempt to destroy the royal house of Athens had already been portrayed by Euripides.

[58] ἀνθρωποκτόνος ('man-killing') and ἀγ[ών]ον ἀθλήσαντα ('taking part in a contest', 11b and 11c Sn.). I am not convinced by Webster 1967: 77, who refers 11a Sn. κρηνῆς πάροιθεν ἀνθεμόστρωτον λέχος ('a flower-strewn bed in front of a fountain') to the story that Sinis' daughter hid from Theseus' advances in a place full of plants (Plut. *Thes.* 8. 2). For Theseus' unknown identity, see fr. 1, ποίαν σε φῶμεν γαῖαν ἐκλελοιπότα | πόλει ξενοῦσθαι τῇδε; τις πάτρας ὅρος | τίς ἔσθ' ὁ φύσας; τοῦ

main adversary in Euripides if fr. 4, πέφυκε γάρ πως παισὶ πολέμιον γυνὴ | τοῖς πρόσθεν ἡ ζυγεῖσα δευτέρῳ πατρί ('for the woman who marries their father is somehow hostile by nature to his previous children') refers to her hostility to her stepson Theseus: the lines presuppose that Theseus' real identity is known, so either they were spoken by Theseus himself, or Medea who has recognized him before anyone else does, or they come from the end of the play when all had been revealed. Later writers record that Medea had a son, Medos, by Aegeus. It has been suggested that the tradition preserved by Diodorus, that Medea left Athens with Medos and went to Colchis, reflects the end of a tragedy, but Medos is so shadowy a figure that it is unwise to assume that he had a part in Euripides' *Aegeus*.[59]

Nauck contended that the plot of Euripides' *Aegeus* is preserved in outline by *ΣΙl.* 11. 741.[60] According to this narrative, Medea leaves Corinth after the infanticide, comes to Athens and marries Aegeus. When Theseus arrives at Athens, she recognizes him, but his father does not, and Medea persuades him that the young man is a threat to the king and should be poisoned.[61] As Theseus is about to take the poison, his father recognizes the sword and sandals which he had left for him in Trozen, dashes the cup from Theseus' mouth and expels Medea, who settles in Ephyra. The account of Plutarch (*Thes.* 12) is very similar, but it is more overtly

κεκήρυξαι πατρός; ('What land are we to say that you left, to be welcomed in this city? What is the boundary of your homeland? Who begot you? From what father are you proclaimed to be?'), and fr. 2, τί σε μάτηρ ἐν δεκάτα τόκου ὠνόμαζεν; ('What did your mother name you when you were born in the tenth month?'). ἦ που κρεῖσσον τῆς εὐγενείας | τὸ καλῶς πράσσειν ('Right conduct is more important than noble birth,' fr. 9) may be someone's judgement on Theseus' heroism before he has revealed himself, and perhaps also the words of fr. 6 τί γὰρ πατρῴας ἀνδρὶ φιλτέρον χθονός; ('What is dearer to a man than his native land?') belong to Theseus on his arrival.

[59] Medos: D.S. 4. 55. 5; Apollod. 1. 9. 28; Hyg. 26–7; Paus. 2. 3. 8; cf. Hdt. 7. 62; see Mayer 1883: 61 f.; Buchwald 1939: 44. Mayer suggests that Theopompus 17K–A (*Theseus*, written after 390), ἥξῃ δὲ Μήδων γαῖαν ἔνθα καρδάμων | πλείστων ποιεῖται καὶ πράσων ἀβυρτάκη ('You will come to the land of the Medes where sauce is made of much cardamom and leeks,') is parodying the end of Euripides: Sourvinou-Inwood 1979: 56 refers the fragment to a parody of Sophocles' *Aegeus*; see also Kassel and Austin 1989: vii. 717.

[60] Nauck 1964: 363.

[61] Aegeus seems to have been decidedly naïve: cf. Page 1958: xiv on his characterization in the *Medea* and below. Perhaps δειλῶν γυναῖκες δεσποτῶν θρασύστομοι ('The wives of cowardly masters have bold tongues', fr. 3) refers to Aegeus and Medea.

dramatic than that of the scholiast, since he adds that the poison was to be administered at a feast, and that Theseus, cleverly wishing to give a discreet sign of his identity to his father, drew his sword as if he were about to cut the meat with it. Aegeus recognized the sword and dashed down the poison on a place where subsequently the enclosure in the Delphinion stood, and recognized him (ἐγνώριζεν) in front of the citizens who received him because of his courage.

Plutarch's banquet scene clearly resembles that described by the messenger in *Ion* 1122 ff., which ends with a recognition of the bond between father and son, while the link between myth and currently existing objects or conditions (the Delphinion and the hostility between the Athenians and the Medes), is also a familiar tragic device. This version of the story is distinct from that of Apollod. *Ep.* 1. 5. 6 or the vase paintings discussed above, in which Medea's hostility to Theseus is linked with his capture of the Marathonian bull, and if the accounts of the Homeric scholiast and Plutarch do draw on Euripides, then Sophocles' *Aegeus* may, after all, be a more plausible candidate as the originator of the version which links Medea with the bull. In the present state of the evidence, however, nothing is very certain, and from the fragments alone, excluding any other evidence, it would appear that the bull definitely features in Sophocles' *Aegeus* and Medea very probably in Euripides, but which (if either) linked Medea with the bull is not at all clear.[62]

A recently found Euripidean fragment contains a description of an encounter between Theseus and a dangerous horned beast.[63]

> $. . . . \overset{\times - \cup}{?\cdot?\cdot?} . . .]$ θε κιόνῳ [ν
> $. . \overset{\times - \cup}{?\cdot?\cdot?} . .] . ατ᾽ εἶχον$ [
> $. . \overset{\times - \cup}{?\cdot?} . .]$ ακρον καὶ δα[
> $. . . . . .]$ ων θεατὴς ἀσφ[αλ
> λεύσσω] δὲ τὸν μὲν βο[
> $. . . . . .]$ τα κυρτὸν εἰς κ[έρας θυμούμενον
> γλώσσῃ|ι διαψαίροντα μ|υκτήρων πόρους

---

[62] Thus I am sceptical of Buchwald 1939: 43–4, who leaves *ΣIl.* 11. 741 out of account and 'reconstructs' the plot of the *Aegeus* as a combination of Plut. *Thes.* 12 and Ap. *Ep.* 1. 4–6: it would be possible, but in themselves, his arguments are not decisive given the difficulties surrounding the relationship between Sophocles' *Aegeus* and that of Euripides.

[63] *POxy* 3531 in vol. 50 of the *Oxyrhynchus Papyri* (Parsons 1983), 25–8; l. 7 fits with E. fr. 926N.

......] . ι θαρσοῦντα . [
......]τα μηρῶν εντος[
ὁ δ' Αἰγέ]ως μὲν τῶι λόγωι [κεκλημένος,
ἔργωι] δὲ Θησεὺς ἐκ Ποσε[ιδῶνος γεγώς
......]ματ' ἐκδὺς θηρὸς [
.....κο]ρύνηι δεξιὰν ὡ[πλισμένος

A snorting (διαψαίροντα μ[υκτήρων πόρους, ll. 6–7) animal with horns (κ[έρας, l. 6) could be the bull or the Minotaur and the fragment has been claimed both for the *Aegeus* and the *Theseus*. The uniquely peculiar appearance of the Minotaur is clearly worth describing—perhaps more so than that of an ordinary animal such as a bull[64]—but there are difficulties in assuming that the speaker is describing Theseus in the labyrinth (implied by κιόνω[ν, 'of columns', l. 1): who could have accompanied him there as a spectator (θεατής, l. 4)? In spite of this, however, to my mind, ll. 10–11 tip the balance in favour of an ascription to the *Theseus*, since the speaker describes Theseus as 'supposedly the son of Aegeus but really the son of Poseidon'. The assumption that Theseus' identity was already known in the bull scene would detract from its climactic revelation in the poisoning scene at the end of the play.[65] I would therefore assign the fragment to Euripides' *Theseus*, in which case the suggestion that Euripides' *Aegeus* included Theseus' encounter with the bull must remain unproven.

Vase painters portray Theseus with the bull and his recognition by Aegeus as separate episodes rather earlier than the composite scenes of Medea with the bull. The two stories are perfectly coherent without the inclusion of Medea and it is reasonable to ask what she adds to Theseus' homecoming, and at what date she was included in the story.[66] Euripides' *Medea*, in which she plays on Aegeus' thoroughly Athenian concern for the oppressed so as to secure the promise of asylum in his city, is the definite *terminus ante quem* for her appearance in the Theseus story, but vase painting (leaving aside the problem of Neophron's date), may take her first

[64] Compare E. *Kretes* 2a Cant., ll. 12–23, a dialogue between Minos and the Coryphaeus, which dwells in detail on the monstrous appearance of Pasiphae's progeny.

[65] Parsons 1983: 25 f.

[66] Cf. Herter 1939: 278–80; Shefton 1962: 351 n. 86; Sourvinou-Inwood 1979: 51. For Theseus and the Marathonian bull, see §1.4. For pictures of Aegeus' recognition of his son, see Kron 1981a: 362, nos. 27–32: the theme is especially popular from 480/470 to 430/420.

certain appearance back to *c*.460.[67] Her only part in Athenian mythology is her attempt to kill the national hero, and one might guess that accounts of her attempt to assassinate Theseus emphasized her dishonesty and ingratitude to Aegeus. Athens welcomes the oppressed, and is normally rewarded for its generosity. Medea, the dangerous foreign woman who destroys families,[68] attempts to subvert Athenian generosity, but she fails and is driven out. In this case, uniquely, Athens is not rewarded for its generosity because its recipient is unworthy, but the city is not harmed either, and Athenian invincibility is emphasized all the more as Medea is successfully driven out to the Medes (who in their turn will come close to, but not succeed in, destroying Athens). The theme of ἀρετή and reward, which is a dominating principle in the Theseus tragedies, also shapes the story of Medea and the Athenian royal house: the basic principles of the Athenian mission are so sound that the city will not be damaged by a mistake which arises from the most honourable motives, and 'typical' Athenian courage will remove any threat of danger to the city.

> πῶς οὖν ἱερῶν ποταμῶν
> ἢ πόλις ἢ φίλων
> πόμπιμός σε χώρα
> τὰν παιδολέτειραν ἕξει,
> τὰν οὐχ ὁσίαν μετ' ἄλλων;

('how all the city of holy waters, the city that looks after its friends, receive the child-killing, unholy woman?')

Thus ask the chorus of E. *Med.* 846 ff., horrified at Medea's planned infanticide. Ultimately, however, 'the holy city that looks after its friends' will remove her from Greece altogether, punishing her as she deserves. Athens will succeed where the Corinth of the *Medea* fails.

It would be interesting to know more about the portrayal of Aegeus in these plays, because everything we know about him suggests that he was notably outclassed in wisdom and heroism by his son. Although fifth-century Athens does not dwell on Theseus' responsibility for his father's death, if Aegeus is thought to be

---

[67] Cf. Buchwald 1939: 44.

[68] Whether she was said to have murdered her children before Euripides is disputed, but her crimes against Pelias and Absyrtos were already part of the myth at this time: Sourvinou-Inwood 1979: 53 and n. 179.

inferior to his son (whether consciously or unconsciously) his removal is 'justified', since it enables Athens to acquire a greater king under whom the Amazons are repelled and the Argive dead are buried.[69]

Herodotus makes an explicit etymological connection between the Medes and Medea (Hdt. 7. 62; cf. Paus. 2. 3. 8, Hyg. *Fab*. 27). The aetiological possibilities of the story in the aftermath of the Persian wars are obvious, and it may be that Medea is incorporated into the story after Athens' near-fatal encounter with the Medes. It has been suggested that Theseus' original enemy was not Medea, but another stepmother, who was overshadowed by her after the Persian wars. It is common in stories of a hero's youth for him to encounter and outwit persecutors—indeed, a hero must have the combination of ability and good fortune to overcome what would destroy an ordinary man—and such a story would not have been out of place in the *Theseid*.[70] It would, however, be an exaggeration to claim that the Medea story is just a symbolic re-enactment of the struggle against the Persians. Like the Amazons, who acquire Persian features after the Persian wars, but who are mythical enemies of Athens before 470 BC,[71] Medea (or the wicked stepmother)

---

[69] Sourvinou-Inwood 1979: 18–28 argues that there was always antagonism between father and son because Aegeus abandoned Theseus, and that this hostility first led Aegeus to send him against the bull and ultimately made Theseus responsible for his father's death: thus Medea, or another stepmother (see below) was introduced to divert this hostility to a more acceptable source. However, Bacch. 18 is not real evidence for hostility between them (as Sourvinou-Inwood, 26), since Aegeus does not know who the young man really is. Moreover, all narratives of Theseus' early life focus exclusively on his triumphant return to Athens, not his early abandonment. Coming to Athens proves that Theseus is now an adult, and Aegeus specifically prepared for this moment by leaving the sword and sandals for him. He did *not* want his son to be killed, and it is a proof of Theseus' special destiny that he is saved from death in the nick of time. He then went out against the bull of his own accord to further his heroic reputation and because truly Athenian heroes are expected to volunteer for danger.

[70] *ΣΕ*. *Med*. 673 and Apollod. 3. 15. 6 mention other, less famous wives of Aegeus. See also Rank 1964: 159; Sourvinou-Inwood 1979: 50–6.

[71] Although 460/450 is the surest *terminus post quem* for the story of Medea and Theseus, Sourvinou-Inwood 1979: 27f., 51ff. argues that a cup by Makron (*ARV*² 460,13 = Kron 1981*b*: 422, no. 25, datable to 500/480), which shows 'Theseus' attacking 'Aethra' should read 'Theseus' and 'Medea'. Other interpretations of the cup are possible (Sourvinou-Inwood 1979: 3–7; Neils 1987: 103; Kron 1981*b*: 429), but if her interpretation is correct, then the story of Theseus and Medea, like that of Athens and the Amazons, could even antedate the Persian wars. Even if Makron's cup must be left out of account, there is also a group of vases on which a youth attacks a woman, dating from *c*.480/475 (first on *ARV*² 242,80) which may illustrate the scene.

symbolizes danger and the threat to order; but so, of course, do the Persians themselves, in a metaphorical sense separate from their literal historical existence. The relationship between what actually happened in the Persian wars and how it was subsequently told, in a highly mythicizing structure of hubris punished and virtue rewarded, makes it difficult to regard Medea's attempt to kill Theseus purely as a symbol of the Persian attack on Athens,[72] and the myth of a wicked stepmother and a virtuous hero has a potency which is not explicable simply by what it 'really' stands for.

7.5 THE THESEUS PLAYS OF SOPHOCLES AND EURIPIDES

7.5.1 *Sophocles' Theseus (?)*

Only two words are definitely ascribed to Sophocles' *Theseus*, and the name may simply be an alternative title for his *Aegeus* or *Phaedra*, but the contents of *POxy* 2452 are often identified with it.[73] The papyrus contains part of a play by an Attic author, and although Achaeus and Heraclides (?) as well as Sophocles and Euripides wrote plays called *Theseus*, so little of the minor tragedians survives that the ascription of the fragments to one of them is unlikely on grounds of probability. Linguistic considerations just about tip the balance in favour of Sophocles, but an ascription to Euripides' *Theseus* cannot be excluded.[74] 730a (*POxy* 2452, col. ii. 6–13):

---

[72] Or the wicked stepmother as a symbol of the tyrants, as Sourvinou-Inwood 1979: 50–6.

[73] Full commentaries are provided by Turner 1962 (rev. by Lloyd-Jones 1963); Diotti 1966; Carden 1974: 110–35. I use the text of Kannicht in Radt 1977.

[74] For the linguistic arguments in favour of Sophocles, see Turner 1962: 1–2; cf. also Lloyd-Jones 1963: 436; Diotti 1966: 53–5. If the papyrus did contain Euripidean material, the mathematical probability that the papyrus could not be matched to one of the existing fragments would be extremely low: Kannicht 1977: 498. Even so, all the material we have here would suit what we know of Euripides' *Theseus*, which was also set in Crete, and Webster 1967: 105–9 maintains that Euripides is the author of these fragments. Eucken 1979 sees similarities between the Theseus of these fragments and that of *Oedipus Coloneus*, and suggests that the *Coloneus* is recalling another play by Sophocles (that of *POxy* 2452) in which Theseus also defended the young from oppression by a tyrannical figure. His argument convincingly demonstrates that Athenian drama tends to assign a fixed role to Athens' national hero, but not that Sophocles is the author of *POxy* 2452.

ἐ]πεὶ ἄφατα κε[
ἄναυδοι δυς.[
ΑΡΙΑΔΝΗ δύστηνα τέκνα. [- ∪ - × - ∪ -   8
δοκῶ πρὸς ὑμᾶς [- ∪ - × - ∪ -   (4)
ΕΡΙΒΟΙΑ οἰκτρὰ φρο[ν
οὐ γὰρ ἀλε.[
λέγηι κνω[12
]μ.[. .]. δὲ δεσπότι[∪ - × - ∪ -[75]   (8)

Eriboia has a cameo role in the Theseus myth, as one of the Athenian girls destined for the Minotaur, who had the further misfortune of being the object of Minos' unwanted attentions on the way to Crete in Bacchylides' seventeenth poem: it is tempting to assume that this story has some connection with the play.[76] As for Ariadne, although she is the daughter of the enemy king of Crete, she seems here to be sympathetic to the plight of the Athenians, calling them 'unlucky children' (l. 8), and οἰκτρὰ (l. 10) may indicate that Eriboia was attempting to win further sympathy from her.[77] Perhaps such sympathy was intended to contrast with Minos' cruelty.[78] Likely supplements to l. 12 include κνωσία ('Cretan') and κνωδάλον ('monster'). If the latter is accepted, Eriboia may have been referring to Ariadne's kinship with the Minotaur, and Kannicht suggests that the next line referred to Pasiphae.[79] In the uncanny, un-Greek world of Crete, so unlike the world which Theseus represents in tragedy, mothers can fall in love with bulls and half-brothers can be half-animal.[80]

]ρωπ. . [
].λιν' αορ[
].ουντά . [
× - ∪]. οἰκτίρουσα[- × - ∪ -   4

[75] From l. 13 on, with the possible exception of l. 21's δα]κρυτο, the fragment is too scrappy for us to deduce anything about the play. For the full text, see Kannicht 1977: 498–9.

[76] Sutton 1984: 76. Eriboia appears among the twice seven on the François vase of *c*.570; for Bacchylides' account of her harassment by Minos, see §1.7.

[77] Iambic trimeters, ll. 8–9, indicating Ariadne's calm, are answered by emotionally agitated dochmiacs from Eriboia: cf. Carden 1974: 123.

[78] I assume that he appeared in person in the play: Lloyd-Jones 1963: 435 supplements l. 73 to read Ἀν]δρόγε[ω, Minos' son, whose death in Attica was the reason that Athens had to pay tribute to Minos: cf. §1.3.3.

[79] Kannicht 1977: 498.

[80] Cf. §7.1.2, my interpretation of *POxy* 3531 above, and fr. 2a Cant. of Euripides' *Cretans*.

x -　　]α. γὰρ τοιαῦτα[- x - ∪ -
x - ∪　]ᾳι παῖ μὴ φε[- x - ∪ -
x -　　]αρ οἱ ξένοι τι·[- x - ∪ -
x -　　]μ' ἀπ' ἀνδρῶν φιλτατ[- x - ∪ -　　　　8
　　　].ει βίοτον· τόιτ' ἰανδ' ε[
　　　κα]κοπαθεῖ μόρωι φερομε[- ∪ -
　　　κα]τελεήσατε κατελεή[σατε
　　　ἄρ]ιστοι βροτῶν[　　　　　　　　　　　　12
x - (∪)]εων ἄτερθε καὶ πατρ[- ∪ -⁸¹
x - ∪ -　] ἄφυκτον αἷμα[- ∪ -
　　　].ος ἐχθρότερος[
　　　]ησία πάρει　　　　　　　　　　　　　16
　　　]' ἀλκά
　　　].θ' ἡμιν⁸² ἥδε
　　　].λᾶ
　　　]πω　　　　　　　　　　　　　　　20
　　　]έπὸ ὡ[
　　　. . .

(730b R)

The similarities between the preceding passage and 730b may suggest that they both come from the same part of the play. Ariadne
may be the first speaker, again in trimeters, again pitying the
Athenians (l. 4);⁸³ while Eriboia may reply to her in dochmiacs
from l. 8 on.⁸⁴ If this distribution of parts is correct, it is not easy to
determine who the 'dear men' are, from whom Ariadne is being
dragged away (reading φιλτάτ[ων ἀποσπάσας, l. 8), unless we
assume that she is being moved by pity to help the Athenians,
against her family's interests. If ἄρ]ιστοι is the correct supplement
for l. 12, Eriboia may have been appealing to a chorus composed of
Cretan men ('best of men') to pity her (κατελεήσατε, l. 11).⁸⁵

⁸¹ το]κέων ἄτερθε καὶ πάτρ[ας ἀπὸ ('far from my parents and homeland'—
Snell); γόν]εων ἄτερθε καὶ πάτρ[ας πλανώμενη ('wandering far from my parents
and homeland'—Lloyd-Jones).
⁸² This word would strongly suggest that we are dealing with Sophocles, not
Euripides: Turner 1962: 18; Kannicht 1977: 500 with Ellendt 1872: 192.
⁸³ Radt suggests τί μηχαν]ᾷ, παῖ; ('what are you devising, child?') as a supplement for l. 6, which would suit an attribution to Ariadne; cf. also Turner 1962: 18.
⁸⁴ Carden 1974: 124; Sutton 1984: 77.
⁸⁵ A mixed chorus would be unparalleled in extant tragedy, and a chorus of
Cretan men is the obvious alternative: Kannicht 1977: 500. Perhaps the twice seven
appeared as a supplementary chorus (like that of the Epigonoi at the end of
Euripides' *Suppliants*) whose youth and vulnerability would be an effective foil for
Theseus' dynamic heroism. Sutton 1984: 77 suggests that since the *Niobe* also

Ariadne may then reply to Eriboia, and she seems to say something about being far away from home and possibly from her parents, if the supplements for l. 13 of Snell or Lloyd-Jones are right; l. 14 may refer to the pollution she will incur in killing her monstrous brother (cf. 730a. 12 f.).[86] Could Eriboia be finally about to prevail upon Ariadne to help them, by promising her safe conduct from Crete in return? A promise by Eriboia herself that the Athenians would take Ariadne away from Crete might also serve to divert attention from Theseus' relations with the Cretan girl.

οὔκ· ἀλλὰ [
ἅ σ' ἐξεκ[
⟨ΘΗΣΕΥΣ⟩ ἥκιστ'· ἀ[
ἀλλ' οὖσα[4
παθων[
τίνειν α[
τούτων [
οὔτ' ἐμε[λ]ον]ο]ῦτ' ἤσκησα [(?)μηκύνειν ὅσα   8
μὴ μ' εἰκ[ὸ]ς ε[ἰ]πεῖν· ἀλλ' α[
καὶ πρόσθε δὴ 'γὼ πολλάκ[ις (?) πολλῶν ὕβριν
καθεῖλον αὐτὸς ταῖν ἐμ[αῖν χεροῖν σθένει
καὶ νῦν π[έ]ποιθα τοῦτον [12
ληφθήσεται πάροιθεν [
θη.[ ].ναθ[.]..ν μήποθ['
δασμὸν τρίφ[υλ]ον ἠιθέων ἄξ[
ἢ [γ]άρ ποτ[. . .]τρέφουσα χ[16
χθὼν Ἰσθμίοις κρημνοῖσι φ[
χὠ ξυμπάραυλος Κρομμυὼ[ν
σὺν ἐμπόρω[ν] δηλήμον' ἥν [
ἔπαυσα δειν[ ].ς κἀνυποστάτ.[20
ἔπαυ]σα δὲ Σκ[είρ]ωνα τὸν θα[
. . . . .]ονων [. . .]ερθε ποντ[
]πλ[
. . .

(730c, ll. 1–26)

The speaker is Theseus, cast in his familiar role of defender of the just order. The Athenian mission of punishing the wicked dominates the passage, to judge from παθών ('suffering') and τίνειν

required a supernumerary chorus of seven boys and seven girls, the two plays were performed in the same year (before 422; Ar. *Vesp.* 579 with Σ).

[86] ἄφυκτον αἷμα or αἵματος μύσος ('inescapable bloodshed' or 'taint of bloodshed'): Kannicht 1977: 500.

('paying') with Lloyd-Jones's supplement of ἀμοιβάς ('recompense', ll. 5–6).[87] The killing of the Minotaur is probably intended as the Cretan tyrant's just punishment for his cruelty in imposing the tribute (cf. δασμὸν, l. 15); it is not an excessive punishment but only what he deserves.[88] Lines 8–11 portray Theseus with the combination of humility and justice allied to power that is conventional for him: 'I have never cared for, or practised, speaking at length about what I should not, but often before, I have crushed the [violent arrogance of many, with the strength of my hands'. Such sentiments are rather similar to his modest refusal to boast about retrieving Antigone and Ismene from Creon's clutches at S. *OC* 1139–44.[89] Lines 10–21 reassuringly recount the familiar list of those who are no longer a danger to humanity, thanks to Theseus' righteous strength:[90] Sinis (l. 16) and the Crommyonian sow (l. 18), who is Homericized as the ἐμπόρω[ν] δηλήμονα ('destroyer of travellers', cf. *Od.* 18. 85, 116, 21. 308), and lastly Sciron. The absence of Periphetes at the start of the list might indicate that the play was written before *c*.450. The Minotaur and Minos' despotic power will be yet another addition to Theseus' already splendid heroic record, and Theseus is supremely (and rightly) confident in what he must do.[91]

> χρή [. . . .]λείπειν η[
> απερ[.] . . [ ]ς ἡμῖν τεν[
> δοκεῖ[ς[ἅπασιν· ουδεγ.[
> ΘΗ]ΣΕΥΣ ἄπειμι τοίνυν [ ]κλυ[4
> δίκαια πράσσει[ν[κε.[
> ⟨ΧΟΡΟΣ⟩   εἴην ὄθι[
>
>   (730d)

[87] For Theseus' concern for due ἀμοιβάς in a different context, compare E. *HF* 1169.

[88] Compare Theseus' treatment of the Thebans in Euripides' *Suppliants* and of Creon in *Oedipus Coloneus*.

[89] Note esp. *OC* 1144–5: οὐ γὰρ λόγοισι τὸν βίον σπουδάζομεν | λαμπρὸν ποεῖσθαι μᾶλλον ἢ τοῖς δρωμένοις ('I am not keen to make my life glorious in words, but in deeds.').

[90] Cf. E. *Hipp.* 976ff.; E. *Supp.* 316–17: for the form of l. 12, compare S. *Aj.* 768–9. The identity of Theseus' interlocutor here is entirely uncertain: see Sutton 1984: 75–8; Diotti 1966: 58. I include in the text some possible supplements which echo motifs which are extremely familiar by now: cf. also Page 1967: 34. Turner supplemented l. 14 as θής ὤν, so that Theseus' services to his city would be foreshadowed in his name, but this is difficult: Lloyd-Jones 1963: 434–5; Carden 1974: 118; Kannicht 1977: 501.

[91] Cf. Carden 1974: 119. He rather resembles the Homericized Theseus of Bacchylides 17.

In this fragment, someone is commanding Theseus to leave (l. 1), perhaps for the labyrinth, and he seems to say something about accomplishing justice (l. 4). The chorus then begin an ode of a type common in tragedy, in which they wish that they were somewhere else. Often choruses wish to be far away from the scene of impending trouble, but at S. *OC* 1044, the chorus is so confident that Theseus will conquer Creon that they wish they could watch the battle. It is an attractive conjecture that they wish for something similar here.[92]

Two other major fragments of the papyrus are too scrappy to be of much assistance in determining the action and the characters of the play. In 730e, a stargazer reports a portent which he has seen in his night watch (to Minos, near the start of the play?), but how this relates to Theseus' adventures in Crete is unclear.[93] It would certainly be attractive to suppose that the thunder and calm of ll. 14 and 18 come from an account of the story told by Bacchylides, in which Theseus jumps into the sea to prove to Minos that Poseidon is his father after Minos has induced his father Zeus to thunder for him, particularly if Eriboia's encounter with Minos featured in the play.[94] 730f is even scrappier, but the fragment may be from a messenger's speech referring to the ξένος Theseus,[95] and ll. 14 and 16 refer to a prayer. Kannicht suggests tentatively that we should think of the tradition that Poseidon granted three wishes to his son, and that Theseus was to rescue himself from the labyrinth by using one of them.[96] Although Ariadne was normally inextricably linked with Theseus' escape from the labyrinth, her presence in the play does not rule out Kannicht's suggestion, because it is fundamental to the ideal image of Athens that the city and its representatives bestow benefits, rather than accepting them. In only two adventures—in Crete and in the underworld—does Theseus have to accept help from another. In chapter four, we saw how attention

---

[92] As Eucken 1979: 138. See *Hipp.* 732; cf. *Ba.* 403, *IT* 1138.

[93] Turner 1962: 17 suggests that the dual forms at ll. 10, 15 refer to the two constellations of the crown of Ariadne and the 'Engonasis', interpreted as Theseus, as at Hyg. *Poet.Astr.* 2. 5. 6. This cannot be deduced from the fragment as it stands: see also Carden 1974: 115–17. Diotti 1966: 50 wonders if the Dioscuri could be involved, but they have no known connection with the story of Theseus in Crete.

[94] Carden 1974: 117. Indeed, Hyg. *Poet.Astr.* 2. 5 who also tells the story, sets the challenge on the coast, rather than the open sea of Bacchylides' version.

[95] See Kannicht 1977: 505; Carden 1974: 127.

[96] *Contra* Herter 1939: 315 n. 371. For Theseus' three wishes, cf. ΣΕ. *Hipp.* 46, 888, 1348 and above, pp. 213–14.

was diverted from the weakness of Theseus in the underworld to the active service that he does for Euripides' Heracles.[97] Theseus was also helped by Ariadne, but repaid her, at least in non-Attic literature, by deserting her, and an alternative version of the story in which Theseus used one of his wishes to save himself has advantages for an Athenian audience, not only because it saves Theseus' reputation, but because it actively emphasizes his links with divinity.[98]

Whatever his relations with Ariadne were in this play, one may surely assume that he was not the faithless lover of non-Athenian tradition. Sophocles' extant plays contain up to five episodes, and it is possible that (for example) scenes of Minos and Eriboia, Eriboia pleading for the sympathy of Ariadne and the chorus, perhaps some kind of *agon* between Theseus and Minos, the adventure in the labyrinth, and preparation to escape, would provide enough material for a tragedy without any need to make love the motivation for Ariadne's departure with Theseus and the Athenians. The fifth-century Attic vase painters' lack of interest in such a picturesque story is striking; and when they do illustrate it, they tend to exculpate Theseus from abandoning Ariadne, by making it clear that he leaves her through divine intervention, not of his own will, as in the apologetic version of the story told by Pherecydes (*FGrH* 3 F148). Roughly contemporary with Pherecydes' *Histories* is *ARV²* 252,52 (*c*.480), on which Ariadne is borne off by Dionysus while Athena commands a submissive Theseus to go in the opposite direction, and she is equally authoritative on a lecythus from Taranto of a similar date (*ARV²* 560,5). In general Ariadne's encounter with Dionysus is a much more popular subject in Athenian vase painting than her desertion by Theseus.[99] Whereas Athens is loyal to others and helps the weak, Theseus' actions in the traditional Ariadne story are the opposite of such behaviour: it was not a good role model for Athens' relations with other states.[100]

---

[97] See also my comments on the *Peirithous* below. On *ARV²* 1086,1, Theseus saves himself from Hades by his own efforts while Heracles looks on.

[98] Was this the version preferred by the *Theseid*?: see Barrett 1964: 40; Herter 1939: 314–16.

[99] *ARV²* 405,1 seems to be the only 5th-cent. vase on which Theseus deserts Ariadne without any direct divine intervention, although Hermes is portrayed alongside the departure scene. For a full list of scenes of the desertion and its more popular aftermath, see Bernard 1986: 1057–62.

[100] Thus I doubt the suggestion of Diotti 1966: 59 that the play made Ariadne and Eriboia rivals in love for Theseus.

We have very little idea of the proper order of the fragments, but it is likely enough that 730c preceded 730d, and that 730a–b came from an early episode in the play.[101] If Eriboia was able first to win over Ariadne, and then the chorus, perhaps swearing them to secrecy, this would leave the Cretan king in an unsympathetic position, as might be expected. Even Minos' own sailors are impressed by Theseus' courage in Bacchylides 17 (l. 50), and Theseus' relationship with the Cretans was perhaps similar in this play as well: though he is a foreigner in a strange and dangerous land, Theseus' native courage and wisdom will ensure his success and will impress even those who would not naturally be sympathetic to him, so that the wicked are punished and the oppressed are saved.

7.5.2 *Euripides*

Many of the same question marks which hang over the play preserved by *POxy* 2452, such as the identity of the chorus and the treatment of Theseus' relations with Ariadne, also hang over Euripides' *Theseus*, but it was certainly set in Crete (cf. Tzetz. *Chil.* ii. 255), and it may be conjectured that Euripides' portrayal of Theseus was highly conventional, since the Cretan triumph is the model for so many of his subsequent exploits, in which he comes from afar to assert himself as he restores order, a pattern which has analogies with Athenian imperial expansionism. In the *Aegeus* plays, he returns from abroad to his own city to be recognized by his father: in the *Theseus* plays, he moves into the unknown and will bring the Athenian combination of power and justice to those who are unfamiliar with it. The most substantial fragment of the play (382) is a riddle spoken by a Cretan herdsman, who describes the shapes of the letters of Theseus' name, unaware of who he is; he, and Minos, will come to know him by the end of the play. The distinction the riddle makes between *H* and *E* dates the *Theseus* after *c*.450.[102] The illiteracy of the Cretan herdsman is a mark of the distance between Crete and 'normal' civilization,[103] and fr. 381, σχεδὸν παρ' αὐτοῖς κράσπεδοις Εὐρωπίας ('by the very edges of

---

[101] For the papyrological reasons for putting 730e immediately after 730c, see Turner 1962: 16.

[102] Webster 1967: 102. The same riddle is found in Agathon's *Telephus* (*TGrF* 39 F4) and Theodektas (*TGrF* 72 F6); cf. Athen. 453c. Perhaps the herdsman has seen the name written on Theseus' ship or on his famous sword: Webster 1967: 106–7.

[103] Cf. Kiso 1984: 78.

Europe's land') may refer to the island's remote position. Theseus will go to a dangerous land not his own, but, he will make it his own: πᾶσαν μὲν θάλασσαν καὶ γῆν ἐσβατὸν τῇ ἡμετέρᾳ τόλμῃ καταναγκάσαντες γενέσθαι ('by our daring, making every land and sea accessible': Thuc. 2. 41. 4).[104]

The play included an abrasive exchange between Theseus and Minos, from which fr. 384,

> κάρα τε γάρ σου συγχέω κόμαις ὁμοῦ
> ῥανῶ τε πεδόσ' ἐγκέφαλον ὀμμάτων δ' ἄπο
> αἱμοσταγῆ πρηστῆρε ῥεύσονται κάτω

('I'll mix your head with your hair, and spatter your brain on the ground, and from your eyes bloody jets will pour down')

is quoted in ΣAr. *Ran.* 473. Such violent language is utterly unlike that used by Theseus elsewhere: one would guess that it is more appropriate to Minos,[105] although the scholia on Ar. *Ran.* 467 say that very similar words to the string of curses uttered by Aeacus to Dionysus in the *Frogs* were spoken by Theseus to Minos (cf. ΣAr. *Ran.* 475). However, according to ΣAr. *Ran.* 470V, material invented by Aristophanes is mixed with the reminiscences of Euripides and it is unwise to assume that the quarrel between Minos and Theseus can be recovered from Aristophanes.[106] This part of the *Frogs* concentrates so heavily on the dangers of the underworld that it is hard to imagine an appropriate context for similar words in a dispute between Theseus and Minos, and the only fragment of the *Theseus* which is quoted verbatim by the scholia (384) is not very close to anything in Aristophanes.[107]

---

[104] E. fr. 964 (ap. DK 59a. 33) is attributed to a speech of Theseus from an unknown play. ἐγὼ δὲ παρὰ σοφοῦ τινος μαθὼν | εἰς φροντίδ' ἀεὶ συμφορὰς ἐβαλλόμην | φυγάς τ' ἐμαυτῷ προστιθεὶς πάτρας ἐμῆς | θανάτους ἀώρους καὶ κακῶν ἄλλας ὁδούς | ἵν' εἴ τι πάσχοιμ' ὧν ἐδόξαζον φρενί | μή μοι νεωρὲς προσπεσὸν μᾶλλον δάκοι ('I learnt from some wise man always to lay difficulties in my mind, setting before myself exile from my homeland and untimely deaths and other routes to evil, so that if I were to suffer anything of what I expected, nothing new would fall on me and sting me.'). Such a speech of calm acceptance would be appropriate for Theseus as he prepares to meet the Minotaur. It is also reminiscent of S. *OC* 562 f.

[105] Cf. Sutton 1978: 49. Although he suggests here and in 1985: 359 that the violent language of these fragments is only appropriate for a satyr play, compare e.g. E. *HF* 565 ff.

[106] τὰ μὲν ἑαυτῷ πλάττων λέγει, τὰ δὲ ἐξ Εὐρίπιδου: ΣAr. *Ran.* 470V; cf. ΣAr. *Ran.* 467; Nauck, however, prints *Frogs* 470–7 as E. fr. 383.

[107] Wilamowitz 1875: 172 (cf. van Leeuwen 1896: 78–9) assigned the lines to an

The *Theseus* was also parodied in Aristophanes' *Wasps* of 422 BC. *ΣAr. Vesp.* 312 quotes τί με δῆτ᾽ ὦ μέλεα μῆτερ, ἔτικτες; ('why, then, did you bear me, wretched mother?') as part of the lament of the twice seven children sent to the Minotaur (fr. 385 and cf. *ΣAr. Vesp.* 303), and *ΣAr. Vesp.* 313–14 assigns ἀνόνητον ἄγαλμ᾽ ὦ πάτερ, οἴκοισι τεκών ('begetting a useless delight for the house', fr. 386), to a speech by Hippolytus in the *Theseus*. If Hippolytus had appeared in this play, Euripides' version of the Cretan story would be unique and chronologically extremely awkward. However, the suspicion must remain that ἀνόνητον of Ar. *Vesp.* 314 reminded the scholiast of a line spoken by Hippolytus, but not necessarily in Euripides' *Theseus*; the first *Hippolytus* is an obvious alternative.[108] The confusion would be easy because Theseus appeared in both plays and Hippolytus in fact would have nothing to do with this play.

Although λίνου κλωστῆρα περιφέρει λαβών ('taking a linen thread, he carries it around', fr. 1001N) is not ascribed to the *Theseus*, the line would most obviously refer to the traditional means by which Theseus escaped from the labyrinth, but it must also remain a possibility that he escaped by using one of the three wishes which Poseidon had given him, to avoid incurring the debt to Ariadne.[109] In *ΣAr. Ran.* 850 Ariadne is listed along with Pasiphae and Phaedra as one of the Cretan women portrayed unflatteringly by Euripides. The extant *Hippolytus* may imply that she put love for Theseus before duty to her divine husband (E. *Hipp.* 339), but the reference is too brief for certainty, and it is at least plausible that it was in Euripides' *Theseus* that a full portrait of her misdemeanours was painted.[110] Fr. 388 could, in fact, be assigned to a speech of Theseus repelling her advances.

encounter between Heracles and Aeacus in the *Peirithous*, but the surviving fragments of their encounter do not point to a violent scene between Heracles and the porter: cf. Dover 1993: 253–4; Rau 1967: 116–18.

[108] Compare Hippolytus' reproach to Theseus, ὦ τάλαινα μᾶτερ ἔτεκες ἀνόνατα ('O wretched mother, in vain did you give birth', E. *Hipp.* 1145): cf. Diotti 1966: 54; Webster 1967: 101.

[109] If *POxy* 3531 is assigned to the *Theseus* rather than the *Aegeus*, the distinction made between Theseus' apparent and real paternity in ll. 10–11 would be especially suitable for a version of the story in which Poseidon's gift, rather than Ariadne, rescued him from the labyrinth: Parsons 1983: 26 and cf. §7.4.2.

[110] Webster 1967: 27 suggests that the line καίτοι φθόνου μὲν μῦθον ἄξιον φράσω ('and I will tell you a blameworthy story', fr. 387) refers to her unseemly conduct. Her love for Theseus could be represented as simple *akrasia*. Compare the story of Phyllis and Demophon: Apollod. *Ep.* 6. 1. 6; *ΣAeschin.* 2. 31; Tzetz. *Lycophr.* 490.

ἀλλ' ἔστι δή τις ἄλλος ἐν βροτοῖς ἔρως
ψυχῆς δικαίας σώφρονός τε κἀγαθῆς
καὶ χρῆν δὲ τοῖς βροτοῖσι τόνδ' εἶναι νόμον
τῶν εὐσεβούντων οἵτινες τε σώφρονες
ἐρᾶν, Κύπριν δὲ τὴν Διὸς χαίρειν ἐᾶν.[111]

However, more than one context is suitable for a fragment of such
high moral tone. It resembles Theseus' admonition of Minos in
Bacchylides 17. 20ff., in which he admonishes the Cretan king
politely but firmly to keep his hands off Eriboia and let fate and justice take their course, and it has also been assigned to a speech of
Athena as a *dea ex machina* at the end of the play, either warning
Theseus to desist from pursuing Ariadne further, or admonishing
Ariadne that her destiny does not lie with him. If so, Euripides
would be following the exculpatory Athenian version of the story.
On a vase of 430/420, perhaps roughly contemporary with this
play, although any connection between the two is merely conjec-
tural, Aphrodite has dressed Ariadne as a bride, and she sits wait-
ing for Dionysus, while on the other side Theseus looks back in
wonder as he meekly retreats to his ship; Athena places a wreath on
his head, while his father Poseidon looks on. It is clear that the part-
ing between them is sanctioned by the gods, and certainly not
caused by Theseus' 'dreadful passion' for Aegle, as Hesiod once
alleged.[112]

[111] 'But there is another love among mortals, of a just, and moderate and good
spirit, and this law should exist for whichever mortals are right-minded: to love
what is virtuous, and bid farewell to Cypris, daughter of Zeus.' Webster 1967: 107
notes that it is quoted along with a speech of Bellerophon, and although he interprets
E. fr. 388 as a speech warning Theseus not to pursue Ariadne, Bellerophon was the
object of the attentions of a predatory woman: were both Bellerophon and Theseus
trying to fend off unwanted passion?

[112] *ARV²* 1184,4 by the Cadmus painter: see Simon 1963: 14; cf. Webster 1966:
27f. and 1967: 105; Bernard 1986: 1060. Compare also an early 4th-cent. Apulian
stamnos (Boston 00. 349) on which Theseus sees Dionysus and retreats from
Ariadne while Athena looks on. Finally, I cannot resist speculating that it would be
possible to turn the traditional story entirely on its head, so that Ariadne's love
induces her to help Theseus and he kindly agrees to rescue her from Minos, but
Athena intervenes to tell him that his loyalties must lie elsewhere.

7.6 OTHER THESEUS PLAYS OF EURIPIDES

7.6.1 *Alope*

It is commonly assumed that the essence, if not the exact structure, of the plot of Euripides' *Alope* is preserved by Hyginus 187, who tells a traditional tale of a young woman who becomes pregnant by a god.[113] After Alope, daughter of king Cercyon of Eleusis, had given birth to Poseidon's child (cf. fr. 106), she gave him to her nurse so that he could be exposed, but he survived by being suckled by a mare[114] until a shepherd found him and took him home, still wrapped in his royal clothes. When a fellow shepherd asked him for the child, the first shepherd handed him over, but without his royal garments. A quarrel developed between them and they went to Cercyon to ask him to adjudicate between their claims, only to have him recognize the garments in which the child had been wrapped. Alope's nurse revealed the truth to Cercyon, who was enraged[115] and ordered that Alope should be imprisoned and the child exposed yet again; but once more, he was saved, first by the mare, and then by some more shepherds, who brought him up under the name of Hippothoon. (The double exposure is probably not Euripidean.) When Theseus came to Eleusis he killed Cercyon and Hippothoon came to Theseus and asked for his kingdom, which Theseus willingly gave him when he learnt that Poseidon was Hippothoon's father as well as his own. Poseidon turned Alope into a fountain. Harpocration 13. 7 asserts that the *Alope* made a specific connection between Hippothoon and the Hippothoontid tribe at Athens (cf. Hellanicus *FGrH* 323a F6). It is awkward that Hippothoon should be a baby at the start of the play and a prospective king of Eleusis at its end. Perhaps the action of the play stopped at the moment when Theseus came to kill Cercyon, but even if Theseus' intervention was only prophesied as a warning to Cercyon that his cruelty would not go unpunished,[116] Theseus' role in the *Alope* would be familiar,

---

[113] Compare the plots of the *Ion*, *Melanippe Desmotis*, *Auge* and *Danae*: Schmid and Stählin 1940: iii. 592. For a full account of the evidence, see Borecký 1955; also Séchan 1926; Kron 1976: 178–9. It is called *Cercyon* by the sources which cite frs. 106 and 107. For the fragments, see Nauck[2] 1964: 389–92 and Mette 1967: 42–4.

[114] The scene is portrayed in a 4th-cent. Attic vase (*ARV*[2] 612,1): see Kron 1981*b*: 572.

[115] Cf. frs. 107, 109, 110, 111 and probably 108. A mid-2nd-cent. Roman sarcophagus probably portrays this scene: see Kron 1981*b*: 573.

[116] Borecký 1955: 82, 84–6; Kron 1976: 178–9.

as that of a secondary figure who rescues the powerless from cruelty. Not only Cercyon's cruelty was at issue here, perhaps, since the suffering inflicted on Alope by Poseidon's desire for her recalls Creusa's experiences with Apollo in the *Ion*. Similarly, in the *Heracles*, Theseus' treatment of Heracles was contrasted with the behaviour of the gods towards him.

7.6.2 *Peirithous*

The Peirithous of Euripides or Critias is the last Theseus tragedy to be discussed in this chapter, and with it, we return to a thoroughly orthodox portrayal of Theseus. Substantial papyrus fragments of the play are extant, as well as a hypothesis, which states that Peirithous went with Theseus to Hades to get Persephone as his wife. He was duly punished for this impiety by being bound to a rock by snakes. Theseus, thinking it shameful to abandon his friend, willingly chose to stay in Hades with him, but on his mission to abduct Cerberus, Heracles released both men, by the grace of the gods of the underworld.[117] Such a plot is entirely what we would expect of a fifth-century Athenian dramatization of the ill-fated journey of Theseus and Peirithous to the underworld. In Athenian narrative, Theseus always accompanies his friend out of loyalty, although sometimes he tries to persuade him not to go on such an obviously impious mission (Isoc. 10. 20; cf. D.S. 4. 63. 4): the *Peirithous* extends that loyalty so that Theseus actually prefers staying in Hades to deserting his friend.

Much of the critical energy expended on this play has been used in trying to establish whether it is by Critias or Euripides. There is no incontrovertible proof for either authorship, although the balance of critical opinion inclines towards Critias.[118] However, the

---

[117] Joh.Logoth. 144 and Greg.Cor. 1312. See Nauck[2] 1964: 546–7; Cf. Wilamowitz 1875: 168; Snell 1971: 170–1.

[118] For Critias: Snell 1971: 170–1, though cautiously (cf. Diels and Kranz 88F15a); Dover 1993: 53–4; Fossati 1950; Körte 1932; also Wilamowitz 1875: 161–6. For Euripides: Page 1950; Mette 1983: 16; cf. also Kannicht 1991: 109. Criteria of language or content do not help: certain features of the language strike Mette as typically Euripidean; for Wilamowitz, other features are clearly Critian. The cosmological fragments 592–3 (not discussed here, but see Cataudella 1932 and Tièche 1945) are sometimes enlisted for Critias because their Anaxagorean influence is held to be inappropriate for Euripides, but without knowing their context, I do not see how we can be sure of this, and Euripides is associated with the teaching of Anaxagoras by DK 59 A1. 7, 20a–c, 62, 91; 33 quotes a speech of Theseus from an unknown tragedy (E. fr. 964 N, quoted above, n. 104) in connection with Anaxagoras. The confusion is evident in early times: Athen. 11. 496a professes

Theseus of this play seems to be indistinguishable from those of Euripides and Sophocles, and such a conventional portrayal as he is given in the *Peirithous*, which reaffirms his traditional association with democratic and imperial Athens, seems rather surprising for the arch-oligarch Critias.[119] The *Hypothesis* implies that the powers of the Underworld were moved by the human loyalty of Theseus towards Peirithous to release him and this emphasis on human relations is highly reminiscent of Euripides in the *Hippolytus* and *Heracles*.[120]

Of all the plays discussed so far, the *Peirithous* has benefited most from papyrological discoveries.[121] *POxy* 2078 yielded a fragment of what was probably an opening dialogue in which Aeacus sees Heracles approaching and asks him who he is (*TGrF* 43 F1). Heracles explains to him that he has been ordered by Eurystheus to take Cerberus from Hades. At some point after this, he must have encountered Peirithous, probably before he met Theseus, since Heracles and Theseus already know one another, and it is more dramatic if Heracles first comes across an unfamiliar figure bound by snakes, who tells him why he is there. From this first meeting, we possess a fragment of Peirithous' speech (*TGrF* 43 F5) in which he describes the fate of his father Ixion, who was a sexual transgressor against the gods (ll. 7, 13–15, 19): his attempt to seduce Hera was foiled by a cloud, and he was bound to a wheel as punishment. Peirithous seems to compare his own fate to that of his father now that he has been bound to his rock by snakes.[122] Theseus himself was probably not bound, because it would be awkward for two main characters to be immobile,[123] and also because

uncertainty as to its author and the *Vit.Eur.* 3,2 Schw. declares it spurious, but it was probably included in Euripides' works by *IG* II² 2363. 45 (cf. *ΣOr.* 982); *POxy* 2455, 56 regard the disputed *Sisyphus* and *Tennes* as Euripidean but the parts of the papyri where the *Peirithous* ought to be are lost. Fr. 592 refers to Eleusinian initiates, from which the inference is often drawn that the *Peirithous* influenced Aristophanes' *Frogs*: Wilamowitz 1875: 171–2; Lloyd-Jones 1967: 218–20; but see now Dover 1993: 50–4. Sutton 1987 came to my notice belatedly, but his excellent analysis favours Euripidean authorship and our conclusions are broadly similar.

[119] See esp. the discussion of Theseus and Heracles in *POxy* 2078, frs. 2–3 below.

[120] Cf. Fossati 1950: 107–8, cf. 113. Although she interprets the emphasis of the play on human ties as anti-religious and concludes that its author was Critias, the fragments seem to me to posit a more traditional view of the world in which the gods do exist and can reward or punish as they see fit; or at least, the *Peirithous* seems to be no more 'irreligious' than Euripides' *Heracles*.

[121] For the texts of the fragments not quoted here, see Snell 1971: 172–8.

[122] See Körte 1932: 50–3; Hunt 1927.   [123] Cockle 1983: 32.

the moral difference between Theseus and Peirithous is emphasized by leaving him free. Since the publication of Snell's edition of
the fragments of the minor tragedians, a dialogue between Heracles
and Peirithous which should come from the same part of the play
has been found (*POxy* 3531) which Cockle places above the extant
fragment of Peirithous' speech in *POxy* 2078, fr. 1.[124] Here,
Peirithous' transgression is emphasized, as the Chorus say something about learning late and honouring the gods (l. 5). Heracles
seems to be guardedly sympathetic to him: though he talks of ἄτη
('infatuation', l. 14), he also regards what has happened as
δυσπραξία ('bad luck', l. 11).

The action of the play between the arrival of Heracles and the
eventual rescue of Theseus and Peirithous is a mystery, but frs. 2
and 3 of *POxy* 2078 give an unusually rewarding insight into the
characterization of Theseus in the *Peirithous*. The main part of the
more or less complete text is as follows:

   . . .

             *c.*25 ll.   ].σης[

             *c.*26 ll.   ]πη[

             *c.*25 ll.   ]ν πόνου

. . . .].σοι τọ[. . . . .] ἡδὺ ν[ῦ]ν δοκεῖ   4 (24)

⟨ΘΗΣΕΥΕ⟩ . . . .]τος, Ἡράκλεις, [σὲ] μέμψομαι

. . . .]η, πιστὸν γὰρ ἄνδρα καὶ φίλον

. . . . . .πρ]οδοῦναι δυσμ[εν]ῶς εἰλημμένον.

⟨HP⟩   σαυτῶι τε,] Θησεῦ, τῆι τ' Ἀθηναίων πό[λει   8 (28)

         πρέπουτ' ἔλεξας· τοῖσι δυσ[τυ]χοῦσι γὰρ

         ἀεί ποτ' εἶ σὺ σύμμαχος· σκῆψιν [δ' ἐμ]οὶ

         ἀεικές ἐστ' ἔχοντα πρὸς πάτραν μολεῖν.

         Εὐρυσθέα γὰρ πῶς δοκεῖς ἄν, ἄσμενọν   12 (32)

         εἴ μοι πύθοιτο ταῦτα συμπράξαντά σε,

         λέξειν ἂν ὡς ἄκραντος ἤθληται πόνος;

⟨ΘΗΣ⟩   ἀλλ' οὐ σὺ χρήιζεις π[. . . . .] ἐμὴν ἔχεις

         εὔνοιαν, οὐκ ἔμπλ[ηκτον, ἀλλ' ἐλ]ευθέρως   16 (36)

         ἐχθροῖσί τ' ἐχθρὰν [καὶ φίλοισι]ν εὐμενῆ.

         πρόσθεν σ' ἐμοὶ τ[. . . . .]ει λόγος,

         λέγοις δ' ἂν [. . . .].[   ]ους λόγους

⟨HP⟩   ὦ φ[   ]   20 (40)

             *c.*25 ll.   ]ιας

             *c.*24 ll.   ὑ]πηρετῶ

             *c.*21 ll.   ]. θν[η]τῶ[ν] φρένας

             *c.*19 ll.   ]γνώμης ἄτερ   24 (44)

[124] Cockle 1983: 30–1.

c.17 ll.   τοῦ]τό σοι φίλον
12 ll.   ]δικωτατ' αἰτιᾷ θεούς

(15a D)

(*Theseus*: . . . I will blame you, Heracles . . . to betray a trusty friend caught in a bad way. *Heracles*: What you have said is worthy of yourself and of the city of the Athenians. For you are always an ally of the unfortunate. But it is shameful for me to go home with this pretence. How do you think Eurystheus would gladly say that the endless labour was accomplished if he learned that you had helped with it? *Theseus*: But what you need . . . you have my good will, not unstable, but freely an enemy to enemies and friendly to friends. For before me . . . you might say . . . words.)

From here, the text becomes more fragmentary, although odd phrases in Heracles' reply to Theseus such as]γνώμης ἄτερ . . . ('without reason', l. 24) and]δικώτατ' αἰτιᾷ θεούς ('you blame the gods (?) most justly', l. 26) would be compatible with a speech advising him how he should persuade the gods to release Peirithous. In this passage, Theseus epitomizes Athens' steadfast loyalty to friends—especially those who are vulnerable and can be turned into clients of the city or its representatives—as he refuses to desert his 'dear and trusted friend', thinking it shameful to abandon him in Hades (ll. 6–8). By this part of the play, if not long before, he must have been free to leave Hades with Heracles, and, as might be expected, Peirithous, not Theseus, will have taken any blame for the attempted abduction of Persephone.[125] Not only is Theseus not responsible for the deed, however, but he is even loyal enough to his friend to stay in Hades with him. By valuing friendship more than his individual life, he makes a choice analogous to that made by the heroes and heroines of myth who offer themselves so that the city might be saved, the anonymous soldiers of the *epitaphioi*, who die for the good of Athens, and even that made by the idealized imperial Athens, which prefers the effort of helping friends and punishing the wicked to leading a pleasant life of ἡσυχία. The connection between Theseus the ideal friend and Athens the ideal city is underlined by Heracles' reply to him: both Theseus and Athens are known for their adherence to the highest

---

125 Wilamowitz 1907 assigned the fragment Ἀφίδνε, γαίας υἱὲ τῆς ἀμήτορος ('Aphidnus, son of the motherless earth', 955c Sn.) to this play. Aphidnus' only importance in Attic myth was as Helen's guardian when Theseus went to Hades. Could this exploit have been mentioned in a play so apparently flattering to Theseus? However, the attribution is far from certain.

moral codes, and especially concern for the unfortunate (ll. 8–10). Both heroes seem to agree that Peirithous is unfortunate, rather than impious (ll. 7, 9, cf. *POxy* 3531, l. 11): if Theseus had previously explained to Heracles that his friend was unlucky or simply foolish and did not deserve eternal punishment, he would be acting fully in accord with the flexibility and ἐπιείκεια that encomia classify as unique to democratic Athens.[126]

Theseus' role as the wise and kindly representative of his city is entirely familiar by now, and at ll. 12 ff., he exhibits an equally familiar, but more traditional heroism, as we learn that he had even offered to help Heracles capture Cerberus.[127] That Theseus could even consider helping Heracles in this 'unaccomplishable task' (ἆθλον ἀνήνυτον, fr. 1. 13–14) is an indication of how far the conception of his heroism has advanced from the early days of Minotauromachy.[128] However, the author of the play does not go as far as making the radical change in the story necessary for Heracles to be able to accept Theseus' kind offer, and he explains that Eurystheus will not be satisfied with the capture of Cerberus, if Theseus has had a hand in it (ll. 12–14). A comparison may be made here with the end of the *Heracles*: although Heracles does ask Theseus for assistance with Cerberus at *HF* 1386 f., Euripides, like the author of the *Peirithous*, does no more than suggest that Theseus could displace Heracles in his greatest feat, and the suggestion lies outside the action of the play itself. In the *Peirithous*, Theseus graciously accepts Heracles' refusal, and asserts his voluntary good will towards him, and consequent hatred towards his enemies, upholding a familiar principle of Greek ethics (ll. 15–17). Line 18 seems to refer to a service previously done by Heracles to Theseus (cf. *HF* 1169, 1220): naturally Theseus, like Athens, never forgets a service done to him, and always tries to repay it at least in full.[129] Frs. 595–6, αἰδοῦς ἀχαλκεύτοισιν ἔζευκται πέδαις ('he has been bound in the chains of reverence, that are not made of bronze')

---

[126] Would Critias have contented himself with something so conventional?

[127] In return for Peirithous' rescue? Mette 1983: 17.

[128] For συμπράξαντα (l. 13), compare the συν- compounds at *HF* 1202, 1220, 1225.

[129] In the *Heracles*, of course, Theseus repays Heracles for the rescue from the underworld, but the Hypothesis to the *Peirithous* implies that because he was not responsible for what Peirithous did, Theseus himself did not need to be rescued. Hunt 1927: 45 suggests that the service which Heracles has done Theseus is connected with the Amazons (cf. E. *Hcld.* 215 f.).

and οὔκουν τὸ μὴ ζῆν κρεῖσσόν ἐστ᾽ ἢ ζῆν κακῶς; ('isn't death better than living in shame?') are closely related to the themes of this speech, and 595 is cited several times by Plutarch as an outstanding sentiment of friendship (*Mor.* 482a, 533a, 763a; cf. 96c). The shift from the literal bonds, which once kept the transgressor in the underworld, to the metaphorical chains of friendship which detain the morally sanitized representative of Athens in this play is remarkable. It may be assumed that the play ended with the release of Peirithous, thanks to Theseus' persuasive abilities and loyalty to his friend.[130] Heracles, or perhaps one of the underworld gods, may have killed or called off the snakes by which Peirithous had been guarded.[131] This version of the story is probably more suited to tragedy than the version in which Heracles had to pull both men off a rock into which their flesh had grown.[132] Heracles had performed the supreme feat of overcoming death: thanks to his innate Athenian virtue, Theseus manages, in a slightly different way from him, to equal that achievement. The act of helping Peirithous exemplifies courage and intelligence on Theseus' part and—of course—demands gratitude from his 'client' Peirithous, as well as the admiration of Heracles and of the gods of the underworld. No longer Peirithous' accomplice in an act of folly and impiety, once more he is made to personify the ideals and aspirations which shape the dealings of Athens with the rest of Greece in the fifth century. Out of loyalty to a friend, Theseus takes the ultimate risk—accepting a life in the underworld—and is rewarded with success, in Peirithous' release, his undying gratitude, and—perhaps most important, at least for the Athenian audience—the reaffirmation of his (and their) reputation for wise courage and courageous wisdom in the eyes of all.

---

[130] Compare ΣTzetz. *Chil.*, *Anecd.Gr.Oxon.* iii. 359,22; D.S. 4. 26. 1; Ov. *Tr.* 1. 9. 31–2.

[131] If adespota 658 belongs to this *Peirithous* (Carlini 1968), perhaps Persephone herself forgave and helped them (ll. 16–20) but the attribution is so uncertain that it should be left out of account: cf. Kannicht and Snell 1985: 240–2; Cockle 1983: 31.

[132] See Ch. 1 n. 36.

Afterword

Recent scholarship has emphasized the problematic aspects of Theseus in his role as the national hero of Athens.[1] His mother's Trozenian nationality, especially after Pericles' citizenship law of 451/0,[2] makes his very status as an Athenian dubious, and, with the exception of the triumph over the Minotaur, the deeds for which he is famous in early narrative are moral failures in their conception and actual failures in their results. It seems very strange that the Athenians should focus on such an apparently unsuitable character as their representative in tragedy and other art-forms. However, all this admitted, I do not think that what some modern scholars analyse as the contradictory or disturbing elements of the figure of Theseus were necessarily of innate relevance or concern in themselves to the Athenians.[3] The actions of the Theseus of early narrative would, indeed, hardly pass scrutiny by the Committee for Un-Athenian Activities, but all figures of myth can be constantly remade, and Theseus is no exception.

Every myth is essentially a collection of stories about a particular character, whose actions need not necessarily be consistent from one story to the next. Narrating, or believing in, a myth is a selective process: narrators or their audience need take only what they want from the whole range of stories comprising the myth, and its discarded elements need not necessarily have any bearing on the parts of it that are to the fore. Everyone will want to share in the glorious feat of the Minotauromachy, but nobody in Athens need feel connected to Theseus' desertion of Ariadne or his responsibility for Aegeus' death. Some writers, such as Pherecydes (*FGrH* 3 F148), do take trouble to explain away Theseus' treatment of Ariadne, but I suspect that others could simply ignore it, or anything else about Theseus that was unpalatable to them, concentrating instead on the unambiguously virtuous side of him, which is, of

---

[1] The theme runs through much of Walker 1995; cf. Garland 1992: 98.

[2] Cf. Walker 1995: 172.

[3] *Contra* Garland 1992: 98, who sees the ambivalent nature of Theseus as symbolic of the Athenians' ambivalent attitude to the empire, and Walker 1995, *passim*.

course, the side that is built up and expanded by various Athenian authors. Excuses for Theseus are there when they are needed, and the moral flavour of the visit to the underworld, in particular, is changed out of all recognition. What the Athenians do not like, they either change, or simply ignore. They would hardly be unique in altering or ignoring unpalatable 'facts'. Even if it is possible to interpret Theseus as a rather ambivalent figure between good and bad in the context of the Theseus myth in all its various elements, I doubt that this actually was how he was seen by the Athenians, and I believe that the view—that they recognized, and were interested in, his darker side—has been somewhat overstated. I have argued instead throughout this book that the Athenians created and maintained an unambiguous character who reflected their unambiguously favourable self-image, and that those who write about Theseus do not direct their audiences to question the nature of Theseus and what he is supposed to represent, but rather to reaffirm their 'common knowledge' of their heroic ancestry and the Athenian way of life.[4] Of course, non-Athenians have much less stake in Theseus, and the continuing existence of older narratives of stories such as the desertion of Ariadne may partly explain why Theseus remains very much the representative of Athenian virtues inside Athens.

Although mythical figures are vibrantly alive in the many, everchanging stories told about them, they are also safely dead: Theseus can belong to everyone, whereas a figure in the more recent past, especially a historical figure who may have descendants, and whose enemies may also have descendants, is not far away enough in time to be the property of the whole city.[5] A figure such as Theseus, who lived so long ago as to be everyone's ancestor, provides a direct line from the great heroes of old, who lived even before the Trojan war, down to their modern ancestors. Theseus was the only hero with Athenian connections who was famous outside the borders of Attica. His triumph over the

[4] Compare my remarks in §§6.3 and 6.5, and 1.7 on the ways in which Euripides and Bacchylides detach Theseus in *Hippolytus* and Minos in Bacchylides 17 respectively from their normal roles, and make it clear that these are 'different' characters by directing us away from thinking of them as they normally appear.

[5] Cf. Walker 1995: 6. Compare the modern Greek numismatic custom of reserving notes of larger denominations for the less controversial (but still glorious and important) figures of the ancient past, and consigning more recent figures to their small change.

Minotaur transcends his failures with Ariadne, Helen and Persephone, and it is as the Minotauromachist that he acquires a position of importance among the Athenians. In killing the strange and malevolent creature, he is essentially a civilizing hero. Civilizing heroes range from humans who are simply stronger than dangerous non-humans to those who represent the conception of civilization for a particular society in its most complex ethical sense. Theseus begins as the first type and ends as the other, as the killer of the Minotaur becomes the upholder of all the civilized virtues which the Greeks defined as Greek, rather than non-Greek, and the Athenians, as Athenian most of all among the Greek.

Athenian conceptions of the civilizing power of their city and its people antedate the Persian wars by several decades, but the wars undoubtedly confirm the 'truth' of this idealized self-image. Athenian conduct in 490 and in the campaigns of 480–479 created the Athenian empire. Athens the civilizer gradually became Athens the imperialist, but the role of the self-serving imperialist is less attractive than that of the altruistic civilizer: thus the imperialist must, to a very large extent, be subsumed within the civilizer. I have attempted to sketch what such a self-perception entails, because the image of Theseus which Athenian tragedy provides conforms so closely to broader trends in Athenian self-perception. In tragedy, Theseus is almost always the active helper, rather than the helped, and the altruistic champion of the common good of Greece. Precisely because he is the representative and symbol of Athens, his characterization is so consistent in most tragedy as to be rather limited, since he is almost exclusively confined to the role of civilizer, helper or comforter. Only the rather more daring Euripides tries to transcend convention, in the Hippolytus plays. The first of these, which almost certainly did not flatter Theseus, proved unpopular among the Athenians. The second, which was much more favourably received, distances Theseus, not only from responsibility for Hippolytus' death, but also from the city of Athens, making him almost into a different character from the Theseus of the other tragedies. It is worth noting, however, that although Euripides defied convention with the Hippolytus plays, he also wrote the *Suppliants*, in which, as I argue in Chapter 3, the Athenian image of Athens is presented to the audience without reservation or criticism.

Even this most blatantly patriotic of plays, however, does

not pretend that the Athenian ideal is a panacea for all suffering. In Greek thought, human beings are distinguished from the gods by their limitations in power and knowledge, which impose moderation and caution on them. The Theseus of most tragedy is a human hero subject to human limitation in a world in which humanity is at the mercy of more powerful forces. Theseus and the Athenian ideal can never cure sufferings inflicted by the gods, and in tragedy, Theseus is always aware of his own limitations as a human being, while simultaneously exemplifying the very best of humanity in all areas of action. Through Theseus, a train of thought which pervades Greek culture and which is summed up in the old maxim μηδὲν ἄγαν ('nothing in excess') is offered to Athens as an alleged description of what the 'national character' was and a prescription for what it should be in the wider context of Athenian self-definition. The Theseus plays, especially those whose primary dramatic concern is something other than the glorification of Athens, are brilliant vehicles for the propagation and reaffirmation of the idealized image of Athens precisely because they accept the inevitability of suffering, while simultaneously presenting a city which, through its own wisdom, courage and virtue, ultimately avoids any such suffering and is rewarded with human and divine approval. It is hard to imagine a subtler and more seductive way of validating the audience's national and personal pride in being Athenians, and of justifying whatever Athenian policy needed to be justified.

The recreation of myths by Athenian playwrights is symbolic of Athenian imperial attitudes to the rest of the Greek world, and in particular, the relationship between Heracles and Theseus is symbolic of wider trends. Like Theseus, Heracles is a civilizer, though originally he is far greater and more famous than Theseus throughout Greece. Athenian writers assimilate Theseus to Heracles, and also tend to minimize Heracles' services to their national hero: in older narratives, Heracles saved Theseus from eternal punishment in the underworld, but in Athenian literature the emphasis of the story is changed, so that the balance of services rendered no longer favours Heracles exclusively. Thus in Euripides' *Heracles*, Theseus saves Heracles from committing suicide, even though earlier narratives concerning the madness of Heracles had no place for the Athenian king, and in the *Peirithous*, Theseus' own wisdom and humanity, as much as Heracles' intercession, saves Peirithous from everlasting punishment. Even more striking is the role assigned by Sophocles to Theseus in the Oedipus myth, since Oedipus' connections with Attica—unlike those of Heracles—were minimal, and his crimes against the family made him an exceptionally problematic candidate for Athenian aid. In general, Athenian tragedians exhibit a curious mixture of restriction, in the functions their plays assign to Theseus, and freedom, in the innovations they make to include their national hero in myths with which he had no traditional connection. Such *polypragmosyne* in myth-making is one aspect of a more general active, interventionist attitude to the surrounding world, whether it is called 'helping others' or merely 'interfering'. In this *polypragmosyne*, whether it moulds mythological narrative or the image of the ideal Athens that was so influential in Athenian foreign policy, Athenian risk-taking must always have its reward.

BIBLIOGRAPHY

ADKINS, A. W. H. (1966), 'Basic Values in Euripides' *Hecuba* and *Hercules Furens*', *CQ* 16: 193–219.

——(1976), '*Polypragmosyne* and "Minding One's Own Business": A Study in Greek Social and Political Values', *CP* 71: 301–27.

ALLISON, J. W. (1979), 'Thucydides and Πολυπραγμοσύνη', *AJAH* 4: 10–22.

AMANDRY, P. (1960), 'Sur les épigrammes de Marathon', in *Theoria: Festschrift für W. A. Schuchardt*, ed. F. Eckstein (Baden-Baden), 1–8.

AMEIS, F., and HENTZE, C. (1877), *Anhang zu Homers Ilias 1–3*, 2nd edn. (Leipzig).

AMEIS, F., HENTZE, C., and CAUER, P. (1913), *Ilias* (Leipzig).

AMPOLO, C., and MANFREDINI, M. (1988), *Le vite di Teseo e di Romolo* (Milan).

ANDREWES, A. (1956), *The Greek Tyrants* (London).

——(1959), 'Thucydides and the Causes of the War', *CQ* 9: 223 ff.

——(1960), 'The Melian Dialogue and Pericles' Last Speech', *PCPS* 6: 1–10.

——(1970), Commentary on Thucydides book 5, in A. W. Gomme, A. Andrewes and K. J. Dover, *Historical Commentary on Thucydides*, vol. 4 (Oxford).

——(1982a), 'The Tyranny of Pisistratus', *CAH* 3. 3. 2: 392–416.

——(1982b), 'The Growth of the Athenian State', *CAH* 3. 3. 2: 360–91.

APTHORP, M. J. (1980), *The Manuscript Evidence for Interpolation in Homer* (Heidelberg).

ARROWSMITH, W. (1969), Introduction to the *Heracles*, in Grene and Lattimore (1969), 266–81.

ASHMOLE, B., and YALOURIS, N. (1967), *Olympia* (London).

AUBERSON, P., and SCHEFOLD, K. (1972), *Führer durch Eretria* (Berlin).

AUDIAT, J. (1933), *Le Trésor des Athéniens* (Paris).

BACON, H. H. (1961), *Barbarians in Greek Tragedy* (New Haven).

BAIN, D. (1977), *Actors and Audience: A Study of Asides and Related Conventions in Greek Drama* (Oxford).

BARLOW, S. A. (1982), 'Structure and Dramatic Realism in Euripides' *Heracles*', *G&R* 29: 115–24.

——(1986), *The Imagery of Euripides*, 2nd edn. (Bristol).

BARRETT, W. S. (1964), *Euripides: Hippolytus* (Oxford).

BARRON, J. P. (1972), 'New Light on Old Walls', *JHS* 92: 20–45.

——(1980), 'Theseus, Bacchylides and a Woolly Cloak', *BICS* 27: 1–8.

BATTEGAZZORE, A. M. (1970), 'Il termine Καθέδρα nella hypothesis del *Piritoo* di Crizia', in *Mythos—Scripta in honorem Mario Untersteiner* (Genoa).

BAŽANT, J. (1982), 'The Case of Symbolism in Classical Greek Art', *Eirene* 18: 21–31.

BEAZLEY, J. D. (1986), 'The Development of Attic Black Figure', 2nd edn. (Los Angeles).

BECATTI, G. (1937), 'I tirannicidi di Antenore', *RAC* 9. 1: 97–107.

BECKEL, G. (1961), *Götterbeistand in der Bildüberlieferung griechischer Heldensagen* (Waldsassen).

BECKER, M. (1939), *Helena—Ihr Wesen und ihre Wandlungen im Klassischen Altertum* (Leipzig, Strassburg and Zurich).

BENEDETTO, V. DI (1961), 'Responsione strofica e distribuzione delle battute in Euripide', *Hermes* 89: 298–321.

——(1971), *Euripide, teatro e società* (Turin).

BENGL, H. (1929), *Staatstheoretische Probleme im Rahmen der attischen, vornehmlich euripideisch Tragödie* (Munich).

BÉRARD, C. (1989), *A City of Images: Iconography and Society in Ancient Greece* (Princeton).

BÉRARD, V. (1946), *L'Odyssée* (Paris).

BERGER, E. (1968), 'Die Hauptwerke des Basler Antiken Museums zwischen 460 und 430 v.Chr.', *AK* 11: 63–4, 125–36.

BERNARD, M.-L. (1986), 'Ariadne', in *LIMC* 3. 1 1050–70.

BERNABÉ, A. (1987), *Poetarum Epicorum Graecorum; testimonia et fragmenta* (Leipzig).

BETHE, E. (1895), *Thebanische Heldenlieder: Untersuchungen über die Epen des thebanisch-argivisch Sagenkreis* (Berlin).

——(1910), 'Minos', *Rh.Mus.* 65: 200–32.

——(1922), *Homer: Dichtung und Sage*, ii (Leipzig and Berlin).

BETTELHEIM, B. (1976), *The Uses of Enchantment* (London).

BICKNELL, P. J. (1972), *Studies in Athenian Politics and Genealogy* (Wiesbaden).

BIEHL, W. (1989), *Euripides:* Troades (Heidelberg).

BLAMIRE, A. (1989), *Plutarch: Life of Kimon* (London).

BLECH, M. (1982), *Studien zum Kranz bei den Griechen* (Berlin and New York).

BLEGEN, C. W. (1940), 'Athens in the Early Age of Greece', *HSCP* Supp. 1: 1–9.

BLOK, J. (1990), 'Patronage and the Pisistratidae', *BABesch* 65: 17–28.

BLUNDELL, M. W. (1989), *Helping Friends and Harming Enemies: A Study in Sophocles and Greek Ethics* (Cambridge).

—— (1990), *Sophocles' 'Oedipus at Colonus'* (Newburyport).

BOARDMAN, J. (1972), 'Herakles, Peisistratos and Sons', *RA* 1972: 59–72.

——(1975), 'Heracles, Peisistratus and Eleusis', *JHS* 95: 1–12.

——(1978*a*), 'Herakles, Delphi and Kleisthenes of Sicyon', *RA* 1978: 227–34.

——(1978*b*), 'Exekias', *AJA* 82: 11–25.

——(1982), 'Herakles, Theseus and Amazons', in D. Kurtz and B. Sparkes (eds.), *The Eye of Greece: Studies in the Art of Athens* (Cambridge), 1–28.

——(1984), 'Image and Politics in Sixth Century Athens', in H. A. G. Brijder (ed.), *Ancient Greek and Related Pottery: Proc. of the International Vase Symposium in Amsterdam* (Amsterdam).

——(1985), *The Parthenon and its Sculptures* (London).

BOEGEHOLD, A. L. (1982), 'A Dissent at Athens ca. 424–421 BC', *GRBS* 23: 146–56.

——(1994), Introduction in Boegehold and Scafuro (1994).

BOEGEHOLD, A. L., and SCAFURO, A. C. (1994), *Athenian Identity and Civic Ideology* (Baltimore and London).

BOERSMA, J. S. (1970), *Athenian Building Policy from 561/0–405/4* (Groningen, 1970).

BOLLING, G.M. (1925), *The External Evidence for Interpolation in Homer* (Oxford).

BOND, G. W. (1981), *Euripides: Heracles* (Oxford).

BORECKÝ, B. (1955), 'La Tragédie *Alope* d'Euripide', *Studia Antiqua Salač Oblata* (Prague), 81–9.

BOTHMER, D. VON (1957), *Amazons in Greek Art* (Oxford).

BOWRA, C. M. (1944), *Sophoclean Tragedy* (Oxford).

——(1961), *Greek Lyric Poetry*, 2nd edn. (Oxford).

——(1963), 'The Two Palinodes of Stesichorus', *CR* 13: 245–52.

BRADEEN, D. W. (1960), 'The Popularity of the Athenian Empire', *Historia* 9: 258–309.

BRASWELL, B. K. (1988), *Commentary on the Fourth Pythian Ode of Pindar* (Berlin).

BRELICH, A. (1956), 'Theseus e i suoi avversari', *SMSR* 27: 136–41.

——(1958), *Gli eroi greci* (Rome).

BREMMER, J. (1987), *Interpretations of Greek Mythology* (London and Sydney).

BRÖCKER, W. (1971), *Der Gott des Sophokles* (Frankfurt).

BROMMER, F. (1953), *Herakles* (Munster).

——(1979), 'Theseusdeutungen', *AA* 1979: 487–511.

——(1982), *Theseus* (Darmstadt).

——(1984), *Herakles II: Die unkanonischen Taten des Helden* (Darmstadt).

BROWN, A. L. (1978), 'Wretched Tales of Poets', *PCPS* 24: 22–30.

——(1984), 'Eumenides in Greek Tragedy', *CQ* 34: 260–81.

BRUNT, P. A. (1978), 'Laus Imperii', in Garnsey and Whittaker (1978), 159–91.

BUCHWALD, W. (1939), *Studien zur Chronologie der attischen Tragödien 455–431* (Königsberg).

BURIAN, P. (1974), 'Oedipus as Suppliant and Saviour,' *Phoenix* 28: 408–29.

——(1985), '*Logos* and *Pathos*: The Politics of the *Suppliant Women*', in P. Burian (ed.), *Directions in Euripidean Criticism* (Durham, NC), 129–55.

BURKERT, W. (1979), *Structure and History in Greek Mythology and Ritual* (Berkeley and Los Angeles).

——(1985), *Greek Religion*, trans. J. Raffan (Oxford).

BURNETT, A. P. (1971), *Catastrophe Survived* (Oxford).

——(1985), *The Art of Bacchylides* (Harvard).

BURTON, R. W. B. (1980), *The Chorus in Sophocles' Tragedies* (Oxford).

BUSS, H. (1913), *De Bacchylide Homeri Imitatore* (diss., Giessen).

BUTTERWORTH, E. A. S. (1966), *Some Traces of the Pre-Olympian World in Greek Religion* (Berlin).

BUXTON, R. G. A. (1980), 'Blindness and Limits: Sophokles and the Logic of Myth', *JHS* 100: 22–37.

——(1982), *Persuasion in Greek Tragedy* (Cambridge).

CAIRNS, D. (1993), *Aidos* (Oxford).

CALAME, C. (1990), *Thésée et l'imaginaire Athénien* (Lausanne).

CAMBITOGLU, A., and TRENDALL, A. C. (1992), *Second Supplement to Red Figure Vases of Apulia*, *BICS* Supp. 60 (London).

CANNATÀ FERA, M. (1986), 'Euripide "Supplici" 176–9', *GIF* 1986: 255–61.

CANTARELLA, R. (1963), *I Cretesi* (Milan).

CANTARELLI, F. (1974), 'Il personaggio di Menesteo nel mito e nelle ideologie politiche greche', *RIL* 108: 459–505.

CARDEN, R. C. (1974), *The Papyrus Fragments of Sophocles* (Berlin and New York).

CARLINI, A. (1968), 'Un nuovo frammento di tragedia greca', *ASNP* 1968: 163–71.

CARTER, L. A. (1986), *The Quiet Athenian* (Oxford).

CATAUDELLA, Q. (1932), 'Sulla Teogonia di Antifane e sui frammenti del *Piritoo* di Euripide', *Athenaeum* 10: 259–68.

——(1969), *Saggi sulla tragedia greca* (Messina).

CHALK, H. H. O. (1962), '*APETH* and *BIA* in Euripides' *Heracles*', *JHS* 82: 7–18.

CHANDLER, L. (1926), 'The North West Frontier of Attica', *JHS* 46: 1–21.

CLAIRMONT, C. (1983), *Patrios Nomos: Public Burial in Athens during the Fifth and Fourth Centuries* (Oxford).

CLARK, R. J. (1979), *Catabasis: Vergil and the Wisdom Tradition* (Amsterdam).

CLAVAUD, R. (1980), *Le Ménexène de Platon et la rhétorique de son temps* (Paris).

CLOTA, J. A. (1957), 'Helena de Troya—historia di un mito', *Helmantica* 8: 373–94.

COCKLE, H. M. (1983), in *Oxyrhynchus Papyri*, vol. 50 (London), 29–36.

COGAN, M. (1981), *The Human Thing* (Chicago).

COLDSTREAM, J. N. (1977), *Geometric Greece* (London).

COLLARD, C. (1972), 'The Funeral Oration in Euripides' *Supplices*', *BICS* 19: 39–53.

——(1975), *Euripides' Supplices, Edited with Introduction and Commentary* (Groningen).

——(1981), *Euripides* (Oxford).

CONACHER, D. J. (1956), 'Religious and Ethical Attitudes in Euripides' *Suppliants*', *TAPA* 87: 8–26.

——(1967), *Euripidean Drama: Theme, Myth and Structure* (Toronto).

CONNOR, W. R. (1990), 'The City Dionysia and Athenian Democracy', in W. R. Connor and others (eds.), *Aspects of Athenian Democracy* (Copenhagen), 8–32.

——(1994), 'The Problem of Athenian Civic Identity', in Boegehold and Scafuro (1994), 34–44.

COOK, A. B. (1900), 'Iostephanos', *JHS* 20: 1–13.

COOK, R. M. (1987), 'Pots and Pisistratan Propaganda', *JHS* 107: 167–9.

COSTE-MESSELIÈRE, P. DE LA (1957), *Les Sculptures du trésor des Athéniens, Fouilles de Delphes*, vol. 4. 4 (Paris).

CRAMER, J. A. (1886), *Anecdota Graeca Oxoniensia*, 3 vols. (Oxford).

CROPP, M. J., and FICK, G. (1985), *Resolutions and Chronology in Euripides* (London).

CROSBY, M. (1949), 'The Altar of the Twelve Gods in Athens', in *Commemorative Studies in Honour of Theodore Leslie Shear* (Baltimore), 82–103.

DAVIE, J. N. (1982), 'Theseus the King in Fifth Century Athens', *G&R* 29: 25–34.

DAVIES, A. M. (1963), *Myceneae Graecitatis Lexicon* (Rome).

DAVIES, J. K. (1971), *Athenian Propertied Families 600–300 BC* (Oxford).

DAVIES, M. (1982), 'The End of Sophocles' O.T.', *Hermes* 110: 269–77.

——(1988), *Epicorum Graecorum Fragmenta* (Göttingen).

——(1989), 'The Date of the Epic Cycle', *Glotta* 67: 89–100.

DAVISON, J. A. (1955), 'Peisistratus and Homer', *TAPA* 86: 1–21.

DAY, J. W. (1980), *The Glory of Athens: The Popular Tradition as Reflected in the Panathenaicus of Aelius Aristides* (Chicago).

DELEBECQUE, E. (1951), *Euripide et la Guerre du Péloponnèse* (Paris).

DELVOYE, E. (1975), 'Art et politique à Athènes à l'époque de Cimon', in *Le Monde grec: Hommages à Claire Préaux* (Brussels), 801–7.

DENNISTON, J. D. (1954), *Euripides:* Electra, 2nd edn. (Oxford).

DEONNA, W. (1920), 'Le Portrait de Phidias sur le Bouclier d'Athéna Parthénos', *REG* 33: 291–308.

DETIENNE, M. (1970), 'L'Olivier: un mythe politico-religieux', *RHR* 178: 2–23.

DEUBNER, L. (1932), *Attische Feste* (Berlin).

——(1942), *Oidipusprobleme* (Berlin).

DILLER, H. (1950), *Göttliches und menschliches Wissen bei Sophokles* (Kiel).

DIMOCK, G. (1977), 'Euripides' *Hippolytus*, or Virtue Rewarded', *YCS* 25: 239–58.

DINSMOOR, W. B. (1941), *Observations on the Hephaesteion, Hesperia* Supp. 5 (Baltimore).

——(1946), 'The Athenian Treasury as Dated by its Ornament', *AJA* 50: 86–121.

DIOTTI, U. (1966), 'Il "Teseo" di Sofocle', *Dioniso* 40: 43–62.

DODDS, E. R. (1925), 'The *aidos* of Phaedra and the Meaning of the *Hippolytus*', *CR* 39: 102–4.

——(1951), *The Greeks and the Irrational* (Los Angeles).

——(1974), *The Ancient Concept of Progress* (Oxford).

DONLAN, W. (1973), 'The Tradition of Anti-Aristocratic Thought in Early Greek Poetry', *Historia* 22: 145–54.

DOVER, K. J. (1957), 'The Political Aspect of Aeschylus' *Eumenides*', *JHS* 77 (pt. 2): 230–7.

——(1970), A. W. Gomme, A. Andrewes and K. J. Dover, *Historical Commentary on Thucydides*, vol. 4 (Oxford).

——(1974), *Greek Popular Morality in the Time of Plato and Aristotle* (Oxford).

——(1993), *Aristophanes'* Frogs (Oxford).

DRAGE, G. (1890), *Eton and the Empire* (Eton).

DREXLER, H. (1943), 'Zum Herakles des Euripides', *NGG* 1943: 311–63.

DUBOIS, P. (1979), 'On Horse/Men, Amazons and Endogamy', *Arethusa* 12: 35–49.

EASTERLING, P. E. (1967), 'Oedipus and Polynices', *PCPS* 13: 1–13.

——(1973), 'Repetition in Sophocles', *Hermes* 101: 14–34.

——(1982), *Sophocles:* Trachiniae (Cambridge).

——(1985), 'Anachronism in Greek Tragedy', *JHS* 105: 1–10.

——(1989), 'City Settings in Greek Poetry', *PCA* 86: 5–17.

EDMUNDS, L. (1975), *Chance and Intelligence in Thucydides* (Harvard).

——(1981), 'The Cults and Legends of Oedipus', *HSCP* 85: 221–38.

EHRENBERG, V. (1946), 'Tragic Heracles', in *Aspects of the Ancient World* (Oxford), 144–66.

EHRENBERG, V. (1947), 'Polypragmosyne: A Study in Greek Politics', *JHS* 67: 46–67.

——(1954), *Sophocles and Pericles* (Oxford).

EISNER, R. (1977), 'Ariadne in Art, Prehistory to 400 BC', *RSC* 25: 165–81.

ELLENDT, R. (1872), *Lexicon Sophocleum*, 2nd edn. (Berlin).

ELSE, G. (1957), *Aristotle's Poetics: The Argument* (Harvard).

EUCKEN, C. (1979), 'Das Anonyme Theseus-Drama und der O.C.', *MH* 36: 136–41.

EUBEN, J. P. (1986), *Greek Tragedy and Political Theory* (Los Angeles).

FARNELL, L. (1900), *Cults of the Greek States*, vol. 5 of 5 (Oxford, 1896–1900).

——(1932), *The Works of Pindar*, 3 vols. (London).

FARRAR, C. (1988), *The Origins of Democratic Thought* (Cambridge).

FERGUSSON, W. S. (1913), *Greek Imperialism* (London).

FESTUGIÈRE, A. J. (1973), 'Tragédies et tombes sacrées', *RHR* 184: 3–13.

FINLEY, J. H., jr. (1938), 'Euripides and Thucydides', *HSCP* 49: 23–68.

FINLEY, M. I. (1978), 'The Fifth Century Athenian Empire: A Balance-Sheet', in Garnsey and Whittaker (1978), 103–26.

FITTON, J. W. (1961), 'The Suppliant Women and the Heraklidai of Euripides', *Hermes* 89: 430–61.

FITTSCHEN, K. (1969), *Untersuchungen zum Beginn der Sagendarstellung bei den Griechen* (Berlin).

FOLEY, H. (1985), *Ritual Irony* (Cornell).

FORREST, W. G. (1956), Review of *Fouilles de Delphes* 3. 4, in *RBPh* 34: 541–2.

——(1960), 'Themistocles and Argos', *CQ* 10: 220–41.

——(1975), 'Aristophanes and the Athenian Empire', in B. Levick (ed.), *The Ancient Historian and His Materials: Essays for C. E. Stevens* (Farnborough), 17–29.

FOSSATI, V. (1950), 'Il mito nelle tragedie di Crizia', *Dioniso* 13: 105–16.

FRAENKEL, E. (1963), 'Zu den Phoenissen des Euripides', *SB München* 1963.

FREY, V. (1947), *Die Stellung der attischen Tragödie und Komödie zur Demokratie* (diss., Zurich).

FRIIS JOHANSEN, K. (1945), *Thésée et la danse à Délos: étude herméneutique* (Copenhagen).

——(1967), *The Iliad in Early Greek Art* (Copenhagen).

FRITZ, K. VON (1962), *Antike und moderne Tragoedie* (Berlin).

FUCHS, W., and FLOREN, J. (1987), *Die griechische Plastik*, vol. 1 (Munich).

FURLEY, D. (1986), 'Euripides on the Sanity of Heracles', in J. H. Betts, J. T. Hooker, and J. R. Green (eds.), *Studies in honour of T. B. L. Webster*, 2 vols. (Bristol, 1986, 1988), i. 102–13.

GALINSKY, G. K. (1972), *The Herakles Theme* (Oxford).

GALLET DE SANTERRE, H. (1958), *Délos primitive et archaique* (Paris).

GAMBLE, R. B. (1970), 'Euripides' *Suppliant Women*: Decision and Ambivalence', *Hermes* 98: 385–405.

GANSCHIENITZ, W. (1919), 'Katabasis', *RE* 10. 2 (Stuttgart), 2359–449.

GANTZ, T. J. (1978), 'The Aischylean Trilogy: Prolegomena', *CJ* 74: 287–304.

GARDINER, C. (1987), *The Sophoclean Chorus* (Iowa).

GARLAND, R. (1992), *Introducing New Gods* (London).

GARNSEY, P. D. A., and WHITTAKER, C. R. (1978), *Imperialism in the Ancient World* (Cambridge).

GARVIE, A. F. (1969), *Aeschylus'* Supplices: *Play and Trilogy* (Cambridge).

GASTALDI, E. C. (1976), 'Propaganda e politica negli Eleusini di Eschilo', *CISA* 4: 50–71.

——(1977), 'L'Amazzonomachia "teseica" nell'elaborazione propagandistica ateniese', *AAST* 111: 283–96.

GAUER, W. (1968), *Weihgeschenke aus den Perserkriegen* (Tübingen).

GELLIE, G. H. (1972), *Sophocles: A Reading* (Melbourne).

GENTILI, B. (1977), 'Eracle "Omicida Giustissimo"', in *Il Mito Greco: Atti del Convegno Internazionale*, ed. B. Gentili and G. Paioni (Rome, 1977), 299–305.

GHALI-KAHIL, L. B. (1955), *Les Enlèvements et le retour d'Hélène dans les textes et les documents figurés* (Paris).

GIANFRANCESCO, L. (1975), 'Un frammento sofistico nella *Vita di Teseo* di Plutarco?', *CISA* 3: 7–18.

GIESEKAM, G. J. (1977), 'The Portrayal of Minos in Bacchylides 17', in Francis Cairns (ed.), *Papers of the Liverpool Latin Seminar 1976*, 237–52.

GILES, P. R. (1890), 'Political Allusions in the "Supplices"', *CR* 4: 95–8.

GOETZE, H. (1938), 'Die attischen Dreifigurenreliefs', *Röm.Mitt.* 53: 184–280.

GOLDHILL, S. (1987), 'The Great Dionysia and Civic Ideology', *JHS* 107: 58–76.

——(1988), *Reading Greek Tragedy* (Cambridge).

——(1991), *The Poet's Voice* (Cambridge).

GOMME, A. W. (1956), *Historical Commentary on Thucydides*, vol. 2 (Oxford).

GOOSSENS, R. (1932), 'Périclès et Thésée à propos des Suppliantes', *BAGB* 35: 9–40.

——(1962), *Euripide et Athènes* (Brussels).

GOULD, J. P. (1973), 'Hiketeia', *JHS* 93: 74–103.

GOULD, T. (1965), 'The Philosophers on Oedipus the King', *Arion* 4: 363–86.

GRECO, G. (1985), 'Un cratere del pittore di Talos da Serra di Vaglio', *RSA* 8: 5–35.

GREENWOOD, L. (1953), *Aspects of Euripidean Tragedy* (Cambridge).

GREGORY, J. (1977) 'Euripides' *Heracles*', *YCS* 25: 259–75.

——(1991), *Euripides and the Instruction of the Athenians* (Michigan).

GRENE, D. (1965), *Greek Political Theory* (Chicago).

GRENE, D., and LATTIMORE, R. (1969), *The Complete Greek Tragedies* (Chicago).

GRIFFIN, A. (1982), *Sikyon* (Oxford).

GRIFFIN, J. (1977), 'The Epic Cycle and the Uniqueness of Homer', *JHS* 97: 40–53.

——(1980), *Homer on Life and Death* (Oxford).

——(1990), 'Characterisation in Euripides' *Hippolytus* and *Iphigeneia in Aulis*', in C. B. R. Pelling (ed.), *Characterisation and Individuality in Greek Literature* (Oxford), 128–49.

GRIFFIN, M. T. (1991), 'Urbs Roma, Plebs and Princeps', in L. Alexander (ed.), *Images of Empire* (Sheffield), 19–46.

GRIFFITHS, M. (1978), 'Aeschylus, Sicily and Prometheus', in *Dionysiaca: Nine Studies in Greek Poetry by Former Pupils Presented to Sir Denys Page* (Cambridge), 105–39.

GRIMAL, P. (1964), review of Zintzen (1960), in *REA* 65: 210f.

GROSSMANN, G. (1950), *Politische Schlagwörter aus der Zeit des peloponnesischen Krieges* (Basel).

GRUBE, G. M. A. (1941), *The Drama of Euripides* (London).

GUTHRIE, W. K. C. (1957), *In the Beginning* (London).

——(1962–81), *A History of Greek Philosophy*, 6 vols. (Cambridge).

HÄGG, R., and MARINATOS, N. (1984), *The Minoan Thalassocracy: Myth and Reality* (Stockholm).

HALL, E. M. (1989), *Inventing the Barbarian* (Oxford).

HALLERAN, M. R. (1985), *Stagecraft in Euripides* (London and Sydney).

HALLIWELL, S. (1991), 'Comic Satire and Freedom of Speech in Classical Athens', *JHS* 111: 48–70.

HARDING, P. (1981), 'In Search of a Polypragmatist', in G. S. Shrimpton and D. J. McCargar (eds.), *Classical Contributions, Studies for M. F. McGregor* (New York), 41–50.

——(1994), *Androtion and the Atthis* (Oxford).

HARDWICK, L. (1990), 'Ancient Amazons—Heroes, Outsiders or Women?', *G&R* 37: 14–36.

HARRISON, A. R. W. (1968), *The Law of Athens*, i (Oxford).

HARRISON, E. B. (1966), 'The Composition of the Amazonomachy on the Shield of Athena Parthenos', *Hesperia* 35: 107–33.

——(1967), 'Athena and Athens in the East Pediment of the Parthenon', *AJA* 71: 27–58.

——(1972), 'The South Frieze of the Nike Temple and the Marathon Painting in the Painted Stoa', *AJA* 76: 353–78.

——(1981), 'Motifs of the City Siege on the Shield of Athena Parthenos', *AJA* 85: 290–317.

HAUVETTE, A. (1898), 'Les Eleusinies d'Eschyle', *Mélanges Henri Weil* (Paris), 159–78.

HEATH, M. (1987), *The Poetics of Greek Tragedy* (London).

——(1989), *Unity in Greek Poetics* (Oxford).

HEIMBERG, U. (1968), *Das Bild des Poseidon in der griechischen Vasenmalerei* (Freiburg).

HENDERSON, J. L. (1964), 'Ancient Myths and Modern Man', in C. G. Jung (ed.), *Man and his Symbols* (London).

HERTER, H. (1936), 'Theseus der Ionier', *Rh.Mus.* 85: 177–91, 193–239.

——(1939), 'Theseus der Athener', *Rh.Mus.* 88: 244–86, 289–336.

——(1940), 'Theseus und Hippolytos', *Rh.Mus.* 90: 273–92.

——(1973), 'Theseus', *RE Supp.* XIII (Munich, 1973), 1045–238.

HITZIG, H., and BLÜMNER, H. (1901), *Pausaniae Graeciae Descriptio*, 3 vols. (Leipzig).

HOBSON, J. A. (1938), *Imperialism: A Study*, 3rd edn. (London).

HOBSBAWM, E. (1987), *The Age of Empire* (London).

HOEKSTRA, A., and HEUBECK, A. (1989), *A Commentary on Homer's Odyssey, Books ix–xvi* (Oxford).

HOFKES-BRUKKER, C. (1966), 'Die Liebe von Theseus und Antiope', *BABesch* 41: 14–27.

HOLLOWAY, R. R. (1967), 'Panhellenism in the Sculpture of the Zeus Temple at Olympia', *GRBS* 8: 93–101.

HÖLSCHER, T. (1973), *Griechische Historienbilder des 5. und 4. Jahrhunderts* (Würzburg).

HÖLSCHER, T., and SIMON, E. (1976), 'Die Amazonschlacht auf der Schild der Athena Parthenos', *JDAI* 91: 115–48.

HOOG, I. (1973), 'Ariadne', *Lexikon des frühgriechischen Epos*, vol. 7 ed. E. M. Voigt, 11 vols. (1955–84), 1269–70.

HOPE SIMPSON, R. (1981), *Mycenean Greece* (Park Ridge).

HORNBLOWER, S. (1982), *Mausolus* (Oxford).

——(1987), *Thucydides* (London).

——(1991), *Commentary on Thucydides 1–3* (Oxford).

HOW, W. W., and WELLS, J. (1912), *A Commentary on Herodotus*, 2 vols. (Oxford).

HUDSON-WILLIAMS, T. (1950), 'Conventional Forms of Debate and the Melian Dialogue', *AJP* 71: 156–69.

HUNT, A. S. (1927), *Oxyrhynchus Papyri*, vol. 17 (London).

HUXLEY, G. (1960), 'Homer's Amazons', *PdP* 15: 122–4.

——(1969), *Early Epic Poetry from Eumelus to Panyassis* (Cambridge, Mass).

278   Bibliography

Isler-Kerényi, C. (1972), *Lieblinge der Meermädchen* (Zurich).

Jacobsthal, P. (1911), *Theseus auf dem Meeresgrunde* (Leipzig).

Jacoby, F. (1944), 'Patrios Nomos: State Burial in Athens and the Public Cemetery in the Cerameicus', *JHS* 64: 37–66.

——(1945), 'Some Athenian Epigrams from the Persian Wars', *Hesperia* 14: 157–211.

——(1947a), 'The First Athenian Prose Writer', *Mnemosyne*, 3rd ser. 13: 13–64.

——(1947b), 'Some Remarks on Ion of Chios', *CQ* 41: 1–17.

——(1949), *Atthis* (Oxford).

——(1954), *Fragmente der griechischen Historiker*, vol. 3b *Supplement* (text, commentary and notes in 3 vols.) (Leiden).

Jaeger, W. (1947), *The Theology of the Early Greek Philosophers* (Oxford).

James, C. (1969), 'Whether 'tis Nobler', *Pegasus* 12: 10–20.

Jeanmaire, H. (1933), *Couroi et Courètes* (Lille).

Jebb, R. C. (1898), 'Bacchylidea', in *Mélanges Weil* (Paris), 225–242.

——(1900), *Oedipus Coloneus* (Cambridge).

——(1905), *Bacchylides: The Poems and Fragments* (Cambridge).

Jeffery, L. H. (1965), 'The "Battle of Oenoe" in the Stoa Poikile', *BSA* 60: 41–60.

Jeny, H. (1989), 'Troizen as the setting of *Hippolytos Stephanephoros*', *AJP* 110: 400–4.

Jouan, F. (1966), *Euripide et les Chants Cypriens* (Paris).

Kakridis, J. T. (1928), 'Der Fluch des Theseus im Hippolytus', *Rh.Mus.* 77.

——(1949), *Homeric Researches* (Lund).

——(1961), *Der Thukydideische Epitaphios* (Munich).

——(1971), *Homer Revisited* (Lund).

Kalkmann, A. (1882), *De Hippolytis Euripideis* (Bonn).

Karusu, S. (1972), 'Choeur de tragédie sur un lécythe à figures noires', *RA*, 195–204.

Kamerbeek, J. C. (1966), 'Unity and Meaning of Euripides' Heracles', *Mnemosyne*, 4th ser. 19: 1–16.

Kamptz, H. von (1982), *Homerische Personnamen* (Göttingen).

Kannicht, R. (1977): text of Sophocles fr. 730 in S. Radt (1977).

——(1991), *Musa Tragica: Die griechische Tragödie von Thespis bis Ezechiel* (Göttingen).

Kardara, C. P. (1951), 'On Theseus and the Tyrannicides', *AJA* 55: 293–300.

Karsai, G. (1982), 'Le Monologue de Thésée', *AAnt Hung* 30: 113–27.

Kassel, R., and Austin, C. (1983), *Poetae Comici Graeci*, vol. 4 (Berlin and New York).

——(1984), *Poetae Comici Graeci*, vol. 3. 2 (Aristophanes) (Berlin and New York).

——(1989), *Poetae Comici Graeci*, vol. 7 (Berlin and New York).

KEARNS, E. (1982), 'A Homeric Theoxeny', *CQ* 22: 1–8.

——(1989), *The Heroes of Attica* (London).

KERÉNYI, K. (1976), *Dionysus: Archetypal Image of Indestructable Life*, trans. Ralph Manheim (London).

KERFERD, G. (1981), *The Sophistic Movement* (Cambridge).

KIERDORF, W. (1966), *Erlebnis und Darstellung der Perserkriege* (Göttingen).

KIERNAN, V. G. (1969), *The Lords of Human Kind: European Attitudes towards the Outside World in the Imperial Age* (London).

KIRK, G. S. (1962), *The Songs of Homer* (Cambridge).

——(1974), *The Nature of Greek Myth* (Harmondsworth).

——(1985), *The Iliad: A Commentary*, vol. 1 (Cambridge).

KIRKWOOD, G. M. (1986), 'From Melos to Colonus', *TAPA* 116: 99–117.

KIRSTEN, E. (1973), 'Ur-Athen und die Heimat des Sophokles', *WS* 7: 5–26.

KISO, A. (1973), 'Sophocles' Phaedra and the Phaedra of the first *Hippolytus*', *BICS* 20: 22–36.

——(1984), *The Lost Sophocles* (New York).

KITTO, H. D. F. (1939), *Greek Tragedy* (London).

KJELLBERG, E. (1922), 'Zur Entwicklung der Theseussage', *Strena Philogica Upsaliensis: Festskrift tillagnad Professor Per Persson* (Upsala).

KLUWE, D. (1965), 'Das Marathonweihgeschenk in Delphi—eine Stattsweihung oder Privatweihung des Kimon', *Wiss. Ztschr. Jena* 1/14: 21–7.

KLUWE, E. (1968), 'Das Perikleische Kongressdekret, das Todesfahr des Kimon und seine Bedeutung für die Einordnung des Miltiadesgruppe in Delphi', *Rostock Wiss. Ztschr.* 17.

KNOX, B. M. W. (1952), 'The Hippolytus of Euripides', *YCS* 13: 3–31.

——(1957), *Oedipus at Thebes* (New Haven).

——(1963), *The Heroic Temper* (Los Angeles).

——(1966), 'Second Thoughts in Greek Tragedy', *GRBS* 7 reprinted in *Word and Action* (Baltimore, 1979), 321–74.

KOLF, M. C. VAN DER (1924), *Quaeritur quomodo Pindarus fabulas tractaverit quidque in eis mutaverit* (diss., Rotterdam, 1924).

——(1929), 'Skiron', *RE* IIIA (Stuttgart), 537–45.

——(1952), 'Polypemon', *RE* 20 (Stuttgart), 1790.

——(1957), 'Prokoptas' and 'Prokrustes', *RE* 23 (Stuttgart, 1957), 599, 609–13.

KÖRTE, A. (1918), 'Bacchylidea', *Hermes* 53: 113–47.

——(1932), 'Literarische Texte mit Ausschluss der christlichen', *APF* 10: 19–70.

KOSTER, W. J. W. (1942), 'De Euripidis Supplicibus', *Mnemosyne*, 3rd ser. 10: 161–203.

KOUMANOUDES, S. (1976), 'Θησέως σηκός', *AE* 1976: 194–216.

KOVACS, D. (1982), 'Tyrants and Demagogues in Tragic Interpolation', *GRBS* 23: 31–50.

KRAAY, C. M. (1956), 'The Archaic Owls of Athens: Classification and Chronology', *Num. Chron.*, 6th ser. 16: 43–68.

KRETSCHMER, P. (1912), 'Mythische Namen', *Glotta* 4: 205–9.

KRON, U. (1976), *Die zehn attischen Phylenheroen* (Berlin).

——(1981*a*), 'Aegeus', *LIMC* 1. 1.

——(1981*b*), 'Aethra', *LIMC* 1. 1.

——(1981*c*), 'Alope', *LIMC* 1. 1.

KÜHNER, R., and GERTH, B. (1898), *Ausführliche Grammatik der griechischer Sprache*, vol. 1 (Hanover).

KUIPER, C. (1923), 'De Euripidis Supplicibus', *Mnemosyne*, 2nd ser. 51: 102–28.

KUNZE, E. (1950), *Archaische Schildbänder: ein Beitrag zur frühgriechischen Bildgeschichte und Sagenüberlieferung* (Berlin).

LANDMANN, G. P. (1974), 'Das Lob Athens in der Grabrede des Perikles', *MH* 31: 65–95.

LATTIMORE, R. (1962), 'Phaedra and Hippolytus', *Arion* 1: 5–18.

——(1964), *Story Patterns in Greek Tragedy* (Ann Arbor, Mich.).

LAWLER, L. B. (1964), *The Dance in Ancient Greece* (London).

LAWSON, J. C. (1910), *Modern Greek Folklore and Ancient Greek Religion* (Cambridge).

LEEUWEN, J. VAN (1896), *Aristophanes: Ranae* (Leiden).

LEFKOWITZ, M. R. (1969), 'Bacchylides Ode 5: Imitation and Originality', *HSCP* 73: 45–96.

——(1989), '"Impiety" and "Atheism" in Euripides', *CQ* 29: 70–82.

LEGON, R. P. (1981), *Megara: The Political History of a Greek City State to 336 BC* (Cornell).

LEO, F. (1878), *Seneca* (Berlin).

LESKY, A. (1952), 'Zwei Sophokles-Interpretationen', *Hermes* 80: 91–105.

——(1956), *Greek Tragedy* (London).

——(1960), 'Psychologie bei Euripides', *Fondation Hardt: Entretiens sur les Études Classiques*, vol. 6 (Geneva), 123–68.

——(1962), *A History of Greek Literature*, trans. J. Willis and C. van der Heer (New York).

LINFORTH, I. M. (1951), 'Religion and Drama in "Oedipus at Colonus"', *UCPCP* 14: 75–191.

LLOYD, M. (1992), *The Agon in Euripides* (Oxford).

LLOYD-JONES, H. (1957), *Aeschylus*, vol. 2 (Harvard).

——(1963), review of Turner (1962), *Gnomon* 35: 433–6.

——(1967), 'Heracles at Eleusis: P Oxy 2622 and PSI 1391', *Maia* 19: 206–29.

——(1983), *The Justice of Zeus*, 2nd edn. (Berkeley).

LORAUX, N. (1973), ' "Marathon", ou l'histoire idéologique', *REA* 75: 13–42.

——(1974), 'Socrates contrepoison de l'oraison funèbre: Enjeu et signification du Ménexène', *AC* 43: 172–211.

——(1978) 'Mourir devant Troie, tomber pour Athènes: De la gloire du héros à l'idée de la cité', *Information sur les Sciences Sociales* 17: 801–17.

——(1981), *Les Enfants d'Athéna* (Paris).

——(1986), *The Invention of Athens*, trans. A. Sheridan (Harvard).

McDEVITT, A. M. (1972), 'The Nightingale and the Olive', in A. Lesky, H. Schwabl and R. Hanslik (eds.), *Antidosis: Festschrift für Walther Kraus zum 70. Geburtstag* (Vienna), 227–37.

MACDOWELL, D. M. (1963), *The Athenian Homicide Law* (Manchester).

MACLEOD, C. (1974), 'Form and Meaning in the Melian Dialogues', *Historia* 23: 385–400 (repr. in *Collected Essays* (Oxford, 1983), 52–67).

——(1983), 'Rhetoric and History: Th. 6. 16–18', *Quaderni di Storia* 1975 (repr. in *Collected Essays* (Oxford, 1983), 68–87).

——(1978), 'Reason and Necessity, Thuc. 3. 9–14, 37–48', *JHS* 98: 64–78.

MANUWALD, B. (1983), 'Der Mord an der Kindern', *WS* 17: 27–61.

MANIET, A. (1941), 'Le Caractère de Minos dans l'Ode XVII de Bacchylide', *LEC* 10: 35–54.

MARCH, J. R. (1987), *The Creative Poet* (London).

MASARACCHIA, A. (1978), *Erodoto* 9 (Milan).

MASSARO, V. (1978), 'Herodotus' Account of the Battle of Marathon and the Picture in the Stoa Poikile', *AC* 47: 458–75.

MASSON, O. (1972), 'Remarques sur quelques anthroponymes mycéniens', *Acta Mycenea: Proceedings of the Fifth International Colloquium on Mycenean Studies* (Salamanca), 287–9.

MASTRONARDE, D. J. (1979), *Contact and Discontinuity: Some Conventions of Speech and Action on the Greek Tragic Stage* (Berkeley).

——(1987), 'The Optimistic Rationalist in Euripides: Theseus, Jocasta, Teiresias', in M. Cropp, E. Fantham and S. E. Sunley (eds.), *Greek Tragedy and Its Legacy: Essays Presented to D. J. Conacher* (Calgary), 201–11.

MATTHEWS, V. J. (1974), *Panyassis of Halicarnassus: Text and Commentary* (Leiden).

MATTHIESEN, K. (1979), 'Euripides: Die Tragödien', in G. A. Seeck (ed.), *Das griechische Drama* (Darmstadt).

MAYER, M. (1883), *De Euripidis Mythopoeia* (Berlin).

MÉAUTIS, G. (1940), *L'Oedipe à Colone et le culte des héros* (Neuchâtel).

MEIER, C. (1993), *The Political Art of Greek Tragedy*, trans. A. Webber (Cambridge and Oxford).

MEIGGS, R. (1972), *The Athenian Empire* (Oxford).

MEIGGS, R., and LEWIS, D. M. (1988), *A Selection of Greek Historical Inscriptions to the end of the Fifth Century BC* (Oxford).

MERKELBACH, R. (1950), '*ΠΕΙΡΙΘΟΥ ΚΑΤΑΒΑΣΙΣ*', *SIFC* 24 (1950), 255–63.

——(1952), 'Nachtrag zur *ΠΕΙΡΙΘΟΥ ΚΑΤΑΒΑΣΙΣ*', *SIFC* 26: 255–63.

METTE, H. J. (1963), *Der verlorene Aischylos* (Berlin).

——(1967), 'Euripides', *Lustrum* 12.

——(1983), 'Peirithous-Theseus-Herakles bei Euripides', *ZPE* 50: 13–19

MICHELINI, A. N. (1989), 'Neophron and Euripides' Medea', *TAPA* 119: 115–35

MINTO, A. (1960), *Il vaso François* (Florence).

MORGAN, C. H. (1962*a* and *b*), 'The Sculptures of the Hephaesteion 1 and 2', *Hesperia* 31: 210–19 and 221–35.

MORGAN, C. (1990), *Athletes and Oracles* (Cambridge).

MÜLLER-GOLDINGEN, C. (1985), *Untersuchungen zu der Phönissen des Euripides* (Stuttgart).

MYLONAS, G. E. (1953), 'Anaskaphe nekrotapheiou Eleusinos', *Praktika* 1953, 71–81.

——(1961), *Eleusis and the Eleusinian Mysteries* (Princeton).

MYRES, J. L. (1906), 'On the "list of thalassocracies" in Eusebius', *JHS* 26: 84–130.

NAUCK, A. (1964), *Tragicorum Graecorum Fragmenta*, 2nd edn. (Hildesheim).

NEILS, J. (1981), 'The Loves of Theseus: An Early Cup by Oltos,' *AJA* 85: 177–9.

——(1987), *The Youthful Deeds of Theseus* (Rome).

NILSSON, M. P. (1932), *The Mycenean Origins of Greek Mythology* (Cambridge).

——(1950), *The Mycenan-Minoan Religion and its Survival in Greek Religion*, 2nd edn. (Lund).

——(1951), *Cults, Myths, Oracles and Politics* (Lund).

——(1953), 'Political Propaganda in Sixth Century Athens', in G. Mylonas and D. Raymond (eds.), *Studies Presented to David M. Robinson*, 2 vols. (St Louis).

NORDEN, E. (1926), *P. Vergilius Maro: Aeneis Buch VI*, 3rd edn. (Leipzig and Berlin).

NORWOOD, G. (1953), *Essays in Euripidean Drama* (Los Angeles).

OBER, J. (1994), 'Civic Ideology and Counterhegemonic Discourse: Thucydides on the Sicilian Debate', in Boegehold and Scafuro (1994), 102–126.

OLIVER, J. H. (1955), 'Praise of Periclean Athens as a Mixed Constitution', *Rh.Mus.* 98: 37–40.

OSBORNE, R. (1983), 'The Myth of Propaganda and the Propaganda of Myth', *Hephaistos* 5: 61–70.

PADUANO, G. (1966), 'Interpretazione delle *Supplici* di Euripide', *ASNP* 35: 193–249.

PAGE, D. L. (1950), *Select Papyri*, vol. 3 (Harvard).

——(1958), *Euripides: Medea*, 2nd edn. (Oxford).

——(1959), *History and the Homeric Iliad* (Los Angeles).

——(1967), 'Notes on Euripides' "Cretans" and Sophocles' "Theseus"', *PCPS* 193: 134.

PALLAT, L. (1891), *De Fabula Ariadnae* (diss., Berlin).

PALMER, M. (1992), *Love of Glory and the Common Good: Aspects of the Political Thought of Thucydides* (Lanham).

PARKE, H. W. (1977), *Festivals of the Athenians* (London).

PARKER, R. C. T. (1983), *Miasma: Pollution and Purification in Early Greek Religion* (Oxford).

PARRY, A. (1981), *Logos and Ergon in Thucydides* (Salem).

PARSONS, P. J. (1977), 'The Lille Stesichorus', *ZPE* 26: 7–36.

——(1983), text and commentary of *POxy* 3531, in vol. 50 of the *Oxyrhynchus Papyri* (London).

PATTERSON, C. B. (1981), *Pericles' Citizenship Law of 451/0* (Salem).

PAVESE, C. (1967), 'The New Heracles Poem of Pindar', *HSCP* 72: 47–88.

PEARSON, A. C. (1917), *The Fragments of Sophocles*, 3 vols. (Cambridge).

PFEIFFER, R. (1949), *Callimachus*, 2 vols. (Oxford).

PICKARD-CAMBRIDGE, A. (1962), *Dithyramb, Tragedy and Comedy*, 2nd edn., rev. T. B. L. Webster (Oxford).

——(1968), *The Dramatic Festivals of Athens*, 2nd edn., rev. J. Gould and D. M. Lewis (Oxford).

PODLECKI, A. J. (1966), *The Political Background of Aeschylean Tragedy* (Michigan).

——(1968), 'Simonides: 480', *Historia* 17: 257–75.

——(1971*a*), 'Cimon, Skyros and "Theseus' bones"', *JHS* 91: 141–3.

——(1971*b*), 'Stesichoreia', *Athenaeum* 49:, 313–27.

——(1975*a*), *Themistocles* (Montreal and London).

——(1975*b*), 'Theseus and Themistocles', *RSA* 25: 1–23.

——(1975–6), 'A Pericles Prosôpon in Attic Tragedy', *Euphrosyne* 7: 7–27.

——(1986), 'Polis and Monarch in Early Greek Tragedy', in Euben (1986), 76–101.

POHLENZ, M. (1954), *Die griechische Tragödie* (Göttingen).

PORTER, D. H. (1987), *Only Connect* (Lanham).

POST, C. R. (1922), 'The Dramatic Art of Sophocles as Revealed by the Fragments of the Lost Plays', *HSCP* 33: 1–22.

PRELLER, L., and Robert, C. (1920–1), *Griechische Mythologie*, 2 vols. (Berlin).

PRIDIK, A. (1892), *De Cei Insulae Rebus* (Berlin).

QUINN, T. J. (1964), 'Thucydides and the Unpopularity of the Athenian Empire', *Historia* 13: 257–66.

RAAFLAUB, K. A. (1987), 'Herodotus, Political Thought and the Meaning of History', *Arethusa* 20: 221–48.

RADERMACHER, L. (1938), *Mythos und Sage bei den Griechen* (Zurich).

RADT, S. (1977), *Tragicorum Graecorum Fragmenta*, vol. 4 (Sophocles) (Göttingen).

——(1982), 'Sophokles in seinen Fragmenten', *Entretiens Hardt* 1982 (Geneva), 185–222.

——(1985), *Tragicorum Graecorum Fragmenta* iii (Aeschylus) (Göttingen).

RANK, O. (1964), *The Myth of the Birth of the Hero and Other Writings*, ed. P. Freund (New York). First published 1914.

RAU, P. (1967), *Paratragodia: Untersuchungen einer komischen Form des Aristophanes* (Munich).

RAUBITSCHEK, A. E. (1973), 'The Speech of the Athenians at Sparta', in P. A. Stadter (ed.), *The Speeches of Thucydides* (Chapel Hill, NC), 32–48.

RECKFORD, K. J. (1972), 'Phaethon, Hippolytus, Aphrodite', *TAPA* 113: 414–16.

——(1974), 'Phaedra and Pasiphae—The Pull Backwards', *TAPA* 104: 307–28.

REED, P. D. (1990), *The Idea of the Labyrinth* (Cornell).

REEVE, M. D. (1972), 'Interpolation in Greek Tragedy II', *GRBS* 13: 451–74.

REINHARDT, K. (1979), *Sophokles*, trans. H. and D. Harvey (Oxford,).

RHODES, P. J. (1981), *Commentary on the Aristotelian Athenaion Politeia* (Oxford).

RICHARDSON, N. (1979), *The Homeric Hymn to Demeter*, 2nd edn. (Oxford).

RIVIER, A. (1975), *Essai sur le tragique d'Euripide*, 2nd edn. (Paris).

ROBERT, C. (1878), *Eratosthenes Catasterismorum Reliquiae* (Berlin), 66 ff.

——(1892), *Die Nekyia des Polygnot* (Halle).

——(1895), *Die Marathonschlacht in der Poikile und weiteres über Polygnot* (Halle).

——(1898), 'Theseus und Meleagros bei Bacchylides', *Hermes* 33: 130–59.

——(1915), *Oidipus* (Berlin).

ROMILLY, J. DE (1963), *Thucydides and Athenian Imperialism*, trans. P. Thody (Paris).

——(1968), *Time in Greek Tragedy* (Cornell).

——(1979), *La Douceur dans la pensée grecque* (Paris).

——(1980), 'Le Refus du Suicide', *Archaeognosia* 1: 1–10.

——(1987), 'La Notion des classes moyennes dans l'Athènes du 5ᵉ. s. av. J.C.', *REG* 100: 1–17.

RONNET, G. (1969), *Sophocle: Poète tragique* (Paris).

ROSENMEYER, T. G. (1952), 'The Wrath of Oedipus', *Phoenix* 6: 92–112.

RUSSO, C. F. (1950), *Hesiodi Scutum: Introduzione, testo critico e commento con traduzione* (Florence).

RUSTEN, J. S. (1989), *Thucydides: The Peloponnesian War, Book 2* (Cambridge).

SAID, S. (1993), 'Tragic Argos', in A. Sommerstein and others (eds.), *Tragedy, Comedy and the Polis: Papers of the Greek Drama Conference, Nottingham, 18–20th July 1990* (Bari).

SAMUEL, R., and THOMPSON, P. (1990) (eds.), *The Myths We Live By* (London and New York).

SARKADY, J. (1969), 'Die Theseussage und die sogenannte theseische Verfassung', *Act. Ant. Hung* 17: 1–10.

SAUER, B. (1899), *Das sogennante Theseion und sein plastisches Schmuck* (Leipzig).

SCHEFOLD, K. (1946), 'Kleisthenes', *MH* 3: 59–93.

——(1978), *Götter- und Heldensagen der Griechen in der spätarchaischen Kunst* (Munich).

SCHMID, W., and STÄHLIN, O. (1929–48), *Geschichte der griechischen Literatur*, 5 vols. (Munich).

SCHMIDT, D. A. (1990), 'Bacchylides 17—Paean or Dithyramb?', *Hermes* 118: 18–31.

SCHMIDT, J. (1929), 'Sinis', *RE* IIIA (Stuttgart).

——(1988), 'Heraclidae', *LIMC* 4. 1 (Zurich).

SCHROEDER, O. (1914), *De Laudibus Athenarum* (diss., Göttingen).

SCHWARTZ, J. (1960), *Pseudo-Hesiodea* (Leiden).

SCHWARZE, J. (1971), *Die Beurteilung des Perikles durch die attische Komödie und ihre historische und historiographische Bedeutung* (Munich).

SCHWINGE, M. (1972), *Die Funktion der zweiteiligen Komposition im 'Herakles' des Euripides* (Tübingen).

SCOTT, J. A. (1911), 'Athenian Interpolations in Homer', *CP* 1911: 1–20.

SEAFORD, R. (1984), *Euripides' Cyclops* (Oxford).

SÉCHAN, L. (1911), 'La Légende d'Hippolyte dans l'antiquité', *REG* 24: 105–51.

——(1926), *Études sur la tragédie grecque dans ses rapports avec la céramique* (Paris).

SEGAL, C. P. (1971), *The Theme of the Mutilation of the Corpse in the Iliad* (Leiden).

——(1974), 'The Raw and the Cooked in Greek Literature', *CJ* 69: 289–306.

——(1976), 'Bacchylides Reconsidered', *QUCC* 22: 99–130.

——(1981), *Tragedy and Civilisation* (Harvard).

SEVERYNS, A. (1928), *Le Cycle épique dans l'école d'Aristarche* (Paris and Liège).

——(1933), *Bacchylide: Essai biographique* (Liège).

SHAPIRO, H. A. (1977), *Personification of Abstract Concepts in Greek Art and Literature to the End of the Fifth Century BC* (Ph.D diss. Princeton).

——(1983), 'Amazons, Thracians and Scythians', *GRBS* 24: 103–14.

——(1989), *Art and Cult under the Peisistratids* (Mainz).

——(1990), 'Old and New Heroes: Narrative, Composition and Subject in Attic Black Figure', *CA* 9: 114–48.

——(1991), 'Theseus: Aspects of the Hero in Archaic Greece', in *New Perspectives in Early Greek Art*, ed. D. Buitron Oliver (Washington).

——(1992), 'The Marriage of Theseus and Helen', in H. Froning, T. Hölscher, and H. Mielsch (eds.), *Kotinos, Festschrift für Erika Simon* (Mainz am Rhein), 232–6.

SHAW, M. H. (1982), 'The *Ethos* of Theseus in the "Suppliant Women"', *Hermes* 109: 3–19.

SHEFTON, B. B. (1956), 'Medea at Marathon', *AJA* 60: 159–63.

——(1962), 'Heracles and Theseus on a Red Figured Louterion', *Hesperia* 31: 330–68.

SHEPPARD, J. T. (1916), 'The Formal Beauty of the *Hercules Furens*', *CQ* 10: 72–9.

SHIELDS, M. G. (1961), 'Sight and Blindness Imagery in the *Oedipus Coloneus*', *Phoenix* 15: 63–73.

SILK, M. S. (1985), 'Heracles and Greek Tragedy', *G&R* 32: 1–22.

SIMMS, R. M. (1983), 'Eumolpos and the Wars of Athens', *GRBS* 1983: 179–208.

SIMON, B. (1978), *Mind and Madness in Ancient Greece* (Cornell).

SIMON, E. (1963), 'Polygnotan Painting and the Niobid Painter', *AJA* 67: 43–62.

SIX, J. (1919), 'Mikon's Fourth Picture in the Theseion', *JHS* 39: 130–43.

SMITH, A. H. (1898), 'Illustrations to Bacchylides', *JHS* 18: 267–80.

SMITH, W. D. (1966), 'Expressive Form in Euripides' "Suppliants"', *HSCP* 71: 151–70.

SNELL, B. (1964), *Scenes from Greek Drama* (Los Angeles).

——(1971), *Tragicorum Graecorum Fragmenta*, vol. 1 (Göttingen).

SOKOLOWSKI, F. (1969), *Lois sacrées des cités grecques* (Paris).

SOMMERSTEIN, A. (1989), *Euripides:* Eumenides (Cambridge).

SOURVINOU-INWOOD, C. (1971), 'Theseus Lifting the Rock and a Cup near the Pithos Painter', *JHS* 91: 94–109.

——(1979), *Theseus as Son and Stepson: A Tentative Illustration of Greek Mythological Mentality* (London).

SOURY, G. (1943), 'Euripide rationaliste et mystique d'après Hippolyte', *REG* 56: 29–52.

STADTER, P. A. (1989), *A Commentary on Plutarch's Pericles* (Chapel Hill, NC).

STANFORD, W. B. (1983), *Greek Tragedy and the Emotions* (London).

STARR, C. G. (1955), 'The Myth of the Minoan Thalassocracy', *Historia* 3: 282–91.

——(1962), 'Why Did the Greeks Defeat the Persians?', *PdP* 17: 321–32.

STE. CROIX, G. E. M. DE (1954), 'The Character of the Athenian Empire', *Historia* 3: 1–14.

STEVENS, E. B. (1944), 'Some Attic Commonplaces of Pity', *AJP* 65: 1–25.

STINTON, T. C. W. (1975), 'Hamartia in Aristotle and Greek Tragedy', *CQ* 25: 221–54.

——(1976a), 'Si credere dignum est: Some Expressions of Disbelief in Euripides and Others', *PCPS* 22: 60–90.

——(1976b), 'The Riddle at Colonus', *GRBS* 17: 323–8.

STRASBURGER, H. (1968), 'Thukydides und die politische Selbstdarstellung der Athener', repr. in H. Herter (ed.), *Thukydides* (Darmstadt), 498–520. First in *Hermes* 86 (1958), 17–40.

STRAUSS, B. S. (1993), *Fathers and Sons in Athens: Ideology and Society in the Era of the Peloponnesian War* (London).

——(1994), 'Oikos/polis: Towards a Theory of Athenian Paternal Ideology', in Boegehold and Scafuro (1994), 101–27.

SUTTON, D. F. (1974), 'A Handlist of Satyr Plays', *HSCP* 1974: 107–43.

——(1978), 'Euripides' "Theseus"', *Hermes* 106: 49–53.

——(1984), *The Lost Sophocles* (Lanham).

——(1985), 'Lost Plays about Theseus: Two Notes', *Rh.Mus.* 108: 358–60.

—— (1987) *Two Lost Plays of Euripides* (New York).

TANNER, R. H. (1916), 'The *Drapetides* of Cratinus and the Eleusinian Tax Decree', *CP* 11: 65–94.

TAPLIN, O. P. (1977), *The Stagecraft of Aeschylus* (Oxford).

——(1978), *Greek Tragedy in Action* (London).

——(1986), 'Fifth-Century Tragedy and Comedy: A Synkrisis', *JHS* 106: 163–74.

TARKOW, T. A. (1977), 'The Glorification of Athens in Euripides' *Heracles*', *Helios* 5. 1: 27–35.

TARRANT, R. J. (1978), 'Seneca's Drama and its Antecedents', *HSCP* 82: 213–63.

TAYLOR, M. W. (1981), *The Tyrant Slayers* (New York).

THOMAS, R. (1989), *Oral Tradition and Written Record in Athens* (London).

THOMPSON, E. A. (1944), 'Neophron and Euripides' Medea', *CQ* 30: 10–14.

THOMPSON, H. A. (1937), 'Buildings on the West Side of the Agora', *Hesperia* 6: 37–9, 64–7.

THOMPSON, H. A. (1950), 'Excavations in the Athenian Agora 1949', *Hesperia* 19: 313–37.

——(1952), 'The Altar of Pity in the Athenian Agora', *Hesperia* 21: 47–82.

——(1966a), 'The Sculptural Adornment of the Hephaesteion', *AJA* 62: 339–47.

——(1966b), 'Activity in the Athenian Agora 1960–5', *Hesperia* 35: 37–54.

THOMPSON, H. A., and WYCHERLEY, R. E. (1972), *The Athenian Agora*, xiv, *The Agora of Athens* (Princeton).

THOMPSON, S. (1955–8), *Motif Index of Folk Literature: A Classification of Narrative Elements in Folktale, Ballads, Myths, Fables, Mediaeval Romances, Exempla, Fabliaux, Jest-Books and Local Legends*, 6 vols. (Copenhagen).

TIÈCHE, E. (1945), 'Atlas als Personifikation der Weltachse', *MH* 2: 65–86.

TIGERSTEDT, E. N. (1965), *The Legend of Sparta in Classical Antiquity* (Uppsala).

TILLYARD, E. M. W. (1913), 'Theseus, Sinis and the Isthmian Games', *JHS* 33: 296–312.

TURNER, E. G. (1962) (ed.), *Oxyrhynchus Papyri*, vol. 27 (London).

TURNER, V. (1974), *Dramas Fields and Metaphors* (Ithaca, NY, and London).

TYRELL, W. B. (1984), *Amazons—A Study in Athenian Myth-Making* (Baltimore).

UNTERSTEINER, M. (1956), *Senofane: Testimonianze e frammenti* (Florence).

VALGIGLIO, E. (1963), 'Edipo nella tradizione pre-attica', *RSC* 11: 8–43.

VALK, M. H. A. L. H. VAN DER (1964), *Researches on the Text and Scholia of the Iliad*, 2 vols. (Leiden).

VELLACOTT, P. (1975), *Ironic Drama* (London).

VENTRIS, M., and CHADWICK, J. (1973), *Documents in Mycenean Greek*, 2nd edn. (Cambridge).

VERDENIUS, C. (1962), '*ΑΒΡΟΣ*', *Mnemosyne* 15: 392–3.

VERMEULE, E. (1958), 'Mythology in Mycenean Art', *CJ* 54: 97–108.

VERNANT, J. P. (1975), *Les Origines de la pensée grecque*, 3rd edn. (Vendôme).

——(1988), 'Tensions and Ambiguities in Greek Tragedy', in Vernant and Vidal-Naquet (1988), 29–48.

VERNANT, J. P., and VIDAL-NAQUET, P. (1988), *Myth and Tragedy in Ancient Greece* (Brighton).

VICKERS, B. (1973), *Towards Greek Tragedy* (London).

VICKERS, M., and FRANCIS, E. D. (1985), 'The Oenoe Painting in the Stoa Poikile and Herodotus' Account of Marathon', *BSA* 80: 99–113.

VIDAL-NAQUET, P. (1986), 'An Enigma at Delphi', in *The Black Hunter*, trans. A. Szegedy-Maszak (Baltimore), 302–24.

——(1988), 'Oedipus between Two Cities', in Vernant and Vidal-Naquet (1988), 329–59.

VISSER, M. (1982), 'Worship Your Enemy: Aspects of the Cult of Heroes in Ancient Greece', *HThR* 75: 403–28.

VOLLKOMMER, R. (1988), *Herakles in the Art of Classical Greece* (Oxford).

WADE-GERY, H. T. (1931), 'Eupatrids, Archons and Areopagus', *CQ* 25: 1–11.

——(1933), 'Classical Epigrams and Epitaphs', *JHS* 53: 71–104.

WALKER, H. J. (1995), *Theseus and Athens* (New York and Oxford).

WALLACE, R. W. (1994), 'Private Lives and Public Enemies: Freedom of Thought in Classical Athens', in Boegehold and Scafuro (1994), 127–55.

WALTERS, K. R. (1980), 'Rhetoric as Ritual—The Semiotics of the Attic Funeral Oration', *Florilegium* 2: 1–27.

——(1981), ' "We Fought Alone at Marathon": Historical Falsification in the Attic Funeral Oration', *Rh.Mus.* 124: 204–11.

WALTON, F. R. (1952), 'Athens, Eleusis and the Homeric Hymn to Demeter', *HThR* 45: 105–14.

WASSERSTEIN, A. (1969), 'Réflexions sur deux tragédies sophocléennes', *BAGB* 1969: 189–200.

WEBSTER, T. B. L. (1965), 'A Note on the Date of Euripides' Aegeus', *AC* 34: 519–20.

——(1966), 'The Myth of Ariadne from Homer to Catullus', *G&R* 13: 22–31.

——(1967), *The Tragedies of Euripides* (London).

——(1968), *Introduction to Sophocles*, 2nd edn. (London).

——(1972), *Potter and Patron in Ancient Athens* (London).

WEILL, N. (1959), 'Céramique thasienne à figures noires', *BCH* 83: 430–54.

WEIZSÄCKER, P. (1877), 'Neue Untersuchungen über die Vase des Klitias und Ergotimos', *Rh.Mus.* 33: 364–99.

WELCKER, F. G. (1835, 1849), *Der epische Cyclus oder die Homerische Dichter* (Bonn).

——(1839, 1841), *Die griechische Tragödie mit Rücksicht auf der epische Cyclus geordnet*, 2 vols. (Bonn).

WEST, M. L. (1966), *Hesiod: Theogony* (Oxford).

——(1972), *Iambi et Elegi Graeci*, vol. 2 (Oxford).

——(1989), 'The Early Chronology of Attic Tragedy', *CQ* 39: 251–4.

WEST, S. R. (1982), review of Apthorp 1980, *CR* 32: 1–2.

——(1987), in A. Heubeck, S. R. West and J. B. Hainsworth, *A Commentary on Homer's Odyssey, Books i–viii* (Oxford).

WEST, W. C. (1970), 'Saviours of Greece', *GRBS* 11: 271–82.

WHITEHEAD, D. (1977), *The Ideology of the Athenian Metic* (Cambridge).

WHITMAN, C. H. (1951), *Sophocles: A Study in Heroic Humanism* (Harvard).

WILAMOWITZ-MOELLENDORF, T. VON (1917), *Die dramatische Technik des Sophokles* (Berlin).

WILAMOWITZ-MOELLENDORF, U. VON (1875), *Analecta Euripidea* (Berlin).

——(1880), *Aus Kydathen* (Berlin).

——(1884), *Homerische Untersuchungen* (Berlin).

——(1893), *Aristoteles und Athen*, 2 vols. (Berlin).

——(1895), *Euripides:* Herakles (Berlin).

——(1907), 'Zum Lexikon des Photius' (=*Kleine Schriften* 4. 534).

——(1925), 'Die griechischen Heldensagen II', *S.B. Preuss.* 1925: 214–42.

——(1926), *DLZ* NS 47: 853–4.

WINNINGTON-INGRAM, R. P. (1954), 'A Religious Function of Greek Tragedy', *JHS* 74: 16–24.

——(1954), *Sophocles: An Interpretation* (Cambridge).

WOLGENSINGER, F. (1935), *Theseus* (diss., Zurich).

WOODFORD, S. (1971), 'Cults of Heracles in Attica', in D. G. Mitten, J. G. Pedley and J. A. Scott (eds.), *Studies Presented to George M. A. Hanfmann* (Mainz), 211–25.

——(1974), 'More Light on Old Walls', *JHS* 94: 158–65.

WÜST, E. (1956), 'Eumenides', *RE* Supp. 8 (Stuttgart), 86–91.

—— (1968), 'Der Ring des Minos', *Hermes* 96: 527–38.

WYCHERLEY, R. E. (1953), 'The Painted Stoa', *Phoenix* 7: 20–35.

——(1954), 'The Altar of Eleos', *CQ* 34: 143–57.

——(1957), *The Athenian Agora*, vol. 3, *Literary and Epigraphical Testimonia* (Princeton).

YOUNG, E. ROBERTS (1972), 'The Slaying of the Minotaur: Evidence in Art and Literature for the Development of the Myth, 700–400 BC' (unpub. doctoral thesis, Bryn Mawr).

ZEITLIN, F. (1986), 'Thebes: Theater of Self and Society', in Euben (1986), 101–41.

ZIELINSKI, T. (1925), *Tragodoumenon Libri Tres* (Crakow).

——(1931), 'The Reconstruction of the Lost Greek Tragedies', *Iresione* 1931: 425–42.

ZINTZEN, C. (1960), *Analytisches Hypomnema zu Senecas Phaedra* (Meisenheim).

ZIOLKOWSKI, J. E. (1981), *Thucydides and the Tradition of Funeral Speeches at Athens* (Salem).

ZSCHIETZSCHMANN, W. (1931), 'Homer und die attische Bildkunst um 560', *JDAI* 46: 45–60.

ZÜRCHER, W. (1947), *Die Darstellung des Menschen im Drama des Euripides* (Basel).

ZUNTZ, G. (1955), *The Political Plays of Euripides* (Manchester).

ZWIERLEIN, O. (1987), *Senecas Phaedra und ihre Vorbilder* (Mainz).

INDEX